THE HUMAN VOYAGE OF SELF-DISCOVERY

Brendan Leahy is the Bishop of Limerick. He is Professor of Systematic Theology at Saint Patrick's College, Maynooth, and author of numerous publications. A von Balthasar scholar, he is involved in ecumenical and inter-religious dialogue.

David Walsh is Professor of Politics at the Catholic University of America. Originally from Clonmel in Tipperary, he studied in both University College Dublin and the University of Virginia. He has authored and edited numerous publications, most recently *The Modern Philosophical Revolution* (Cambridge University Press, 2008).

The Human Voyage of Self-Discovery

Essays in Honour of Brendan Purcell

Edited by Brendan Leahy and David Walsh

Published 2013 by
Veritas Publications
7–8 Lower Abbey Street
Dublin 1
Ireland
publications@veritas.ie
www.veritas.ie

ISBN 978 1 84730 430 8

Copyright © the editors and the individual contributors, 2013

10 9 8 7 6 5 4 3 2 1

The material in this publication is protected by copyright law. Except as may be permitted by law, no part of the material may be reproduced (including by storage in a retrieval system) or transmitted in any form or by any means, adapted, rented or lent without the written permission of the copyright owners. Applications for permissions should be addressed to the publisher.

Excerpt from 'The Love Song of J. Alfred Prufrock' by T. S. Eliot is reprinted by permission of Faber and Faber Ltd in the UK and Houghton Mifflin Harcourt Publishing Company in the US (from *Collected Poems 1909–1962*. Copyright © 1936 by Houghton Mifflin Harcourt Publishing Company. Copyright © renewed 1964 by Thomas Stearns Eliot. Reprinted by permission of Houghton Mifflin Harcourt Publishing Company. All rights reserved).

Line from 'If I Were Tickled by the Rub of Love' by Dylan Thomas, from *The Poems of Dylan Thomas*, copyright © 1939 by New Directions Publishing Corp. Reprinted by permission of New Directions Publishing Corp (US); David Higham Associates, London, as agents for the Trustees of the Copyrights of Dylan Thomas (UK).

Line from 'Allegro' by Tomas Tranströmer, taken from *Friends, You Drank Some Darkness: Three Swedish Poets: Martinson, Ekelöf, and Tranströmer*, Robert Bly, trans. and ed., Beacon Press, 1975.

Line from 'Calmly We Walk Through This April's Day' by Delmore Schwartz, taken from *Selected Poems: Summer Knowledge*, New Directions, 1967.

'Canal Bank Walk' by Patrick Kavanagh is reprinted from *Collected Poems*, edited by Antoinette Quinn (Allen Lane, 2004), by kind permission of the Trustees of the Estate of the late Katherine B. Kavanagh, through the Jonathan Williams Literary Agency.

A catalogue record for this book is available from the British Library.

Designed by Dara O'Connor, Veritas
Printed in Ireland by Hudson Killeen Ltd, Dublin

Veritas books are printed on paper made from the wood pulp of managed forests. For every tree felled, at least one tree is planted, thereby renewing natural resources.

CONTENTS

7
A PORTRAIT OF BRENDAN PURCELL
BRENDAN LEAHY

15
INTRODUCTION
DAVID WALSH

27
THE BRAZEN CONTOURS OF PHILOSOPHICAL ANTHROPOLOGY
CYRIL O'REGAN

44
NEANDERTHAL POLITICS
BARRY COOPER

70
THE WEALTH OF PERSONS: RE-CAPTURING A PERSON-CENTRED ECONOMIC PERSPECTIVE
JOHN MCNERNEY

89
THE ROLE OF CONSCIENCE IN THE ADVENTURE OF HOLINESS ACCORDING TO BLESSED JOHN HENRY NEWMAN
THOMAS NORRIS

104
THE RHETORICAL POWER OF SOCRATIC DIALECTIC: SOCRATES' REFUTATION OF GORGIAS
EMESE MOGYORÓDI

125
PERSON AND SPIRIT
FRAN O'ROURKE

138
EXISTENCE AND WILL: THE POLITICAL INHERITANCE OF WILLIAM OF OCKHAM
JAMES GREENAWAY

161
WHY CHICKENS HAVE NO MYTHS: WALKER PERCY ON LANGUAGE AND MAN
GERARD CASEY

178
REFUGEE FIDEISTS: TEACHING RELIGION IN A SCIENTIFIC CULTURE
EOIN G. CASSIDY

203
MERLEAU-PONTY ON SENSIBILITY, ALTERITY AND TRACE
TIMOTHY MOONEY

225
ERIC VOEGELIN'S USE OF METAPHOR
GLENN HUGHES

248
'LEAFY-WITH-LOVE': PATRICK KAVANAGH'S 'CANAL BANK WALK'
JOSEPH MCCARROLL

264
EPIC AS THE SAVING TRUTH OF HISTORY: SOLZHENITSYN'S *RED WHEEL*
DAVID WALSH

284
RELIGIOUS FREEDOM AND DIALOGUE: THE PROPHESY OF *DIGNITATIS HUMANAE*
PIERO CODA

301
CHIARA LUBICH AND THE SCIENCE OF THE 'WHY?'
BRENDAN LEAHY

320
BRENDAN PURCELL BIBLIOGRAPHY

323
LIST OF CONTRIBUTORS

A Portrait of Brendan Purcell

BRENDAN LEAHY

To most readers of this work, Brendan Purcell hardly needs any introduction. A priest-philosopher who has inspired many, a spiritual friend to people in all kinds of situation, and a gifted media commentator, he is one of life's greats. This Festschrift in his honour is an expression of gratitude on the part of its contributors.

'WHO WE ARE ENTERS INTO THE KIND OF QUEST WE UNDERTAKE'

Born on 4 December 1941, Brendan Purcell grew up in Rathmines, Dublin, studying at Synge Street Christian Brothers School and then pursuing his undergraduate studies at Clonliffe College, University College Dublin, the Irish College, Rome and the Lateran University. He went on to do further studies at the Catholic University of Leuven. He has written that 'who we are very much enters into the kind of quest we undertake' in life.[1] In his case the intellectual quest has taken a twisting and turning path precisely because of his love of Truth and obedience to conscience as he seeks to interpret humanity's journey.

The doctoral thesis that he began at the Catholic University of Leuven and completed in UCD in 1980 marks a specific turn in his life. It was to become the launching point in a life project of unravelling the theme of what it is that makes us human. The title of his thesis – *Wewards: Theoretical Foundations for a Psychology of Friendship* – indicates a base note that will be heard at several points in his work. Commenting a few years ago, Brendan described the big discovery he made as he concluded his thesis research: 'The thesis tried to work out a framework for exploring the full range of human relationships: friendship; deepening love; its opposite, enmity; and finally, going beyond enmity in reconciliation. But it was only after I'd finished it that I understood that, all along, I'd been trying to get inside what is meant by the word "we".'[2]

There was a turning point in his life at this stage when his focus shifted from psychology to philosophy because he realised that 'as a human being,

I myself wasn't really, at least not exclusively, "an object", the kind of a thing science could wholly encompass and explain. Fundamentally, I realised I'm something other than a world-immanent thing – a subject – and that there's an inexhaustibility to the within-ness that marks me out as a human being as distinct from a galaxy, an ecosystem or an animal.'[3] In the preface to the unpublished thesis work, he comments on how he felt 'immeasurably enriched thanks to the human hugeness of the many greatsouled people I encountered or who befriended me on the way'.[4]

The quest for what it is to be human, exploring the exclusively inner dimension that characterises human beings, has continued unabated since then. In the process of this quest, Brendan has encountered 'a thousand and one mirror quests in the unanticipatable multiplicity and variety of quests other individuals and cultures have undertaken throughout history'.[5] It has brought him to glimpse behind each human creation or artefact an expression of the quest of others.

With a generous openness to the Truth that is found in others, Brendan found forming within him a deepening conviction that the human family is profoundly united in this quest no matter how far apart in time and space, in the style or medium of expression: 'what this quest has shown me is that the self-appropriation of the questing nature of our humanity, through meditative re-enactment of the expressions of the quests of others animates our existence with a heightened sense of the worth of human existence – our own and others' – and grounds a sense of human family that is universal across space and time: showing us that we human beings are a big mystery, both individually, and as a humankind that's one, yet has to become so much more so'.[6]

KEY INFLUENCES

Apart from the thousands Brendan Purcell has met in life, in a wide range of circumstances, each of whom he appreciated as having something important to contribute, a few key people have been central in his research.

Chiara Lubich (1920–2008) and the Focolare Movement: In the late 1960s, in the context of a personal crisis, he encountered the Focolare Movement founded by the Italian Chiara Lubich, a major prophetic figure of the twentieth century. On the one hand, the movement provided him with what he described as a 'community of friends' when he returned to Dublin after his studies in Leuven. He remarks that 'it was they who showed me the meaning of friendship ... from them I learned that love is stronger than death ... '.[7] His encounter with the Focolare Movement also introduced him to a communitarian spirituality centred on love, unity and Jesus' 'why-question' on the Cross ('my God, my God, why have you forsaken me?' [Mk 15:34; cf. Mt 27:46]).

The spiritual doctrine of the movement opened up for Brendan a perspective on how to read the interrelationship of persons and cultures, events and circumstances. He wrote that 'because inability to reach out to the other person or society as different has characterised the various 'isms' we are now trying to leave behind, Chiara Lubich's way of living Jesus Forsaken is by no means only a way of individual asceticism, but is also a practicable answer to the crisis of our times ... Because at the heart of all our dialogues is our love of the One whose quest was derailed into Godforsakenness, and Who, through loving beyond that apparently absolute lostness, found a way to a new and deeper oneness with his Father – not just for his own humanity, but for all humanity.'[8]

Bernard Longeran (1904–84): The writings of the Canadian philosopher-theologian, Bernard Lonergan, were very important for Brendan, in particular Lonergan's major texts, *Insight* and *Method in Theology*. He appreciated particularly Lonergan's writings on the notion of a universal viewpoint that contributed to the problem of clarifying the 'bias' of relativism or historicism in interpretation.

Noting that with reference to the natural sciences Lonergan had spoken of a scissors-like operation of empirical method, 'whose upper theoretical blade is a heuristic structure, an ordered set of general questions demanding specific determinations in the data. The lower, experimental, blade, is constituted by the techniques by which specific determinations of the data may be provided'.[9] Brendan realised that what Lonergan has said about the hermeneutic 'upper blade' can be extended on the basis of his own articulation of a philosophy of the person in social and historical community.

In terms of hermeneutics and epistemology in general, Brendan Purcell relied much on Lonergan's notion of the cognitive precepts found in the levels of consciousness – being attentive, understanding, judging, being responsible and loving. He saw Lonergan's universal viewpoint as 'simply the application of the intrinsic exigencies of human perceptual-imaginative-affective/cognitive/volitional consciousness in its orientation towards the beauty/truth/goodness of being, to the specific application of that conscious orientation we called hermeneutics or interpretation.'[10]

Eric Voegelin (1901–85): The author that has been the most considerable academic influence on Brendan Purcell is Eric Voegelin. Initially captivated by reading his multivolume *Order and History*, Brendan's reading of Voegelin brought him to see that he would have to expand his search of what it is to be human beyond psychology to take into account other experiences such as the ancient near Eastern world, the Old Testament, the Greek experience from Homer to Aristotle. He built up a personal relationship with Voegelin having been struck by this 'empirical anthropologist', as Voegelin termed himself. He learned that philosophy had to go back to the earliest expressions of the human if we want to grasp the full story of our humanity.

Brendan himself would become very interested in early archaeological discoveries and experiences such as the Egyptian myths of order, the Irish Neolithic evidence and Australian Aboriginal experiences.

TEACHING AND RESEARCH

Years of lecturing in University College Dublin brought Brendan into contact with thousands of students, many of whom today recall fondly his lively, effervescent, always fascinating lectures. Meticulously prepared and with generous handouts, Brendan (as well as joking about the Fulham football team) conveyed excitement as he taught about the Greek discovery of mind, the odyssey of the human spirit from Homer to the mystic philosophers before Plato, through to the Greek tragic poets. Through his teaching, Brendan himself was learning: 'Early on in teaching philosophical anthropology I realised that the quest for an understanding of the human couldn't be limited to the western world, so I taught classes on the Chinese Tao Te Ching, the Indian Bhagavad Gita and the Old and New Testament revelation on the meaning of human existence in Job and the Gospel of St John'.[11] He attempted to summarise a lot of his teaching in a 1996 publication entitled *The Drama of Humanity: Towards a Philosophy of Humanity in History*.[12]

Anyone who sets out on the quest must face the fact of evil, humanity's systematic failure to be human. And Brendan did this in particular by reflecting on how two great countries like Russia and Germany could have ended up taking such a wrong turn in the twentieth century. He engaged the ideological experiences of the left and right of these countries expressed in mass movements like Communism and National Socialism. He co-translated and co-edited Voegelin's lectures on Hitler and the Germans.[13] In his introduction to the work, Brendan explored the philosophical framework underlying the lectures. He noted how Voegelin felt a descriptive sociological and historic account of the Holocaust is only one dimension of history. The true criterion for judgement and assessment needs to include an explicit consciousness of the nature of the human. Social structures surrounding us may deeply influence us, corrode our moral personality, cause us fear. And yet, the moral personality of the individual is not determined by this. For Voegelin, 'personal achievement or failure to achieve moral and spiritual character would … be the explanatory ground of the goodness or evil of socio-political structures'.[14]

Throughout these years there was a growing realisation in Brendan that it is not enough to research where written records began. There are so many unwritten expressions of the human quest. His fascination with the Boyne Valley and Newgrange moved to a new level. As he writes, 'With Mircea Eliade's invaluable *Patterns in Comparative Religion* as my guidebook, I felt as if I had been sent a love letter in a foreign language – I could make out the most important words'.[15] He interpreted Newgrange, also with the help of Voegelin's writings, in terms of an expression of a yearning to outlast death, and be in tune with that oneness at the heart of being, a sense of belonging to the ultimately kind cosmic ground, the source of peace beyond the struggle between life and death.[16] He would go on to study other places such as Chaco Canyon, New Mexico, Carrowmore and Carrowkeel in Co. Sligo, Lascaux in France and Kakadu in Australia's Northern Territory.

Going back further and further, he was left with the question, how far back can we go? Do we have to resign ourselves to recognising that the far distant past, the beginnings of the human, its history and culture, is beyond our grasp?

A sabbatical leave in America and Australia launched him into a new phase of his quest: 'It became obvious that any adequate philosophical understanding of what makes human beings human would have to deal with our very beginnings in time.'[17] He tried to make up for a lack he and others had noted – that there is nothing in literature by philosophers on human origins. It's not that materials on human origins are lacking but rather *philosophical* reflection on them.

So in his work, *From Big Bang to Big Mystery*, he reflected philosophically on the vast material continuously emerging on the question of human origins. He wanted to facilitate a dialogue between important developments in philosophy and the many new discoveries in palaeontology, burial rituals etc. With Aquinas-like confidence in Truth in whatever form it comes, Brendan felt no fear in undertaking this as there are two different orders of questions that precisely as such, in their distinction, can dialogue. So factual questions need to be analysed scientifically. But there are issues that go beyond natural scientific questions such as what do 'rites of passage' mean? Or 'when we speak about human origins, what does the word "human" mean for us? It's this kind of question that philosophers raise explicitly and try to answer.'[18]

It has to be recalled again that Brendan's interest was driven along by a desire to serve his students better. He explains this when he comments on how a course entitled 'philosophical anthropology' in the English-speaking world 'is far more likely to focus on that question in the context of science, ethics, politics, and of course, human origins than on more specifically philosophical topics like metaphysics or theory of knowledge. So spurred on by my earlier interest in psychology, then in an applied philosophy of humanity in history, and aware of the questions that culture around me asks regarding human origins, I began to work up a course on the topic'.[19] He realised how closely intertwined our understanding of the unfolding of the cosmos, biological evolution and human emergence were: 'That meant I'd need to go back to the beginning, to what we know as the Big Bang … And once the process that began with the Big Bang moved on to living things, I'd have to see just how human origins fitted into that long process of evolutionary development. As a philosopher I'd be asking further questions about how the whole process started, whether human beings simply derive from that process or if their existence poses questions of a different sort to the questions asked by natural scientists.'[20]

So the book that could be considered his magnum opus, *From Big Bang to Big Mystery*, was born. In it Brendan writes about human origins in the context both of evolution and of creation, noting the difference between creation and 'creationism'. The main argument of the book is that human beings are both continuous with the evolutionary process and discontinuous with it. In many ways, *From Big Bang to Big Mystery* is a unique contribution to the understanding of human origins. It can be considered a great contemporary summa of science and faith. It shows how the external record meticulously charted by science must be integrated with the equally vast internal record of the human search for meaning. Deepening and expanding Lonergan's notion of emergent probability as the theoretical linchpin of the understanding of origins, Brendan reads together the external record meticulously charted by science with the equally vast internal record of the human search for meaning.

CONCLUSION

This short profile has focused mainly on Brendan Purcell's academic works. Apart from his main works, he has written many articles for specific occasions or in response to particular requests. He has explored topics such as faith and reason; education; politics; friendship. Some of these are listed in the appendix to this work. He continues his research today as adjunct at the University of Notre Dame Australia in Sydney. A full profile of Brendan Purcell would require a longer treatment than this brief profile permits, covering also his years of caring for the sick and elderly in the Holy Family Residence of the Little Sisters of the Poor in Dublin. Many involved in social and cultural initiatives would want to attest to his enormously encouraging influence, good cheer and wisdom at difficult moments for them. His engagement with journalists and media commentators would also deserve greater attention. But this volume is primarily about his academic work. The contributors to this book, along with many other academics, are grateful to him for his wise counsel and wish him well in his ever-deepening quest which he allows us all participate in as fellow travellers.

NOTES

1. Brendan Purcell, *From Big Bang to Big Mystery: Human Origins in the Light of Creation and Evolution* (Dublin: Veritas, 2011), p. 16. For a review of this work, see Paul O'Hara, 'Book Review: From Big Bang to Big Mystery', *Claritas: Journal of Dialogue and Culture*: Vol. 1: No. 2, Article 10. Available at: http://docs.lib.purdue.edu/claritas/vol1/iss2/10
2. Ibid., p. 16.
3. Ibid.
4. Preface to *Wewards: Theoretical Foundations for a Psychology of Friendship* (UCD, 1980), p. ix.
5. *Big Bang to Big Mystery*, p. 17.
6. Ibid.
7. Preface to *Wewards*, p. x.
8. See Brendan Purcell, 'Introduction' to Chiara Lubich, *The Secret of Unity* (London: New City, 1997), 7–18, at 15–18.
9. Brendan Purcell, *The Drama of Humanity: Towards a Philosophy of Humanity in History* (Frankfurt am Main: Peter Lang, 1996), p. 16.

10. Ibid., p. 20.
11. Ibid., p. 19.
12. Ibid.
13. Eric Voegelin, *Hitler and the Germans* in *The Collected Works of Eric Voegelin*, Vol. 31 (Columbia and London: University of Missouri Press, 1999).
14. Ibid., p. 38.
15. *Big Bang to Big Mystery*, p. 20
16. Brendan Purcell, 'In Search of Newgrange: Long Night's Journey into Day', *The Irish Mind: Exploring Intellectual Traditions*, Richard Kearney, ed., (Dublin: Wolfhound Press, 1985), pp. 39–55.
17. *Big Bang to Big Mystery*, p. 23.
18. Ibid., p. 24.
19. Ibid., pp. 24–25.
20. Ibid., p. 25.

Introduction

DAVID WALSH

'Yes, man is broad, too broad, indeed. I'd have him narrower.'[1] So remarks Dmitri Karamazov, echoing the complaint that arises in every attempt to understand who we are as human beings. Somehow the goal eludes us or recedes as we approach it. We realise that we have not comprehended what we sought but have, rather, been led deeper into the mystery that comprehends us. Each one of us, St Augustine observes, is 'an abyss so deep as to be hidden from him in whom it is'. How then can we have any hope of understanding who we are, of defining what it means to be human and finding the way toward our true good? How can we know where we are if we cannot even know who we are? These are the questions that Brendan Purcell has taken as his life's work. In a sense that is their answer. They are the questions that a man can spend his whole life pursuing without ever reaching their end and, most importantly, without regarding it as an inconclusive quest.

In a sense the questions have no answer but the deepening self-understanding they yield. They are not questions that must be answered before we set upon the path of life, for they are themselves the way through which we live our lives. The answer is present in the question as the source from which it arises. We would not even be able to begin the search if we did not already know that for which we search. Yet we can never definitively reach the end, at least not in this life. It is that inexhaustibility that guards the vitality of the search at once so ancient and so new. All temporality is bounded by the questions that open it up yet exceed what can be known within time. This is why talk of human nature, of the definition of man or the person, is somehow precipitous. At best we have hints and glimpses of what it means to be human, especially from those who exemplify it most completely. We are not at the destination but are launched on the voyage of human self-discovery.

In this quest for self-understanding we are at once the participant and the observer. This is the peculiar situation of the human sciences, as it is of philosophy, literature and theology. The separation between those who study and what is studied is minimal. In contrast to the science of nature, the science of humanity affords no vantage point for the observer that is not included within it. Social and human sciences do not investigate phenomena from which they can safely detach themselves. Rather the lines of meaning and responsibility they seek to comprehend simultaneously include the scientists themselves. The impression that the objective method of the natural sciences might pervade all systematic inquiry has been difficult to dislodge. Science, we are told, will eventually understand what still remains obscure about human beings. From his early days in experimental psychology Brendan Purcell has been a vigorous opponent of 'scientism', as this particular prejudice has been called. But this has never meant opposition to the application of science where its methods are appropriate. Much about human beings can be measured and quantified, for they are physical, chemical and biological entities in the same way as everything else in the natural world. Indeed one of the hallmarks of Purcell's work has been an abiding respect and enthusiasm for the discoveries of science in cosmology, archaeology, genetics, neurophysiology and all the other disciplines that bear on the great question of human origins. One does not have to be a proponent of natural science exclusivity to recognise that it is indispensable to the narrative of our human descent. Science has opened up the marvels of the universe, both large and small, of which we are a part. Like Aristotle, Purcell exemplifies the fearless pursuit of the empirical that is the mark of the true scientist. Far from being intimidated by what natural science may find, he has sought to keep up with the breathless pace of discoveries from that great collaborative enterprise.

Yet that does not mean that we must be in thrall to the imperious claims to which every discipline is tempted, especially one of such unquestioned authority as natural science. At the back of our minds there lingers the awareness that we are not simply a part of nature. For one thing we are capable of studying nature, a possibility that is only available to one who can stand outside of it. Science itself is a spiritual activity, and finds its meaning within the world of intellect that can neither be reduced nor translated into material terms. This is why it has long been acknowledged that the study of human beings must include a philosophical perspective. It cannot simply be left to the sciences that observe from the outside. What is needed is the admission that human beings already understand themselves even before any investigator comes on the scene. No truly scientific approach can neglect the wealth of data that humanity has already provided in the form of its self-interpretation. This is the whole literary, philosophical, artistic, religious and revelatory outpouring that has accompanied the rise of human beings from the very earliest records up to the present. But what is to be the intellectual framework that organises that vast historical trail of symbols through which the human voyage of self-discovery is actually carried forth? How are we to bring together the external sciences with the internal meditation by which the meaning of human existence is unfolded? What is the theoretical horizon that is broad enough to include the broadness of human nature itself? Neither one of the phenomenal sciences nor one of the humane disciplines, it must be capable of including all of them within its remit. This has been a longstanding issue ever since the rise of modern science challenged the supremacy of philosophy and theology at the dawn of the modern era. The essays in this volume address the overarching question that has defined the enduring preoccupation of Brendan Purcell's work.

They begin with Cyril O'Regan's reflection on the category or discipline by which Purcell's work may be identified. Most often the encompassing framework that has been proposed is 'philosophical anthropology', a term that has its origins within the German Enlightenment, especially Kant and Herder. They explained that human nature is appropriately understood through the empirical record deposited both in nature and in culture. Yet they also recognised that it is not simply a descriptive enterprise. A mere catalogue of what humanity has been and done is not sufficient. It must reach up to the point at which we grasp its significance, for we students of humanity are human too and our existence is implicated in what we discover. We cannot dispense with our own humanity, which is to be gained or lost in the undertaking. Somehow the empirical record of human history must be subsumed within the existential drama that is more than historical. What happens in history signifies the transcendence of history. In the absence of any disciplinary conception of what is simultaneously immanent and transcendent, philosophical anthropology became in O'Regan's words an indispensable 'placeholder'.

The problem is that like all placeholders, the grip on reality is not quite what is required. After its German Idealist inception, philosophical anthropology is dislodged by the more radical philosophical track of Heidegger, and the more relentless empiricism of anthropology itself. Purcell's own invocation of philosophical anthropology to name his project is really part of its second wave that begins with Max Scheler and is carried forward by Eric Voegelin and others. Yet even there it begins to modulate, as indicated in Voegelin's later replacement with the term 'philosophy of consciousness'. Nor has 'philosophical anthropology' succeeded in establishing itself within the rubrics of academic departments and disciplines. It remains an orphan, a marker for what is not otherwise demarcated. The contributors to the present volume do not so much offer an alternative as continue the search, already evident in Purcell's own work, for the more perspicuous identification that is required. Philosophical anthropology may be provisionally adequate, but is there not within the notion of a placeholder the suggestions of something more? The metaphor of a voyage of self-discovery already hints at the most crucial feature of our situation. That is, that those who search have already departed from the place from which they set out. An empirical inquiry into the external and the internal record of humanity is indispensable, but it cannot overlook the extent to which the inquiry is made possible by our own humanity. The scientists too are voyagers on the same journey of self-discovery.

It is the horizon of personhood that reaches across space and time and beyond them to encounter that which is. The beginning is carried within as that by which the search is guided. How that encompassing framework, simultaneously embracing the interior and the exterior paths, is denominated is less important to the contributors than the recognition of its scope. It is that convergence that marks the unity of this anthology. There may not be an academic discipline that names what it is that all the disciplines have in common, but we cannot deny that they are all sustained by the persons who stand outside of them. The study of human beings is an exercise in deepening not only our knowledge but also our humanity. Eric Voegelin explained it to his friend Robert Heilman:

> The occupation with works of art, poetry, philosophy, mythical imagination, and so forth, makes sense only if it is conducted as an inquiry into the nature of man ... The basis of historical interpretation is the identity of substance (the psyche) in the object and the subject of interpretation; and its purpose is participation in the great dialogue that goes through the centuries among men about their nature and destiny. And participation is impossible without growth in stature (within the personal limitations) toward the rank of the best; and that growth is impossible unless one recognises authority and surrenders to it.[2]

We can never simply adopt an extrinsic point of view in regard to human beings for it is always what they carry within that is most decisive.

This is well illustrated in Barry Cooper's essay on 'Neanderthal Politics' where the case for genetic continuity with modern human beings is laid out with impressive empirical weight. What for Cooper is dispositive, however, is how they act in organising themselves for collective political action, especially in regard to the most existential event of war. It is that readiness for political action that attests to the inner life that sustains it. A similar revelation occurs in the realm of economics where the implementation of an impersonal system of exchange would seem to eliminate the human factor. But that is only an appearance, as John McNerney's 'The Wealth of Persons' demonstrates. The whole mutuality of trade, the condition of the possibility of wealth, lies in factors that cannot be traded or quantified within the market. It is the relationship of trust that makes a modern economy possible and when trust evaporates it is not easily restored. We know in each of these cases about the bonds that make human communities possible, not from what we observe, but from what we already experience ourselves. These opening essays begin to build the suggestion that philosophical anthropology might be more appropriately conceived as the priority of the person.

Many of the following essays converge on such a personalist thesis. In many ways they sketch a personalist alternative to philosophical anthropology, one that avoids the objectivist implications of the latter and concedes that it is the interiority of the person that underpins all possibility of mutual understanding. We can understand the human voyage of self-discovery only because we are defined by the same quest. 'Heart speaks to heart' was the motto that Newman chose for himself. Thomas Norris reminds us in 'The Role of Conscience in the Adventure of Holiness According to Blessed John Henry Newman' of this thoroughly personalist quality of Newman, who saw more clearly than most that the assent of faith cannot be notional or propositional. At its core, faith is the response of a person to the person who reveals himself. Whether it is God or another human being, we cannot communicate until we enter into the interior life of the other. Persons can only meet as persons. The problem is that our philosophical language has been hard-pressed to name what cannot be named. Plato opened a line that he never fully exploited when, in the *Gorgias*, he has Socrates suggest the question to be posed to the famous teacher. 'Ask him who he is,' is the astonishingly blunt proposal. It is the question that penetrates to the core of the person, the question that Emese Mogyoródi shows in her probing essay 'The Rhetorical Power of Socratic Dialectic: Socrates' Refutation of Gorgias', the celebrated master of rhetoric dared not ask himself. He has, Mogyoródi shows, a persona of arrogant self-confidence but he has never allowed his gaze to slip beneath the surface to who he really is. It is for this reason that, like the other participants in the dialogue, Gorgias eventually withdraws before the searing light of judgement that Socrates shines upon him. None can withstand the deathless truth to which every human being must eventually submit. The *Gorgias* is thus a striking demonstration of the invisibility of the person who is in every instance always more than the mask they wear, the *prosopon*, from which we get the term person. It is a dialogue in which the reality of the person is displayed yet it remains silent about the very condition of its own possibility.

In 'Person and Spirit', Fran O'Rourke lays out Aristotle's approach in his work on the soul, where the question of human immateriality first comes up. Never one to dodge a difficult issue, Aristotle simply bequeathed the problem that human beings are constituted by what is immaterial yet cannot exist apart from the materiality of the body. It was Aquinas, O'Rourke shows, who first understood that the question could be resolved only if immateriality was seen, not as a quality within human beings, but as their very mode of existence. To be a person is to be immaterial. A far more oblique path toward the same realisation is opened up by the late medieval discovery of autonomy that James Greenaway narrates in 'Existence and Will: The Political Inheritance of William of Ockham'. Without tackling the theoretical problem that stumped Aristotle and that even Aquinas's resolution left incomplete, Ockham found his way to the enunciation of an inalienable core of every human being. Even if they renounced all property, the Franciscans could not alienate what made their own lives possible. They possessed and were defined by inalienable rights, a discovery with momentous political consequences for the political self-understanding of the whole modern world.

The irony of course is that we understand ourselves as marked by a moral indestructibility and still cannot find any way of conceiving how it is possible. The situation is perceptively lampooned in Walker Percy's withering critique of reductionism that Gerard Casey takes as his starting point in 'Why Chickens Have No Myths: Walker Percy on Language and Man'. The lostness that Percy laments is thus never as complete as it appears. The human person remains indefatigable because we always know what can never be lost. Percy reminds us, even if he does not quite formulate it this way, that one can only lose what one has somehow possessed. This is why, as Casey points out, even though our whole account of semiotics seems to have a place for everything except the person who grasps the significance of signs as such, we can still never entirely overlook that invisible presence within which we live. But without a philosophical language that can do justice to the person as transcendence, of saying who we are, we cannot readily navigate the different spheres within which the life of persons unfolds. This is amply displayed in Eoin Cassidy's essay, 'Refugee Fideists: Teaching Religion in a Scientific Culture'. If we are unwilling to be 'refugee fideists', conceding the irreconcilability of faith and science at the outset, then we must be prepared to undertake the search for continuity that Brendan Purcell has opened up for us in thinking about human origins as a simultaneously scientific and spiritual inquiry. Purcell exemplifies that enlarged understanding of science and of faith that Cassidy regards as the only viable way of discovering their deeper compatibility. It is a project sustained ultimately by the knowledge that it is the openness to truth, an openness that defines what it means to be a person, that is the key to their underlying unity.

A similar recognition of transcendence is reached by Timothy Mooney in 'Merleau-Ponty on Sensibility, Alterity and Trace', although he begins from a very different starting point. Rather than the person or the self, Merleau-Ponty begins with the body in order to explore the question of whether the body exists as a sheer physicality. In some ways this is the obverse of Aristotle's question of the survival of the soul, for here it is whether the body exists apart from the soul that illumines it inwardly. Mooney follows the analysis by which Merleau-Ponty shows it is impossible to arrive at the non-signifying body, for even in its most elementary condition it is already subsumed into the interiority of the person that aims at self-disclosure. This in turn means that there is no such thing as pure sensation from which the touch or the face of the other has been scrubbed clean. The mutual openness of persons is ineliminable, even when mediated by the most elemental realities. This is an insight, Mooney explains, that was more fully developed by Lévinas, Derrida and Ricoeur with their prioritising of the relationship to the other as what marks the person. What this means is that the world is saturated with the trace of otherness from which at any moment the epiphany of meaning may arise.

This is the capacity for metaphor that Glenn Hughes explores by way of 'Eric Voegelin's Use of Metaphor'. Beginning with the literary conception of metaphor, Hughes shows us that it is far more than a literary device for it is reality itself that is metaphorical. Literary metaphors work only because we respond to the metaphorical call of experience. Everything can become a vehicle for the address that the whole of reality extends to us. Ultimately, metaphor is an indispensable vehicle because it is the nature of the whole that is disclosed in every trace. That which can never be fully present speaks to us in what can be present, and we can hear its call only because we are in continuity with the whole. The enchanted cosmos that speaks to us is perfectly illustrated in the Patrick Kavanagh poem 'Canal Bank Walk', which is the subject of Joseph McCarroll's essay. Even a setting as humble as a bench beside a canal in Dublin can occasion an outburst of transcendence. A whole cosmion is revealed in the experience into which the poet is drawn and communicated to us through the evocative miracle of language. 'Leafy with love' is a phrase that resonates in the mind of the poet and the reader, and in the radiance of nature itself. It is difficult to say where one ends and the other begins. Metaphor is thus not so much something we grasp but something that lays hold of us, compelling us to see what we had not perceived so clearly before yet never without intimating that it is something already known all along. Beauty so ancient and so new cannot merely be an invention of our imagination. It would be more accurate to suggest that we possess imagination only because we are responsive to the unfathomable depths of existence.

The artist is simply the one whose infinite sensitivity is allied to a miraculous evocative capacity. This is why the artist can function as an alternate public authority, as Solzhenitsyn exemplified in relation to his own society. Beyond a bare recounting of the facts of the Russian Revolution, Solzhenitsyn could artistically penetrate their significance to the point of clarifying the redemptive possibility hidden within them. Art has become the means of reaching the truth beyond history in David Walsh's account of 'Epic as the Saving Truth of History: Solzhenitsyn's *Red Wheel*'. Yet even that saving capacity of art does not finally reach the redemptive capacity of the person whose self-transcendence is drawn forth by the redemptive suffering of God. Philosophical anthropology in the end is not extensive enough to capture the kenotic gift of what it means to be a person whose exemplar is the self-giving of the members of the Holy Trinity.

The source of human dignity, Piero Coda shows in 'Religious Freedom and Dialogue: The Prophecy of *Dignitatis Humanae*', is that its source is more than human. Coda skilfully traces the twin streams that flow into the Vatican

II document on religious liberty as the anthropological and the personalist. The former invokes the familiar acknowledgement of man as a rational animal, possessing the autonomy of self-determination and therefore entitled to the liberty of conscience conceded as indispensable. But Coda also calls attention to a deeper, if more elusive thread that ultimately is the binding force within the declaration. Religious liberty is rationally requisite, but it is even more deeply imperative in the personal invitation that God extends to each person. Freedom is not just indispensable to this encounter but is constitutive of it. The self-giving of persons that is the event of meeting can only occur freely. That realisation, Coda insists, is not a recent discovery in the history of the Church but one that reaches all the way back to the revelatory events themselves. The imperative of the free assent of faith has been inextinguishable, but what has not always prevailed is the theological personalism that renders it unmistakable. Instead, the language of persons has often been assimilated to the language of substances whose self-subsistence guaranteed their independence but raised doubts about their mutual openness to one another. The classic expression of this was when the dogma of the Trinity was formulated as three hypostases rather than three persons.

The restoration of a very different 'ontology of the Trinity' is the suggestion of Brendan Leahy's 'Chiara Lubich and the Science of the "Why?"' Its attainment would be nothing less than the recovery of the most profound access to the meaning of what it is to be a person. That is, that to be a person is to already be in relation to other persons. It is perfectly exemplified in the complete self-giving that constitutes the community of persons within the Trinity. The human voyage of self-discovery culminates in the recognition that the self that is discovered is defined by the priority of the other in every instance. There is no self apart from the other to whom the self has already been given. This was the discovery, as Leahy explains, of the profound exploration of unity undertaken by Chiara Lubich and her companions who went on to found the Focolare movement in the aftermath of World War II. Intuiting the mystical path along which she was drawn, Chiara Lubich set in motion a deepening of the theological and philosophical understanding of the Christian message. Meditating steadfastly on the central moment of Christ's self-expiation on the cross, she underlined the significance of the cry 'My God, my God, why hast though forsaken me?' It was, she saw, the ultimate loss that Jesus underwent, for he had lost his relationship with God. But it was also in that moment that he regained his unity with the Father, for love had reached the limit when it had given all. No more separation is possible when love is so complete.

The radical overturning of all the categories of thought that have dominated our metaphysics for two millennia naturally gives rise to the demand for a new ontology. A new way of thinking about being must be found when being *is* most fully by not being:

> In the light of the Trinity, being reveals itself, if we can say this, as guarding deep within itself the non-being that is the gift of self; not the non-being that negates being, rather the non-being that reveals being as love: being that is the three divine Persons. In the light of Jesus Forsaken, the subject, the being of all created things and the Absolute Being itself, find a new explanation that can serve as the basis for a new philosophy of being.[3]

Leahy also quotes Joseph Ratzinger to the same effect that now the hold that substance had on our thinking is over and we discover that relation to the other is the more primordial mode. This is a thought to which he returns as Benedict XVI in *Caritas in Veritate* in declaring the philosophical deepening Christianity must now undergo. 'The Christian revelation of the unity of the human race presupposes a metaphysical interpretation of the "humanum" in which relationality is an essential element.'[4]

It is that unconditionally dynamic quality that is missed in the older language of human nature, for to be fully human is to continually go beyond what is natural. That is the love of Christ, and the reason why we are called to become participants in the life of God that limitlessly transcends the self. It may not be quite true to say that human beings have no nature, but it is a state we are called to surpass. This is not a new idea, for the Church Fathers and especially St Thomas built their whole understanding of the difference between natural and supernatural virtues upon it. The problem was that their philosophical language, a language of fixed entities and natures, was never quite adequate to the infinite outpouring of self that Jesus modelled for them. How can that which is, that which is in being, give more than what it has? How can there be a limit to love? It is only if being is not the ultimate category or at least not a category that can capture the supererogatory being that the person is. 'God without being' is the title of a very important book by Jean-Luc Marion that aims at correcting this persistent prejudice in favour of what possesses being.⁵ Yet even he does not quite foreground the essential reason for the transcendence he identifies. That is, that the necessity arises from personhood as such, for a person, whether human or divine, is always one who has relinquished any interest in merely being. From the very beginning they have always already given themselves away. A static account of who they are inevitably fails to capture what is most decisive about them.

This is why we are made so uneasy by the objective tone of the social sciences that attempt to categorise and explain human reality. It is not just that human beings regularly defy the laws of social science because they are free. They delight in surprising their putative examiners. The deeper problem is that persons are precisely what cannot be studied for they have always evanesced beyond the state in which they seem to exist. Transcendence is not just a future possibility for them. It is their mode of being. And, in recognising that, we invite a far-reaching revision in our understanding of being. 'Beyond being' is not another level of being, an implication that has been difficult to dislodge ever since Plato gave us the term 'transcendent' (*Republic*, 508). We must recognise that beyond being is that which is so little attached to being that it gives its being away. It pours out its being as its mode of being. Only that which is personal *is* in that way. This is why the question of whether the transcendent is a personal God is redundant. We can conceive of no other reality, other than a person, that could so prodigally dispense its being. To participate in the life of the transcendent is to participate in the life of a person or more correctly of the Three Persons who cannot be other than in the mode of complete mutual self-giving.

It is something of that transcendent luminosity that the contributors of the present volume have beheld in their honouree. Brendan Purcell has been a teacher, a mentor and a friend to every one of them and they welcome this small opportunity to celebrate his munificence. The relationship is one that attests to the impossibility of containing unity within any of the terms that describe it. Everything about Brendan Purcell radiates the eschatological excessiveness that reveals what it is to be a person in the fullest sense. He has exemplified what we have each individually sought. This is why we so joyfully join him on the voyage of self-discovery that is at once personal and collaborative. He has been Brendan the Navigator who, like his famous namesake of the sixth century, has dared to set sail toward unknown regions, discovering along the way many marvels as enchanting and surprising as the Birds of Paradise, the submersible islands and the invisible hands of hospitality the companions of the first Brendan encountered.[6] The tale that is brought back, represented in part by the fascinating range of contributions of the present volume, is also something of a latter-day report of the travellers. Yet none of the exploits or discoveries is as great as that of the voyage itself. If there is one thing we have begun to appreciate since the first St Brendan it is that friendship surpasses all that friends may collaboratively undertake. This may not seem much and may even be viewed as a commonplace, but it is really the most remarkable of all. Even the account of the voyage is made possible by the fact that we are no longer on it.

Where we go and what we encounter is really less significant than the possibility of departing from where we are. The human voyage of self-discovery is neither a travelogue nor a catalogue but the very movement of self-transcendence that is the life of persons. The destination is not one that awaits us in the future but one we carry within as the condition of possibility of setting forth. It is those mystical bonds that make possible our reaching out toward all human history, as well as the whole world in which it is, and the loving embrace of God that contains it all. That is the great intuition our Navigator has taught us. The voyage is only undertaken because it is already completed. Nothing more marvellous can be discovered than the companionship that makes it possible for us to embark on the journey together. What we discover on the way is that we are not alone in the enterprise but are sustained on a vast ocean of personhood that has streamed forth from the beginning in which all are united. The human voyage of self-discovery is not a task we set ourselves, but an invitation reaching toward us long before we have even begun.

NOTES

1. *The Brothers Karamazov*, Constance Garnett, trans. (New York: Modern Library, 1950), p. 127.
2. Voegelin, *Collected Works Vol. 30: Selected Correspondence, 1950–1984*, Thomas Hollweck, ed. (Columbia: University of Missouri Press, 2007), pp. 293–94.
3. Chiara Lubich, *Essential Writings: Spirituality, Dialogue, Culture* (New York: New City Press, 2007), p. 754.
4. *Caritas in Veritate* (29 June 2009), n. 54.
5. Jean-Luc Marion, *God Without Being*, Thomas A. Carlson, trans. (Chicago: University of Chicago Press, 1991).
6. The famous *Navagatio* is provided in several of its versions in *The Voyage of Saint Brendan*, W. R. J. Barron and Glyn S. Burgess, eds. (Exeter: University of Exeter Press, 2002).

The Brazen Contours of Philosophical Anthropology

CYRIL O'REGAN

I begin with two observations: (1) Philosophical anthropology is given broad extension in *From Big Bang to Big Mystery*[1] in that (a) it includes an account of human beings as human beings arrived at self-understanding in their immediate responses to nature and in what they take to have ultimate meaning and value through what, following Paul Ricoeur, we might call 'the detour of their symbolisation',[2] (b) philosophical anthropology covers both the emergence of civilised human being from their non-civilised ancestors and the evolutionary movement that begins seven million years ago that results in *Homo sapiens*. (2) It is not only clear from Purcell's visionary text what the operative methodology is, but who provides the main inspiration for his method, that is, Eric Voegelin on the one hand, and Bernard Lonergan[3] on the other. Still questions can be raised in both areas. First, the range of phenomena covered by philosophical anthropology raises the question as to whether 'philosophical anthropology' functions more nearly as placeholder than concept, but also whether its deployment is idiosyncratic or belongs to a particular philosophical tradition. It bears noting that Purcell thinks of *From Big Bang to Big Mystery* as a text of philosophy rather than, say, science (which is not per se reflective about its methodology) or theology, which operates with or from assumptions rather than argues towards them. For Purcell, this distinction is a purely analytic one and indicates neither hostility towards science, nor animus towards theology. Not to engage science in inquiring into the human would make little philosophical sense to Purcell, and if theology is not the chosen method of Purcell's investigation, this is not to say that philosophy and theology are not open to each other. Second, while the general fit between Lonergan and Voegelin with respect to a methodology that would not totally separate the *Geisteswissenschaften* from the *Naturwissenschaften* (thereby leaving the human sciences in an very exposed apologetic situation) is evident enough, it is not as transparent how their respective methodological protocols cohere in practice, given somewhat different commitments to the analysis of history and different levels of methodological self-consciousness.[4] Procedurally, I address these questions separately, even if it quickly becomes apparent that answering the first involves using information adduced to answer the second, and answering the second supposes that one has grasped in a provisional way the model of philosophical anthropology that Purcell deploys.

I argue the following: while it is not intentional on his part, the model for Purcell's forms of philosophical anthropology represents a creative extension of a model for an encompassing form of German philosophical anthropology that has both Herder and Kant as ancestors and can be traced up through Wilhelm von Humboldt and Alexander von Humboldt to Ernst Cassirer and beyond to Eric Voegelin. This model is at once historically sensitive, open to different forms and levels of symbolisation, and in general maintains a positive relation with natural science. It is to this background model that Purcell adds the complexity of evolutionary theory which bears on the core issue of what it is to be to human and not simply the relation-distinction between human beings over the millennia whose cultures, technologies and symbolisation not only differ, but operate at very different levels of complexity. I am insisting here on the verb 'adds', and do so because the rich story that Purcell presents of the emergence of *Homo sapiens* and his criticisms of various forms of reductionism in evolutionary theory will necessarily be misunderstood unless the background frame of philosophical anthropology is made transparent.

PHILOSOPHICAL ANTHROPOLOGY: RANGE AND PRECEDENT

The poem by the great Australian poet Les Murray, which opens *From Big Bang to Big Mystery*, is at once metaphor and synecdoche of unity in Purcell's book. In the poem 'A Walk with O'Connor', two modern individuals come to see what unites them to those humans who have gone before, that is, 'the Quest that summons all men', and thereby makes them human. Although this seeing in 'evening light' is provoked by the traces that Aboriginal people have left behind, it is a kind of miracle to reanimate and find our way into their amazement at a world. Here seeing is a double participation, first by recollecting their wonder and, second, by recreating their sense of the depth and mystery of the world. Purcell, who is interested in ethnography and archaeology, wants to track this amazed and thus amazing creature over the widest geographical and temporal domain. He wishes to provide at least in outline something like a universal history of mankind. Purcell gives credit where credit is due to biblical revelation and Greek philosophy. He does this in synoptic fashion in Part 1, but clearly evoked is the more compendious treatment he provides in *The Drama of Humanity*.[5] He agrees with Bruno Snell in thinking that history owes to the Greeks the discovery of critical mind,[6] but is less parochial than Snell in thinking that critical mind is not coextensive with mind as such. For Purcell, mind is more nearly defined as the complex of desire and intelligence, given to searching, astonishment and communicative expression. In Part 1 of *From Big Bang to Big Mystery,* Purcell demonstrates an interest in broadening beyond the biblical civilisation and Greek philosophy when it comes to defining who human being is as such. He insists on the contributions that come from the East when he underscores the importance of Vedic religion (*BB*, 65). Vedic religion exemplifies the dominance of mythic construction of reality, even as it serves as the backdrop for the emergence of the reflective philosophical discourse of the *Upanishads*, which authorises the quite different practices of meditation and contemplation (*BB*, 66).[7] This more nearly philosophical form of knowing in turn gives rise to and is surpassed in the religious sensibility of the *Bhagavad Gita* (*BB*, 68), which dates from the first century BCE. Thus Purcell, at the very least, sketches in *From Big Bang to Big Mystery* what he amply demonstrates elsewhere,[8] namely that he knows of a number of civilisations which have preceded biblical revelation and Greek philosophy. Satisfied merely to give highlights,[9] Purcell's ambit extends beyond these regional geographical horizons to encompass the entire globe and the entire arena of human production, both utilitarian and non-utilitarian, which preceded the great historical civilisations. The reach of *From Big Bang to Big Mystery* is nothing less than universal and is coterminous with human being in history and pre-history defined as the being with the disposition for quest, a capacity for wonder and the ability to speak.

A salient mark of *From Big Bang to Big Mystery* is that it offers definitions of the sort found in philosophy since the Greeks to mark off one class of entity from another – here human beings from other hominids and from the monkey family in general. Human beings are defined by their wonder and search which is made possible by language.[10] But in a world in which Darwin's model of evolution enjoys near absolute authority, Purcell is convinced that an account of the emergence of human being from the hominids is every bit as essential as definition which has an atemporal character. In Part 2 of his text, Purcell qualifies rather than rejects evolution. He does recognise that overclaims have been made on its behalf and continue to be made up to the present day. Indeed, it is likely that, as relayed in and through its bullish devotees, first Spencer and now Richard Dawkins and Daniel Dennett, a Darwinian theory of evolution constitutes the single-most egregious instance of scientism currently in circulation (*BB*, 99–104). Importantly in *From Big Bang to Big Mystery*, Purcell does not confound Darwin's own view with that of his more reductionist followers. While by no means arguing for an absolute separation between the original and the imitators, and fully acknowledging that some of Darwin's reflections encourage precisely the more tendentiously naturalistic view of his followers,[11] like Conor Cunningham in his magisterial *Darwin's Pious Idea*,[12] Purcell does not believe that Darwin is through and through a naturalist. Again in line with Cunningham, but definitely not dependent upon him, Purcell's antipathy to scientism is matched by his reservations towards creationism. Purcell is succinct: essentially the creationist is the obverse of the naturalist: both confuse two distinct domains of inquiry, thereby confounding why with what questions (*BB*, 119–20).[13] Precisely because he is writing a constructive book rather than presenting a genealogy,[14] Purcell does not proceed to challenge creationism's inadequate hermeneutic, which ignores complexity and depth of the biblical text, as well as the belatedness of their mode of interpretation which has little sanction in the Christian theological and philosophical tradition.

Now, if one were forced to summarise what is distinctive and distinctively original about *From Big Bang to Big Mystery*, it would be Purcell's ambition to provided a general philosophical anthropology that refuses to unlink discussion of the relation between historical and pre-historical human being from discussion of human being's relation to other hominids and those in the genetic pool from which human being emerged.[15] This naturally raises the question however as to whether Purcell fails to recognise that he is including under the umbrella of 'philosophical anthropology' at least three distinct areas of inquiry that careful thinkers would almost certainly keep apart, thereby suggesting that his originality is indistinct from idiosyncrasy. I submit, however, that as evinced in *From Big Bang to Big Mystery*, Purcell's overall theoretical framework is not intrinsically eccentric. Granted that it looks odd in the circle of Anglophone culture, this framework becomes immediately more recognisable when we shift focus to the tradition of continental philosophy. Here we are saying more than that Purcell acknowledges a profound intellectual debt to Eric Voegelin; we are suggesting that Purcell's broad view of philosophical anthropology has a very definite German history on which he, as well as Eric Voegelin, inheres. Immanuel Kant, and even more Johann Gottfried von Herder, provide starting points for the emergence of a field of inquiry which offers an account of the history of human beings in different cultures and in different contexts, civilised and uncivilised, while being interested in human being's basic definition whether that be primarily a rational or linguistic being. As John H. Zammito elaborates in his authoritative *Kant, Herder, and the Birth of Anthropology*, Kant is not simply the author of the three critiques, but a thinker who even before the critical turn wrote on physical geography and had the ambition to map the human species, and who even after the turn demonstrated a tendency to illustrate his non-empirical points about human perception, conception and willing by reference to peoples of ancient civilisation and especially travel reports concerning so-called primitive peoples.[16] That Kant's apriorism does not sit well with this empirical emphasis is a given. Nonetheless, according to Zammito, however counterintuitive, throughout the nineteenth and twentieth centuries Kant functions as a major authority in sanctioning the empirical study of human being. Promoters of Kantian method may have differed in their specific emphases and on the question of whether or not Kant's own philosophy regulated empirical inquiry, but they were united against Idealist constructions of human being which, in the name of 'science', effectively immunised reflections from the empirical. Hegel's speculative Idealism and even more Schelling's *Naturphilosophie* offered two of the more egregious examples of this foreswearing of the empirical.

The sanctioning of the empirical study of human being is evident in the case of the brothers Wilhelm and Alexander von Humboldt in the nineteenth century and in Ernst Cassirer in the twentieth, where in all three cases Kant functions as a major – if not necessarily exclusive – authority. In the case of Wilhelm von Humboldt (1767–1835), the founder of the University of Berlin, and the writer of one of the most famous treatises on language in the nineteenth century, and his brother, Alexander von Humboldt (1769–1859), ethnographer, naturalist and linguist, Kant's view of the 'architectonic' or progressive nature of science was to the fore and informed their respective views of research which had an irreducible empirical component. This commitment very much outweighed reservations concerning Kant's view of reason being defining human being and his lack of historical sense. If Wilhelm provided the theoretical foundation for considering language rather than reason as defining what it is to be human, and thereby pointing to culture and society rather than the individual as being constitutive of human being, it was Alexander von Humboldt, who spent years in the field compiling data on vocabulary and grammar of non-European languages, especially in South and Central America, who invented the field of comparative linguistics. Interestingly, despite or perhaps because of their interest in language, both von Humboldts also had a less hierarchical sense than Kant about the rational and non-rational expressions of human beings. While it would be going too far to say that they transcended the Eurocentric point of view which placed reason on a pedestal, they could see the value of all human expressions, whether humane or not, even if a theoretical framework was not available to dismantle the hierarchy altogether.[17]

Something similar could be said about the thought of Ernst Cassirer, whose truly humanist sensibility showed great openness to data about the various linguistic and non-linguistic expressions of human beings throughout the ages.[18] The famous debate between this scholar, who attempts to articulate a broad-band anthropology in line with Kant but surpassing him, and Heidegger at Davos in 1929,[19] reveals a striking contrast between a scholar who is still committed to a broad-band anthropology, which can synthesise general principles and empirical results, and a philosophical radical[20] who insists not only on phenomenological description but on a situatedness that annuls contrasts between modern and ancient, civilised and uncivilised, and discourages philosophical discussion concerning the relation between human beings and animals. On Heidegger's account such inquiries are anachronistic sophistications. They also are beholden to a conventional Kant, who is not the only Kant. This unconventional – but truly authentic – Kant is not the friend of science; rather he gives us access to who we are as we adopt a stance of refusal or acceptance of Being. Given the depth of the opposition, from a Heideggerian point of view it is entirely irrelevant, or relevant only in the wrong way, how Cassirer modifies Kant by opening him up beyond his narrow rationalist perspective in accounting for and thinking positively of modes of western thought that could easily be passed over as sub-rational, and especially for the subtlety of his contouring of human expression and the richness of his account thereof.[21] Heidegger's reservations with respect to Cassirer are different in tone and form to those of Voegelin. In a famous review of Cassirer's *The Myth of the State*, Voegelin's tone is considerably more respectful, but shares to some extent Heidegger's view that Cassirer's philosophy is bedeviled with compromise. Of particular concern to Voegelin is the way in which in his work in general, and in *Philosophy of Symbolic Forms* in particular, Cassirer compromises his huge advantage over Kantian rationalism, by construing myth as inferior to concept and happily gradually giving way in western society.[22] Although it would be somewhat anachronistic, if we take the work of the later Voegelin as a model in the way that Purcell does (*BB*, 18), another way in which Voegelin goes beyond Cassirer, undoubtedly, is the greater confidence in the prospect of a rapprochement of a science of universal history with a more nearly naturalist description of human being.

A good argument can be made in the case of the very Kantian Cassirer, as with Wilhelm and Alexander von Humboldt, that a condition of the possibility for the kind of comprehensive philosophical anthropology in evidence is the reflection of Kant's contemporary, Johann Gottfried von Herder, and thus in a sense Kant's refraction through his sometime Romantic opponent. Through such texts as *This Too a Philosophy of History for the Formation of Humanity* (1774), *A Metacritique on the Purism of Pure Reason* (1784), and *Ideas for the Philosophy of History of Humanity* (1784–91), it is Herder rather than Kant who more nearly integrates descriptive accounts of human beings with normative evaluations, and who shows a disposition to avoid constructing rigid hierarchies between the civilised and uncivilised cultures, as well as between distinct civilised cultures.[23] And similarly it is Herder who in *Treatise on the Origin of Language* (1772)[24] critiques Kant *avant la lettre* by insisting that it is language rather than rational thought that constitutes the unity of man and ties together civilised and uncivilised human beings. Of course, here one should not ignore also Herder's copious literary criticism, especially his expostulations on Hebrew poetry and his more general reflections on aesthetics which get to the idea of human beings being symbol makers.[25] And finally, it is Herder who, as he enjoins the study of other cultures (ancient and modern) and other languages, also recommends the need for those interested in the universal humanity to possess the capacity of *Einfühlung*.[26] This term, which can be literally translated as 'feeling one's way in', bespeaks a sympathy with those human beings whose cultures and customs are so different from ours, whether living or dead. It is not difficult to see the link here between the disposition towards the ancestors described in Les Murray's extraordinarily humane poem, and a notion that functions in Herder at once as creed and the condition of the possibility of an empirical science that does not end in the dead-end of the apriorism of Kant's critical philosophy. Herder provides perhaps the best summary of his project carried out in a wide variety of venues over a period of thirty years when he writes near the end of *Essay on the Origin of Language* (1772) to the effect that his aim has been to collect 'firm (solid) data of the human soul, human organisation, the structure of all ancient and savage (primitive) languages and from the whole economy of the human races and at proving his thesis in the way that the firmest philosophical truth can be proved.'[27]

Herder is often called a Romantic, and is so for good and bad reasons. The bad reasons include a disinterest in issues of verification and complete conceptual determination; the good reasons include a more holistic, historical account of human beings whose actual symbolic productions should be the object of or interest rather than the possibility of such production. If Purcell is our *terminus ad quem*, then one would expect that the debits of the Romantic constructions are reduced, while the virtues are enhanced. I think this is the case in *From Big Bang to Big Mystery*, and that for Purcell Eric Voegelin provides his basic compass in this regard, especially in Voegelin's turn to the empirical investigation of human beings in both the historical and pre-historical periods, but most especially in the latter (*BB*, 20). Voegelin is quite obviously in the tradition of Herder when it comes to the emphases on symbolisation and avoiding Kantian hierarchies between the pre-rational and the rational.[28] Given Voegelin's German background he is in a better situation than Purcell to grasp Herder and Kant as the horizon of philosophical anthropology. Voegelin certainly has written on Herder, but nowhere does he provide him with the kind of role that I am suggesting. I am convinced, however, that in terms of the kind of brand of philosophical anthropology practised, it is Herder who provides the basic form – if not necessarily the content – of historical work such as *Order in History* and the need to extend beyond literate cultures. By extension this is true also in the case of Purcell. Purcell's performance of philosophical anthropology in *From Big Bang to Big Mystery* is – whether consciously or not – the heir of the tradition of Herder. This tradition has undergone modification in that the call for the empirical becomes even more urgent as the level of empirical knowledge explodes, and the relevance of biology and human physiology, merely intimated in Herder, comes to be seen as crucial. But none of these extensions or developments fundamentally alters the template. Moreover, although in one sense Herder and Kant represent fundamental options, in another Kant's view of the architectonics of science, as elaborated especially in the latter part of *Critique of Pure Reason*, can be used to reinforce Herder's model of philosophical anthropology by adding its voice to the legitimation of the empircal.

PHILOSOPHICAL ANTHROPOLOGY: AIDS FOR THE REFORMULATION OF THE PROTOCOLS FOR DISCUSSING EVOLUTION

Tracking in genealogical fashion the ultimate backdrop of the model of philosophical anthropology exhibited in *From Big Bang to Big Mystery* is truly useful if and only if one can map onto it Purcell's foreground double commitment to Voegelin and Lonergan and see how he avails of the latter to make his own unique contribution to the articulation of a form of philosophical anthropology that is unusually encompassing in scope. It is not difficult to see within the field of elaboration of philosophical anthropology in *From Big Bang to Big Mystery* the following general isomorphism, which is at once an analogy of proportionality and something more: Herder: Kant: Voegelin: Lonergan. It is good to be reminded that in his *The History of the Race Idea,* Voegelin not only has very positive things to say about Herder's philosophical anthropology,[29] but expresses a decided preference for his thought over that of Kant whose anthropology is judged to be relatively 'paltry' by comparison.[30] In addition, as indicated already, Voegelin repeats in fundamental respects Herder's commitment to a universal history of human being as a symbolic and linguistic animal whose expressions are historically and culturally specific. Similarly, one can think of Lonergan as presenting a methodological guide to the comprehension of the universe and human being, which continues the best of the more empirically inclined Kant that one finds in his tracts on anthropology. Given this empirical inflecting of Kant, the notion of the architectonic of science, which is so important in *Critique of Reason*, finds its complement rather than contradiction in such Lonerganian notions of the sequence of sciences being correlative to the levels of reality (*BB*, 96–8) and emergent probability (*BB*, 93–6). I would like to comment briefly on how Purcell develops Voegelin within the horizon of Herder, and how Purcell develops Lonergan within the horizon of a non-apriorist Kant before summing up what I take to be the real contribution of Purcell's text.

I begin with Purcell's development of Voegelin in *From Big Bang to Big Mystery*, although to be fair Voegelin functions as an aid to his own supplementation. Purcell is convinced that philosophical anthropology needs to include not only as broad a history of cultures and their dominant expressions and meaning as possible – something heroically exemplified throughout Voegelin's work and in his five-volume *Order and History* in particular – but philosophical anthropology must attempt to be truly universal by tracking human being further and further back into the twilight of prehistory in and through their fragmentary traces. If Purcell here is in line with the later Voegelin, he is also responding in a positive way to the programme of universal history suggested by Herder and enacted in German intellectual culture by the von Humboldts and Cassirer. Of course, historically to develop Voegelin is at the same time to develop the commitment to empirical research on Neolithic and Paleolithic human being. This Purcell does copiously in *From Big Bang to Big Mystery*, as he discusses in some detail the cave paintings at Lascaux (*BB*, 219–21), as well as even more ancient burial sites (*BB*, 221–23). Against the backdrop of Herder's empiricism and his openness to description of human being that would not exclude physiology, Purcell has no compunction about discussing the human brain (*BB*, 197–203) and vocal tract (*BB*, 203–06). More specifically, as is abundantly evident in Chapter 8, Purcell is more emphatic than Voegelin was on the importance of language, and more nearly in line with Herder, the von Humboldts and Cassirer in this respect.[31] At the very least, Purcell evinces in *From Big Bang to Big Mystery* as much conviction about the essential community of human being as Voegelin, and as broad a sensibility towards human responsiveness to a reality that excites and incites because of its overwhelming power and fascination. In this respect, Purcell is absolutely clear that wonder (*thaumazein*) does not merely mark the philosopher, but each human being as such.[32] With respect to wonder or amazement, one sees clearly how Purcell's framing of his text through Murray's poem makes more explicit than Voegelin did the pathos that characterises our interest in our ancestors who responded wholeheartedly to a world that was mysterious in its depth as well as its breadth.

Purcell also develops as well as repeats Lonergan in a text in which Voegelin and Lonergan are regarded as complementary. In *From Big Bang to Big Mystery*, Purcell enthusiastically adopts Lonergan's model of scientific rationality with particular emphasis on the notions of emergent probability and the epistemological distinction between how and why questions (Part 2, Chapters 3 and 4). 'What Lonergan opens up,' Purcell writes in a passage of unqualified endorsement, 'is the possibility of a radically non-deductivist philosophical formulation of a cosmological-anthropological view of the world' (*BB*, 94). Of course, both notions have general range and apply to domains of inquiry other than evolution, and both are intended to pick out and resist reductionism, whatever forms it takes. For example, the distinction between how and why questions usefully exposes the confusions of Stephen Hawking when, having indicated that science cannot deal with the questions of beginning, he then proceeds to answer the question of the ultimate origin of the universe by means of a reductively naturalistic explanation (BB, 81–2). Hawking, however, is just one of any number of scientists guilty of this conceptual confusion which turns science into bad philosophy. For Purcell, Lonergan's notion of 'emergent probability' (BB, 93–8) is key. Here I will neither reproduce Lonergan's highly condensed explanation of the principle, nor Purcell's lucid description. I simply point to the correlation between the sequences of sciences and the sequence of levels of reality (BB, 96–8). Instead of taking the tack of explaining human beings in terms of biology, this method requires a discipline that responds and corresponds to the complexity of a phenomenon, which is irreducible to animal or plant. To recur to biology leaves unexplained what look to be specifying features of human beings: language, technology, etc. This is ideology or more specifically scientism, that is, science overstepping its limits by offering an explanation of phenomena too complex to fall within its domain of competence. As already indicated in the first section, the crucial question is whether Darwin's theory of evolution flouts Lonergan's methodological strictures. For Purcell, the question is perhaps more important than the answer.[33] In any event, Purcell seems to think that Darwin simultaneously displays non-reductive and reductive tendencies; both are capitalised on and emphasised in his reception. As Purcell points out, Lonergan (BB, 108) and humanists such as Cassirer (BB, 108) both commend the first tendency in Darwin, and thus a theory of evolution to the degree to which it is self-restricting and open to development and correction in obedience to the recursive shape of science. Purcell himself shows no interest either in rejecting Darwin or the theory of evolution. Indeed, in Chapter 4 he points to those healthy developments within Darwinism that usefully complicate Darwin's original theory. Since other essays herein will, undoubtedly, speak to these developments, both at the theoretical level and at the level of genetics, I will confine myself to making the point that, for Purcell, a theory of evolution of broad Darwinian vintage need not be rejected because of religious or philosophical convictions. The discourse of biology and the discourses of religion and philosophy operate on entirely different levels: a theory of evolution operates at the level of what or how, religion and philosophy at the level of why. But keeping the levels of discourse in mind also rules out any requirement to sign onto creationism or even intelligent design (*BB*, 119–24) which, at different levels of intensity, confuse very different levels of inquiry.

One consequence of Lonergan being strategically deployed rather than being explicated is that Purcell has no obligation to excavate the philosophical traditions upon which Lonergan calls to construct his method. This kind of genealogical inquiry is essentially kept in suspension in *From Big Bang to Big Mystery*; for practical purposes Lonergan is cast as a modern Thomist with an intellectually responsible empirical bent. Thus the question whether Kant might anticipate Lonergan's elaboration of method in any positive sense is not necessarily to the fore, indeed perhaps is necessarily not to the fore. Moreover, there is much in Kant to which Lonergan would, undoubtedly, be allergic, including his apriorism, his unreserved Newtonian commitments and his philosophical and anthropological dualism. But if I am correct in drawing attention to another, more empirical Kant, one who more truly heeds his arguments about scientific openness and the recursiveness of science, one interested in historical and comparative inquiry into human beings, and one less stipulative about modern reason being the norm for defining human being, then there is a sense that Kant and Lonergan form a pair – if not necessarily an ideal pair. Certainly, Lonergan does not reduce to Kant, any more than Voegelin reduces to Herder. It also goes without saying that *From Big Bang to Big Mystery* is itself much more than the sum of Voegelin and Lonergan.

Moreover, although Voegelin and Lonergan provide Purcell with distinct intellectual goods, these goods are not totally separable. It is not only that one can find both commenting on the possibility and even fact of reductionism in Darwinism, but that each illustrates – albeit at weaker levels – the quite definite strengths of the other. In his work as a theologian, Lonergan illustrates at the level of interpretive practice and at a level of method a real interest in history that might not be evident from reading *Insight*.[34] Similarly, throughout his voluminous writings, Voegelin shows a keen sense of what appropriate method looks like or does not look like when the subject is human being. This is evident in his history of political thought, in his five-volume *Order and History*, and in his numerous essays on major figures and movements of modern thought. Thus, there are real overlaps between these two main thinkers who play a major role in Purcell's argumentation, as well as genuine complementarity. This too mirrors what is the case for Kant and Herder, both of whom attempted to found a philosophical anthropology whose reach was truly universal. If the former had a tendency towards emphasising reason too much in defining human beings, the latter suggested that symbolic expression and language functioned at a more primordial level; if the former thought that a philosophical anthropology should be genuinely scientific, the latter allowed perhaps considerable latitude as to what counted as evidence for the definition of human being. The advantages here go both ways. Similarly with respect to the emphasis upon history and its extent: if Kant has an idea of universal history, it is not evident that it is not Eurocentric all the way through, whereas in Herder one witnesses the first sketch of the kind of universal history that one can see in Voegelin and in Purcell. At the same time, as both allow for the study of human being as a material entity, it is Kant who is clearest about the impossibility of reducing human being to matter.

CONCLUSION

The question that I have addressed here is what historically makes sense of the model of philosophical anthropology enacted by *From Big Bang to Big Mystery*. One perfectly legitimate way of answering the question is simply to give a good account of the book, which among other things would involve some discussion of Purcell's dependence on the thought of Voegelin and Lonergan respectively. After all, the book is an argument, and arguments persuade or fail to persuade. In this essay I did not follow this tack, largely because I feared that Purcell's sense of the dimensions of philosophical anthropology might appear eccentric and that, in any event, the dimensions of 'philosophical anthropology' could conceivably come across as somewhat underdetermined. Thus the genealogical style of the paper, in which I paint *From Big Bang to Big Mystery* against the background of late-eighteenth-century German attempts to articulate a philosophical anthropology which is universalistic in scope, one essentially foresworn in the twentieth century with the exceptions of Cassirer and Voegelin. Here the two main figures are Herder and Kant who, although in some fundamental respects irreducible to each other, set the terms for nineteenth- and twentieth-century attempts to articulate an universalistic philosophical anthropology. This kind of philosophical anthropology was called into question in the twentieth century by changes in philosophical style, for example, the emergence of analytic philosophy on the one hand, and an anti-humanist form of phenomenology (Heidegger) on the other. It also found itself on the defensive with the rise in the authority of science and the newfound prestige of empirical anthropology, but also by scepticism with regard to the reach of philosophy and doubts as to whether anything more than placeholder definitions of human being are possible, not only because of difficulties distinguishing human beings from other hominids and primates, but also because of a sense that what we call human being is a creature of environmental and historical circumstances and thus variable or equivocal in principle. To attempt to advance a philosophical anthropology on the scale that *From Big Bang to Big Mystery* does is essentially to row against all these currents.

In this all-too-brief essay, I make some attempt to move from the primogenitors of this large-scale visionary philosophical anthropology to the two figures, Voegelin and Lonergan, who are crucial to Purcell, and to map the latter in terms of the former. The mapping is extremely sketchy and is so both for conceptual and practical reasons. Practically speaking, even if one had mastered the four major discourses, mapping would require both a host of intermediate figures and focused attention to differences. Perhaps even more importantly, I am not convinced that it is conceptually necessary, or at the very least interpretively necessary. The purpose of the paper is to allow the challenging question of coherence to be asked and to show that one has heard it by understanding that not every model of philosophical anthropology would allow a thinker to connect what is in fact connected by Purcell in *From Big Bang to Big Mystery*. I suggest that one model does permit such connection, and this is the German model inaugurated by Herder and Kant and which established a specific tradition into which one can obviously insert Voegelin and somewhat more probatively Lonergan. Importantly, I do not intend this essay to be demonstrative in any way. Its sole ambition is to illuminate what is going on in Purcell's fabulous book by referring to those traditions of philosophical anthropology – perhaps no longer consciously remembered – which make *From Big Bang to Big Mystery* intelligible.

NOTES

1. Brendan Purcell, *From Big Bang to Big Mystery: Human Origins in the Light of Creation and Evolution* (Dublin: Veritas, 2011). Hereafter *BB*.
2. In this respect *From Big Bang to Big Mystery* is continuous with Purcell's earlier *The Drama of Humanity: Towards a Philosophy of Humanity in History* (Frankfurt am Main: Peter Lang, 1996). While more than a summary, Part 1 of *From Big Bang to Big*

Mystery can be regarded as a recapitulation of the earlier text with a view to placing a philosophy of history with an emphasis on symbolisation in a more encompassing account of humanity.
3. This is obvious throughout the reading of *From Big Bang to Big Mystery*. It is confirmed by looking at the index. Moreover, the presence of Voegelin and Lonergan is consistent throughout the five parts of the book. The only places where references are thin are precisely where you would expect. Voegelin is not cited much in Part 2 where the issue is the relation between anthropology and scientific method. Similarly, Lonergan is not prominent in Part 1 which presents a history of human being's most differentiated symbolisations that express human wonder, searching and participation in a transcendent order. In this chapter it should come as no more a surprise that Voegelin is the major interlocutor than in Part 2 that Lonergan plays this role.
4. This is not to deny, however, that in the case of both Voegelin and Lonergan both elements are in play. The issue here is more nearly that of dominance-recessive relation.
5. See *The Drama of Humanity*, Chapters 3–7. Chapters 3–5 are on Greek material. There, in addition to the two classical philosophers, Plato and Aristotle, Purcell discusses in some detail Greek Tragedy and the Presocratic philosophers. Chapters 6 and 7 are on Revelation, with the first devoted to Hebrew scripture and featuring the book of Job, the second on the New Testament and featuring the Gospel of John.
6. See Bruno Snell, *The Discovery of the Mind: The Greek Origins of European Thought*, T. G. Rosenmeyer, trans. (New York: Harper & Row, 1960).
7. As Purcell points out, the Vedas essentially are a collection of hymns, many of which accompany rituals of sacrifice (*BB*, 65–6).
8. Purcell treats the Neolithic period of humanity and its expression more explicitly in *The Drama of Humanity* (Chapter 2), where he provides a brilliant analysis of Newgrange, the Irish Neolithic tomb in the Boyne valley. Just how continuous *From Big Bang to Big Mystery* is with this earlier book is evident in that the first chapter of this book concerns human origins and evolution.
9. Throughout *From Big Bang to Big Mystery*, Purcell draws our attention to the Paleolithic period of symbolism and is especially drawn to cave paintings such as those found at Lascaux over 16,000 years ago (*BB*, 219–22).
10. There can be no doubt that in *From Big Bang to Big Mystery* Purcell understands the possession of language to be a key discrimen between human beings and primates (pp. 225–38, esp. 235–36).
11. Purcell's discussion of Darwin and his heritage in Chapter 4 (pp. 107–43) is exquisitely balanced, and shows intimate knowledge of Darwin's work, the history of interpretation of *On the Origin of Species*, and the history of effects of his views.
12. See Conor Cunningham, *Darwin's Pious Idea: Why the Ultra-Darwinists and Creationists Both Get it Wrong* (Grand Rapids, MI: Eerdmans, 2010). In a note on page 115, Purcell states that that book is the best account he has read on the relation of science and religion that arise from Darwin's theory of evolution. He indicates, however, that its publication came too late to aid the argument of his own text.
13. Obviously, an important role Voegelin and Lonergan play is that of presenting an alternative to creationism as well as scientism. For Purcell, Aquinas can also play this role (*BB*, 139–44).
14. This is the distinctive mark of *Darwin's Pious Idea*.
15. Purcell explicitly names his enterprise as one of 'philosophical anthropology' (*BB*, 24).

16. I am very much influenced here by John H. Zammito's wonderful book, *Kant, Herder, and the Birth of Anthropology* (Chicago: University of Chicago Press, 2002). As Zammito makes clear, the purpose of the book is to suggest that together Kant and Herder are responsible for the 'disciplinary calving' of anthropology from philosophy (pp. 1–13). At the same time, at least implicitly, the book is an argument for the continuing relevance in anthropology of philosophical construction, which ironically is marginalised once anthropology comes to be interpreted as an empirical science. Zammito devotes a profound chapter to Kant in which he draws attention to the fact that Kant routinely taught an anthropology course after as well as before his 'critical turn'. Even the later versions of the course remain committed to the empirical and, crucially, none of the apriorism that one might expect from the author of *Critique of Pure Reason*. Within this generally empirical matrix Kant could ask the question of origins. Zammito draws particular attention to Kant's 1775 essay 'Von den verschieden Racen des Menschen', in which Kant argues against the view of multiple origins of humanity, which at the time served the cause of underwriting the distinction between Caucasians and blacks.
17. Obviously lacking was an intellectual framework that enabled them to dismantle the hierarchy.
18. Of course, the classical expression of this sensibility is Cassirer's three-volume *Philosophie des symbolischen Formen* (1928–31), but it is found throughout his work.
19. For the full text and commentary on this eventful meeting, see Peter E. Gordon, *Continental Divide: Heidegger, Cassirer, Davos* (Cambridge, MA: Harvard University Press, 2010). Although there are deep substantive issues between Cassirer and Heidegger, their disagreements are staged as competing interpretations of Kant, one the Enlightenment critic of reason who, nonetheless, can see value not only in theoretical and practical, but also aesthetic reason, the other who sees in Kant not an Enlightenment thinker, but a thinker who offers before his time a phenomenological-ontology of finitude.
20. For a very illuminating discussion on Cassirer's commitment to enlarge on Kant's idea of a *Menschenkenntnis*, which included under it an examination of the phenomena attributed to human cultures (pragmatics) and an examination of phenomena attributed to nature, for example, anatomy, psychology and geography, see David Bidney, 'On the Philosophical Anthropology of Ernst Cassirer and Its Relation to the History of Anthropological Thought', *The Philosophy of Ernst Cassirer* (The Library of Living Philosophers) (La Salle, IL: Open Court, 1949, pp. 465–544). Bidney underscores how Cassirer acknowledges Kant's contribution (p. 484), develops him by construing human being as a 'symbolic animal' (p. 493), but also is fundamentally limited by Dilthey's tendency to separate the natural and human sciences.
21. Heidegger places no interpretive value on the fact that for Cassirer *Third Critique* is as important as *Critique of Pure Reason* and *Critique of Practical Reason*. For Heidegger, Cassirer's concern with aesthetics in general, and more specifically how by thinking of symbols which are sub-rational (in that they are not categories), does not mean that the conventional picture of Kant, which rests on a narrow reading of the first two Critiques, is being fundamentally challenged.
22. Eric Voegelin, *The Journal of Politics* 9.3 (1946), pp. 445–47. For a similar opinion of Cassirer, see *Order and History, Volume 2: The World of the Polis*, Athanasios Moulakis, ed. (Columbia and London: University of Missouri Press, 2000), p. 247, note 13.
23. Once again Zammito is a reliable guide. See especially *Kant, Herder, and the Birth of Anthropology*, Chapter 8.

24. For a convenient English translation of this hugely important text, see *Johann Friedrich von Herder: Philosophical Writings*, Michael N. Forster, ed. (Chicago: University of Chicago Press, 2002), pp. 65–164. This text is of special interest, given Purcell's Voegelin-like insistence on language, symbolic expression in general, and wonder being constitutive of human being as human beings disclose themselves over time. Herder returns to these features of human being time and again. *This Too: A Philosophy of History for the Formation of Humanity* (1774) is a case in point.
25. It is interesting that Voegelin thought it worthwhile to comment on this aspect of Herder's thought in his essay 'Gospel and Culture', *Published Essays, 1966–1985*, Ellis Sandoz, ed. (Baton Rouge: Louisiana State University Press, 1990), pp. 172–212.
26. For a good discussion of the meaning and range of this term, see Forster's introduction in *Herder: Philosophical Writings* (pp. vii–xxxviii, esp. p. xvii)
27. See *Herder: Philosophical Writings*, p. 164. Forster's translation is a bit awkward. I have put in parenthesis a few adjectives that would more aptly capture Herder's meaning.
28. This by no means suggests that Voegelin thinks – or that Purcell believes that he thinks – the difference between human beings functioning, for example, at the level of myth and at the level of reason is unimportant, or that relativising the distinction between rational and pre-rational modes of symbolisation indicates a regressive hostility to reason. Purcell, who is a distinguished scholar of Voegelin, would likely agree that while Voegelin goes further in both regards than Cassirer, in the end he is nearer to Cassirer than he is to Heidegger who in his later work simply inverts the hierarchy.
29. Eric Voegelin, *The History of the Race Idea: From Ray to Carus (Collected Works of Eric Voegelin, Volume 3)*, Klaus Vondung, ed., Ruth Hein, trans. (Columbia, MO: University of Missouri Press, 2000), pp. 66–71. The original German text is from the 1930s.
30. Eric Voegelin, *The History of the Race Idea*, pp. 68–9.
31. Doubtless, however, Purcell would be the first to point out that in his unpublished correspondence Voegelin was more inclined to stress the fundamental importance of language.
32. See *From Big Bang to Big Mystery* (pp. 47–8), where Purcell hugs very close to Voegelin's interpretation of Aristotle in which, in line with Herder but against Cassirer, he refuses the hierarchy of 'lover of wisdom' (*philosophos*) and 'lover of myth' (*philosmythos*) (BB, p. 48).
33. That this is a question for Voegelin becomes clear in Voegelin's brief but lucid reflections on Darwin in *The New Order and Last Orientation*.
34. In the case of the former I am thinking of *The Way to Nicaea: The Dialectical Development of Trinitarian Theology* (Philadelphia: Westminster/John Knox, 1976). In the case of the latter, I am thinking of *Method in Theology* (London: Darton, Longman & Todd, 1972). In the latter the study of history is a functional speciality.

Neanderthal Politics[1]

BARRY COOPER

By the middle of the nineteenth century, natural historians were able to argue persuasively and on the basis of geological phenomena that the earth was older than the 6,000 or so years calculated on the basis of counting 'begats' in the Old Testament. Some natural historians got carried away and thought that geology was a kind of metaphysics or theology. Today some of their successors, particularly biologists and geneticists, have voiced similar sentiments. In fact, however, the appearance of a new species, *Homo sapiens* is, for biologists, simply a biological event, but inasmuch as it is an *event* it also has a historical aspect. In other words, the subject matter of very early human history appears to overlap with biology even though the approaches to this subject matter by historians (and *a fortiori* by political scientists) are not the same as those used by biologists.

In *From Big Bang to Big Mystery*, Brendan Purcell raised the question: 'Are hominid studies a branch of zoology or anthropology?' as well as a tributary one: 'Was there a human revolution?'[2] For philosophical anthropology the answer to the first question is: both. One could even add physics and history, which is another way of introducing the major hermeneutical question for which Purcell's book provides a subtle and magisterial answer. The goal of this chapter is more modest than an exegesis of his argument. I take it as given, as Purcell wrote in an earlier book, that all human societies 'were burdened with the task of wresting the order of their existence from ever-threatening disorder.'[3] The rather unusual question I would like to introduce is whether or to what extent Neanderthals are to be understood in that context as constituting a 'human society'. Because it is impossible to engage in conversation with Neanderthals, much of the discussion is inferential and necessarily makes use of the work of archaeologists and other paleoscientists. Whether they would approve of the use made of their work is a separate matter.

Let us begin by considering Purcell's second question, whether there was a 'human revolution'. Gordon Childe may not have been the first to apply the notion of 'revolution' to human affairs, but his 1930s Marxism has certainly been influential in archaeology and paleoanthropology.[4] One of the consequences that follows from insisting upon revolutions, particularly in archaeology and paleoanthropology, is that 'researchers, perhaps unwittingly, create a gulf separating humans from the rest of the biological world.'[5] Apart from the conflicting paleoanthropological accounts, what is at issue here is the question of continuity and discontinuity, which is a problem of interpretation because the fossil record does not speak for itself.

I have already introduced the biological term for this new species, *H. sapiens*. What constitutes a species, however, is not self-evident. Let us therefore consider what a biological species conventionally is understood to be today.

Richard G. Klein began his comprehensive thousand-page book, *The Human Career: Human Biological and Cultural Origins*, with an account of what the term means. 'The species,' he said, 'is the least arbitrary and most fundamental evolutionary unit … Evolutionary biologists define a *species* as a group (or a population) of organisms that look more or less alike and that interbreed to produce fertile offspring.' The necessity of producing fertile offspring is usually called the 'biological species definition' and is usually grounded in genetics whereas more or less looking alike is usually called the 'typological species definition', and is grounded in morphology.[6] The contemporary biological definition has largely replaced the older typological definition, in part because of the acceptance by biologists of the major tenets of Darwinian evolution. So far as the fossil record is concerned, however, the typological definition is still widely applicable for the obvious reason that fossils don't breed even though fossil DNA is sometimes available for analysis.

Until very recently, the biological barrier between *H. sapiens* and *H. neanderthalensis* was assumed to be impermeable.[7] The theoretical possibility of interbreeding had occasionally been raised,[8] but because most of the argument was based on morphological differences between Neanderthals and Anatomically Modern Humans, Cro-Magnons, or 'Moderns', as we will call them in this essay, the results were inconclusive.[9] Conventional biology was formalised as 'rules' (Bergmann's Rule and Allen's Rule) according to which, 'if Neanderthals and modern humans are separate species, they cannot be compared reliably' in terms of morphology because such 'rules' permit comparisons only among members of the same species. On the other hand, 'if they are the same species, then the comparison would be appropriate, but then ... the Neanderthals. ... would not be extinct'.[10] It was not until 2010 that an international team of paleogeneticists published a paper showing that both Europeans and Asians shared between 1 per cent and 4 per cent of their nuclear (not mitochondrial) DNA with Neanderthals, but Africans did not share any. This finding suggested 'that gene flow from Neandertals into the ancestors of non-Africans occurred before the divergence of Eurasian groups from each other'.[11] Genetic theory[12] would predict what the paleogeneticists found.[13] Moreover, genetic theory would also predict that a relatively small number of events of interbreeding can have appreciable frequencies of Neanderthal alletes in contemporaneous Modern populations.[14] As Gibbons said, the estimated frequency, around 2 per cent, is 'not trivial' but not 'wholesale' either.[15] The most likely site for initial interbreeding was the Levant.[16] Moreover, genome comparisons suggest a date between 45ky and 80ky ago, well within the period when Neanderthals and Moderns shared the same Levantine and European ranges.[17]

In short, the geneticists argued that beneficial Neanderthal alletes would, on conventional Darwinian grounds, provide a selective 'fitness' advantage to carriers that was akin to hybrid vigour in cattle. Moreover, by the standard statistical accounts of population genetics it would not have taken much: 'even a few dozen half-Neanderthal babies over thousands of years would have allowed modern humans to acquire most of the Neanderthal's genetic strengths'.[18] The discoveries by the paleogeneticists may not put to rest the disputes between the theory of the 'rapid replacement' of Neanderthals by Moderns[19] and the 'slow assimilation' theory,[20] but they do certainly favour the latter. If so, and without even considering the validity of the assumptions of population genetics regarding mutation rates, the characteristics of a 'slow' process needs to be explained. In particular, it is not clear why genetic change is given more weight than behavioural changes that for one reason or another are creative, volitional and innovative and thus, biologically considered, are uncaused.[21]

The philosophical limits to biological explanations of human being are by now familiar themes in philosophical anthropology so there is no need to reiterate the arguments here.[22] We would add only the observation that a series of chance historical factors combined to constitute the view that Neanderthals were a distinct species: (1) the discovery of Neanderthal fossils in nineteenth-century Europe; (2) that because of European climate during the Pleistocene, Moderns developed in a particular way so that (3) Neanderthals did not look like contemporary Europeans. 'Thus, about 100 years ago,' as Henneberg pointed out, 'a separate taxonomic category for Neandertals was created' and new fossil discoveries were categorised in light of it.[23] Since the self-understanding of archaeology and the various paleosciences is both incremental and positivist, once the category 'Neanderthal' was created it remained pretty much unquestioned as a taxonomic unit. The significance of gene flow between Neanderthals and Moderns for our purposes is that it provides clear evidence that the two groups interacted in close physical proximity. This is politically important not because of what it tells us about Neanderthals but because of what we already know about Moderns.

There is widespread agreement that the common ancestor of both Neanderthals and Moderns was *Homo heidelbergensis*,[24] a fossil dating back over half a million years. Mitochondrial DNA analysis confirmed the separation of *H. neanderthalensis* and *H. sapiens* between ca.410–440kyBP during the mid-Pleistocene. This DNA analysis is generally consistent with a paleoanthropological interpretation of distinct lineages of humans north and south of the Mediterranean commencing around the same time.[25] In other words, 'in evolutionary terms it does not matter what we call Neanderthals or Moderns. The point is that the genetic evidence ... indicates that Neanderthals and Moderns had a common ancestry that can be approximately dated around 500–400kyr and that these two lineages apparently went along separate paths, one in Eurasia and one in Africa.'[26] The question of species and taxonomy by contemporary accounts therefore is subordinate to the evolutionary ecology of populations or, more simply, to population history. We may, accordingly, think of the human lineage as a single paleospecies comprised of geographically separate populations displaying varying degrees of cultural and morphological distinctiveness at different times in their history.

Considered by themselves rather than in the context of a transition to Modern culture, the chief characteristic of Neanderthal society, just about everyone who has considered the question agrees, is its stability because the collections of artifacts and assemblages from Neanderthal sites were homogeneous, at least as compared to the much more variable assemblages from roughly contemporaneous Modern sites.[27] 'Stability' in the context of evolution, which is to say, in the context of historical adaptation to alterations in the physical, biological, social or cultural environment, is not necessarily a blessing when one or more of these contextual factors change.

Regarding the other attributes of Neanderthal society, there also appears to be widespread agreement on several points. Given that the earliest domestication of fire, by *H. erectus*, has been dated in the Levant at 790kyBP,[28] and in Europe ca.400ky ago,[29] it is not surprising that Neanderthals could as they wished make fires for protection, warmth, sociability and cooking.[30] Without being cooked, meat is difficult to digest,[31] and meat-eating Neanderthals were hunters of fresh as well as scavengers of 'aged' or 'naturally cooked', which is to say, sometimes rotten meat.[32] Hunting, moreover, is a cooperative enterprise; most Neanderthal hunts were ambushes of herding animals in open landscapes, which meant they were able to communicate with some accuracy.[33] There is even evidence of mass killing; much as North American Indians would stampede bison over cliffs or 'buffalo jumps', Neanderthals could stampede mammoths and rhinoceroses as well as bison.[34] They were not, however, as accomplished 'endurance runners' as Moderns and so were unable to run ungulates, for example, to a standstill before dispatching them.[35] As a consequence they would have been subjected to greater risk of injury either from prey that was not immobilised or had been immobilised by less effective techniques, such as running them into a swamp or a trap.[36]

Neanderthals also buried their dead, which is one reason for the relative abundance of surviving fossils, a fact that has inspired yet another major controversy.[37] Tattersall and Schwartz made the commonsensical observation that perhaps the Neanderthal corpses were buried only for hygienic reasons or to remove them from the attention of animal scavengers,[38] but d'Errico has recently pointed out that of fifty-eight burials dating from the Middle Paleolithic, thirty-five are of Neanderthals in Europe and the Near East. The remaining twenty-three from this period are of Moderns and are found only in the Near East. Some graves for both types of hominin in both places were accompanied by grave goods – stones and antlers.[39] Such evidence led him and his colleague Joao Zilhao to argue that the Neanderthals 'could well have been the acculturators, not the acculturated,'[40] inasmuch as burial was interpreted as *prima facie* evidence that Neanderthals questioned the meaning of existence by implicitly raising the question of the place of the protected dead in the story of life.[41] Conard and Bolus more cautiously argued that the newly arriving Moderns had much to profit 'from the local knowledge of the region [Swabia in the Upper Danube Valley] that the indigenous Neanderthals no doubt possessed.'[42] Neanderthals also apparently were cannibals,[43] though it is not clear whether those consumed were dietary sources or participants in a ritual. And they were as right-handed as modern humans.[44] There are additional controversies regarding the Neanderthals' means of communication, their use of ochre, and their capacity to symbolise.[45] About the only firm conclusion one can make is that the population history of Eurasian hominins including (but not limited to) Neanderthals and their replacement by Moderns is complex. In recent years it has been rewritten practically on an annual basis.[46] One thing however seems clear: the rapid biological replacement narrative or 'human revolution' has come under increasing criticism. As Nowell said, the European 'human revolution' ca.40ky ago is 'effectively dead', which answers in part Purcell's tributary question.[47]

A more interesting line of thought that also conforms to Darwinian orthodoxy is that the replacement of Neanderthals was effected by cultural rather than biological competition. In this context, paleoscientists often speak of a 'cultural stimulus' that (somehow) caused pre-Modern organisms morphologically identical to *H. sapiens* to turn into Moderns. This 'stimulus' was the cause of language and a new capacity to symbolise.[48] In its simplified Darwinian form, one finds an almost *a priori* assertion that 'interspecies competition' resulted in the extinction of the Neanderthals. The causes have been variously identified as climate change,[49] poor diet leading to high infant mortality,[50] especially a dearth of micronutrients (they did not eat enough veggies!),[51] lengthy breast feeding, leading to demographic decline because of longer mean birth-spacing than Moderns,[52] an inability of Neanderthals to pursue successfully low-risk generalised hunting strategies,[53] a reduced 'social brain' that impaired their ability to use symbols and develop extensive social networks for mating and risk reduction through mutual obligations,[54] and bad luck.[55] The way Moderns lived apparently contradicted Neanderthal traditions and culture and so increased their vulnerability, much as European civilisation did to North American Indians.[56] In short 'what became extinct by some 25,000 BP was not a taxon but a way of living and relating to others.'[57] The addition of culture as a relevant variable adds considerable complexity to the euphemistic narrative of 'replacement'.

For example, Francesco d'Errico argued not only that the Neanderthals created their own Upper Paleolithic technology in France but did so without help from the Moderns.[58] Granted that Neanderthals did not produce spears with bone points though they were able to haft stone, so why no bone-tipped spears? Were they too stupid to figure out how to do the trick? Or, since stone-tipped spears have some obvious advantages in sharpness and penetrating power, though they are not a stand-off weapon and so are more dangerous to employ, did they simply use a hunting strategy that did not require bone?[59] It is difficult to know which interpretation is preferable, though the implications for our understanding of Neanderthal consciousness, intelligence and cognitive capabilities are quite distinct.[60] For his part, d'Errico argued at length that there is 'no material support for the ... notion of "Neanderthal inferiority". On the contrary, the evidence points to 'an original and independent cultural evolution of western Europe's late Neanderthals'.[61] Or, in his more cautious later formulation, 'the hypothesis of separate but converging cultural trajectories for archaic hominins in Europe and anatomically modern *Homo sapiens* before the Middle/Upper Paleolithic transition is not proven, but cannot be rejected.'[62] If these arguments are sound, they give additional poignancy to the question: what happened to the Neanderthals?

Consider the Iberian situation. D'Errico and his colleagues argued that south of the Ebro river Neanderthals and Moderns 'were contemporary for at least 5,000 and probably for 10,000 years, during which, inevitably, some form of contact must have taken place'. But nothing fundamental changed in the material culture of the Iberian Neanderthals, which challenges the hypothesis of the biological superiority of Moderns that led to acculturation of Neanderthals. It may be that the Ebro was 'a major biocultural frontier'; to the north, Europe was occupied between 40ky and 38kyBP by Moderns. To the south 'the rest of Iberia continued to be occupied, until ca.30,000–25,000 years BP by Neanderthals with a Middle Paleolithic material culture'. And then, in a relatively short period, ca.2ky, 'replacement seems to have taken place quite suddenly' following a 1500-year cold snap (40–38.5kyBP) called the Heinrich 4 event, which saw Arctic ice rafts drifting south into the Bay of Biscay and the eastern Atlantic.[63] It is no doubt true, as Tattersall and Schwartz said, that for hunters, cold times are not necessarily hard times because pursuing herding ungulates in a more or less open landscape is a lot easier than killing boar in an oak forest,[64] but there is a limit to the benefits of cold weather and gradually, the argument goes, the Neanderthals were driven south toward the Mediterranean and Black Seas.[65]

The reason for the existence of the Ebro frontier was 'unclear', though several theories were available – it was more heavily wooded in the south, for example, or relatively warm micro-climates in the north provided plenty of space for the Moderns. In any event, at least 5,000 years of possible contact, which was plenty of time for 'acculturation' to occur, provided no evidence of changes in Neanderthal culture south of the Ebro. As Zilhao observed,

> ... unless we go back to nineteenth-century notions of a north-south gradient in human intelligence – i.e. Iberian Neanderthals were even dumber than French ones, which at least were able to imitate [the Moderns] – the Ebro frontier pattern cannot be explained at all in the framework of the paradigm of a biologically based intellectual inferiority of Neanderthals.[66]

However, because Moderns living on the south shore of the Mediterranean did not attain the cultural achievements of the European Upper Paleolithic until well after 30kyBP, cultural achievement must be independent of biology. Accordingly, the contact between Neanderthals and Moderns was

> ... a traditional problem of contact between populations with different cultural trajectories; in this case, as has often been documented in both the historical and the ethnographic record, the long-term outcome of contact was that one of those trajectories was truncated and the corresponding genetic lineage became extinct.[67]

In this respect, the example of the extinction of the Viking colonies in Greenland during the Little Ice Age and the survival of the Inuit provides a parallel.[68]

Zilhao and colleagues recently discovered evidence in southern Spain of Neanderthal use of body decoration. They began with the uncontroversial statement that, so far as Moderns are concerned, body decoration in Africa and southwest Asia has been accepted widely as evidence of symbolic thinking. But when the same kind of evidence is found at Neanderthal sites in Europe, claims that they, too, engaged in symbolic behaviour 'are disregarded on different grounds', such as poor recording techniques, uncertain or ambiguous interpretation, imitation of Moderns and so on. 'Here, we report secure evidence that approximately 50ky cal BP, ten millennia before modern humans are first recorded in Europe, the behaviour of Neandertals was symbolically organised and continued to be so until the very end of their evolutionary trajectory'.[69] What made the evidence secure was that it was found at a brecciated remnant of a site 50ky old so that 'the association of this material with the Neandertals is, literally, rock-solid'.[70] He drew the conclusion that body-painting and the use of shells for decoration at about the same time in Iberia and South Africa 'among two different lineages ... is inconsistent with cognitive-genetic explanations and implies that these innovations were fulfilling a need – aiding in the personal or social identification of people – that did not exist in the preceding two million years of human evolution'.[71] Their conclusion, bluntly stated, is that cultural barriers between Neanderthals and Moderns would have been as permeable as biological ones.

The use of colourants, 'representations' and engravings, 'personal ornaments and decorated bone tools with sets of notches' show no dramatic differences with similar 'depictional ... representations' produced by Moderns.[72] The significance of such ornamentation is that it represents 'a profound shift in technologies for encoding and transmitting information'.[73] With contemporary humans, decorations can indicate marital status, ethnicity, religion, wealth and other marks of social identity. Why should Neanderthals be exempt from such concerns? Denying Neanderthals ability to symbolise, d'Errico said, was simply an 'anti-Neanderthal prejudice'.[74]

The significance of the capability of symbolisation, which paleoscientists shorten to symboling, has been analysed from a paleoscientific perspective by Marin Byers. According to him, *all* the activities of a symboling population are rule-governed and *all* their material culture has a rule-governed style. In contrast, non-symboling behaviour is directed by ends or goals, not rules, which guide (rather than direct) actions (as distinct from behaviour).[75] For example, consider two observably different stone tools, both of which are capable of slicing and cutting, which is to say both can be used to perform the same material behaviour. But one is used only for sacrifice and the other only for butchering – two rule-guided actions. Accordingly, 'non-symboling human populations perform only material behaviours, symboling human populations material actions'.[76] This distinction between behaviour and action, which Byers borrowed from the contemporary language philosopher, John Searle, is practically identical with that of Hannah Arendt.[77] The 'rules' governing distinct actions are surplus to the material behaviour *and* they endow the actions with meaning – as sacrifice or butchery, for example. The ability to symbolise, moreover, rests on our ability to monitor what we are doing – to monitor our monitoring, which Byers (and Searle) call 'reflexivity'.

In other words, the ability to engage in symbolic action is self-conscious as well as 'effortless'.[78]

The editors of *Current Anthropology* (where Byers published this article) often invite critical comments from other scholars and give the author an opportunity to reply. Much of the criticism in this instance did not bear on the questions considered here. Michael Shanks, however, made the highly pertinent remark that Byers's 'real topic is the sudden emergence of *social* order and the character of this order; indeed, he is writing of the origins of society and morality. This is, of course, a traditional interest of political philosophy'.[79] Shanks was, in my view, essentially correct, whether the 'emergence' was sudden or gradual. Byers agreed and made the following concluding observation:

> To state the obvious, humans are animals, and as such we are subject to the same range of constraints in nature as are other animals. But we are not quite like any other animals, for as effortlessly reflexive beings we are responsible for the conditions of our life in ways that cannot be claimed for any other species we know.[80]

Ex hypothesi, if the cultural barriers between Neanderthals and Moderns were permeable, this has a major implication for their replacement by Moderns. By analogy it is not simply wrong to say, for example, that cattle 'replaced' buffalo on the great plains of North America, but such language does obscure the political and human dimension whereby a European culture extinguished, suppressed or subordinated an indigenous one. The means of doing so may have varied north and south of the border between Canada and the United States (or so Canadians like to think) but the result was pretty much the same: the 'replacement' of wild buffalo with domestic cattle. Let us consider the 'replacement' of Neanderthals in the same way. This has the important implication that the biological process involved, whether the agent of replacement was a hybrid Modern-Neanderthal hominin, a purebred Modern with a random genetic mutation that conferred some sort of Darwinian advantage, or a Modern that endured some other kind of neuroplastic alteration, is secondary.

Suppose the population dynamics of Neanderthals and Moderns as roughly analogous to the human changes that accompanied the replacement of buffalo with cattle. Suppose as well, as Tattersall and Schwartz noted, Upper

Paleolithic Moderns, 'were us: humans with all the attributes, appalling as well as admirable'. Now, 'we only have to know one side of the equation to realise that encounters between Neanderthals and modern humans cannot always have been happy ones' so that 'it seems highly unlikely that they usually brought out the best in the strangers who invaded their territory ... it is staying well within the bounds of science to suggest that the extinction of the Neanderthals involved at least a certain amount of direct conflict as well as of more generalised economic competition'.[81]

In a similar vein, Nicholas Wade asked:

> What does it mean to say that the Aurignacian culture was succeeded by the Gravettian? ... when the last Glacial Maximum made northern latitudes uninhabitable and the glaciers pushed their populations south, is it likely that they were welcomed with open arms by the southerners whose territory they invaded? If warfare was the normal style of affairs, it would have shaped almost every aspect of early human societies.[82]

In other words, the first option of 'population dynamics' can be called conflict, war, even what we now call genocide. In this context, the implication regarding gene flow would be equally stark.

In contrast to a simple assault, others have argued for simple avoidance because 'direct competition or fighting' would be 'probably too risky'.[83] In support of the 'peaceful competition leading to extinction' narrative, Zubrow offered the observation that an increase in mortality rates of Neanderthals of only 2 per cent would extinguish the population in a millennium.[84] Other accounts speak of 'absorption' or 'blending' without specifying in detail what such metaphors might mean.[85] It seems to me that the one basic fact that we should not lose sight of is, as Tattersall put it: 'our species became an irresistible force in Nature, clearly not only intolerant of competition but able to indulge that intolerance'.[86] I quoted Purcell above that *all* human societies 'were burdened with the task of wresting the order of their existence from ever-threatening disorder'.[87] There is no reason to think Neanderthals were exempt or that they were incapable of understanding the Moderns as an exemplar of ever-threatening disorder.

Let us, however, consider some ancillary evidence. Exhibit A: much to her surprise and dismay, Jane Goodall observed what she called chimpanzee warfare in Gombe.[88] In fact, monkey wars have become almost a subfield in primatology.[89] It would probably be prudent, therefore, to expect that warfare, which is to say organised and collective violence, to be an attribute of primate and so of human existence. To be more anthropologically precise: a predisposition to kill is present in nonhuman animals, especially when they are in conditions that stimulate aggressive behaviour, anger, self-protection, jealousy, and so on, any of which may lead to violence. This does not mean that the death of another is sought even in primates. Baboons apparently treat a dead companion 'as if the latter were alive but passive'.[90] For humans at least it is likely true, as Azar Gat said, 'fighting was probably an integral part of hunter-gatherers' existence throughout the genus Homo's evolutionary history'.[91]

We noted Neanderthal cannibalism above. Eudald Carbonell and his colleagues presented evidence of cannibalism by *H. antecessor*, ca.800ky ago, which Keith F. Otterbein took to be the earliest evidence of warfare.[92] Even if cannibalism is not the result of homicide, there is strong circumstantial evidence of Neanderthal homicide. During the 1950s, excavation of Shanidar Cave in the Zagros mountains of northeastern Iraq produced partial skeletons of nine Neanderthals. Four of the six reasonably complete skeletons show some form of 'trauma-related abnormality'.[93] The most interesting individual was Shanidar 1, who was at least 45ky old. All his injuries were described in great detail, including head trauma that crushed his left eye orbit, 'probably causing blindness in the left eye'. Three interpretations were advanced to account for his other injuries including 'a penetrating wound to the shoulder' that eventually resulted in an infection of the clavicle. Almost as interesting was Shanidar 3, also an adult male. He was injured on the ninth rib leaving a parallel-sided groove 'caused by a penetrating wound between the eighth and ninth ribs' that punctured the lung. 'The angle and precision of the wound make it unlikely that the injury was self-inflicted'. Indeed, it was just what one would expect if a right-handed individual stabbed Shanidar 3 while standing face to face. It could, of course, have been an accident; and in any event, Shanidar 3 was nursed for several weeks and then buried. Shanidar 5, of which little remains, was scarred on the head and suffered a scalp wound deep enough to impact the periostium.[94]

In 1979 a partial Neanderthal skeleton was discovered near the village of St Césaire, Charente Maritime, France. It was about 36ky old and provided 'the first direct evidence for the association of Neanderthals with Châtelperronian implements'. The Châtelperronian period, dated between 45 and 36kyBP, overlapped with the late Mousterian, which used to be exclusively identified with Neanderthals, and early Aurignacian, which used to be identified exclusively with Moderns; these fossils constituted the material basis for much of the archaeological discussion of the relationship of Neanderthals and Moderns during the early Upper Paleolithic. What is interesting about this fossil in the present context is that when the skull was reconstructed using computer-assisted imagery, it revealed a healed fracture in the cranial vault. 'When paleopathological diagnostic standards are applied, this bony scar bears direct evidence for the impact of a sharp implement, which may have been directed toward the individual during an act of interpersonal violence' followed by burial.[95] If we accept that blades are 'a marker of the Upper Paleolithic culture complex',[96] this Neanderthal may have been killed by one of his Modern contemporaries. The direction of the slash indicated that he suffered a blow or thrust that was intentional and was accomplished by an implement, not a natural object. 'To attain the kinetic energy necessary to penetrate bone, considerable acceleration, probably through hafting, would have been essential.' The immediate effects were probably serious, with heavy bleeding and temporary impairment. He did however survive for several months, which meant the trauma was not fatal.[97] Both Moderns and Neanderthals were capable of hafting.[98]

Both the St Césaire and Shanidar 3 individuals indicate that Neanderthals were capable of using tools as weapons – unless both Neanderthals were killed by Moderns. It seems more plausible that Neanderthals knew how to use an implement in a context other than that for which it was originally designed. The relative dearth of direct evidence of weapons may reflect the low frequency of such aggressive actions or it may 'reflect the limits of paleopathological diagnosis'.[99] If it is the latter, a reexamination of Neanderthal fossils with weapons-induced trauma in mind, might produce a more violent picture of 'replacement', especially if we bear in mind that, face to face, a person's skeleton occupies a little over half the target area that a body presents to an attacker.[100]

In any event, two things seem clear: first, the use of hunting or food-processing tools as weapons in interpersonal violence increased the potential for intergroup damage.[101] More interesting for our concerns, Zollikofer wrote, with this use of weapons 'no major "transition" from Neanderthal to EMH-specific [i.e. Modern] behavioural patterns during the Upper Paleolithic took place'. That is, Neanderthals and Moderns were 'largely similar' in their ability 'to balance between aggressive and cooperative tool-mediated behavioural patterns.'[102] In short, both groups were capable of using weapons and practising warfare of some kind.

In addition, there is some indirect evidence of Neanderthal war-making capability. Their elevated frequencies of head and neck trauma, which have been compared in its distribution to that of injuries sustained by rough-stock rodeo cowboys, may reflect their high-risk hunting of medium- and large-size game using thrusting spears, 'given the tendency of ungulates to react strongly to being impaled'.[103] Elevated trauma rates may also reflect a lot of fighting.

The evidence for hostile contact or warfare is admittedly thin because Neanderthal populations, already small at their maximum, were under climate-induced stress, as were Moderns. The estimates of Upper Paleolithic meta-populations vary over a fairly large range,[104] but the ratio of Modern to Neanderthals has been estimated to have been around 10:1.[105] This is why some archeologists and paleoanthropologists argue quite reasonably that it is highly unlikely that they ever met.[106]

Granted, then, that absolute population numbers of Neanderthals were small and that they were increasingly outnumbered by the new arrivals, we must note as well that tenure in historical hunter-gatherer societies is not a matter of controlling a surface area but of controlling sites and pathways within a surface landscape, which is to say that boundaries clearly exist, but they are connected to the use of specific sites and paths, not to specific real estate or a general surface area.[107] Moreover, the examples of Inuit, Australian Aborigines, or North American plains Indians indicate low population densities and mobility over low-yield terrain does not mean little or no conflict and competition. All it means is that larger low-yield territories are needed to survive. Even in Tasmania, before the modern European settlers murdered the inhabitants, the combination of low population density and primitive military and hunting technology (Tasmanians lacked even the stand-off weapon of a boomerang) did not prevent the maintenance of territorial frontiers and lethal raiding – warfare.[108]

At the very least, all the elements for Neanderthal-Modern conflict were in place. In this context, as with the problem of choosing a narrative,[109] we must note that, historically, contemporary anthropologists and archaeologists have, until fairly recently, typically overlooked or de-emphasised violence. Partly this is because archaeological evidence of annihilation of a population through war is difficult to find,[110] but also because of pre-scientific commitment to peaceful primitives.[111] In what has become a kind of minor classic, *War Before Civilization*, Lawrence H. Keeley offered an explanation for the comparative understudying of prehistoric conflict: 'archeologists of the postwar period had artificially "pacified the past" and shared a pervasive bias against the possibility of prehistoric warfare.'[112]

Partly because of the impact of Keeley's book in changing the minds of archeologists, Steven A. LeBlanc was able to undertake an extensive survey of conflict among hunter-gatherers, including prehistoric humans. 'One common thread' of hunter-gatherer conflict, he said, was that it was correlated with human beings exceeding the carrying capacity of the area in which they live.[113] In this respect war is an alternative to starvation and population control by disease or predators. Moreover, if resource stress is the normal human condition, then warfare is endemic. The historical absence of 'ecological balance' means that Rousseauian peaceful savages living in harmony with nature can be summarily dismissed because first, societies have always lived in a changing environment and second, they always have had neighbours. 'The best way to survive in such a milieu is not to live in ecological balance with slow growth, but to grow rapidly and be able to fend off competitors as well as take resources from others.'[114] Stealing resources of others is likely to be resisted by them, and the result is conflict.

LeBlanc mentioned two other considerations directly relevant to our admittedly speculative notion of conflict between Neanderthals and Moderns. The first is an apparent desire to dominate other males that may be innate to primates and certainly is present among chimpanzees. This is a significant consideration because it lies outside the conventional assumptions that raiding and stealing the resources of one's neighbours is economically rational. Of course one can reduce observations to a 'selfish gene' model, which is basically economic, but that is not where the phenomenal evidence leads a normal observer. Chimps, said LeBlanc, 'seem to enjoy dominating other males of their own group, but they usually do this in ways that are not lethal. They extend this behaviour by attacking and killing the males of other groups.'[115] Among humans one would speak, by analogy, of a desire for recognition, of the enjoyment of *thymos*, pride and self-respect, or even of manliness. At the very least, the notion that either modern hunter-gatherers or Neanderthals and Moderns did not fight because they had few possessions and thus had nothing to fight about or could have easily declined confrontation and wandered away rests on the assumption that all conflict is over territory or possessions. A moment's reflection indicates that this is not so. All wars, even chimpanzee wars, are dangerous, and the chimps know it. Indeed, the ability to face danger looks to be part of all primate conflict. Bands or societies that avoid danger, especially the danger of confrontation and conflict (and this applies equally to chimps as to contemporary humans), lose. As Winston Churchill said, every country has an army; either its own or somebody else's.

Another equally significant consideration concerns hunting. The connection between group hunting and group fighting has often been noted. Stalking, attacking a target in a coordinated way, being able to throw things accurately or to stab or thrust a spear with force and precision are all useful hunting arts. 'And they are useful when executing an ambush on an unsuspecting camp of nearby humans.' Moreover, generally speaking big-game hunting is a 'specialised male activity the world over. With very few exceptions, it is these same men who engage in warfare.'[116] There is practically unanimous agreement that Neanderthals were skilled big-game hunters and we have seen that the change from a hunting tool to a weapon is entirely within their imaginative capability.

A third consideration concerns emotion, which is always involved in facing danger, and self-respect or *thymos*. Fighting, battle, and even war are all at least as much an emotional experience as a calculative or cognitively rational one. Like territorial chimps, surely Neanderthals would take offence and become angry at the migration of these other humans into 'their' home range, even if it is only sites and pathways, not real estate. Indeed, if Mithen's account of the singing Neanderthals is at all accurate,[117] the emotional power of music might lead us to anticipate great emotional intensity among Neanderthals.

Peaceful accounts of the extinction of the Neanderthals defy commonsense. It seems to me that Jiri A. Svoboda was correct when he suggested that the new arrivals on many occasions faced 'a dangerous aboriginal population, the Neanderthals'. Accordingly, 'if the modern humans benefitted from higher levels of self-awareness, planning and imagination, as we generally expect, then they were also probably more afraid'.[118] If the rather gruesome accounts reconstructed by Keeley of scalping and weapons trauma were not sufficiently persuasive regarding the likelihood of conflict,[119] consider again the analogy of the replacement of wild buffalo with domestic cattle across the prairies of North America. For political science, the notion that Neanderthals would be incapable of fighting Moderns is simply naïve. The process of replacement, we have no reason to expect, was some sort of unarmed peaceful migration. In short, humans, whether Neanderthal or Modern, would fight before they would agree to starve, even though fighting increases the chance of starvation. Given that the carrying capacity of the land of the European Neanderthals was already strained by persistent cold, the invading Moderns would be seen as adding to the problem, even if questions of cultural differences and the inherent danger of dealing with strangers can be ignored. Perhaps William Golding's *The Inheritors* better describes the process of 'replacement' than does the preferred peaceful paleoanthropological narrative.

A strong tradition in anthropology and archaeology does not consider 'primitive warfare' to be an adaptive Darwinian strategy. Indeed, in a rather odd reversal of the usual evolutionary rationale, the conventional argument is that warfare is inherently non-adaptive, at least until the invention of agriculture and the founding of cosmological empires. It seems to me that Azar Gat was correct to argue that warfare is not really a social mechanism for regulating population but one of the strategies that human beings use 'to gain the upper hand in response to increased competition that may arise from demographic growth' or other sources of stress.[120] Such competition and conflict is not necessarily connected either to agriculture or to empire.

This brief account of recent contemporary intellectual history regarding the allegedly peaceful hunter-gatherers, as distinct from the actual historical subject matter of Upper Paleolithic conflict and war has a bearing on the question of Neanderthal 'politics'. Taking some comfort in the fact that 'chimpanzee politics' is an intelligible notion,[121] in principle there is no reason, apart from always sparse and sometimes ambiguous evidence, why Neanderthal politics is impossible. That is my first and relatively straightforward concluding point. As a corollary, one would expect there to be a means by which these conflicts came to an end. The obvious candidate is massacre but given the existence of 'peacemaking' among chimpanzees, one might expect that negotiations would also be possible.[122] And negotiations, one need hardly add, are possible only on the basis of some shared understanding of the rules of the game.[123]

A second conclusion is more elaborate. Often in the paleoanthropological literature scholars draw parallels and analogies between historical hunter-gatherer societies and prehistoric ones. Usually this exercise is undertaken with an abundance of caution since the evidence is so widely separated in time. There is a large anthropological literature on what might be called the politics of small-scale societies. I have not discussed this material here, and no one is more aware than I of this lacuna in the full argument that needs to be made. However, the evidence for Upper Paleolithic warfare seems to me to be suggestive, if not compelling, given the widespread agreement regarding what Modern and Neanderthal humans were like. Accordingly I would propose as a hypothesis or as a heuristic, and not simply as evidence of admiration for Clausewitz, that war constituted a major element of politics during the Upper Paleolithic, especially during the period of 'replacement' of Neanderthals by Moderns.

This second, more contentious conclusion leads to a third that is even less secure. If an analogy with much later human activity might be permitted, one might say that the 'victory' of the Moderns in the long wars against the Neanderthals was the basis for the sustained creative outburst in technology and art during the Mousterian. This is not to imply that there was no conflict among Moderns, no war and no violent politics. Unquestionably there was plenty. Nor is there any suggestion that, with the 'victory' of the Moderns, evolution came to a stop. On the contrary. But it is to suggest that the rules of the game had become more explicit when politics and war did not have to cross a divide (however narrow) that separated two kinds of human beings.

NOTES
1. I would like to thank Joe Donner and the Donner Canadian Foundation for their support for this project.
2. Brendan Purcell, *From Big Bang to Big Mystery: Human Origins in the Light of Creation*, (Dublin: Veritas, 2011), p. 169ff; p. 173ff.
3. Purcell, *The Drama of Humanity: Towards a Philosophy of Humanity in History* (Frankfurt am Main: Peter Lang, 1996), p. 53.
4. Bruce G. Trigger, *A History of Archaeological Thought*, second ed. (Cambridge: Cambridge University Press, 2009), p. 241ff; p. 322ff; G. Clark, 'Prehistory since Childe', *Bulletin of the Institute of Archaeology* 13 (1976), pp. 1–21; Kevin Greene, 'V. Gordon Childe and the Vocabulary of Revolutionary Change', *Antiquity* 73 (1999), pp. 97–106; P. Gathercole, 'Patterns in Prehistory?: An Examination of the Later Thinking of V. Gordon Childe', *World Archaeology* 3 (1971), pp. 225–32.
5. Sally McBrearty and Allison S. Brooks, 'The Revolution That Wasn't: A New Interpretation of the Origins of Modern Human Behaviour', *Journal of Human Evolution* 39 (2000), p. 455. See also McBreaty, 'Down with the Revolution', *Rethinking the Human Revolution: New Behavioural and Biological Perspectives on the Origins and Dispersal of Modern Humans*, Cambridge, McDonald Institute for Archaeological Research, Paul Mellars et al., eds. (Oxford, Oxbow Books, 2008), pp. 133–51.
6. Richard G. Klein, *The Human Career: Human Biological and Cultural Origins*, third ed. (Chicago: University of Chicago Press, 2009), pp. 3–4.

7. Klein, 'Archaeology and the Evolution of Human Behaviour', *Evolutionary Anthropology* 9 (2000), p. 24; Klein, *Human Career*, p. 627, p. 741; Brian Fagan, *Cro-Magnon: How the Ice Age Gave Birth to the First Modern Humans* (New York: Bloomsbury, 2010), p. 12.
8. See for example, W. W. Howells, 'Explaining Modern Man: Evolutionists versus Migrationists', *Journal of Human Evolution* 5 (1976), p. 492; O. Bar-Yosef, 'The Role of western Asia in Modern Human Origins', *Philosophical Transactions of the Royal Society, London: Biological Sciences*, Vol. 337, No. 1280 (29 August 1992), p. 198; Milford H. Wolpoff et al., 'Modern Human Ancestry at the Peripheries: A Test of the Replacement Theory', *Science* 291 (2001), pp. 293–7.
9. See, on the pro-interbreeding side, Erik Trinkaus et al., 'An Early Modern Human from Peșteracu Oase, Romania', *Proceedings of the National Academy of the United States of America*, 100.20 (30 September 2003), pp. 11231–36; and on the anti-interbreeding side, Shara E. Bailey et al., 'Who Made the Aurignacian and Other Upper Paleolithic Industries?', *Journal of Human Evolution* 57 (2009), pp. 11–26.
10. J. R. Stewart, 'The Ecology and Adaptation of Neanderthals During the Non-Analogue Environment of Oxygen Isotope Stage 3', *Quaternary International* 137 (2005), p. 42. See also Stewart, 'Neanderthal-modern Human Competition?: A Comparison Between the Mammals Associated with Middle and Upper Paleolithic Industries in Europe During OIS 3', *International Journal of Osteoarchaeology* 14 (2004), pp. 178–89.
11. Richard E. Green et al., 'A Draft Sequence of the Neanderthal Genome', *Science* 328 (7 May 2010), p. 710. See also Ann Gibbons' introduction, 'Close Encounters of the Prehistoric Kind', *Science* 328 (7 May 2010), pp. 680–84; and Rex Dalton, 'Ancient DNA set to Rewrite Human History', *Nature* 465 (13 May 2010), pp. 148–9.
12. Mathias Currat et al., 'The Hidden Side of Invasions: Massive Introgressions by Local Genes', *Evolution* 62 (2008), pp. 1908–20.
13. Green et al., 'A Draft Sequence', p. 721.
14. John Hawles et al., 'A Genetic Legacy from Archaic Homo', *Trends in Genetics* 24:1 (2007), pp. 14–20.
15. Gibbons, 'Close Encounters', p. 681. See also Chris Stringer, 'Evolution: What makes a Modern Human', *Nature* 485 (3 May 2012), pp. 33–5.
16. See Vania Yotova et al., 'An X-linked Haplotype of Neandertal Origin is Present Among all Non-African Populations', *Molecular Biology Evolution* 28:7 (2011), pp. 1957–62. For a slightly earlier criticism of this position, see John J. Shea, 'The Boulevard of Broken Dreams: Evolutionary Discontinuity in the Late Pleistocene Levant', *Rethinking the Human Revolution*, Mellars et al., eds., pp. 219–32.
17. See also Sriram Sankararaman et al., 'The Date of Interbreeding between Neanderthals and Modern Humans', available at http://www.arXiv:1208.2238 vi [q-bio.PE] (accessed 10 August 2012).
18. Gregory Cochran and Henry Harpending, *The 10,000 Year Explosion: How Civilization Accelerated Human Evolution* (New York: Basic Books, 2009), p. 42.
19. The cause of the rapid replacement of Neanderthals by Moderns was during the 1990s widely claimed to be an unspecified (and unspecifiable) genetic mutation that (somehow) endowed Moderns with new capacities. This was an update on the 'pre-sapiens' models of the 1950s, which in turn were re-writes in the language of natural science of the biblical narrative of the story of the chosen people, only now they were Moderns who went forth and multiplied worldwide after God or Nature gave them light, called language, intelligence and the ability to symbolise.

20. For a clear pre-paleogeneticists' statement of the problem, see John F. Hoffecker, 'The Spread of Modern Humans in Europe', *Proceedings of the National Academy of Sciences of the United States of America* 106:38 (22 September 2009), pp. 16040–45. See also W. W. Howells, 'Explaining Modern Man: Evolutionists versus Migrationists', *Journal of Human Evolution* 5 (1976), p. 480. See also Giorgio Manzi and Pietro Passarello, 'At the Archaic/Modern Boundary of the Genus *Homo*: The Neanderthals from the Grotta Breuil', *Current Anthropology* 36:2 (1995), pp. 355–66.
21. This human capacity, as Hannah Arendt has argued, is the basis for politics. It constitutes a 'second birth' following the biological birth that constitutes our natality. For a discussion, which we cannot even summarise here, see Arendt, *The Human Condition* (Chicago: University of Chicago Press, 1958), pp. 8–9, pp. 62–3, pp. 96–7, pp. 177–8; and Tilo Schabert, *Die zweite Geburt des Menschen: Von der politishen Anfängen menschlicher Existenz* (Freiburg: Verlag Karl Alber, 2009), pp. 21–4.
22. See Purcell, *The Drama of Humanity* and *From Big Bang to Big Mystery*. See also Jonas, *The Phenomenon of Life: Toward a Philosophical Biology* (Chicago: University of Chicago Press [1966] 1982), pp. 3–4.
23. M. Henneberg, 'Comments' to Trinkaus: Modern Human versus Neandertal Evolutionary Distinctiveness', *Current Anthropology* 47 (2006), pp. 610–11. See also M. Henneberg and C. de Miguel, 'Hominins are a Single Lineage: Brain and Body Size Variability does not reflect Postulated Taxonomic Diversity of Hominins', *Homo: Journal of Comparative Human Biology* 55 (2004), pp. 21–37.
24. But as with just about every 'fact' in paleoanthropology, there is disagreement. See Jean-Jacques Hublin, 'What Can Neanderthals tell us about Modern Humans?' in Mellars et al., *Rethinking the Human Revolution*, pp. 237–8. See, for example, D. Curnoe and A. Thorne, 'Number of Ancestral Human Species: A Molecular Perspective', *Homo* 53.3 (2003), pp. 201–24.
25. Phillip Endicott, et al., 'Using Genetic Evidence to Evaluate Four Paleoanthropological Hypotheses for the Timing of Neanderthal and Modern Human Origins', *Journal of Human Evolution*, 59 (2010), 87–95. For a discussion of the archeological evidence, and a slightly different time for separation of the two kinds of humans, see J. J. Hublin, 'The Origin of Neanderthals', *Proceedings of the National Academy of Sciences of the Untied States of America* 106.38 (22 September 2009), pp. 16022–27. Similar estimates of the separation of Neanderthals and Moderns were also established by analysing Neanderthal DNA. See Richard E. Green et al., 'A Draft Sequence', p. 718.
26. Clive Finlayson, *Neanderthals and Modern Humans: An Ecological and Evolutionary Perspective* (Cambridge: Cambridge University Press, 2004), p. 72.
27. Klein and Edgar, *The Dawn of Human Culture*, p. 190; Fagan, *Cro-Magnon*, p. 42, p. 80; Clive Finlayson, *The Humans Who Went Extinct: Why Neanderthals Died Out and We Survived* (Oxford: Oxford University Press, 2009), p. 152, p. 219.
28. Naama Goren-Inbar et al., 'Evidence of Hominin Control of Fire at Benot Ya'aqov, Israel', *Science* 304.5671 (2004), pp. 725–7.
29. John Gowlett, 'The Early Settlement of Northern Europe: Fire History in the Context of Climate Change and the Social Brain', *Comtes Rendus Palevol* 5 1.2 (2006), pp. 299–310.
30. Steven Mithen, *The Singing Neanderthals: The Origins of Music, Language, Mind and Body* (London: Phoenix, 2006), p. 223ff; Finlayson, *The Humans Who Went Extinct*, p. 57ff.
31. Rachel Carmody and Richard Wrangham, 'The Energetic Significance of Cooking', *Journal of Human Evolution* 57 (2009), pp. 379–91.

32. Klein and Edgar, *The Dawn of Human Culture*, pp. 156–7; see also Curtis W. Mavean and Soo Yeun Kim, 'Mousterian Large Mammal Remains from Kobeh Cave: Behavioural Implications for Neanderthals and Early Modern Humans', *Current Anthropology* 39, SI (Special Issue: The Neanderthal Problem and the Evolution of Human Behaviour), (June 1998), pp. 79–114.
33. M. P. Richards et al., 'Isotopic Dietary Analysis of a Neanderthal and Associated Fauna from the Site of Jonzac (Charente-Maritime, France)', *Journal of Human Evolution* 55 (2008), pp. 179–85; Hervé Bochereus et al., 'Isotropic Evidence for Diet and Subsistence Pattern of the Saint-Césaire I Neanderthal: Review and Use of a Multi-Source Mixing Model', *Journal of Human Evolution* 49 (2005), pp. 71–87; Fagan, *Cro-Magnon*, 61–2.
34. Katharine Scott, 'Two Hunting Episodes of the Middle Paleolithic Age at La Cotte Saint-Brelade, Jersey (Channel Islands)', *World Archaeology* 12 (1980), pp. 137–52; Paul Mellars, *The Neanderthal Legacy* (Princeton: Princeton University Press, 1996); C. Farizy et al., 'Hommes et bison du paléolithique moyen à Mauran (Haute-Garrone)', *Gallia Préhistoire* (Paris: CNRS, 1994), supp. 30; A. J. Jelinek et al., 'A Preliminary Report on Evidence Related to the Interpretation of Economic and Social Activities of Neanderthals at the Site of La Quina (Charente), France', *L'Homme de Neandertal: Actes du Colloque International*, Vol. 6, M. Otte, ed. (Liège: Université de Liège, 1986), pp. 99–106.
35. 'Endurance running' is a hunting technique that relies on the inability of quadrupeds to run and pant at the same time. Since panting is a way of cooling off and since humans sweat to cool off, humans can run some game quadrupeds to a standstill and then kill them as they stand panting from hyperthermia.
36. For details, see D. R. Carrier, 'The Energetic Paradox of Human Running and Hominid Evolution', *Current Anthropology* 25 (1984), pp. 483–95; Dennis M. Bramble and Daniel E. Lieberman, 'Endurance Running and the Evolution of Homo', *Nature* 432 (18 November 2004), pp. 345–52; David A. Raichlen et al., 'Calcaneus Length Determines Running Economy: Implications for Endurance Running Performance in Modern Humans and Neanderthals', *Journal of Human Evolution* 60 (2011), pp. 299–308.
37. Gargett, 'Grave Shortcomings: The Evidence for Neandertal Burial', *Current Anthropology* 30.2 (April 1989), pp. 157–90. In addition to the remarks appended to Gargett's original article, the 'et al.' of the citation above, see also the comments in the following issue: L.P. Louwekooijmans et al., 'On the Evidence for Neanderthal Burial', *Current Anthropology* 30.3 (June 1989), pp. 322–30.
38. Ian Tattersall and Jeffrey H. Schwartz, *Extinct Humans* (Boulder: Westview, 2000), p. 213.
39. Francesco d'Errico, 'The Origin of Humanity and Modern Cultures: Archaeology's View', *Diogenes* 54 (2007), pp. 127–8
40. Zilhao and d'Errico, 'The Chronology and Taphonomy of the Earliest Aurignacian and Its Implications for the Understanding of Neanderthal Extinction', *Journal of World Prehistory* 13 (1999), p. 3.
41. Henry de Lumley, 'The Emergence of Symbolic Thought: The Principal Steps of Hominisation Leading towards Greater Complexity', *Becoming Human: Innovation in Prehistoric Material and Spiritual Culture*, Colin Renfrew and Iain Morley, eds. (Cambridge: Cambridge University Press, 2009), p. 21.
42. Nicholas J. Conard and Michael Bolus, 'Radiocarbon Dating the Appearance of Modern Humans and Timing the Cultural Innovations in Europe: New Results and Challenges', *Journal of Human Evolution* 44 (2003), p. 364.

43. Alban Defleur et al., 'Neanderthal Cannibalism at Moula-Guercy, Ardèche, France', *Science* 286 (1 October 1999), pp. 128–31.
44. Natalie T. Uomini, 'Handedness in Neanderthals', *Neanderthal Lifeways, Subsistence and Technology: One Hundred and Fifty Years of Neanderthal Study*, Conard and Jürgen Richter, eds. (Dordrecht: Springer, 2011), p. 150.
45. April Nowell, 'Defining Behavioural Modernity in the Context of Neandertal and Anatomically Modern Human Populations', *Annual Review of Anthropology* 39 (2010), pp. 437–52. Ella Hovers et al., 'An Early Case of Colour Symbolism: Ochre Use by Modern Humans in Qafzeh Cave', *Current Anthropology* 44.4 (2003), pp. 491–522.
46. P. Brown et al., 'A New Small-Bodied Hominin from the Late Pleistocene in Flores, Indonesia,' *Nature* 4312 (2004), pp. 1055–61; M. J. Morwood et al., 'Preface: Research at Liang Bua, Flores, Indonesia', *Journal of Human Evolution* 57 (2009), pp. 437–9; David Reich et al., 'Genetic History of an Archaic Hominin Group from Denisova Cave in Siberia', *Nature* 468 (23 December 2010), pp. 1053–60; Reich et al. confirmed an earlier DNA sequencing of Neanderthal remains from Uzbekistan and the Altai region of Siberia.
47. Nowell, 'Defining Behavioural Modernity', p. 441.
48. Tattersall, *The Monkey in the Mirror: Essays on the Science of What Makes Us Human* (New York: Harcourt, 2001), pp. 160–1.
49. Paul Mellars, 'A New Radiocarbon Revolution and the Dispersal of Modern Humans in Eurasia', *Nature* 439 (23 February 2006), pp. 931–5; Jean-Jacques Hublin and Wil Roebroeks, 'Ebb and Flow or Regional Extinctions? On the Character of Neandertal Occupation of Northern Environments', *Comtes Rendus Palevol* 9 (2009), p. 503; Bert Sørensen, 'Demography and the Extinction of European Neanderthals', *Journal of Anthropological Archaeology* 30 (2011), p. 17. On the other hand, if migratory herds moved south during periods of environmental degradation, the hunters could follow them, thus increasing the local carrying capacity. Francesco d'Errico and Maria Fernanda Sanchez Goni, 'Neandertal Extinction and the Millennial Scale Climatic Variability of OIS 3', *Quaternary Science Reviews* 22 (2003), p. 769. Leslie C. Aiello and Peter Wheeler, 'Neanderthal Thermoregulation and the Glacial Climate', *Neanderthals and Modern Humans in the European Landscape During the Last Glaciation*, Tjeerd H. van Andel and William Davies, eds. (Cambridge: Cambridge University Press, 2003), pp. 147–66.
50. Bryan Hockett and Jonathan A. Haws, 'Nutritional Ecology and Diachronic Trends in Paleolithic Diet and Health', *Evolutionary Anthropology* 12 (2003), pp. 211–16.
51. Hackett and Haws, 'Nutritional Ecology and the Human Demography of Neandertal Extinction', *Quaternary International* 137 (2005), pp. 21–4.
52. P. Pettitt, 'Neanderthal Lifecycles: Development and Social Phases in the Lives of the Last Archaics', *World Archaeology* 31 (2000), pp. 354–5.
53. Curtis W. Marean, 'Heading North: An Africanist Perspective on the Replacement of Neanderthals by Modern Humans', *Rethinking the Human Revolution*, Mellars et al., eds., p. 376.
54. See Robin I. M. Dunbar, 'The Social Brain and the Cultural Explosion of the Human Revolution', *Rethinking the Human Revolution*, Mellars et al., eds., p. 91ff; Clive Gamble, 'The Social and Material Life of Neanderthals', Conard and Richter, eds., *Neanderthal Lifeways*, 160ff; Dunbar, 'The Social Brain Hypothesis,' *Evolutionary Anthropology* 6 (1998), pp. 178–90.
55. Finlayson, *The Humans Who Went Extinct*, p. 102, p. 218. See also Joao Zilhao, 'Fate of the Neanderthals', *Archaeology* 53:4 (July–August 2000), pp. 24–32.

56. Conard, 'The Demise of the Neanderthal Cultural Niche and the Beginning of the Upper Paleolithic in Southwestern Germany', *Neanderthal Lifeways*, Conard and Richter, eds., pp. 223–40. See also J. Lear, *Radical Hope: Ethics in the Face of Cultural Devastation* (Cambridge: Harvard University Press, 2006).
57. Olger Soffer, 'Defining Modernity, Establishing Rubicons, Imagining the Other and the Neanderthal Enigma', *An Enquiring Mind: Studies in Honor of Alexander Marshack*, Paul Bahn, ed. (Cambridge: Oxbow Books, 2009), p. 301.
58. Francesco d'Errico et al., 'Neanderthal Acculturation in western Europe? A Critical Review of the Evidence and Its Interpretation', *Current Anthropology* 39.51 (*Special Issue: The Neanderthal Problem and the Evolution of Human Behaviour*) (1998), pp. 1–44, p. 2. See also Jean-Jacques Hublin et al., 'A Late Neanderthal Associated with Upper Paleolithic Artefacts', *Nature* 381 (16 May 1996), pp. 224–6; and J. Hahn, 'L'Orígine du Paléolithique supérieure en Europe centrale: Les Datations C14', *El Orígen del Hombre moderno en el Suroeste de Europa*, Cabrerra Valdés, ed. (Madrid: Universidad Nacionale d'Educación a Distancia, 1993), pp. 61–80.
59. Steven Lithen, *The Prehistory of the Mind: The Cognitive Origins of Art, Religion and Science* (London: Thames and Hudson, 1996), p. 167.
60. Francesco d'Errico et al., 'Archaeological Evidence for the Emergence of Language, Symbolism, and Music: An Alternative Multidisciplinary Perspective', *Journal of World Prehistory* 17 (2003), p. 13.
61. D'Errico et al., 'Neanderthal Acculturation', pp. 3–4. Of course, d'Errico has received a good deal of criticism as well. See Paul Mellars, 'The Neanderthal Problem Continued', *Current Anthropology* 40.3 (1999), pp. 341–64; Mellars, 'Neanderthals and the Modern Human Colonization of Europe', *Nature* 432 (25 November 2004), pp. 461–5; Mellars et al., 'Confirmation of Neanderthal/Modern Interstratification at the Châtelperronian Type-Site', *Publications of the National Academy of Science of the United States of America* 104:9 (27 February 2007), pp. 3657–62.
62. D'Errico, 'Archaeological Evidence for the Emergence of Language, Symbolism and Music', p. 19. This argument did not convince those who held the orthodox or traditional views regarding acculturation of Neanderthals by superior Cro-Magnons. See P. Mellars, 'The Impossible Coincidence: A Single Species Model for the Origins of Modern Human Behaviour in Europe', *Evolutionary Anthropology* 14 (2005), pp. 12–27. See also P. G. Chase, 'The Significance of Acculturation Depends on the Meaning of Culture', *Rethinking the Human Revolution*, Mellars et al., eds., pp. 55–66. G. A. Clark, 'Neandertal Archaeology: Implications for Our Origins', *American Anthropologist* N.S. 104.1 (2002), p. 61. See also April Nowell and Francesco d'Errico, 'The Art of Taphonomy and the Taphonomy of Art: Layer IV, Moldova I, Ukraine', *Journal of Archaeological Method and Theory* 14 (2007), pp. 1–26. Taphonomy considers the process to which an organism is subject from its death until its recovery. See Gisela Grupe, 'Taphonomic and Diagenetic Processes', *Handbook of Paleoanthropology, Vol. 1: Principles, Methods and Approaches*, Winfried Henke and Ian Tattersall, eds. (Berlin: Springer, 2007), pp. 241–59.
63. See H. Heinrich, 'Origin and Consequences of Cyclic Ice Rafting in the Northeast Atlantic Ocean During the Past 130,000 Years', *Quaternary Research* 29 (1988), pp. 142–52; G. Bond et al., 'Correlations Between Climate Records from North Atlantic Sediments and Greenland Ice', *Nature* 365 (1993), pp. 143–7. D'Errico et al., 'Neanderthal Acculturation', p. 19; D'Errico and Goni, 'Neandertal Extinction', p. 784.
64. Tattersall and Schwartz, *Extinct Humans*, p. 205.

65. Finlayson, *The Humans Who Went Extinct*, p. 125ff.
66. Zilhao, 'The Ebro Frontier: A Model for the Late Extinction of Iberian Neanderthals', C. B. Stringer et al., eds., *Neanderthals on the Edge: Papers from a Conference Marking the 150th Anniversary of the Forbes Quarry Discovery, Gibraltar* (Oxford: Oxbow Books, 2000), p. 119.
67. D'Errico et al., 'Neanderthal Acculturation', pp. 21–2.
68. See also Curtis W. Marean, 'Heading North: An Africanist Perspective on the Replacement of Neanderthals by Modern Humans', *Rethinking the Human Revolution*, Mellars et al., eds., pp. 367–79.
69. Joao Zilhao et al., 'Symbolic Use of Marine Shells and Mineral Pigments by Iberian Neandertals', *Proceedings of the National Academy of Science of the USA* 107 (19 January 2010), p. 1023. D'Errico was also part of this research team.
70. Zilhao et al., 'Symbolic Use of Marine Shells', p. 1027. Brecciated archaeological sites contain artifacts that are surrounded by minerals or rock fragments that cement the artifact in place, making it 'literally rock-solid'.
71. Zilhao et al., 'Symbolic Use of Marine Shells', p. 1027.
72. D'Errico, 'The Invisible Frontier', p. 199.
73. Steven L. Kuhn and Mary C. Stiner, 'Paleolithic Ornaments: Implications for Cognition, Demography and Identity', *Diogenes* 214 (2007), p. 41.
74. D'Errico, 'The Invisible Frontier', p. 196. See also the earlier argument by Zilhao and d'Errico, 'The Chronology and Taphonomy of the Earliest Aurignacian and Its Implications for the Understanding of Neanderthal Extinction', *Journal of World Prehistory* 13 (1999), pp. 1–68. Whether animated by 'anti-Neanderthal prejudice' or not, Eric Trinkaus downplayed the Southern African evidence as presenting 'few distinctively modern human features', notwithstanding evidence of modern human symbolic behaviour dating from a very early period. See C. W. Mavean et al., 'Early Human Use of Marine Resources and Pigment in South Africa during the Middle Pleistocene', *Science* 449 (18 October 2007), pp. 905–09; Trinkaus, 'European Early Modern Humans and the Fate of the Neandertals', *Proceedings of the National Academy of Sciences of the United States of America* 104.18 (1 May 2007), p. 7368.
75. Byers, 'Symboling and the Middle-Upper Paleolithic Transition: A Theoretical and Methodological Critique', *Current Anthropology* 35.4 (1994), pp. 369–99.
76. Byers, 'Symboling', p. 370.
77. See n. 20 above.
78. Byers, 'Symboling', p. 372.
79. Shanks, 'Comment' on 'Symboling', p. 390.
80. Byers, 'Symboling', p. 397.
81. Tattersall and Schwartz, *Extinct Humans*, p. 221.
82. Wade, *Before the Dawn: Recovering the Lost History of Our Ancestors* (New York: Penguin, 2006), p. 157. My emphasis.
83. John J. Shea, 'Neanderthals, Competition and the Origin of Modern Human Behaviour in the Levant', *Evolutionary Anthropology* 12 (2003), p. 184, p. 187. See also Sørensen, 'Demography and the Extinction of European Neanderthals', p. 25.
84. E. Zubrow, 'The Demographic Modelling of Neanderthal Extinction', *The Human Revolution: Behavioural and Biological Perspectives on the Origins of Modern Humans*, P. Mellars and C. Stringer, eds. (Edinburgh: Edinburgh University Press, 1989), pp. 212–31.
85. An exception is Pierre-Yves Demars who noted in response to d'Errico's paper on 'Neanderthal Acculturation' that 'none of the definitions' of 'assimilation' or

'acculturation' assumes 'the "inferiority" of a population, except perhaps in war technology'. D'Errico, 'Neanderthal Acculturation', p. 24.
86. Tattersall, 'Evolution and the Human Capacity', *An Enquiring Mind*, Bahn, ed., p. 320.
87. Purcell, *The Drama of Humanity*, p. 53.
88. Goodall, *Through a Window: My Thirty Years with the Chimpanzees of Gombe* (Boston: Houghton Mifflin, 1990), pp. 98–111.
89. See Michael P. Ghiglieri, *The Dark Side of Man: Tracing the Origins of Male Violence* (Cambridge: Perseus Books, 1999), pp. 156–204; R. W. Wrangham and D. Peterson, *Demonic Males: Apes and the Origins of Human Violence* (Boston: Houghton Mifflin, 1996); see also Frans de Waal, *Peacemaking among Primates* (Cambridge: Harvard University Press, 1989).
90. Vijender Bhalla, 'Comments' to Marilyn Keyes Roper, 'A Survey of the Evidence for Intrahuman Killing in the Pleistocene', *Current Anthropology* 10.4 (October 1969), p. 450.
91. Gat, *War in Human Civilization* (Oxford: Oxford University Press, 2006), p. 25.
92. Carbonell et al., 'Cultural Cannibalism as a Paleoeconomic System in the European Lower Pleistocene', *Current Anthropology* 51 (2010), p. 439; Carbonell et al., 'A Reply to Otterbein', *Current Anthropology* 52 (2011), p. 441.
93. Erik Trinkaus and M. R. Zimmerman, 'Trauma Among Shanidar Neandertals', *American Journal of Physical Anthropology* 57 (1982), p. 61. See the complete report as well; Trinkaus, *The Shanidar Neandertals* (New York: Academic Press, 1983), esp. pp. 206, p. 414ff.
94. Trinkaus and Zimmerman, 'Trauma Among Shanidar Neandertals', p. 69, pp. 71–2, p. 75.
95. Christopher P. E. Zollikofer et al., 'Evidence for Interpersonal Violence in the St Césaire Neanderthal', *Proceedings of the National Academy of Sciences of the United States of America* 99.9 (April 30 2002), p. 6444.
96. Klein, *The Human Career*, p. 489. Archaeologists define blades as stone tools that are significantly longer than they are wide, which means they embody a greater length of cutting edge per unit volume of stone than either core or flake tools; that is, they are an improvement.
97. Zollikofer et al., 'Evidence for Interpersonal Violence', p. 6447. Hafting, that is attaching a handle to a point, dates from the Mousterian about 40kyBP. See Eric Boëda et al., 'Bitumen as a Hafting Material on Middle Paleolithic Artefacts', *Nature* 380 (28 March 1996), pp. 336–8.
98. Johann Koller et al., 'High-Tech in the Middle Paleolithic: Neandertal-Manufactured Pitch Identified', *European Journal of Archaeology* 4.3 (2001), pp. 385–97.
99. Zollikofer et al., 'Evidence for Interpersonal Violence', p. 6647.
100. Phillip L. Walker, 'A Bioarcheological Perspective on the History of Violence', *Annual Review of Anthropology* 30 (2001), p. 584. Studies of arrow wounds to US Army personnel during the Indian wars indicated that 'fewer than a third of the arrows struck bone and that 61 per cent of fatal arrow wounds were to the abdomen'. See Samuel Bowles, 'Did Warfare Among Ancestral Hunter-Gatherers Affect the Evolution of Human Social Behaviour?', *Science* 324 (5 June 2009), p. 1296. See also Ruth Mace, 'On Becoming Modern', *Science* 324 (5 June 2009), pp. 1280–1. Possibly the same percentage would obtain with spear thrusts, since bows and arrows were not invented until after the Neanderthals were long gone.
101. In this context, Lawrence Guy Straus used the image of an 'arms race' to describe intergroup competition around the last Glacial Maximum (ca.25kyBP). 'The Upper Paleolithic of Europe: An Overview', *Evolutionary Anthropology* 4 (1995), p. 10.

102. Zollikofer et al., 'Evidence for Interpersonal Violence', p. 6448.
103. Thomas D. Berger and Erik Trinkaus, 'Patterns of Trauma among the Neanderthals', *Journal of Archaeological Science* 22 (1995), p. 8489. See also the earlier survey by Marilyn Keyes Roper, 'A Survey of the Evidence for Intrahuman Killing in the Pleistocene', 427ff.
104. Jean-Pierre Bocquet-Appel et al., 'Estimates of Upper Paleolithic Meta-Population Size in Europe from Archaeological Data', *Journal of Archaeological Science* 32 (2005), pp. 1663–4. A meta-population is a population that is geographically dispersed, fragmented or isolated but of the same species.
105. Paul C. Mellars and Jennifer C. French, 'Tenfold Population Increase in western Europe at the Neanderthal-to-Modern Human Transition', *Science* 333 (29 July 2011), pp. 623–7. See also Adrian W. Biggs et al., 'Targeted Retrieval and Analysis of Five Neandertal mtDNA Genomes', *Science* 325 (17 July 2009), pp. 318–21.
106. Sørensen, 'Demography and the Extinction of European Neanderthals', p. 25.
107. See Tim Ingold, *Territoriality and Tenure: The Appropriation of Space in Hunting and Gathering Societies* (Iowa City: University of Iowa Press, 1986), p. 153.
108. W. Lloyd Warner, *A Black Civilization: A Social Study of an Australian Tribe* (New York: Harper [1937] 1958), pp. 15–90.
109. See Misia Landau, *Narratives of Human Evolution* (New Haven: Yale University Press, 1991). See also Clifford Geertz, *Available Light: Anthropological Reflections on Philosophical Topics* (Princeton: Princeton University Press, 2000), p. 102; Abigail Hackett and Robin Dennell, 'Neanderthals as Fiction in Anthropological Narrative', *Antiquity* 77 (2003), pp. 816–27.
110. S. L. Vencl, 'War and Warfare in Archaeology', *Journal of Anthropological Archaeology* 3 (1984), p. 124.
111. Carol R. Ember, 'Myths about Hunter-Gatherers', *Ethnology* 17 (1978), pp. 438–39; V. Gordon Childe, 'War in Prehistoric Societies', *The Sociological Review* 33 (1941), pp. 126–38.
112. Keeley, *War Before Civilization* (New York: Oxford University Press, 1996), p. vii.
113. LeBlanc, *Constant Battles: The Myth of the Peaceful Noble Savage* (New York: St Martin's, 2003), p. 69.
114. Ibid., p. 73.
115. Ibid., p. 85.
116. Ibid., pp. 90–1.
117. See n. 30 above.
118. Svoboda, 'On Modern Human Penetration into Northern Eurasia: The Multiple Advances Hypothesis', *Rethinking the Human Revolution*, Mellars et al., eds., p. 329.
119. See *War Before Civilization*, pp. 36–9.
120. Gat, *War in Human Civilization*, p. 143.
121. Frans de Waal, *Chimpanzee Politics: Power and Sex Among Apes*, rev. ed. (Baltimore: Johns Hopkins University Press, 1998).
122. See De Waal, *Peacemaking Among Primates*.
123. See Johan Huizinga, *Homo Ludens: A Study of the Play Element in Culture* (Boston: Beacon Press, 1950), Chapter 1, p. 6.

The Wealth of Persons: Re-capturing a Person-Centred Economic Perspective

JOHN MCNERNEY

TRUST: A HUMAN DIMENSION OF THE FREE MARKET ECONOMY
Heinrich Böll, the Nobel Prize-winning German writer wrote a short story called *The Balek Scales*.[1] In it, the Balek family, whose members are depicted as mighty landowners on a feudal estate near Prague in the 1900s, is unable to restore its credibility after the villagers find out that the only scales in town – which are owned by the family – have been manipulated. The scales are used by the family to determine essential economic indicators like prices in their trade with local farmers and field labourers. The story describes how a village boy called Franz Brücher makes the startling discovery, finding out that the hamlet's scales have been rigged at the rate of two ounces per pound in favour of their owners.[2] Protests and pandemonium ensue. The gendarmes are called and even the local priest tries to appease the protesters by demonstrating the accuracy of the scales in public.

Order is eventually restored in the little village, but *trust* is not. The Baleks realise this when at High Mass on New Year's Day the villagers sing a protest hymn pointing out that the family have now 'forsaken its old status and moral authority'.[3] The Baleks 'had expected garlands in the village [to welcome them] … but the village was completely deserted when they drove through it, and in the church the pale faces of the people were turned toward them, mute and hostile'.[4] Böll's description concerns what befalls an old aristocratic family in a sleepy hamlet. I believe if an analogous analysis is applied to the contemporary collapsed economic culture, it can recapture the essential insight into the need for an adequate understanding of the human dimensions, which are often hidden but remain at the core of the economic life of the free market economy. This indicates that the free market process is actually based upon what could be called fundamental 'personcentric' principles. In the Balek story, for example, the centrality of *trust* in the dynamics of economic life is highlighted. There are, of course, many other values that underlie the proper workings of the free economy. Actually, Pope John Paul II reminded us in a social encyclical entitled *Centesimus Annus*, written after the collapse of the Berlin Wall, of some of these essential human characteristics. He wrote, for example, that the market economy allows for initiative and human entrepreneurial creativity and thereby involves such virtues as:

> diligence, industriousness, prudence in undertaking reasonable risks, reliability and fidelity in interpersonal relationships, as well as courage in carrying out decisions that are difficult and painful but necessary, both for the overall working of a business and in meeting possible setbacks.[5]

These human qualities are, if you like, the plate tectonics or fundamental movements that drive the free market economy. Without them there is the risk of total economic and social stasis. There is no doubt in the context of the current economic meltdown that this human dimension has been shattered and eclipsed out of our very comprehension of what it means to live and work within a free market economic dynamic. Increasingly, a number of economists have acknowledged the centrality of human values and virtues in the proper functioning of economic life. In terms of a person-centred economics, for instance, the Jewish Professor Kenneth Arrow from Stanford who won the Nobel Memorial Prize for Economics has thought-provoking clarifications in this regard. Interestingly, he was one of the economists invited to participate in the preliminary consultation during the drafting of *Centesimus Annus*, and later in the Pontifical Academy of Social Sciences.[6] Arrow says that

> ... morality is closely related to the workings of the market ... people do have aims in life, and not just the grand achievement of material gains. They're concerned about others. This concern is the result of moral codes, which are developed and adopted through religion or through inculcation by other ethical sources. Certainly family relationships are marked by sacrifice. People are engaged in these relationships, and therefore, they devote their energies to acquire goods, not for the purpose of using them themselves, but for others.[7]

The American economist Raymond J. Keating also writes about the vital role of trust in the free market process. He remarks:

> Trust as a virtue in the marketplace means having confidence in the honesty, reliability, and integrity of market players. It speaks volumes of our free enterprise system that a stranger can walk into a small business, for example, that he has never patronised before, and yet generally trust that he will be served well, dealt with fairly, and will walk out the door with a product that does what it's supposed to do ... The virtue of trust is critical in a free-market economy ... High degrees of trust must exist in the economic system, in the government, in business, and in consumers.[8]

The Stanford social scientist Professor Francis Fukuyama believes that there are certain basic conditions that must be met for an economy to become free and prosperous. Two essentials are private property and the rule of law (for example, a theory of contract). But there's another element that is crucial and often overlooked – it is what has been called 'social capital',[9] specifically the existence of trust. In his seminal study on the matter he writes:

> Today, having abandoned the promise of social engineering, virtually all serious observers understand that liberal political and economic institutions depend heavily on a healthy and dynamic civil society for their vitality ... there is a mistaken tendency, encouraged by contemporary economic discourse, to regard the economy as a facet of life with its own laws, separate from the rest of society. Seen in this way, the economy is a realm in which individuals come together only to satisfy their selfish needs and desires before retreating back into their 'real' social lives. But in any modern society, the economy constitutes one of the most fundamental and dynamic arenas of human sociability. There is scarcely any form of economic activity, from running a dry-cleaning business to fabricating large-scale integrated circuits that does not require the social collaboration of human being ... one of the most important lessons we can learn from an examination of economic life is that a nation's well-being, as well as its

ability to compete, is conditioned by a single, pervasive cultural characteristic: the level of trust inherent in society.[10]

It is also important to keep in mind that it is not just modern economists who advert to the centrality of 'trust' and the multi-dimensional human aspects of economic life. Luigino Bruni explains how already in the seventeenth century and even before then, the economist-philosopher Antonio Genovesi, and leader of the Neapolitan School of Economics, formulated important economic reflections upon 'the ideas of public happiness, reciprocity, relationships, and trust, which today constitute the theoretical platform of what is called the "civil economy"'.[11] Bruni outlines clearly how Genovesi 'sees market economic relations as relationships of mutual assistance, thus neither impersonal nor anonymous'.[12] Genovesi's 'anthropological and relational view'[13] emerges particularly well in his analysis of 'trust, or "public trust"'.[14] The Italian jurist and philosopher Gaetano Filangieri, also from Naples and within this tradition, wrote, 'Confidence is the soul of commerce ... without it, every part of its edifice collapses on its own.'[15] But this anthropological viewpoint did not become dominant due to the triumph of the Anglo-Saxon perspective.[16] The suggestion here by Bruni is that a particular anthropological perspective was actually eclipsed out of economic thought. I cannot develop this very thought-provoking insight here, but Murray Rothbard similarly argues that, in fact, even the earlier Scholastic tradition was excluded and that Adam Smith:

> ... tragically shunted economics on to a false path, a dead end from which the Austrians had to rescue economics a century later. Instead of subjective value, entrepreneurship, and emphasis on real market pricing and market activity, Smith dropped all this and replaced it with a labour theory of value ... a world where entrepreneurship was assumed out of existence. Under Ricardo, this unfortunate shift in focus was intensified and systematised.[17]

The retrieval of these forgotten anthropological principles slowly emerged in the pioneering work of Joseph Schumpeter during the 1950s and 1960s. Schumpeter wrote his famous *History of Economic Analysis*[18] and his insights were further developed in the works of Raymond de Roover, Marjorie Grice-Hutchinson and John T. Noonan.[19] I could further trace the cultural roots of this eclipse of the 'subjective' dimension within economics back to the 'protestant reformation' but this theme does not directly concern us here.[20]

To return to our central focus, one of the positive things perhaps about the present economic crisis is that it forces us to ask some good questions about what are the fundamental principles which lie at the heart of the free market process.[21] An important insight is to realise that it is fundamentally grounded upon what I term 'the wealth of persons'. In other words, behind the mask or masks, which often occlude this reality, there is the actuality of 'economics with a human face'. Eric Voegelin remarks that an essential part 'of the resistance against ideologies'[22] is the importance of regaining the meaning of words. He mentions how it can often become commonplace among intellectuals, to 'prefer ... the Humpty-Dumpty philosophy of language: determining the meaning of words'[23] themselves without submitting them to criticism. I would apply a similar evaluation to certain public leaders and some economists when they discuss the contemporary crisis and the functioning of the market economy. Observing this debate is somewhat like discovering that we seemingly inhabit a world that is a 'tale of two cities'[24] where it is Keynesians who control one city and roar 'spend, spend' in order to exit the dystopian landscape of financial collapse, and Hayekians emphasising austerity who control the other part and just shout 'cut, cut' in order to regain economic redemption. Or it can seem as if we live in the midst of the shadows of a Tower of Babel, where we all certainly yearn to speak a common language but it becomes so confused that we cannot understand one another. In this scenario we can all end up a little bit like Alice wondering 'whether you [really] can make words mean so many different things'.[25] Indeed, in light of this challenge in terms of understanding, I agree with Voegelin's observation: 'recapturing reality in opposition to its contemporary deformation requires a considerable amount of work.'[26] The same degree of effort is required in regaining an adequate understanding of the critical anthropological elements, which are at the heart of the modern economy.

THE CASE OF 'CREDIT' CRUNCHED

If you simply take the origins of the word 'credit', for example, you'll see that it can be traced back to the Latin word *credere*, which involves the experience 'to trust' in someone, or 'to believe' in something. This human act of 'trusting in' someone else is at the basis of the economic system we live in. If you want to start a bank, for example, your problem will not be in finding borrowers.

There will, in fact, be no shortage of people willing to be your customers. The challenge you will face is getting the money to lend to others. To do this you'll have to find people who *trust you* to deposit their money with your bank. After all, 'why should they trust you not to blow it all and never repay them?'[27] Jamie Whyte, a former Cambridge philosopher, describes it as follows:

> A banker's basic challenge is to create confidence in potential depositors. So it is no surprise that bankers cultivated prudence and integrity at their firms and went to great lengths to signal this culture to depositors. The imposing bank buildings, the formality of manner and dress, the fastidious attention to details of contract and process, the conventional haircuts and absence of tattoos: It is all easily explained. Being boring was an essential selling point for bankers.[28]

If we examine, for instance, the origins of money and banking, you can clearly trace the human dimensions and the workings of the free economy. An important observation to make about the creation of money is that no state intervention is needed, nor is any central direction necessary for its introduction. Money comes into existence thanks to the application of human reason and insight. In other words, human innovation is at the heart of the emergent process when it comes to explaining the origins of money and banking.[29] Once a particular commodity (gold or silver coins, for example) has assumed the character of money and possesses the qualities indispensable to a medium of exchange, as in, durability, portability, divisibility and desirability, the institution of banking quickly follows on from this in human history. Banks now become a storehouse for money where the depositor places his gold or silver for safekeeping and receives a receipt or bank note in return. The depositor is entitled to redeem this at any time for the gold he has placed in the bank. As time goes on the depositors use the notes themselves as currency. There's no need to redeem them at all for that would mean that every time they made a purchase they would have to transport the gold around to the shops. As long as people have *trust and confidence* in the bank issuing the notes, these notes can circulate as money.

Banking and the means of credit have developed greatly since its early origins, but without cultivating and maintaining *public trust* it is simply not possible to have a modern free market economy as we know it. In the current circumstances of financial collapse it is quite obvious that the banking culture has changed profoundly. Robert Sirico describes how the continuing financial crisis, which began in 2008, happened precisely because of a 'breakdown of trust, integrity, and responsible freedom'[30] occurring within the prevailing culture. We hear the terminology of the 'credit crunch' and it is true that people and businesses can no longer easily access sources of financing for their projects. Previously, banks were by and large successful if its directors were habitually prudent in sourcing and holding loans on their own books, and if they were not, the depositors lost trust and the bank would inevitably fail. We cannot sufficiently develop this theme here. Suffice it to say, banks originally operated on the 'originate and hold' model, that is, the banker created the opportunity to extend credit (originate) but in so doing usually held it as a debt on his own books. And he also needed the necessary capital (assets, financial resources) to keep such a loan portfolio solvent. In doing all of this he had to use the critical human faculties of *seeing, judging and acting* in terms of the debtor and it was the banker's judgement (insight or intuition) that ultimately decided the matter. I'd suggest at this point that by phenomenologically 'x-raying' the banker's action, we could usefully apply Bernard Lonergan's analysis of the rational self-conscious subject to the banker's role. In other words, the banker's actions are constituted too by the conscious operations of experiencing, understanding, judging and deciding[31] which are actually constitutive of human economic interaction. In terms of a 'phenomenological x-ray', I have in mind here that we do not just remain at the level of pure description of the banker's action and his relationship to the customer. I use this idea of a 'phenomenological x-ray' because as I argue elsewhere, when it comes to human action, 'pure description is not enough. There is, therefore, secondly, the need to interpret, that is to understand the essence of the phenomenon by seeing it in the context of the whole person and of interpersonal relations.'[32] There is today an even more urgent need to philosophically re-examine the anthropological roots of human economic action so that we can hopefully come up with a more coherent understanding of a person-centred economics.

In contemporary times, of course, the banking model shifted to 'originate and distribute', that is, the banker lends but then sells on the 'hazard' to other financial institutions. The risk was then packaged into new financial instruments and sold on to anonymous parties. Inherently, there is no problem with spreading risk; indeed, it is probably a very wise thing to do humanly. But problems can emerge when we end up in the situation where there is then no 'somebody' to trust, so *credit* (*credere*: 'to trust in') is vitally denuded of its original meaning. Trust becomes no longer necessary or constitutive of banking or economic exchange in itself. This situation, as one university professor of international banking recently described to me, can result in human economic actions, which are inspired by 'malignant intention'.[33] Ludwig von Mises, the Austrian economist, clearly outlined how the whole economy is based on human 'intentionality'. Mises was not satisfied with simply describing economic phenomena but he sought to interpret and explain them as the 'outcomes of countless conscious, purposive actions, choices, and preferences of individuals'.[34] Explaining the acting person in the economic arena, Mises said:

> Human action is purposeful behaviour. Or we may say: Action is will put into operation and transformed into an agency. In aiming at ends and goals, it is the ego's meaningful response to stimuli and to the conditions of its environment. It is a person's conscious adjustment to the state of the universe that determines his life ... For the term *will* means nothing else than man's faculty to choose between different states of affairs, to prefer one, to set aside the other, and to behave according to the decision made in aiming at the chosen state and forsaking the other.[35]

Nonetheless, as the present crisis shows, the *human will* can become subverted in various theatres of action and economic agency is no exception.[36] Of course, this became so evident in the subprime-lending debacle in the United States. Michael Lewis in *The Big Short* explains how 'any business where you can sell a product and make money without having to worry how the product performs is going to attract sleazy people'.[37] Lewis points out that had the market really been *free*, and not interfered with it, those involved 'might have learned a simple lesson: Don't make loans to people who can't repay them. Instead they learned a complicated one: You can keep on making these loans, just don't keep them on your books.'[38] Lewis goes on to explain how the first existing bank to adopt the 'originate and sell' model was Long Beach Savings.[39] In this strange new financial landscape 'credit' does not mean 'credit' any longer; what's essentially going on in 'the extension of credit by instrument'[40] is that 'a lot of people who couldn't actually afford to pay their mortgages the old-fashioned way'⁴¹ now apparently can. But to do this lenders had to dream, 'up new instruments to justify handing them new money.'⁴² In the last analysis 'it was a clear sign that lenders had lost it, constantly degrading their own standards to grow loan volumes'⁴³ and increase their own interest.

Lewis describes an interesting experience of one of the auditors by the name of Vincent Daniel who started his first job in Manhattan. It was to audit the books of the investment bank Solomon Brothers. Alarmingly, Daniel discovers that nobody 'was able to explain why the traders were doing what they were doing'.⁴⁴ He says, 'I didn't know anything either. I asked basic questions – like, Why do they own this mortgage bond? Are they just betting on it, or is it part of some larger strategy? I thought I needed to know. It's really difficult to audit a company if you can't connect the dots.'⁴⁵ But Vincent's manager really grew tired of all the questions. He was told, 'It's not your job. I hired you to do XYZ, do XYZ and shut your mouth.'⁴⁶ Daniel could not take this so he walked out of the job.

In trying to understand the processes of deformation, which occur within ideologies, Voegelin outlined as a central characteristic of the participants 'what Doderer has called the "refusal to apperceive" (*Apperzeptionsverweigerung*).'⁴⁷ I think you can equally apply this to the current economic and social impasse. In this fragmented culture not alone is the question 'what are you doing?' often censored but so too is the first-order question as to 'why' you are doing it in the first place. Voegelin refers to the '"*Denke nicht, frage mich nicht*", Don't think, don't ask me'⁴⁸ attitude which is fundamental to this 'refusal to apperceive'. Daniel's questions at Solomon Brothers were not appreciated because these were questions 'that would immediately explode the system'⁴⁹ or more importantly the persons working there.

I contend that the economic crisis we are in essentially points us to the *crisis* of economics, that is, the continuing danger of the eclipse of the reality of the human person in the whole process. Financial journalists and economic commentators also make reference in their analyses to what I call the 'anthropological' *missing link* in economic activity. Gillian Tett in *Fool's Gold* mentions how people in the financial world had made the assumption that 'it was perfectly valid to discuss money in abstract, mathematical, ultra-complex terms, without any reference to tangible human beings'.⁵⁰ Larry McDonald, author of the book *A Colossal Failure of Common Sense*, written about the Lehman Brothers collapse, concludes his reflections on the crash saying:

It changed me. It stripped away all the careless glances at stock charts I have lived with all my life. The ramifications of those charts have a different meaning now. Where once I stared at the zigzagging lines, and just thought, *Up, down, win, lose, profit, crash, problem, solution, long, short, buy, sell,* now I see mostly people. Because every movement, up or down, has a meaning. I see it because I've been there. Every fraction of every inch of those financial graphs represents hope or fear, confidence or dread, triumph or ruin, celebration or sorrow. There's nothing quite like a total calamity to focus the mind ... And, I say again, it never should have happened.[51]

I have spoken in this chapter of an attempt to recapture a person-centred perspective in economics. There is no doubt that behind the current economic drama, you can trace in Voegelin's sense a deformation of the language and reality of the essential human dimensions which lie at the core of free market enterprise. Trust, which I have given a very brief analysis of in this chapter, is one of these fundamental factors that are at the heart of the free economy. But it has become somewhat like T. S. Eliot's 'patient etherised upon a table'[52] and eclipsed out of the dynamic process of economic and financial life. In the economic landscape we inhabit there is indeed a lot of talk about 'credit', whose creation is as I have discussed ultimately based upon trust, and there is no doubt too that it is seriously 'crunched'. But if one understands in the first place the fundamental 'personcentric' dimensions at the heart of the market economy, there will be no real surprise to realise then if one of these essential elements, as in *trust*, is pulverised out of the bedrock of the process, we are left with a mutant reality. The way towards an adequate retrieval of the true reality is to return to the human origins of the economic process.

A RE-DISCOVERY OF 'LIKEMINDEDNESS'

In this regard, it is, I suggest, interesting how Brendan Purcell in an unpublished essay on the Social Doctrine of the Church, discusses that at the root of the current financial and economic crisis there's a breakdown of what Aristotle would term a 'likemindedness'. Aristotle used the technical term *homonoia* for this. He also mentions the network of relations sustained by friendship as in 'marriage, kinship, social and religious associations –

which are necessary if the polis, as the *community of such communities*, is to achieve its goal of the shared realisation of their humanity by its members'.[53] Purcell observes:

> Aristotle is only too aware of the breakdown of likemindedness, the kind of breakdown of truth, trust, and indeed love, that's at the root of the present financial and economic crisis. For him, the unfriendliness of bad men who only relate on the basis of immediate self-interest results in bickering at the interpersonal level and speedy destruction of the common interest. Enmity or faction is the social expression of this unfriendliness just as *homonoia* is the social expression of friendship.[54]

Aristotle viewed 'likemindedness' as having to do with 'the basic issues, choices and actions of the community'.[55] This actually guarantees the 'inner substance'[56] of the community 'since it springs from the friendship of good men whose real goal is the common good rather than self-interest'.[57] The creation and manifestation of trust and other virtues in economic relationships is similarly, I believe, an example of Aristotle's 'likemindedness'. Indeed, it can be interpreted as an extension of 'political friendship' into the economic horizon. Aristotle observes in his *Ethics* IX, 6:

> Likemindedness is found among good men; for they are likeminded both in themselves and with one another, being, so to say, of one mind, for the wishes of such men are constant and not at the mercy of opposing currents like a strait of the sea, and they wish for what is just and what is advantageous, and these are the objects of their common endeavour as well.[58]

A crisis, therefore, is perhaps an opportune time to try and recapture the truth of the reality of a person-centred 'likemindedness', which is the originating idea at the heart of the free market economic system. The cardinal exemplar of this 'likemindedness' in the market economy is the crucial cultivation of *trust* and similar human virtues. Although it is true that the economic agent in the free economy is often viewed as a *purely self-maximising agent*. But this perspective is an eclipse of the reality of who we are as human persons and it is not how a proper functioning free market operates. The Austrian economist Wilhelm Röpke (1899–1966) states how the prevalent view of the human person as *homo sapiens consumens* loses sight of everything that goes to make up human happiness apart from money income and its transformation into goods.[59] This perspective is, he says, 'a false anthropology, one that lacks wisdom, misunderstands man, and distorts the concept of man'.[60] Are we then just to give in to the interpretation of the market economy as being based upon the 'icy water of egotistical calculation', which 'lets people gain the world but lose their souls?'[61] The Austrian School of Economics I've referred to argues to the contrary and other economists and philosophers do likewise. In Röpke's perspective there is a need, if you like, for a new 'likemindedness'. He calls for a 'new humanism' and believes that:

> ... the chain reaction between the business world's distrust of intellectuals and the intellectuals' retaliating resentment should be broken by both sides: the intellectuals should abandon untenable ideologies and theories, and the capitalists should adopt a philosophy which, while rendering unto the market the things that belong to the market, also renders unto the spirit what belongs to it.[62]

Luigino Bruni, a member of a new and upcoming group of economists called the Bologna School[63] in which a new economic project called the 'Economy of Communion' can be theoretically positioned,[64] also points us toward important insights into regaining the essential human elements of the market economy. Within the Economy of Communion project this new humanism or anthropology is based upon the concept of the human person as *homo donator* and gives rise to a culture of giving. The culture of giving is about the nature of the human person as a being who is open to communion, to a relationship with the transcendent and with others. The market actually presupposes an anthropology that is 'personcentric', but it is true perhaps that we have lost this insight (or even destroyed it!) and there's a great need to recapture it. The free market's foundation is not just built upon *having* but on *being* because it is constructed upon principles like

> self-discipline, a sense of justice, honesty, fairness, chivalry, moderation, public spirit, respect for human dignity, firm ethical

norms – all these things which people possess before they go to the market and compete with each other. These are the indispensible supports, which preserve both market and competition from disintegration. Family, church, genuine communities, and tradition are their sources.[65]

These 'person-centred' principles referred to are, I believe, constitutive of an integral 'likemindedness' which is at the heart of the free economy. Bruni reminds us:

> The market when it functions properly is a place where innovations and human creativity are favoured and rewarded. It is all too clear that we will never emerge from this crisis without a revival of entrepreneurship ... The market, the competition of the market ... can be seen, that is, if we want to understand it in its totality, as a race to innovate: whoever innovates grows and lives, whoever does not innovate, remains behind and exits from the economic and civil game ... The author who has most developed this *virtuous* dynamic of the market (the capacity to innovate is certainly a virtue, because it is an expression of *areté*, of excellence) is the Austrian economist Joseph A. Schumpeter.[66]

In light of this, professor Stefano Zamangi speaks of the urgent need to regain a more 'personalistic perspective' on the market economy. He observes:

> The Economy of Communion [project] says to us that the market ... can become an instrument which can reinforce social ties ... and the creation of an economic space in which it is possible to regenerate those values (such as trust, sympathy, benevolence) on which the existence of the market itself depends.[67]

Having said all of this and in view of the current economic implosion, one could well be tempted to paraphrase Gandhi's approach to Christianity, apply it to the free market economy, and say that 'it would be a great thing if it ever was practised and tried'.[68]

ANTHROPOLOGICAL PRINCIPLE: A HUMAN DIMENSION REGAINED

An observation Brendan Purcell makes in a paper given at the university of Hong Kong is insightful in regard to any recovery of the human dimension at the core of the free economy. He states, 'We must take seriously Voegelin's expansion of Plato's dictum "society is man written large".[69] Voegelin calls this Plato's 'anthropological principle'. It is based upon Plato's often-quoted phrase that a polis, a city, is man written large. It essentially means the society is an expression of the kind of people who make it up. I think the 'anthropological principle' can be equally applied to the economic reality we have created. The economic situation we are in is actually *us* written large and we have been found wanting. The Polish academic Leszek Balcerowicz observes that 'there is a lot of intellectual confusion'[70] about the root causes of our economic problems. He explains:

> For example, the financial crisis has happened in the financial sector. Therefore the reason for the crisis must be something in the financial sector. Sounds logical, but it's not. It's like saying the reason you sneeze through your nose is your nose.[71]

This is why I suggest there is certain urgency in the need to return to the human origins of free market economics.

The current economic crisis and disorder can provide us with positive areas for growth and development in our understanding of the unique anthropological roots of the free market economy. The present experience is truly horrendous for so many people but perhaps, at the same time, it unfolds the fundamental insight that the free economy 'is not just systems, institutions ... it is not just a technique but above all it is a relationship to the world ... to society' and to each other.[72] Applying the 'anthropological principle' to the economy, therefore, also involves developing a 'relational understanding'[73] of this social reality. In doing so we are engaged not just in a diagnostic economic-philosophical analysis but also in a therapeutic recapturing of the forgotten human dimensions that lie at the heart of the economic drama. In carrying out this undertaking we hope, in the words of Eliot, 'we shall not cease from exploration, and the end of all our exploring will be to arrive where we started and know the place for the first time'.[74] That place is hopefully a new horizon of meaning[75] where we can begin to give philosophical dignity to the multi-dimensional reality of a free economy based upon the wealth of human persons.

Actually, it is quite apposite how Bernard Lonergan describes that:

> Workers, foremen, supervisors, technicians, engineers, managers, doctors, lawyers, professors have different worlds. They live in a sense in different worlds. Each is quite familiar with his own world. But each knows about the others, and each recognises the need for the others. So their many horizons in some measure include one another ... they complement one another. Singly they are not self-sufficient.[76]

These horizons of meaning represent 'the motivations and the knowledge needed for the functioning of a communal world'.[77] Such horizons of meaning, I contend, can be understood even in terms of economics as the 'sweep of our interests and our knowledge'.[78] But by virtue of their own specification these horizons also delimit the boundaries of their own knowledge. Lonergan making reference to Joseph de Finance, distinguishes between 'a horizontal and vertical exercise of freedom'[79] within this cognitional dynamic. The horizontal movement is concerned with decisions or choices that occur within an established horizon, as happens for example within the various schools of economics. But there are also vertical transformations that are 'the set of judgements by which we move from one horizon to another.'[80] When we speak of the need for new horizons of meaning in the economic space, we are concerned with this second kind of exercise of freedom. It essentially involves moving into a 'new horizon of meaning' in terms of our economic anthropology and various disciplines like psychology and philosophy can certainly help us in this endeavour. This can indeed entail an 'about-face'[81] or conversion in our original understanding. Nonetheless, as Lonergan suggests and I have outlined in this chapter, the development in itself 'can keep revealing ever greater depth and breadth and wealth.'[82] This is because when it comes to an adequate philosophical elucidation of the *acting person* within the economic drama of human life, the task is as unending as the mystery and uniqueness of the human person is. This is in the end the true wealth of persons upon which our economic life ultimately depends.

NOTES

1. *The Stories of Heinrich Böll*, Leila Vennewitz, trans. (Evanston, IL: Northwestern University Press, 1995), pp. 439–45.
2. The young boy tells Frau Balek von Bilgan when she leaves the church after Mass that the scales had been rigged 'this much, two ounces, is short in every pound of your justice.' See *The Stories of Heinrich Böll*, p. 444.
3. See 'Trust is lost when scales are rigged', letter by Camillo von Mueller, *Financial Times* (2 October 2012).
4. *The Stories of Heinrich Böll*, p. 443.
5. See John Paul II, *Centesimus Annus* (hereafter *CA*), No. 32, 1 May 1991. The encyclical can be accessed via the web at this URL: www.vatican.va. In quoting from such documents I will refer to the section numbers.
6. Mary Ann Glendon, currently professor of Law at Harvard Law School, was the first female president of the Academy. She observed: 'Many people are surprised to learn that among the thirty-three members of our academy are several non-Catholics. That group includes two American economists, Nobel-prize-winners Kenneth Arrow and Joseph Stiglitz, who share many concerns that animate the social doctrine of the Church.' See 'The Pope's Think Tank: Why did Pope John Paul II found the Pontifical Academy of Social Sciences in 1994?', *Religion & Liberty: A Journal of Religion, Economics, and Culture* 15.1 (Summer 2005), p. 3.
7. See 'The Economy of Trust: An Interview with Kenneth Arrow', *Religion & Liberty* 16.3 (Summer 2006), pp. 12–13.
8. See 'Trust and Entrepreneurship', *Religion & Liberty* 16.3 (Summer 2006), pp. 4–5.
9. 'Social capital refers to the value of social relationships ... Social capital facilitates the transmission of human capital both within families (from parents to children) and within society more broadly'. See *The Oxford Handbook of Human Capital*, Alan Burton-Jones and J. C. Spender, eds. (Oxford: Oxford University Press, 2011), pp. 417, 419.
10. Fukuyama in *Trust: The Social Virtues and the Creation of Prosperity* (New York: Free Press, 1995), p. 4, p. 6, p. 7.
11. Bruni, *The Wound and the Blessing: Economics, Relationships, and Happiness* (New York: New City Press, 2012), pp. 63–4.
12. Ibid., p. 66.
13. Ibid., p. 67.
14. Ibid., p. 66.
15. Quoted in Bruni, *The Wound and the Blessing*, p. 66.
16. Ibid., p. 63.
17. Murray N. Rothbard, *Economic Thought Before Adam Smith: An Austrian Perspective on the History of Economic Thought*, Volume I (Auburn, AL: Ludwig von Mises Institute, 2006), p. xi.
18. Joseph Schumpeter, *History of Economic Analysis* (New York: Oxford University Press, 1954).
19. Rothbard, *Economic Thought Before Adam Smith*, p. x.
20. An interesting study in this regard is by Brad S. Gregory. It is entitled *The Unintended Reformation: How a Religious Revolution Secularized Society* (Cambridge, MA: Harvard University Press, 2012). Gregory writes: 'What transpired five centuries ago continues today to profoundly influence the lives of everyone not only in Europe and North America but all around the world, whether or not they are Christians or indeed religious believers of any kind.' See *The Unintended Reformation*, p. 1.

21. See in this regard a recent book authored by Rev. Robert Sirico, entitled *Defending the Free Market: The Moral Case for a Free Economy* (Washington, DC: Regenery Publishing, Inc., 2012).
22. Voegelin, *Autobiographical Reflections*, Ellis Sandoz, ed. (Baton Rouge, LA: Louisiana State University Press, 1989), pp. 17–18.
23. Ibid., p. 97. Humpty Dumpty says to Alice: 'When I use a word ... it means just what I choose it to mean – neither more nor less.' See Lewis Carroll, *Alice's Adventures in Wonderland and Through The Looking Glass* (New York: Barnes & Noble, 2004), p. 219. C. S. Lewis similarly points out the fallibility of language as a guide, but in spite of its defects it still contains 'a good deal of stored insight and experience. If you begin by flouting it, it has a way of avenging itself later on. We had better not follow Humpty Dumpty in making words mean whatever we please.' See *The Four Loves* (London: HarperCollins, 2012), p. 2.
24. We read in Charles Dickens's novel: 'It was the best of times, it was the worst of times, it was the age of wisdom, it was the age of foolishness, it was the epoch of belief, it was the epoch of incredulity, it was the season of Light, it was the season of Darkness, it was the spring of hope, it was the winter of despair, we had everything before us, we had nothing before us, we were all going direct to Heaven, we were all going direct the other way.' See Dickens, *A Tale of Two Cities* (London: Penguin Books, 2003), p. 5.
25. Carroll, *Through The Looking Glass*, p. 219.
26. *Autobiographical Reflections*, p. 96.
27. See Jamie Whyte, 'Who Broke Banking Culture?', *The Wall Street Journal* (5 July 2012).
28. Whyte, 'Who Broke Banking Culture?'
29. See Murray N. Rothbard, *The Mystery of Banking*, second edition (Auburn, AL: Ludwig von Mises Institute, 2008), Ludwig von Mises, *The Theory of Money and Credit*, H. E. Batson, trans. (Indianapolis, IN: Liberty Fund, 1980), pp. 293–445.
30. See *Defending the Free Market*, p. 3.
31. Lonergan in terms of the development of cognitional structure speaks 'of the operations as experiencing, understanding, judging, and deciding.' See Bernard J. F. Lonergan SJ, *Method in Theology* (London: Darton, Longman & Todd, 1972), p. 14.
32. John McNerney, *Footbridge Towards the Other* (New York: Continuum, 2003), p. 13.
33. I thank Professor Ray Kinsella for this insight. He is Professor of Banking and Finance in the Michael Smurfit Graduate School of Business, University College Dublin. He is Visiting Professor at the School of Banking, Accountancy and Finance at the University of Wales Bangor, is on the Faculty of the Management Institute of Paris, and is adjunct Professor at the University of Bryansk. He has published, researched and broadcast extensively in the fields Banking and Financial Services, including Regulation Governance and Ethics.
34. Ludwig von Mises, *Human Action: A Treatise on Economics* (San Francisco, CA: Fox & Wilkes, 1996), p. v.
35. *Human Action*, p. 11, p. 13. [translation slightly altered]
36. I call this the 'OS' factor. 'OS' stands for 'original sin' that is a part of our fallen human nature.
37. Lewis, *The Big Short: Inside the Doomsday Machine* (London: Penguin, 2010), p. 9.
38. *The Big Short*, pp. 23–4.
39. Ibid., p. 24.
40. Ibid, p. 28.
41. Ibid, p. 28.

42. Ibid.
43. Ibid.
44. Ibid., p. 11.
45. Ibid.
46. Ibid.
47. *Autobiographical Reflections*, p. 98.
48. Ibid.
49. Ibid.
50. Gillian Tett, *Fool's Gold: How Unrestrained Greed Corrupted a Dream, Shattered Global Markets, and Unleashed a Catastrophe* (London: Little Brown, 2009), pp. xii–xiii.
51. Larry McDonald and Patrick Robinson, *A Colossal Failure Of Common Sense: The Incredible Inside Story of The Collapse of Lehman Brothers* (Reading, UK: Ebury Press, 2009), p. 339.
52. T. S. Eliot, *The Complete Poems and Plays* (London: Faber & Faber, 2004), p. 13.
53. In speaking of 'community of such communities' Purcell makes reference to Aristotle's concept of the social consequence of friendship as political friendship. Purcell remarks, 'This can be paraphrased as a friendship based on likeness in actualisation of our common participation in the divine *nous* or mind.' See Purcell, 'Some Notes on the Social Doctrine of the Church', Mariapolis Lieta, Focolare Centre, Prosperous, Co. Kildare, Ireland (11 October 2008), pp. 6–7.
54. Purcell, 'Some Notes on the Social Doctrine of the Church', p. 7.
55. Ibid.
56. Ibid.
57. Ibid.
58. Aristotle, *The Works of Aristotle Translated into English: Vol. IX Ethica Nicomachea Moralia, Ethic Eudemia*, ed. David Ross (Oxford: Oxford University Press, 1966).
59. *A Humane Economy: The Social Framework of the Free Market* (Wilmington, DE: ISI Books, 1998), p. 102.
60. *A Humane Economy*, p. 102.
61. Ibid., p. 113.
62. Ibid., p. 116.
63. The writings of a group of economists, philosophers and thinkers, sometimes called the 'Bologna School', are interesting in that they seek to develop the concept of the acting person in the free market process. In their writings certain anthropological principles like human *alertness, insight, choice, initiative and innovation* can be clearly traced and emerge as of central importance for an adequate philosophical understanding of the free market economy. A small example of the studies from these scholars are: Stefano Zamagni, *L'economia di communione: Verso un agire economico: 'a misura di persona'* (Milano: Vita e Pensiero, 2000), *Economia come impegno civile: Relazionalità, benessere ed economia di communione*, eds. Luigino Bruni and Vittorio Pelligra (Roma: Città Nuova, 2002).
64. The 'Economy of Communion' project launched by Chiara Lubich in 1991 in São Paulo, Brazil can be understood as a positive contribution towards recapturing the truth of the reality of a person-centred dynamic in business and economics. Lubich 'argues that all social relationships, including the economic, can be re-interpreted in such a way as to cast light onto the interpersonal dimension of human existence.' See Lorna Gold, *New Financial Horizons: The Emergence of an Economy of Communion* (New York: New City Press, 2010), p. 56.

65. See Röpke, *A Humane Economy* (Wilmington, DE: Intercollegiate Studies Institute, 1998), p. 125. There are close parallels between the Austrian Wilhelm Röpke's economic perspective and the Bologna School of Economics that has grown out of Chiara Lubich's charismatic insights, which inaugurated the whole Economy of Communion project. Had Röpke lived (he died in 1966 while Lubich launched the Economy of Communion in 1991) to see the launching of the proposal, he would have seen, I am sure, its positive contribution towards recapturing the truth of the reality of a person-centred dynamic in business and economics that was so central to his own economic contribution.
66. Luigino Bruni, 'Su imprenditori e concorrenza: Una guida alla lettura nei tempi di crisi,' *Nuova Umanità*, XXXIV (2012/1), 199, pp. 1–14 (my translation).
67. *Towards A Multi-Dimensional Economic Culture: The Economy of Communion*, Luigino Bruni, ed. (New York: New City Press, 2002), p. 134.
68. See Gerard Casey, 'Murray Rothbard' in *Major Conservative and Libertarian Thinkers*, Volume 15, John Meadowcroft, ed. (New York: Continuum, 2010), p. 121.
69. See Plato, *Republic* 368c-d. See Purcell, 'Towards a trinitarian humanism: Piero Coda's development of a heuristic of radical fraternity as a lived theology of history', *Sophia: Ricerche su i fondamenti e la correlazione dei saperi* IV.2 (Rome, 2012), pp. 247–71.
70. Quoted in Matthew Kaminski's 'Leszek Balcerowicz: The Anti-Bernanke', *Wall Street Journal* (14 December 2012), http://online.wsj.com/article/SB10001424127887323981 50457 (accessed 14 December 2012).
71. Ibid.
72. See Václav Havel, *To the Castle and Back*, Paul Wilson, trans. (London: Portobello Books, 2006), p. 68.
73. See Purcell, 'Towards a trinitarian humanism'.
74. T. S. Eliot, 'Four Quartets', *The Complete Poems and Plays*, p. 197.
75. See Bernard Lonergan, *Method in Theology*, p. 235ff.
76. Ibid., p. 236.
77. Ibid.
78. Ibid., p. 237.
79. Ibid.
80. Ibid. This movement is often required because the challenge of explanation necessarily requires going beyond a particular framework. See William A. Matthews, *Lonergan's Quest: A Study of Desire in the Authoring of Insight* (Toronto: University of Toronto Press, 2005), p. 230.
81. Lonergan, *Method in Theology*, p. 237.
82. Ibid., p. 238.

The Role of Conscience in the Adventure of Holiness according to Blessed John Henry Newman

THOMAS NORRIS

> Certainly, I have always contended that obedience even to an erroneous conscience was the way to gain light, and that it mattered not where a man began, so that he began on what came to hand, and in faith; and that any thing might become a divine method of Truth.[1]

INTRODUCTION

As a young man, John Henry Newman chose as the motto of his life, 'Holiness rather than peace', and 'Growth the only evidence of life.'[2] The occasion of his doing so was his reading of Thomas Scott, an Evangelical Anglican clergyman and the man to whom he felt he owed, under God, the salvation of his soul. He describes this great moment in his life in the *Apologia*. From the time of his first conversion at the age of fifteen, this very philosophical teenager aimed at obedience to the Word of God and the following out of the Will of God in the circumstances of life. Since Christianity is the presence of Persons, the goal of Christian life has to consist in looking unto Christ, the pioneer and finisher of our faith (cf. Heb 12:2). Obedience, not a frame of mind, is what matters. And since in the Kingdom of God, those who have will receive even more and they will become rich (cf. Mt 13:12), Newman's life advances from one degree of insight to another, since he had the grace not to betray the kindly light that led him. The students of this itinerary identify three conversions, one as a teenager in 1816, the second as a Fellow of Oriel in 1828 when he started to prefer intellectual to spiritual achievement, and the third in 1845 when he made the ultimate ecclesiological shift in joining the Catholic Church.

From the time of his youth, there was another concern that rose up before him. It was the spectre of an intellectual movement against religion of such depth and magnitude as to challenge all believers and to require an appropriate response. Christians would have to give an account of the hope that was in them (1 Pt 3:15). The response to that challenge is so much the context of Blessed John Henry Newman's life as to constitute a key hermeneutic of his voluminous writing.[3] Convinced of the power of assimilation of revealed truth, and of the need for time and history as the arenas where that assimilation could only occur, he set out to form Christians.[4] 'That goodly framework of society which is the creation of Christianity' was under threat. Accordingly, Newman dedicated much of his long life to propose and design a response to this subtle, ongoing and erosive marginalisation of Faith. Preparing for the 'Year of Faith' called for by Pope Benedict XVI, who speaks of a 'faith fatigue' affecting much of the West, the witness and insight of Newman are most relevant. If an eminent theologian such as Karl Rahner could contend that the Christians of the future will be mystics or they will not exist at all,[5] then John Henry Newman could be seen as a glowing personification of that principle.

His two great works on faith and belief, the *Oxford University Sermons* and *A Grammar of Assent*, cover about forty years of reflection and writing between them. There one might expect to find his most mature and explicit thinking on the assimilation and personal appropriation of divine revelation. That expectation is, in fact, borne out upon reading these seminal texts. Accordingly, it is to these two works we turn, in particular the latter which has his most mature insight as to how we realise the reality of God and personally appropriate the riches of divine revelation. In fact, he sees in realisation the very pulse of religion. The question, in other words, is, 'how we gain an image of God and give a real assent to the proposition that He exists.'[6] Newman proposes conscience as the preferable route to such an assent, because conscience is a 'first principle' and 'we have by nature a conscience'.[7]

WHAT IS CONSCIENCE?

In the *Grammar*, and significantly in the chapter concluding the first half of that original work where he is dealing with the apprehension of faith, he addresses formally the topic of conscience. Conscience is as real an endowment of our humanity as memory, or intellect or will or imagination or the esthetic sense. Conscience for its part is both a moral sense and a sense of duty, a judgement of reason and a magisterial dictate. In the second volume of the *Philosophical Notebook* he defines conscience in these terms:

By conscience I mean the discrimination of acts as worthy of praise or blame. Now, such praise or blame is a phenomenon of my existence, one of those phenomena through which, as I have said, my existence is brought home to me. But the accuracy of praise or blame in the particular case is a matter not of faith, but of judgement. Here then are two senses of the word conscience. It either stands for the act of moral judgement, or for the particular judgement formed. In the former case it is the foundation or religion, in the latter of ethics.[8]

Conscience as a moral judgement makes it the source of ethics, while its second dimension makes it the key to the realisation of the reality of God and, in a second instance, of the mysteries of divine revelation.

Newman concentrates on the second aspect. Why does he do so? First, 'this is its primary and most authoritative aspect; it is the ordinary sense of the word. Half the world would be puzzled to know what was meant by the moral sense; but every one knows what is meant by a good or bad conscience. Conscience is ever forcing on us by threats and by promises that we must follow the right and avoid the wrong.'[9] A second reason for his preference has to do with his focus on how we reach 'real' or 'imaginative' apprehension of God, and, specifically, the question, 'Can I believe as if I saw?' He will show that this primary sense of conscience is the very place where we access the reality of God initially and later *also* the truths of divine revelation. For in conscience as a sense of duty we encounter 'the dictate of an authoritative monitor bearing upon the details of conduct as they come before us.'[10] The whole world, Newman contends, knows what is meant by a good conscience and a bad conscience, whereas only a few would know what the 'Moral Sense' is. We speak of conscience as a voice, since the imperative side of the act of conscience enables us to realise that *we are being addressed*. 'If, as is the case, we feel responsibility, are ashamed, are frightened, at transgressing the voice of conscience, this implies there is One to whom we are responsible, before whom we are ashamed, whose claims upon us we fear.'[11] Already in the *University Sermons* on faith and reason he has brought out vividly the theonomous dimension of conscience when he explains that its 'very existence carries on our minds to a being exterior to ourselves; for else whence did it come? and to a Being superior to ourselves; else whence its strange troublesome peremptoriness? I say, without going on to the question *what* it says ... its very existence throws us out of ourselves, to go and seek for him in the height and depth, whose voice it is.'[12] To the degree that we listen, obey and act consistently with that voice, our realisation of both the being and the attributes of God grows deeper and sharpens.

With his characteristic pedagogical skill, he sets before us the two sets of 'feelings' or 'emotions' that accompany the good and bad conscience. These sets of feelings are such as require an 'exciting cause'. In that way, 'the phenomena of Conscience, as a dictate, avail to impress the imagination with the picture of a Supreme Governor, a Judge, holy, just, powerful, all-seeing, retributive, and is the creative principle of religion, as the Moral Sense is the principle of ethics'.[13] In that way, conscience in its imperative dimension 'is a connecting principle between the creature and his Creator.'[14]

Now this process, though 'independent of the written records of Revelation',[15] impresses on the mind the reality of a Supreme Being, better Person, who speaks to us and addresses us. Conscience in that fashion is a discovery of our identity as 'You's' before the living God who says to us, 'Do this', and 'Do not do that.' In the process, our minds arrive, 'not only at a notional, but at an imaginative or real assent to the doctrine that there is One God, that is, an assent made with an apprehension, not only of what the words of the proposition mean, but of the object denoted by them.'[16]

It is all the while important to realise the *context* of his exposition on conscience. It comes at the conclusion of the first half of the *Grammar* which deals with our apprehension and access to what is real. In this fifth chapter called 'Assent and Apprehension in the Matter of Religion', he applies the insight gained in the first four chapters. Now a key distinction worked out at length has been that of notional and real or imaginative apprehensions and assents. They differ from each other in terms of direction of attention and depth of impact. In real apprehension, we focus our attention on the whole object, while in notional apprehension we focus on an aspect of the object. Furthermore, in real apprehension, the object exercises maximum impact on the perceiving subject by engaging the imagination as well as the moral sense.

'CAN I BELIEVE AS IF I SAW?'

Newman asks this famous question at a key moment in the *Grammar* as he considers our perception of God and his divine attributes. The imperative side of conscience enables him to follow up his own question vigorously. There is a parallel between the function performed by the mind with regard to the external world and the function performed by conscience with regard to the Supreme Being. The fact is that 'from the perceptive power which identifies the intuitions of conscience with the reverberations or echoes (so to say) of an external admonition, we proceed on to the notion of a Supreme Ruler and Judge, and then again we image Him and His attributes in those recurring intuitions, out of which, as mental phenomena, our recognition of his existence was originally gained.'[17] This explains why he identifies conscience as the great internal teacher of religion and as 'a connecting principle between the Creator and the creature', as we have seen.

The implications of that connection should be noted. The objection circulates widely today that conscience disconnects, and so alienates, a person from the true self, setting Another over against the deepest self. This contention is clearly present to Newman, especially in the *Letter to the Duke of Norfolk* where, with the hindsight of four further years from the completing of the *Grammar*, he sees the mounting resistance to conscience and, in particular, the tactic of reduction of its primordial sense. He already addresses that contention in the *Grammar* by highlighting the fact that conscience is the voice of God and that this voice constitutes a call to our deepest humanity. 'For Newman the encounter with God in conscience is a profoundly religious experience, indeed it is for him the foundational religious experience.'[18] This has to be so since conscience is 'a dutiful obedience to what claims to be a divine voice, speaking within us'.

The significance and priority of conscience in the human access to God is a distinctive component in all of Newman's thinking. It enjoys precedence over the classical proofs of the existence of the Supreme Being. It also operates very powerfully within each person, and so is not reserved to theologians who have the time and the opportunity to formulate and defend the classical arguments. In the *Apologia*, he explains vividly the reasons for its importance for his thinking. The passage deserves quotation in full, not least for the clarity with which he articulates his method and his argument:

> Starting then with the being of a God (which, as I have said, is as certain to me as the certainty of my own existence ...) I look out of myself into the world of men, and there I see a sight that fills me with unspeakable distress. The world seems to give the lie to that great truth, of which my whole being is so full ... If I looked into a mirror, and did not see my face, I should have the

sort of feeling which actually comes upon me, when I look into this living busy world, and see no reflexion of its Creator ... Were it not for this voice, speaking so clearly in my conscience and my heart, I should be an atheist ... I am far from denying the real force of the arguments in proof of a God, drawn from the general facts of human society and the course of history, but these do not warm me or enlighten me; they do not take away the winter of my desolation, or make the buds unfold and the leaves grow within me, and my moral being rejoice.[19]

'CONSCIENCE IS A STERN MONITOR'[20]

'Conscience is not a long-sighted selfishness, nor a desire to be consistent with oneself.'[21] It is rather a messenger from God, a God who addresses us with a peremptory candour and evaluates our actions one by one with stern impartiality. In that way, 'its very existence throws us out of ourselves, to go and seek for him in the height and depth, whose voice it is'.[22] One's inconsistency in obeying the imperative of conscience prods us and goads us, assesses us and challenges us. In practice this means that 'the more a person tries to obey his conscience, the more he gets alarmed at himself, for obeying it so imperfectly'.[23] The experience of one's moral fragility, that experience so incomparably described by St Paul in chapter seven of his Letter to the Romans, is a searing one indeed. 'I fail to carry out the things I want to do, and I find myself doing the very things I hate' (7:19). This searing experience brings us face to face with our moral and human fragility, an experience that pierces and that leans upon us. The result is that '[T]he voice of conscience has nothing gentle, nothing of mercy in its tone. It is severe and even stern. It does not speak of forgiveness, but of punishment. It suggests to him a future judgement; it does not tell him how he can avoid it.'[24]

Now it is precisely this experience that Newman explores in order to investigate the appropriateness, or rather the *necessity*, of the gift of divine revelation. The God of natural religion who speaks in and via conscience is a demanding God so that we feel 'thrown between' the holy God and our unholy selves. Now it is precisely this 'being-thrown-between' the holy God and the unholy self that engenders the desire that God might speak a word of pardon to us![25] Conscience in that fashion puts us on the lookout for the word of pardon and the grace of mercy. In fact, it shows us the anthropological truth of our being by which we are expectant hearers of a possible Word of

Grace and Mercy! Already in an early contribution to the *Oxford University Sermons*, he expresses his insight in these terms. 'Those who know nothing of the wounds of the soul, are not led to deal with the question, or to consider its circumstances; but when our attention is roused, then the more steadily we dwell upon it, the more probable does it seem that a revelation has been or will be given to us.'[26] Men and women are the potential or actual hearers of the Word of the revealing God!

'A RESOLUTE WARFARE AGAINST THE RIGHTS OF CONSCIENCE'[27]

Newman was acutely alive to the religious, philosophical and cultural conditions of his time. The principal strand in that scenario was what he called 'doctrinal liberalism' together with the accompanying and rising tide of worldliness. This war on revealed religion – doctrines being portrayed as nothing but religious opinions that happen to be held by groups of people[28] – represented the greatest evil and challenge of the day for the Oxford Movement and for Newman in particular. The eminent Newman scholar, C. S. Dessain, read Newman's life as a response to that evil. In fact, 'Newman had a remarkable mission, the revival of so much of the revealed religion of Christianity.'[29]

The weakening of faith, inevitably consequent upon the undermining of divine revelation, would motivate and stimulate a further attack on the reality and meaning of conscience. Those who failed to see revelation as the provision of the word of Grace and Pardon, the Grace and Pardon which conscience longs for and reaches after even if anonymously, were likely to manipulate and reduce conscience in various ways. Why tolerate this imperious monarch, this annoying prophet, this stern monitor any longer? In 1874 in reply to Gladstone's expostulation against Vatican I's proclamation of papal infallibility, he writes of a 'warfare' and 'conspiracy' against conscience.

Literature and science have been embodied in great institutions in order to put it down. Noble buildings have been reared as fortresses against that spiritual, invisible influence which is too subtle for science and too profound for literature. Chairs in universities have been made the seats of an antagonist tradition. Public writers, day after day, have indoctrinated the minds of innumerable readers with theories subversive of its claims.[30] In that way, a 'miserable counterfeit'[31] subverts the true meaning.

Many philosophers proffered a phalanx of 'reductions'. Newman read these as 'the academic fashions of the time'. Thus conscience is but a twist in primitive and untutored man. Its dictate is an imagination. As to the notion of guilt, it is irrational since we are never quite sure of our freedom and consequent responsibility, caught as we are in a network of cause and effect. He 'simply rejects without elaboration the whole gamut of ethical theories current in his day: Hobbesian egoism, utilitarianism, Kantian ethics, Darwinian selection and the rest. But the rhetoric does not make it easy to disentangle exactly what it is that he most dislikes, let alone to see the reasons he might have given for his rejection.'[32] This is what he thought of the prevailing thought of the philosophers.

As to the advancing reductionism of the reality of conscience in the popular mind, people talk about 'the rights of conscience'. Alas! This rhetoric in no sense means the rights of the Creator, nor the duty to him, in thought and deed, of the creature. They mean 'the right of thinking, speaking, writing, and acting, according to their judgement, or their humour, without any thought of God at all ... in this century conscience has been superseded by a counterfeit, which the eighteen centuries prior to it never heard of, and could not have mistaken for it, if they had. It is the right of self-will.'[33] One does not have to know the truth in order to act! It's enough to will in order to act. Might is right!

Blessed John Henry Newman's life can only be understood against this twofold background of doctrinal liberalism and the gradual counterfeiting of the inner light of conscience. His own journey represents an original, personal and strikingly relevant itinerary during which he had to respond to these twin dangers as they threatened his times. This is the living context of his work, his 'meaning' in the most personal sense of the term.[34] 'Never was a mind so unceasingly in motion. But the motion was always growth, never revolution,' writes an eminent Anglican scholar.[35] The cumulative character of that growth, issuing as it did in an exceptional itinerary, is due in the main to his fidelity to conscience. From that fidelity there issues a consequent accumulation and convergence of insight and discovery. Most of all, however, it is the key to his holiness.

'REVELATION DOES BUT ENLIGHTEN, STRENGTHEN AND REFINE CONSCIENCE'[36]

As our internal monitor, conscience disposes the person to listen to and to welcome divine revelation. One and the same God speaks via conscience and addresses us in divine revelation. This explains why there is not a conflict between conscience and revelation though at times there might be the appearance of one. On the contrary, 'coming from one and the same Author, these internal and external monitors of course recognise and bear witness to each other.' It will be worthwhile to look at this unique reciprocity of conscience and divine revelation where Newman's thinking has gained for him the praise as the 'great synthesiser of interiority and church'.[37]

The God of creation is also the God of the new creation (cf. 2 Cor 5:17; Gal 6:15). The Creator has gifted the human creature with conscience which 'is not a long-sighted selfishness, nor a desire to be consistent with oneself; but it is a messenger from him, who, both in nature and grace, speaks to us behind a veil, and teaches and rules us by his representatives'. The truth is that 'Conscience is the aboriginal Vicar of Christ, a prophet in its informations, a monarch in its peremptoriness, a priest in its blessings and anathemas'.[38] Conscience is the specific gift which, assisted by grace, enables the creature to perceive the light and the life of divine revelation.

Newman loved to unfold the form and content of divine revelation. With Christ's coming that revelation reaches its climax:

> The Invisible God was then revealed in the form and history of man, revealed in those aspects in which sinners most required to know him, and nature spoke least distinctly, as a Holy yet Merciful Governor of His creatures. And thus the Gospels, which contain the memorials of this wonderful grace, are our principal treasures. They are (so to say) the text of revelation.[39]

As the summit of 'salvation history', the Gospels record and preserve the centre and the core of divine revelation. The Holy Spirit of God illumines that history. 'The birth, the life, the death and resurrection of Christ, has been the text which he has illuminated. He has made history to be doctrine.'[40]

C. S. Dessain noticed the concrete character of divine revelation precisely as addressed to each person. Since that revelation is the 'Presence of Persons – to know Christ and through him, the Father', fidelity to the light of revelation as it engages with conscience is the way to life and its fullness. 'To those who have even more will be given and they will be rich; while those who have not ... ' As he succinctly puts it, 'The whole duty and work of a Christian is made up of these two parts, Faith and Obedience; "looking unto Jesus", the Divine Object as well as Author of our faith, and acting according to his will.'[41]

As the Vicar of St Mary the Virgin in Oxford, John Henry Newman set forth the riches of divine revelation for his congregations. With winning perspicacity he expounded the 'unspeakable riches of Christ' (Eph 3:8). Always, however, he feared 'unreality' as the lack of obedience to the word of God. A contemporary of his identifies his pastoral anxiety in these terms. 'Evangelical theology had dwelt upon the work of Christ, and laid comparatively little stress on his example, or the picture left of his personality and life. It regarded the Epistles of St Paul as the last word of the Gospel message.' With the arrival of Newman, however, there was a dramatic change. 'The great Name stood no longer for an abstract symbol of doctrine, but for a living Master, who could teach as well as save ... It was a change in the look and use of Scripture, which some can still look back to as an epoch in their religious history.'[42] Newman invited and motivated his hearers to listen to the Word of God made flesh and sacrifice in order to keep and to do the same word. In a sermon bearing the title 'The Incarnate Son a Sufferer and a Sacrifice',[43] one encounters the standard emphasis of the man as he says, 'Here, then, revelation meets us with simple and distinct facts and actions, not with painful inductions from existing phenomena, not with generalised laws or metaphysical conjectures, but with Jesus and the resurrection ... [F]acts such as this are not simply evidence of the truth of the revelation, *but the media of its impressiveness*.' The net impact of divine revelation on conscientious hearers of the word of revelation may be seen in the fact that 'the life of Christ brings together and concentrates truths concerning the chief good and laws of our being, which wander idle and forlorn over the surface of the moral world ... It collects the scattered rays of light.'[44]

A healthy conscience is, as we have seen at the very outset, one that does what it judges to be right and avoids what it judges to be wrong. Or at least aspires sincerely in that direction. This is the key to the recurring emphasis Newman places upon the need for believers to be obedient to the light of faith, the gift of the word and the wonder of divine grace. In a Catholic sermon he describes the Christian call to holiness in these words, 'If we were created, it was that we might serve God; if we have his gifts, it is that we may glorify him; if we have a conscience, it is that we may obey it; if we have the prospect of heaven, it is that we may keep it before us; if we have light, that we may follow it; if we have grace, that we may save ourselves by means of it.'[45]

Those believers who obey their faith-enlightened consciences, and in that fashion walk worthy of their vocation (cf. Eph 4:1), will gradually but surely learn a new language. It is

> ... that new language which Christ has brought us. Christ has interpreted all things for us in a new way; he has brought a religion which sheds a new light on all that happens. Try to learn this language. Do not try to get it by rote, or speak of it as a thing of course. Try to understand what you say. Time is short, eternity is long; God is great, man is weak; he stands between heaven and hell; Christ is his saviour, Christ has suffered for him. The Holy Ghost sanctifies him, repentance purifies him, faith justifies, works save.[46]

These great facts vouched for in revelation become imperatives as he immediately stresses, 'That a thing is true is no reason that it should be said, but that it should be done; that it should be acted upon; that it should be made our own inwardly.'[47]

The *Grammar* draws out, in a formally philosophical and theological treatise, his understanding of the logic of faith and its development. The key to that intriguing text is the distinction between assent and inference. In assent, the apprehension of the terms is necessary and the conclusion is simply unconditional. By contrast, inference does not presuppose the apprehension of the terms and the conclusion is always conditional upon the truth of the premises. With regard to conscience in the believing subject, however, it is the role of apprehension and assent that deserves our attention. He famously distinguishes 'notional' and 'real' apprehension as well as 'notional' and 'real' assent. Now conscience in fact is the key to the real, providing as it does access to imaginative apprehensions and imaginative assents in religion. Newman shows how this operates in the theology of the Trinity. There theology attempts a global grasp of the great and first mystery of faith.

CONSCIENCE AND REAL APPREHENSION: VALIDATING THE FAITH OF BELIEVERS

It is important to dwell further on his insight in this field. An important point is the distinction between theology and religion at which I have already hinted. 'Religion has to do with the real, and the real is the particular; theology has to do with what is notional, and the notional is the general and the systematic.'[48] He does us the service of applying those distinctions to the central doctrine of the Blessed Trinity. Fascinatingly, he shows how a real apprehension of this great mystery is possible. Convinced that 'this doctrine of the Trinity *is not proposed in Scripture as a mystery*',[49] he aims at demonstrating how sincere believers may attain an imaginative or real apprehension of the truths composing this sublime mystery of faith. For 'the New Testament and the Liturgy bring home to us, as concrete realities, and in living images, that the Son is God and the Holy Spirit is God'.[50]

CONSCIENCE AND REVELATION: THE IMPERATIVE OF HOLINESS
Since the principal meaning of conscience is seen in the fact that it is the Voice of God speaking to us, urging the doing of the good and the avoiding of what is bad, *divine revelation for its part stands out as the very intensification of that address*. 'For the God who said, "Let there be light shining in the darkness", has shone in our hearts, shone with the light of glory on the face of his Son, Jesus Christ' (2 Cor 4:6). In his first Sermon, 'Holiness necessary for future Blessedness',[51] it is clear at once that he 'wants us to hear the Word of God … as it should be understood and accepted: … as the voice of our Lord and Saviour, who calls out to us in order to draw us away from the paths of sin and death, in order to bring us to the one way of life, in holiness.'[52] In fact, the unique focus of all of those wonderful sermons delivered in St Mary the Virgin is, according to Louis Bouyer, 'to make us realise what it means to be called children of God and to make us become such in fact in Christ'.[53]

As a core of revealed religion, doctrine is the goal of his preaching. God's revelation to us and for us is even earlier a revelation of what he is in himself, namely, the life of infinite love among infinite Persons. It is this life that is the light of humanity (cf. Jn 1:4). The unique focus of the Vicar of St Mary's Sermons is 'to make us realise what it means to be called children of God and to make us become such in fact in Christ'.[54] The issue is quite dramatic: to enjoy the beatitude of heaven it is simply necessary to prepare by means of conversion of heart and of life. Divine revelation, following upon and so reinforcing conscience, tells us that life is the very season of repentance in order to be ready for communion with God the holy Trinity. Someone gaining admittance to heaven without preparation would not be happy there!

Nothing will prove eventually 'good' if we have not first of all met with God – and, of course, on His own terms. And that once again means surrendering to his design of making us holy just as He is holy. This can be expressed better still by saying that our life will be a success or a failure according to our response to the offer of his love; more exactly still, to His stupendous offer of making us able to love as only he can.[55]

Now this is the converging message of conscience speaking on behalf of natural religion, and of revelation speaking on behalf of revealed religion. '…both Scripture and conscience tell us we are answerable for what we do and that God is a righteous Judge.'[56]

NEWMAN: *DOCTOR CONSCIENTIAE*?

John Henry Newman is renowned for his insight into judgement on foot of his breakthrough insight that inference and judgement are different operations of the human mind. He worked out this distinction in the context of the religious drama of the day which he perceived as the reduction of reason to one of its operations, namely, that of science and demonstration. He expounded on the topic at length in the *Grammar*, particularly in chapter eight on 'The Illative Sense'. The reduction of reason undermined the unconditional character of judgement or assent, placing it unfavorably under the guidance and probation of formal inference. In that way there had to follow the undermining of the unconditional character of faith.[57] Inevitably it generated an advancing aversion, in the academy and in society, to Christian and Catholic faith. In the course of his work in founding the Catholic University in Dublin, he spoke of this reduction as 'a form of infidelity of the day'.[58] Its perception would inevitably lead to a dislike of the dogmatic teacher. Would it be an exaggeration to see in the widespread aversion in the West to any version of a clearly defined doctrinal Christianity in our times the perfect verification of Newman's prophetical insight?

There is, however, a further score on which Newman's claim to a unique originality may be based. It is his insight into conscience, an insight running through all his writing. That insight was 'the kindly light' that led his steps to obey and to live by the truth he sought out over the long decades of his theological and spiritual itinerary. With his typical sense of the concrete and the historical, he both articulated the nature and the task of conscience in humanity's access to God and analysed the emerging attack on this prophet, priest and monarch of our very humanity. But it was his dovetailing of conscience with revelation, his very personal formulation of the rapport between grace and nature that highlights the higher echelons of his thought. Does this achievement not qualify him for the title *Doctor Conscientiae*?

NOTES

1. *Apologia pro vita sua*, p. 187. References to Blessed John Henry Newman's works are to the uniform edition, which was published by Longmans, Green & Co. of London between 1868 and 1881. Exceptions will be indicated.
2. Ibid., p. 5.
3. See *Stray Essays on Controversial Points*, London, 1890, 104.
4. See Christopher Dawson, 'Newman and the Modern World', *The Tablet* 5 (August 1972), pp. 733–4. It is interesting that the title of his very first Sermon is, 'Holiness necessary for Future Blessedness', *Parochial and Plain Sermons*, Vol. I, pp. 1–14.
5. See Karl Rahner, *The Christian of the Future* (New York: Herder and Herder, 1967), passim.
6. *Grammar of Assent*, p. 105.
7. Ibid. For further references to conscience in Newman, consult the following: Johannes Artz, *Newman-Lexikon*, Mainz, 1975; *Newman-Studien*, volumes IX (1974) and XI (1980) for various articles; S. A. Grave, *Conscience in Newman's Thought* (Oxford: Clarendon Press, 1989); John Finnis, 'Conscience in the *Letter to the Duke of Norfolk*', *Newman after a Hundred Years*, Ian Ker and Alan Hill, eds. (Oxford: Clarendon Press, 1990); Gerard J. Hughes, 'Conscience', *The Cambridge Companion to John Henry Newman*, Ian Ker and Terrence Merrigan, eds. (Cambridge: Cambridge University Press, 2009), pp. 189–220.
8. Edward Sillem, ed., *The Philosophical Notebook of John Henry Newman*, Vol. II (Louvain: Nauwelaerts, 1969–70), p. 47 (Proof of Theism).
9. GA, p. 106.
10. Ibid.
11. Ibid., p. 109.
12. *Oxford University Sermons*, p. 65.
13. GA, p. 110.
14. Ibid., p. 117.
15. Ibid., p. 118.
16. Ibid., p. 119.
17. Ibid., p. 104.
18. J. Crosby, 'What is Anthropocentric and what is Theocentric in Christian Existence? The Challenge of John Henry Newman', *Communio* 2(1989), p. 253; see also his 'The Encounter of God and Man in Moral Obligation', *The New Scholasticism* 3 (1986), pp. 317–55.
19. *Apologia*, Chapter V, 'General Answer to Mr Kingsley', p. 219.
20. *Difficulties of Anglicans*, II, p. 250.
21. Ibid., p. 248.
22. *Oxford University Sermons*, p. 65.
23. Ibid., p. 67.

24. Ibid.
25. See Heinrich Fries' fascinating comparison of Newman with Karl Rahner in *Newman-Studien*, Vol. XI, Sigmaringendorf, pp. 211–15.
26. *Oxford University Sermons*, p. 67.
27. *Diff*, II, p. 249.
28. See his Note A on Liberalism in the *Apologia* where he gives a précis of the principal tenets of doctrinal liberalism, pp. 259–69.
29. C. S. Dessain, *John Henry Newman* (London: Nelson, 1966), p. 44; see his Biglietto Speech on the occasion of the Cardinalate.
30. *Diff*, II, p. 249
31. Ibid., p. 257.
32. Gerard J. Hughes, 'Conscience', *The Cambridge Companion to John Henry Newman*, 2009, pp. 189–220, at p. 191.
33. *Diff*, II, p. 250.
34. See *Apologia*, opening paragraphs.
35. Owen Chadwick, *Newman* (Oxford: Oxford University Press, 1983), p. 5.
36. *Historical Sketches*, III, p. 79.
37. E. Przywara, 'Newman moeglicher Heiliger und Kirchenlehrer der neuen Zeit?', *Newman Studien*, III, Nurnberg 1957, p. 3; quoted by Terrence Merrigan, 'Newman's Catholic Synthesis', *Irish Theological Quarterly* 1 (1994), p. 43.
38. *Diff*, II, p. 248.
39. *PPS*, II, p. 155.
40. Ibid., p. 227.
41. C. S. Dessain, *John Henry Newman* (London: Nelson, 1966), p. 22.
42. R. W. Church, *The Oxford Movement: Twelve Years, 1833–1845* (London: Macmillan & Co., 1891), pp. 191–2.
43. *PPS*, VI, pp. 69–82.
44. *Oxford University Sermons*, p. 27.
45. *Discourses to Mixed Congregations*, p. 121.
46. *PPS*, V, pp. 44–5.
47. Ibid., p. 45.
48. *GA*, p. 140.
49. *PPS*, I, p. 210.
50. C. S. Dessain, ibid., p. 22.
51. *PPS*, I, pp. 1–14. See Bishop Philip Boyce, 'The Birth and Pursuit of an Ideal of Holiness', *Cardinal John Henry Newman: A Study in Holiness* (London: The Guild of Our Lady of Ransom, 1980), pp. 11–26, being a reprint of *John Henry Newman: Commemorative Essays on the Occasion of the Centenary of his Cardinalate, 1879–May–1979*. By courtesy of the Centre of Newman Friends, Via Aurelia, p. 257.
52. Louis Bouyer, CO, *Newman's Vision of Faith* (San Francisco: Ignatius Press, 1986), p. 17.
53. Ibid., p. 18.
54. Ibid., p. 18.
55. Ibid., p. 34.
56. *PPS*, I, p. 21.
57. See Thomas Norris, chapter on 'Faith', *The Cambridge Companion to John Henry Newman*, 2009, pp. 73–97.
58. See *The Idea of a University* (New York: Longmans, Green, 1947), pp. 287–307.

The Rhetorical Power of Socratic Dialectic: Socrates' Refutation of Gorgias[1]

EMESE MOGYORÓDI

Socrates' arguments in Plato's dialogues often leave their readers puzzled, dissatisfied or suspicious in terms of their validity or adequacy. While Socrates time and again asserts that he is concerned with the truth, and the truth alone, and is an adherent of reason,[2] in light of his often contrived and sophistic arguments this might come across as an insidious rhetorical strategy itself. Aren't we merely lured into believing that his arguments are sound and fall victim to the very manoeuvering of which he pretends to be a fervent critic? This might well be objected to Plato's presentation of a number of Socratic arguments (especially in his early dialogues), were they meant to be taken as strict logical deductions. In recent Platonic scholarship, however, there is a growing appreciation for the dramatic setting of Plato's dialogues, including first and foremost his staging full-fledged characters in his dialogues, who subscribe to certain views or positions not in an abstract, impersonal manner, but as pledged by their experiences, passions, sufferings, as 'wisdom' extracted from and warranted by their whole life, as it were. Consequently, Socrates is not only, or rather, not fundamentally dealing with the conceptual coherence of his interlocutors' beliefs, but their moral integrity: his *elenchos* is meant to explore 'whether their life is in agreement with their avowed principles'.[3] In this sense Socrates' arguments are fundamentally *ad hominem*, of the 'circumstantial' variety.[4] They are meant to point out a contradiction between his interlocutors' holding certain views and a special, personal circumstance *in which* they are subscribing to them, rather than to argue for the implausibility of these views for internal, logical reasons, or on external evidence. But is Socrates' procedure illicit for these reasons? If it is not, what is his excuse for rhetorical manoeuvring? Is he merely striving for victory over his interlocutors while hypocritically pretending to be concerned solely with the high-minded values of truth and justice?[5] This essay explores one of the most puzzling examples for a contrived Socratic argument, his exchange with Gorgias in Plato's *Gorgias* (448e–461b), and argues that while Socrates does employ illicit means in his *elenchos*, he has excuses that fundamentally distinguish his aims from those pursued by rhetoric.

Let me first briefly summarise the most crucial points of the arguments between Gorgias and Socrates and then make comments on them. Their conversation is detained at the beginning, for Polus plays the busybody and volunteers to respond to Socrates' and Chaerephon's questions instead of Gorgias, who is worn out by having delivered a long discourse, according to Polus. He intervenes, then, and straightaway exhibits his rhetorical aptitude by diverting attention from the real issue – who is Gorgias? (447d)[6] – and using the occasion both to praise Gorgias and to advertise his craft. While many are the nice and useful crafts, what Gorgias partakes of is, beyond doubt, 'the most admirable of the crafts', possessed by only the best of men (448c).[7] When Socrates corrects Polus for his inadequate attempt at defining Gorgias' craft,[8] and turning to Gorgias finds out from him that the craft at issue is rhetoric, which is a type of discourse (*logoi*) dealing with 'the greatest of human concerns ... and the best' (451d), at last it is revealed why it should be praised above all other crafts (448d–452d). Rhetoric is a sort of superscience (cf. 456a-b), for by its persuasive *dunamis*, operating by words alone (452e), it secures power over all the experts who claim to provide the best for humans, such as the doctor (health), the physical trainer (beauty), or the businessman (wealth) (452d). What is unique and so neat about it, Gorgias boasts, is that the orator needs to know nothing about the subject matter on which he seeks to persuade others, all he needs to know is the art of persuasion (459b-c). Despite lack of any specific knowledge related to the subject matter on which decisions are made in assemblies, courts or other public or private deliberations, orators can be more persuasive than experts (455d–456e). Somewhat as an aside, Gorgias hastens to add that since rhetoric is such a powerful craft, it should be employed with restraint. Just like any other martial art, it should only be used justly, and strongly implies that this is what he is exhorting his students to do. On the whole, it is the responsibility of the student, not of his teacher, whether the student employs oratory for good or for evil ends; on this basis, then, Gorgias declines all responsibility for the misuse of his craft (456c–457c).

After a short interlude (457c–458e),[9] Socrates entangles Gorgias in the contradiction that if he assumes that rhetoric is an art of *logoi* about right and wrong (*dikaia kai adika* 454b7, cf. 455a2, 459d1-2), and, contrary to his former assertion, at Socrates' prompting he assents that he does know right and wrong and is ready to teach them to his students if they happen not to know them (460a), then he cannot reasonably decline responsibility for his students' misuse of his craft (460a–461b). For, Socrates explains, rhetoric is just like any other craft in that the knowledge it imparts turns the student into the sort of man that this knowledge conveys and makes him act accordingly. For example, if one learns carpentry, one becomes a carpenter and builds houses; if one learns music, one becomes a musician and plays music; by the same token, if one learns what is just, one becomes a just man and cannot do anything wrong to anyone (460a-c). Rhetoric can thus not be misused for immoral ends – if indeed the orator knows what is right and instructs his students in it.

The upshot of this argument has been challenged as illegitimate for various reasons, but they ultimately come down to the conclusion that Socrates traps Gorgias into conceding some thesis that he does not honestly endorse, and that his refutation is thus illegitimate because irrelevant.[10] The most obvious and puzzling one of these is Socrates' signature thesis on the sufficiency of knowledge to virtue – or, in another formulation his rejection of *akrasia* (acting against one's better judgement), or in broader terms, moral intellectualism – derived in turn from what is called the 'Socratic twin paradox' that all wrongdoing is involuntary, for everyone strives for the good.[11] This is the thesis that if someone has learnt, that is to say, knows what is right, he or she cannot fail to act justly; thus the orator cannot misuse his craft as long as it entails knowledge of the good. But – the objection goes – Gorgias has been given no reason to accept Socrates' thesis on the sufficiency of knowledge, nor does it seem to follow from anything he has asserted up to this point in the dialogue. On the contrary, if his expertise itself, as he strongly implies, is value-free,[12] and in fact produces conviction without knowledge (454e–455a), then on these premises nothing could be more disagreeable, or simply irrelevant than the Socratic thesis that knowledge is sufficient for virtue. It might well be objected, then, that Socrates cunningly traps Gorgias into accepting a thesis that he does not sincerely subscribe to and that the 'disharmony' he detects in Gorgias' views is in truth one between *their* opposing views, rather than one internal to Gorgias' theses. Thus, they have not been refuted, rather, it merely turned out that Gorgias' views and Socrates' views are different and that, in fact, the latter is in need of defence, for no support for it has been provided so far.[13] Is this not plain rhetorical manoeuvring on the part of Socrates – or rather, of Plato – then? The answer is not without difficulties.

Several fundamental issues need to be clarified. First, why does Gorgias succumb to the Socratic rejection of *akrasia*? Second, by doing so, does he consent to a thesis that is entirely foreign to his avowed assumptions? Third, is this the ultimate explanation for his downfall at all? Finally, what is the bearing of his consent to this thesis on the apparently damning conclusion that he cannot reasonably decline responsibility for his students' misuse of his craft?

Before answering these questions, the crucial moves in Socrates' arguments and Gorgias' responses need to be mapped out. First, Gorgias states that rhetoric concerns right and wrong (454b); second, on Socrates' prompting he – indirectly – acknowledges that he knows right and wrong, and directly assents that he can teach them to his students if they happen not to know them before joining him (459c–460a); finally, he consents that if he knows right and wrong and teaches them to his students, then they cannot misuse his craft (460a-c), yielding thereby to the Socratic rejection of *akrasia*.

Let us first explore the bearing of Gorgias' consent to these theses on his probity as an elite educator, for while this seems to be the most vital issue about their exchange, it has not been sufficiently clarified. Socrates creates the strong impression that once Gorgias has consented to his intellectualist thesis, he is obliged to avow his responsibility for his students' misuse of his craft. But this is highly misleading. It might or might not be unexpected, or out of character that Gorgias succumbs to the Socratic rejection of *akrasia*. However, on closer scrutiny, this seems to be entirely irrelevant to assessing his probity or responsibility. The Socratic rejection of *akrasia* entails the assumption that *once* the good is understood or known, one cannot fail to act in accordance with it. But it does *not* entail that anyone will of necessity understand or know the good, assuming that someone clearly explained or taught it to him or her. We do not have uniform intellectual abilities, and some of us might simply be unable, or even refuse, to conceive of or understand some point, thesis or argument in the first place.[14] Hence, Gorgias' consent to the Socratic intellectualism does not substantiate his responsibility for his students' misuse of his craft. So far, it follows that Socrates' argument *is* inadequate, but not because Gorgias consents to his rejection of *akrasia* while not honestly embracing it.[15] The thesis simply has no bearing on Gorgias' responsibility. Could the challenge on his probity be explained in some other way?

It might be reasonably assumed that Socrates' arguments ultimately hinge not on Gorgias' consent to his intellectualism. Rather, the lethal move is that – albeit with some reluctance – he (indirectly) assents that he knows right and wrong, and explicitly affirms that he can teach them to his students (459c–460a), as Polus points it out later (461b-c).[16] This is doubly surprising, since Gorgias had proudly asserted earlier that rhetoric assumed no knowledge of the subject matter it persuades people on (453a–455a, 459c), and strongly implied that rhetoric itself had no inherent moral values to convey. But, again, this does not seem to have any bearing on his responsibility. If he consents that he does have knowledge of right and wrong and teaches them to his students, he gives away an incoherence lying behind his views and exposes his negligence to make it clear to himself – and to his students – what his craft is all about and what he is up to in offering its instruction. It sheds a somewhat unfavourable light on an elite educator that he is not alert to the theoretical implications and incoherence of some of his avowed principles.[17] But all this merely demonstrates that Gorgias fails as a competent philosopher – which he never claimed to be – and it neither challenges his personal probity, nor proves that he is wrong to disclaim responsibility for the misuse of his craft.[18] For, given his students' different intellectual abilities – which might be assumed whether or not Socrates' intellectualism is accepted – they might not be able to, or refuse to understand his points in the first place. In addition – assuming Socratic intellectualism is to be put aside – they might simply refuse to comply with his instructions on right and wrong, no matter how clearly he might teach morals to them.

Hence, it occurs that unless Gorgias explicitly teaches, or merely exhorts his students to misuse his craft, his probity remains unchallenged, and he cannot be made culpable for its misuse. The reason is that we have different intellectual abilities and we are ultimately free to obey or disobey what we are taught or exhorted to do. On both accounts, Gorgias seems to be justified in disclaiming responsibility for his students' abusive behaviour. Knowing that there is no way of guaranteeing his students' probity, he merely exhorts them not to misuse his craft, and that is the most he can reasonably be expected to do. What is more, while this may again seem incoherent and flawed from a logical point of view, from a moral perspective he arguably goes out of his way to do the most he can in securing his students' uprightness. For, while teaching what he conceives of as an essentially value-free craft to them, he *nonetheless* exhorts them to employ it fairly (456c–457c). This might be incoherent from an intellectual point of view, but it is not unprincipled; on the contrary.[19]

So, what is going on here? Are Socrates' arguments sufficient to raise doubt about Gorgias' probity and to substantiate his responsibility? And if so, in what way?

Let us return to Gorgias' fatal move highlighted by some commentators as the reason for his defeat. Indeed, his consent that he knows right and wrong and teaches them to his students is the ultimate critical move, since this is a vital premiss from which Socrates can derive the intellectualist thesis. It is worthwhile to quote the relevant passage in full, for it raises several difficulties. Gorgias has just consented that he can make an orator of anyone who wants to study with him, who will then be more persuasive in a gathering – that is, among those who are ignorant – about any subject without knowing anything about it, that is to say, he will seem more knowledgeable than an expert (458e–459c). Upon Socrates' summary of his position he strikes a triumphant note:

> GORGIAS: Well, Socrates, aren't things made very easy when you come off no worse than the craftsmen even though you haven't learned any other craft but this one?
>
> SOCRATES: Whether the orator does or does not come off worse than the others because of this being so, we'll examine in a moment if it has any bearing on our argument. For now, let's consider this point first. Is it the case that the orator is in the same position with respect to what's just and unjust, what's shameful and admirable, what's good and bad, as he is about what's healthy and about the subjects of the other crafts? Does he lack knowledge, that is, of what these are, of what is good or what is bad, of what is admirable or what is shameful, or just or unjust? Does he employ devices to produce persuasion about them, so that – even though he doesn't know – he seems, among those who don't know either, to know more than someone who actually does know? Or is it necessary for him to know, and must the prospective student of oratory already be knowledgeable in these things before coming

to you? And if he doesn't, will you, the oratory teacher, not teach him any of these things when he comes to you – for that's not your job – and will you make him seem among most people to have knowledge of such things when in fact he doesn't have it, and to seem good when in fact he isn't? Or won't you be able to teach him oratory at all, unless he knows the truth about these things to begin with? How do matters such as these stand, Gorgias? Yes, by Zeus, do give us your revelation and tell us what oratory can accomplish, just as you just now said you would.

GORGIAS: Well, Socrates, I suppose that if he really doesn't have this knowledge, he'll learn these things from me as well. (459c3–460a4)

The formulation of this sequence of questions is rather cumbersome, so much so that one might well assume that at least part of the reason for Gorgias' hesitant answer is due to the fact that it is difficult to see what Socrates is up to. Commentators suggest, along with Polus (461b-c), that Socrates asks him whether he as a teacher of oratory must know something after all, namely, right and wrong, and whether he teaches them to his students. But there seems to be a lot more entailed in Socrates' unusually long and complicated questioning, and it is a little odd that Gorgias does not explicitly answer the first of these questions, he only responds to the second. It is also somewhat confusing that Socrates starts his interrogation as though it concerned Gorgias as a *teacher* of oratory, but in about the middle of the passage (459 e1-3) it turns out that he has been referring to Gorgias' orator students all along.[20]

Awkward formulation apart, the passage raises the following main issue: why does Gorgias consent that he teaches his students right and wrong if they do not already possess such knowledge before they learn oratory from him? And why does he unspokenly consent that he does know what is right or wrong? Note that while his somewhat hesitant response adumbrates this, what he gives his assent to is that his orator students *must* know right and wrong either before they join him, or upon learning oratory from him at the latest.[21] This is very far from Gorgias' initial position, in terms of which the orator does not need to know anything, except for the craft of oratory to be persuasive on any subject. Now it seems that knowing right and wrong is an overall *prerequisite* for learning oratory. Why should he succumb to such a strong thesis, in stark contrast with his earlier implication that his craft is entirely value-free?

It has been suggested that it is Gorgias' sense of shame, that is, his concern for public opinion, that compels him to grant that he does know right and wrong and that he teaches them to his students, as Polus protests later:

> POLUS: Really, Socrates? Is what you're now saying about oratory what you actually think of it? Or do you really think that just because Gorgias was too ashamed (*êiskhunthê*) not to concede your further claim that the orator also knows what's just, what's admirable, and what's good ... [that] from this admission [...] some inconsistency crept into his statements [...]? [...] Who do you think would deny (*aparnêsesthai*) that he himself knows what's just and would teach others? To lead your arguments to such an outcome is a sign of great rudeness. (461b3-c4)

Polus protests that his master only succumbed because he felt ashamed to deny in public that 'he belongs to the set of, produces or even associates too closely with, moral idiots (who could each well be described as "one who does not know what good or bad or fine or ugly or just or unjust is") (459d4-5).'[22] He complains that 'to involve a man in a contradiction by forcing him into an admission on a point which he is ashamed to deny, betrays gross boorishness (*agroikia*) on the part of Socrates'.[23] The gist of this qualm is that Socrates breaks the rules of dialectical conversation by appealing to an extra-rational factor (the emotion of shame) to compel Gorgias' compliance. Both the complaint that Socrates employs illicit means at this point of their exchange to refute Gorgias, and the suggestion that it is out of shame that he assents seem to be justified at first sight, but neither is without difficulties. In what follows, I would like to challenge both of these suggestions, in order to clarify the reasons for Gorgias' downfall and the upshot of the Socratic challenge to his probity.

Polus' account for Gorgias' defeat consists of two claims that are worth considering separately in order to expose their full implications. Gorgias felt ashamed to deny in public that 1) he *knows* right and wrong and that 2) he *teaches* them to his students. As to the first of these claims, it does seem that as an elite educator Gorgias cannot afford to avow in public that he does not know right and wrong without serious loss of face, but only if this is taken to mean that he does not have the slightest idea about morals.[24] If he does not consider it his job to teach virtue professionally, as it were – which Socrates assumes as a reasonable option in his interrogation quoted above (459e4) – he is not compelled to have expert knowledge about it either.[25] But it would be grossly unfair on Gorgias to assume that he does not have the slightest idea about morals, nor does *he* have any reason to feel ashamed for utter 'moral idiocy'. As I noted, he exhorts his students to employ his craft justly, and this seems to be the most he can do for the reasons given above. The fact that he does so indicates that he has a fair amount of decency, and the fact that he finds it vital to make note of it while advertising the power of his craft (456a–457c) suggests that he is even proud about his probity.[26] As we know from sources independent of Plato, Gorgias did great service to his fellow citizens when, upon an embassy dispatched to Athens in 427 BC he persuaded the Athenians to provide military help for his native city against Syracusean threat (DK 82 A2, A4, A7).[27] In Olympia he exhibited similar high-mindedness in calling for the political alliance of all the Greeks at a time when they were in internal strife (A1). Thus, it is difficult to see why Gorgias would or should feel ashamed to deny that he *knows* right and wrong. Similarly, it is problematic to assume that it is out of shame that he assents to being ready to *teach* right and wrong if needed. Gorgias implied earlier that rhetoric is value-free without any sign of shame. Also, as Meno informs us, Gorgias did not shy away from laughing in the face of those who promised to teach virtue (*Meno* 95c). Last but not least, it is most notable that Socrates himself openly disclaims knowledge, especially knowledge of the good and virtue,[28] and fashions an argument of it in his defence against the charge of 'corrupting the youth' that he has never promised to teach anything, which obviously includes virtue, or rather, concerns virtue in the first place (*Apology* 33a-b, cf. 20c). Why then would or should it be shameful for *Gorgias* to deny in the open either that he knows, or that he teaches right and wrong?[29]

It occurs then that it is not out of shame that Gorgias consents that he knows right and wrong and teaches it to his students if they happen not to know between them.[30] This does not yet prove that Socrates' arguments are sound or legitimate, so we need to explore that issue further. Why does Gorgias consent to the fatal thesis, then, if not out of shame?

Note that Socrates' complicated questioning ends up targeting Gorgias' proficiency as a teacher. If Gorgias answers Socrates' question on whether he *teaches* right and wrong in the positive, that indicates that he is concerned more about his reputation as a teacher than about his probity. This assumption is supported by what I suggest is the cornerstone of Socrates' argumentative strategy and the key to Gorgias' critical concession. Socrates opens his interrogation that leads to the dénouement quoted above by ascertaining with Gorgias the following: 'Do you say that you're able to (*hoios t' einai*) make an orator out of anyone who wants to study with you (458e5-6)?' It is notable that he ends his questioning similarly: 'Or won't you be unable to (*ouk hoios te esêi*) teach him oratory at all, unless he knows the truth about these things to begin with (459e6-8)?' These questions are designed in such a way that Gorgias could not resist the ultimate conclusion Socrates seeks. Could there be anything of concern that Gorgias would be *unable to* teach? That this 'something of concern' in fact contradicts his earlier implication – that is, that his craft is value-free – is somewhat disconcerting for him (hence his hesitant reply), but upon hearing the keynote 'unable to', which challenges his aptitude as a teacher of oratory, he cannot help falling into Socrates' trap.[31]

As opposed to Polus or Callicles, Gorgias does have a sense of decency.[32] There is no reason to believe that he ever misused the power of his craft, on the contrary, drawing on its resource, at least on some occasions he did great service both to his own country and to Hellas.[33] What is more, according to Plato's portrait, he exhorted his students to employ his craft justly in a way that goes beyond the traditional heroic moral code, toward the Socratic-Platonic conception of *aretê*.[34] Thus, it is not shame that Socrates operates on in arguing against him, for he is well aware that Gorgias' weakness lies elsewhere. Polus is wrong to suggest that Gorgias' consented out of (moral) shame.[35] Polus is projecting his own level of existence onto Gorgias. Polus is refuted later because he *is* 'ashamed (*aiskhuntheis*) to say what he thinks', namely that injustice is really admirable (482e2)'.[36] He does not dare to assert that sort of thing in public because he is the type of man who 'will piously praise the rule of law and condemn the tyrant and who fervently envies the tyrant and would love nothing better than to be one himself. In a decadent society he is the representative of the great reservoir of common men who paralyse every effort at order and supply mass-connivance in the rise of the tyrant'.[37] Socrates is well aware of the difference between Gorgias and his vulgar, reckless and petty student.[38] He knows that Gorgias' flaw is far less trivial: it is not unscrupulousness, but arrogance. Gorgias flauntingly asserts his intellectual supremacy over all experts who possess knowledge of their own craft and claims that rhetoric is

> ... the ability to persuade by speeches judges in a law court, councillors in a council meeting, and assemblymen in an assembly or in any other political gathering that might take place. In point of fact, with this ability you'll have the doctor for your slave, and the physical trainer, too. As for this financial expert of yours, he'll turn out to be making more money for somebody else instead of himself; for you, in fact, if you've got the ability to speak and to persuade the crowds. (452e1-8)

Besides, he believes without the slightest doubt that he knows what is 'in actual fact the greatest good' (452d5-6), a pretension that must come across as far-fetched from the perspective of the Socratic *docta ignorantia*.[39] He is also over-confident as a teacher of oratory, claiming that he can teach it to *anyone* who wants to learn it (458e5-6). Gorgias must thus be highly confident about his intellectual capacities, or rather, assume both his *omniscience*[40] and the *omnipotence* of his craft, that is, of his abilities to employ it in a way that is bound to prove irresistible to anyone. Would Gorgias admit to *not knowing* anything of concern and *not* being *able to* exert total control over his own students of all people? Socrates gathers that he would not, and thus in cunningly devising his argument he appeals to Gorgias' intellectual arrogance, or as Wardy formulates it, to his 'aggressive intellectualism'.[41]

But is arrogance a moral flaw? More importantly, does it have any bearing on Gorgias' responsibility for his students' misuse of his craft? Before answering these questions, let us see the conclusions to be drawn about the legitimacy of Socrates' arguments.

If the suggestion that Socrates ultimately appeals to Gorgias' intellectual arrogance in exacting his lethal consent is plausible, his arguments seem to come off no better than they do on the assumption that he foists on him a thesis that he does not sincerely endorse.[42] It was Gorgias who invented rhetoric as a cunning device of persuasion that derives its power from extra-rational – more specifically, emotional – factors. The *Encomium of Helen* illuminates the source of this power:

[13] To see that persuasion, when added to speech indeed molds the mind as it wishes, one must first study the arguments of the astronomers, who replace opinion with opinion: displacing one but implanting another, they make incredible, invisible matter apparent to the eyes of opinion. Second, compulsory debates with words, when a single speech to a large crowd pleases and persuades (*eterpse kai epeise*) because written with skill, not spoken with truth (*ouk alêtheiai lechtheis*). Third, contests of philosophical arguments, when it is shown that speed of thought also makes it easy to change a conviction based on opinion. [14] The power of speech has the same effect on the disposition of the soul as the disposition of drugs (*pharmakon*) on the nature of bodies. Just as different drugs draw forth different humours from the body – some putting a stop to disease, others to life – so too with words: some cause pain, others joy, some strike fear, some stir the audience to boldness, some benumb (*epharmakeusan*) and bewitch (*eksegoêteusan*) the soul with evil persuasion. (DK 82 B11)[43]

The manipulative power of the art of persuasion consists in its appeal to irrational faculties of the mind rather than to reason and, as the phrase 'evil persuasion' suggests, can thus incite people to actions they would refrain from in their sober minds. By drawing on Gorgias' arrogance in his arguments, Socrates similarly appeals to an extra-rational circumstance, a character trait. It might be debated whether or not arrogance qualifies as an emotion – such as shame more clearly does – it is certainly not in the purview of our reasoning faculties. Arguably, Socrates thus 'benumbs' or 'bewitches' Gorgias instead of persuading him by an appeal to his reason. Worse yet, not only does he employ rhetorical manipulation, he does it with a twist of irony, verging on cynicism. By devious irony Socrates demonstrates to Gorgias that others might be able to employ his own devised weapon just as well as he can and that it might easily be misused, that is, used not only for righteous defence, but also for sly attack. Is Socrates playing the cruel game of turning the very weapon against Gorgias that he had devised and producing thereby merely the semblance of an argument and the semblance of victory? It must be granted that he does play a game of sorts on Gorgias, and a smart one at that. This appears to be a serious breach of the rules of dialectical conversation, as Polus protests.

Nonetheless, this does not invalidate his arguments, nor does it line him up with the expert of 'persuasion without knowledge' (454e–455a).

Socrates has two legitimate and vital excuses for employing apparently illicit means in his refutation. The first one is that he is working on Gorgias' own assumptions, taking them to their ultimate logical – albeit absurd – conclusion. Thus, his arguments are not irrelevant to Gorgias' avowed principles, on the contrary, his conclusion is directly derivable from them. The second excuse is that, unlike oratorical discourse, Socrates' words *are* 'spoken with truth', and are meant to teach, rather than to produce persuasion without knowledge, as oratory does. Socrates' *logos* seeks to teach something to the complacent intellectual, a vital lesson about himself, and about the scope of his responsibility as an elite educator. He breaks the rules of dialectic in order to drive home a realisation the only way he can hope to, if he seeks to achieve more than the transient glory of winning an argument. For, as Wardy points out in his analysis of the contrast between rhetoric and dialectic: 'Rhetoric is a *dynamis* promising easy victory over victims to be subjugated: dialectic is a practice fraught with difficulty, typically marked by frustration rather than ease of achievement.'[44] The attainment of truth is certainly fraught with difficulty. But there is nothing more frustrating than the realisation of a truth about ourselves kept deeply buried under dearly cherished delusions.

Let me clarify the legitimacy of Socrates' argument in terms of its relevance to Gorgias' avowed principles. We can thereby also return to the issue of his consent to the Socratic intellectualism, as well as to the reasons for Gorgias' culpability for his students' misuse of his craft.

I have proposed that Socrates appeals to Gorgias' arrogance in exacting his assent that he knows right and wrong and he is able to teach them to his students. That still leaves his acquiescence in the Socratic rejection of *akrasia* unexplained. Neither shame nor arrogance might account for this move. But the ultimate validity of Socrates' argument depends on this thesis, for it serves as an indispensable premiss to the conclusion that Gorgias cannot evade responsibility for his students' misuse of his craft. Is this conclusion legitimate, then? I propose it is, for Socrates is merely drawing a conclusion from Gorgias' outspoken claims that happens to comply with his rejection of *akrasia*. Ironically, Gorgias' avowed principles commit him to a position on the relationship of knowledge – or rather, belief – that entails the rejection of *akrasia* in such a way that it surpasses Socrates' intellectualism in terms of its stringency. Socrates assumes the omnipotence of knowledge (of the *good*), that is, reason's full command over the passions in terms of action. On the assumption that one knows what the good is, he or she cannot fail to act in accordance with it. However, as noted above, there is a vital proviso. If someone – say a student – fails to understand or conceive of the good, or rejects to note it as a fact – which lies beyond his or her teacher's command – he or she might fail to act in accordance with it. In contrast, given the *omnipotence* that Gorgias attributes to his craft, this is impossible. He claims to be able to persuade anyone of anything in such a way that they cannot fail to act as *he* wants them to. Hence, I suggest, Socrates might be reasoning and could address Gorgias in some such fashion:

> Well then, Gorgias, you are considering yourself a decent man, someone who is concerned about the probity of your students, although you do not teach right and wrong in particular, you teach oratory instead. You say that that is the greatest good, for it provides the greatest power. You claim that you are able to persuade anyone of anything by oratory. Well, my dear friend, look what follows. Why don't you use the magical power of your craft to persuade your students *to be good people*, instead of – or beside – teaching them oratory? All the more so, since your craft – as you cannot fail to see it yourself, my friend – is highly likely to attract the sort of licentious men who seek it in order to misuse it, in the first place. Do you want me to believe that you do your best for your students' probity? Can I tell you in all honesty why I don't believe that? First, because I don't think you have any idea about what 'the greatest good' is. You believe it is power. Now, power is neither good nor bad in itself, as you rightly assume. But that means that it is merely instrumental, and thus it cannot be the greatest good. For example, compare your students and yourself. You have used your power to do something really good; but look at Callicles here, he is about to misuse it for sure, if he does not come to some grief before. Second, even if you knew what 'the greatest good' is, you could not care less for teaching it, if it has anything to do with virtue, for you don't believe that virtue can be – or should be? – taught. Third, even if you cared for virtue and taught it, you cannot seriously be concerned about your students' probity, or else you would turn down those who come to learn

oratory from you in order to accomplish their own egotistic and immoral ends by it. And, last but not least, the power of your craft is not irresistible, my friend, or else, I presume, you would have been able to persuade me that your craft is the greatest good, that you know what the greatest good is, that you are a decent man and you do your best to secure your students' probity. Would you perhaps like to give it another try?

By not bringing all this so brutally in the open, Socrates saves Gorgias from utter humiliation, in order to leave him a chance for examining his conscience in private as an intellectual and elite educator, who assumes his omniscience and omnipotence and puts great power into the hands of people who seek his craft in order to misuse it in the first place, while believing that their mere exhortation for the good, or his own example as a decent man might suffice.[45] If he is assuming that he can wash his hands, he is utterly mistaken. Socrates has given him a riddling clue for examining his conscience by arriving at the absurd conclusion that *on Gorgias' own avowed assumptions* his students are bound to act justly, and by implying thereby that he is *fully* responsible for their unscrupulousness. Rather than bringing his real qualms into the open, Socrates ingeniously relies on his own intellectualist thesis to derive this conclusion in a way that seems plausible to their audience, in order to save the face of Gorgias.[46] But for him personally, Socrates' message is harder to swallow. The brilliance of his *elenchos* rests on the assumption that Gorgias' self-conceit concerns not only his omniscience and the omnipotence of his craft – that is, his superior intellectual competence and abilities – but also his decency. Gorgias seems self-assured that he is doing his best in exhorting his students to use his craft justly, but if so, he badly deceives himself about that. Thus, Socrates corners him into the following options: he either admits both to himself – and to his prospective students – that his craft is *not* omnipotent, or that he does *not* know what the (moral) good is, or that he does not *want to* teach it to his students. If Gorgias opts for the former two, he has to give up his delusions about himself as a superior intellectual and openly acknowledge that his craft is far from being as powerful as he makes it out to be. If he opts for the latter, he is to give up his self-assurance about his probity. He wants none of these options, and thus sinks into deep silence. The contradiction Socrates exposes *for their audience* is between Gorgias' earlier claim that the teacher of rhetoric is not responsible for the misuse of his craft and his later consent that he teaches right and wrong to his students, which in some vague way suggests for them that there is something wrong with his integrity.[47] What Gorgias comes to consent to is the rather strong thesis that the knowledge of right and wrong is a *prerequisite* for learning oratory. Gorgias is trapped into this concession by the bait, 'won't you be able to' (*ouk hoisos te esêi* 459e7), which directly challenges him as an omnipotent orator and teacher of oratory. But were he able to distance himself from his own vainglory, he could realise that what renders Socrates' phrase logically coherent is its less obvious meaning: 'will you be completely *disinclined to* (*ê to parapan ouk hoisos te esêi*) teach him oratory, unless he knows the truth about these things to begin with? (459e6-8).'[48] The contradiction Socrates suggests *for Gorgias* to consider is between his self-conceited belief that he is a high-principled man, concerned about propriety and his students' probity, and his more than naïve lack of regard for offering the undoubtedly great – albeit not unlimited – power of his craft indiscriminately to anyone, including in the first place unscrupulous people, bent on, or intent on, misusing it.[49] Thus, Socrates' argument is *ad hominem*, but it is designed for cleansing his interlocutor of a special variant of false belief, notably, self-deceit, rather than producing it as oratory does.

NOTES

1. I would like to express my deep gratitude for the support of the National Humanities Center, North Carolina, where I wrote this essay. Special thanks to my fellow fellows, Susan Wolf, Randolph Clarke and Robert Mitchell for their invaluable remarks made in a discussion about my concerns in this paper, to James H. Lesher for his kindness to read this paper on short notice and for his vital suggestions, and to Judit Horváth for her precious feedback on my interpretation of a Greek phrase. But especially, I would like to gratefully thank Brendan M. Purcell for his generous friendship, unremitting intellectual inspiration and spiritual and emotional support in a difficult period of my life. I am also indebted to him for introducing me to the work of Eric Voegelin.
2. See, for example, *Apology* 17a–18a; *Phaedo* 99e4-6; and n. 8 below.
3. Charles H. Kahn, *Plato and the Socratic Dialogue: The Philosophical Use of a Literary Form* (Cambridge: Cambridge University Press, 1996), p. 133; cf. E. R. Dodds, *Plato: Gorgias: A Revised Text with Introduction and Commentary* (Oxford: Oxford University Press, 1959), p. 15.
4. See, e.g., Irving M. Copi, *Introduction to Logic* (New York: Macmillan Publishing Company, 1986), pp. 93–4.
5. This is a complaint that often comes from one's students, whose sense of fair play is highly developed.
6. The personal upshot of this question is astutely noted by Eric Voegelin, *Order and History, Vol. 3: Plato and Aristotle* (Baton Rouge and London: Louisiana State University Press, 1957), p. 78: 'The substance of man is at stake, not a philosophical problem in the modern sense. Socrates suggests to Chaerephon the first question: Ask him "Who

he is" (447d). That is for all times the decisive question, cutting through the network of opinions, social ideas, and ideologies. It is the question that appeals to the nobility of the soul; and it is the one question that the ignoble intellectual cannot face.'

7. Translations from Plato's *Gorgias* are by Donald J. Zeyl in John M. Cooper, ed., *Plato: Complete Works* (Cambridge, IN: Hackett Publishing Company, 1997), pp. 791–869.

8. Polus conflates a 'what is it?' question with a 'what is it like?' question, that is, a question concerning substance with inquiry about an attribute, to use Aristotelian terminology. This is not unrelated to his (and Gorgias') ignorance about what is at stake in the dialogue. The issue is not what Gorgias is like, but *who* he is (that is, what he is doing).

9. The interlude is significant, for this is where Socrates differentiates between the Gorgianic type of discourse and his own dialectical method. He calls the former 'eristic', for its sole purpose is to achieve victory over one's interlocutor. In contrast, Socratic dialectic seeks to attain knowledge of the truth, which entails the risk of acknowledging that one might be wrong. Socrates, on his part, prefers dialectical to eristic conversation, for he believes that it is more detrimental to entertain false beliefs than it is to avow in public that one was wrong. But if Gorgias prefers the former type of discourse, Socrates adds with tongue in cheek, he suggests to finish their conversation. Gorgias naturally affirms that, together with Socrates, he prefers the latter; since, however, he believes this might be exacting for their audience, let them at least allow anyone to leave if he might wish. Urged by their audience, and lest he should falsify himself in promising to respond to any question, Gorgias stays on. This interlude is meant to prepare the exacting *elenchos* to which Socrates is about to subject Gorgias, which challenges his personal probity.

10. On the most complete list of objections, see Terence Irwin, *Plato: Gorgias* (Oxford: Clarendon Press, 1979), pp. 125–8.

11. On this, see Kahn, *Plato and the Socratic Dialogue*, p. 132. It must be noted that the Socratic-Platonic moral intellectualism entails not only the assumption that the knowledge of the good is sufficient, but also that it is necessary for acting virtuously (see, for example, *Meno* 97a-c).

12. Gorgias nowhere states explicitly that rhetoric itself conveys no moral values. But his disclaimer that the teacher of rhetoric is not responsible for its possible misuse by his students (457a-c) seems to be derivable from this assumption; it also accords with *Meno* 95c, where his student, Meno, reports that Gorgias never promised to teach virtue, indeed laughed at others who undertook to teach it; he believed people needed to be taught to be formidable speakers (*legein oietai dein poiein deinous* 95c4). Finally, it also explains why – over above teaching them rhetoric – he needs to exhort his students to employ it justly, if he is concerned for his students' good behaviour.

13. Cf. Irwin, *Plato: Gorgias*, pp. 127–8.

14. The *Gorgias* provides a good example for the possibility that someone *refuses* to understand what is clearly explained to him concerning the good. This is how, I take it, Callicles' sulking and drop-out from the dialogue at 505c-d is to be interpreted, when Socrates has clearly refuted his standpoint and clarified for him, first, what the good is *not*. When Socrates goes on to discuss what the good *is*, Callicles no longer listens.

15. Irwin, *Plato: Gorgias*, pp. 126–7 suggests that the critical move might also be Gorgias' consent to the application of the analogy of the crafts to moral issues (460b7). But this is hardly a thesis Gorgias should not accept, *once* he claims to be able to teach right and wrong to his students if needed. For he claims that his activity is a craft,

to that, 'the craft of crafts', as it were (449a2-5, 450c1, 456b5, 456c6-7). Once he consents, therefore, that he teaches right and wrong as a requisite for rhetoric, and conceives of it as a craft, the analogy applies.

16. Dodds, *Plato: Gorgias*, p. 205, suggests that the critical move is that Gorgias says that the subject matter of rhetoric is right and wrong. J. Doyle, 'Socrates and Gorgias', *Phronesis* 55 (2010), pp. 16–17 has convincingly argued, however, that Gorgias never claims that the subject matter of oratory is right and wrong, he merely says that the *persuasion* oratory produces is *related to* right and wrong.

17. This is the account of Dodds, *Plato: Gorgias*, p. 217: 'Both dialogues [i.e. *Meno* and *Gorgias*] carry, it seems to me, the same general implication, that Gorgias and his school have failed to think out the relationship between rhetoric and morals.'

18. Dustin A. Gish, 'Rivals in Persuasion: Gorgianic Sophistic *Versus* Socratic Rhetoric', *Polis* 23 (2006), p. 63, suggests that if Gorgias admitted that he has been caught in a contradiction (between his consent that he is able to educate his students in justice and his earlier disclaimer), that 'would surely damage his reputation as a master rhetorician, leading potential students to disdain him.' I do not think that this could be a problem either for Gorgias or for his students. The art of rhetoric was also an art of *paradoxologia* (paradoxical or antithetical thought or expression) (DK 82 A1, A4).

19. James Stuart Murray, 'Plato on Power, Moral Responsibility and the Alleged Neutrality of Gorgias' Art of Rhetoric (*Gorgias* 456c-457b)', *Philosophy and Rhetoric* 34 (2001), pp. 355–63, argues that Gorgias' craft is inherently abusive and unjust because, unlike boxing or wrestling, rhetoric is meant to be used against non-rhetors in order to gain power over them, and to displace the true arts while being ignorant of them. I think that this is insufficient for establishing the inherently abusive nature of rhetoric, for the issue is *what* that power, once gained, is used for. Of course, for Socrates, the problem is that orators are not likely to attain any good by the power gained by rhetoric, unless they devote themselves to a serious exploration of what the good is. See Roslyn Weiss, 'Oh Brother! The Fraternity of Rhetoric and Philosophy in Plato's *Gorgias*', *Interpretation* 30 (2002–2003), pp. 201–2.

20. 'Or is it necessary for him to know, and must the prospective student of oratory already be knowledgeable … ' (459 e1-3). From the Greek it is clearer that in the whole sentence Socrates refers to Gorgias' orator students (so, in this translation 'him' stands for the 'prospective student'), and thus it turns out at this point that when he spoke about 'the orator' earlier, he had Gorgias' students in mind. This is not without significance, to which I shall shortly return.

21. See also Socrates' summary and Gorgias' response, 'Very much so' (*panu ge*) at 460a5-b1.

22. Robert Wardy, *The Birth of Rhetoric: Gorgias, Plato and their Successors* (London and New York: Routledge, 1996), p. 71; cf. Dodds, *Plato: Gorgias*, p. 30, n. 2; Charles H. Kahn, *Plato and the Socratic Dialogue*, pp. 134–5.

23. Voegelin, *Order and History*, Vol. 3, p. 25.

24. Cf. Irwin, *Plato: Gorgias*, p. 129.

25. For example, in the strong Socratic sense of knowledge, which requires that one be able to provide an adequate definition of virtue in general, or of specific virtues.

26. The moral proviso at 456e implies a remarkable high-mindedness in the context of the common Greek imperative, 'help your friends, harm your enemies'. Gorgias apparently exhorts his students to employ rhetoric justly *even against* 'enemies and wrongdoers, and in defense, not aggression'. This is contradicted by Meno, who, as

Gorgias' student, defines virtue in the less high-minded traditional terms (*Meno* 71 e). If this represents not Gorgias' moral code but Meno's, the contrast is meant to highlight Gorgias' integrity in the *Gorgias*.

27. The collection of Hermann Diels and Walther Kranz, eds., *Die Fragmente der Vorsokratiker*. Vol. 2 (Zürich, Hildesheim: Weidmann, 1952) is my source for the fragments and testimonies of Gorgias. 'DK 82' refers to the chapter on Gorgias in this collection, 'A' (and a number) indicates testimonies, 'B' (and a number) refers to fragments.

28. See *Meno* 80d1, where – without the slightest sign of shame – he denies that he knows what virtue is.

29. Cf. Irwin, *Plato: Gorgias*, p. 129.

30. It might be objected – as Doyle, 'Socrates and Gorgias', pp. 15–16 objects to Cooper's 'straight reading' of Gorgias' rhetoric as a craft seriously concerned with justice – that this is incompatible with Socrates' account of the reason for Gorgias' consent at 487a7–487b5, where he points out that both Gorgias and Polus entailed themselves in contradiction because of shame. I do not wish to deny that concern for propriety in general – which the Greek *aischunê* covers – plays no role in Gorgias' downfall (on which see below), I merely contest that it is out of false shame that he succumbs to the thesis that he teaches right and wrong if needed.

31. The suggestion that Socrates seeks to appeal to Gorgias' pride in his aptitude as a teacher of oratory is supported by further traits of the interrogation. First of all, the question, 'Or won't you be able to teach him oratory at all, unless he knows the truth about these things to begin with (459 e6-8)?' strikes as illogical. Why would Gorgias be *unable to* teach oratory to his students, unless they know right and wrong? The phrasing is meant to be a stickler functioning as bait for Gorgias. Second, the apparently clumsy and perplexing formulation, 'will you make him seem among most people to have knowledge of such things when in fact he doesn't have it (459 e5-6)?' underlines his achievement, at the expense of that of his students. For, how could *he* 'make them seem to know' right and wrong? It could only be his students who could make *themselves* seem to know good, obviously, by the help of oratory that they have learnt from Gorgias. Thus, it is Gorgias' achievement as an oratory teacher that is highlighted by Socrates.

32. Cf. Dodds, *Plato: Gorgias*, p. 9, p. 217; Gish, 'Rivals in Persuasion', p. 62, p. 66.

33. In stark contrast with the Syracusean businessman, Cephalus, Socrates' first interlocutor in the *Republic*, who provided shields for the Athenian *hoplites*, by which they attacked his native city on the Sicilian expedition that was catastrophic for Athens. On Cephalus and the tragic irony Plato draws on in his portrayal, see the excellent analysis by Mark Gifford, 'Dramatic Dialectic in *Republic* Book I', *Oxford Studies in Ancient Philosophy* 20 (2001), pp. 35–106. The contrast between Gorgias and Cephalus in terms of their moral stature is thus conspicuous. This may be the reason why Plato abstains from a direct criticism or parody of Gorgias, although, as Dodds, *Plato: Gorgias*, p. 9, points out, he pokes 'unobtrusive fun at Gorgias' complacency (448a, 449c-d), pomposity (451d, 455d) and naïve vanity (449a, 463d)'.

34. This conception rules that one should never do harm to anyone, apparently including one's enemies (i.e. those committing injustice against one). See especially *Crito* 49a-e.

35. There might be some confusion (see e.g. Gish, 'Gorgianic Sophistic *Versus* Socratic Rhetoric', pp. 62–3) about moral shame and what might be called prudential shame as reasons for his consent to the lethal thesis. It would be out of moral shame if he

consented to it because, as an elite educator, he did not dare to acknowledge in public that he was 'a moral idiot'. But it would be out of prudential shame if he succumbed, because, as an allegedly omniscient and omnipotent oratory teacher, he did not dare to acknowledge that he was in fact incompetent. It is in the former sense that I controverted above that shame plays a role in his assent.

36. Kahn, *Plato and the Socratic Dialogue*, p. 135.
37. Voegelin, *Order and History*, Vol. 3, p. 80.
38. Cf. Weiss, 'Oh Brother!', p. 200. It has been debated whether Socrates' appeal to Polus' sense of shame is legitimate as an argumentative strategy. See Jessica Moss, 'Shame, Pleasure and the Divided Soul', *Oxford Studies in Ancient Philosophy* 29 (2005), pp. 137–70 *contra* D. B. Futter, 'Shame as a Tool for Persuasion in Plato's *Gorgias*', *Journal of the History of Philosophy* 47 (2009), pp. 451–61. While this debate, on the whole, is not entirely irrelevant to the present discussion, since I contest that Gorgias' fall is due to the sort of shame that causes Polus' (and Callicles') downfall, discussion of this debate is not vital for our purposes.
39. See Socrates' ironic remark that he greatly admires some people (such as Gorgias, Prodicus and Hippias) for their claim 'to be able to (*hoios t' eiē*) educate people' (*Apology* 19e2). The implication, I take it, is that it would indeed be remarkable if they could educate people in such a way as to achieve a significant reform of their values, that is, in a positive (moral) direction. Gorgias' self-assurance about the scope of his knowledge seems also to be addressed by Socrates' interrogation quoted above and provide the explanation for the apparently awkward formulation noted in n. 19 above. By starting his interrogation as though it concerned Gorgias as a teacher of oratory (rather than his orator students), Socrates directly challenges his over-confident claim to knowledge of anything of concern.
40. Gorgias famously boasted that he could extemporise on any subject and answer any question (DK 82 A 1a; cf. *Gorg.* 447c, 458d-e).
41. It is worthwhile to quote Wardy on this point more fully: 'Gorgias seems in part simply not to gauge the significance of Socratic rationalism, in part to subscribe himself to an aggressive intellectualism. But even were he fully alive to the import of the sufficiency of knowledge thesis, Gorgias might still not admit to an incapacity to make people good. His refusal would not be a matter of logic, but would rather arise from his championship of *dynamis*: the man who claims supremacy as speaker and teacher is not going to concede that his *logos* is powerless to reform values' (Wardy, *The Birth of Rhetoric*, p. 64). Because of his arrogance, Gorgias 'cannot see that from the Socratic perspective, moral idiocy is both rife and unavoidable' (ibid., p. 71).
42. Whether this thesis is the rejection of Socratic *akrasia*, or that he knows and teaches right and wrong to his students, which he would consent to out of shame.
43. Translation by Michael Gagarin and Paul Woodruff, *Early Greek Political Thought from Homer to the Sophists,* Michael Gagarin and Paul Woodruff, eds, (Cambridge: Cambridge University Press, 1995), p. 193 (the translation was prepared by Michael Nill).
44. Wardy, *The Birth of Rhetoric*, p. 68.
45. As we learn from Aristotle, Gorgias taught oratory by example and habituation, inciting his students to imitate his art, rather than explaining to them its rules (Aristotle, *On Sophistical Refutations,* 183b–184b). He might have believed that, apart from his exhortation for using his craft justly, his own personal example could have a good influence on his students' probity.

46. Dodds, *Plato: Gorgias*, p. 218 pointed out that for Socrates' contemporaries his denial of *akrasia* seemed 'less peculiar than it does to us', for from Homer onward moral conduct had been explained in terms of knowledge. 'This was natural in a society which judged men by their actions, not by their intentions [...] The *agathos* was the man who did things well, and doing things well involved knowing how to do them [...] The originality of Socrates lay not in the invention of a private paradox [...] but in making explicit the unconscious presuppositions of traditional Greek thinking about conduct.'
47. As we have seen, unless Gorgias straightforwardly teaches or exhorts them to misuse his craft, in theory, his probity remains unchallenged. (This might be the reason for Polus' uncertainty about the precise nature of the contradiction at 461b8-9: '*some inconsistency crept into his statements*'.) But this is only in theory, independently of the special situation he is in, namely, that he is the teacher of a craft that is much sought for by licentious people in particular.
48. For this meaning see LSJ *hoios* III.b. and III.2.
49. It is, therefore, Gorgias' self-deluded pretension to propriety – as part of his arrogance – that gets him into trouble. Thus, Socrates' account of the reason for his fall at 487a7-487b5 remains correct.

BIBLIOGRAPHY

Cooper, John M., ed., *Plato: Complete Works*, Cambridge, IN: Hackett Publishing Company, 1997.
Copi, Irving M., *Introduction to Logic*, New York: Macmillan Publishing Company, 1986.
Diels, Hermann, and Walther Kranz, eds, *Die Fragmente der Vorsokratiker*, Vol. 2, Zürich, Hildesheim: Weidmann, 1952.
Dodds, E. R., *Plato: Gorgias. A Revised Text with Introduction and Commentary*, Oxford: Oxford University Press, 1959.
Doyle, J., 'Socrates and Gorgias', *Phronesis* 55 (2010), pp. 1–25.
Futter, D. B., 'Shame as a Tool for Persuasion in Plato's *Gorgias*', *Journal of the History of Philosophy* 47 (2009), pp. 451–61.
Gagarin, Michael, and Paul Woodruff, eds and trans., *Early Greek Political Thought from Homer to the Sophists*, Cambridge: Cambridge University Press, 1995.
Gifford, Mark, 'Dramatic Dialectic in *Republic* Book I', *Oxford Studies in Ancient Philosophy* 20 (2001), pp. 35–106.
Gish, Dustin A., 'Rivals in Persuasion: Gorgianic Sophistic *Versus* Socratic Rhetoric', *Polis* 23 (2006), pp. 46–73.
Kahn, Charles H., *Plato and the Socratic Dialogue: The Philosophical Use of a Literary Form*, Cambridge: Cambridge University Press, 1996.
Irwin, Terence, *Plato: Gorgias*, Oxford: Clarendon Press, 1979.
Moss, Jessica, 'Shame, Pleasure and the Divided Soul', *Oxford Studies in Ancient Philosophy* 29 (2005), pp. 137–70.
Murray, James Stuart, 'Plato on Power, Moral Responsibility and the Alleged Neutrality of Gorgias' Art of Rhetoric (*Gorgias* 456c-457b)' *Philosophy and Rhetoric* 34 (2001), pp. 355–63.
Voegelin, Eric, *Order and History*, Vol. 3: *Plato and Aristotle*, Baton Rouge and London: Louisiana State University Press, 1957.
Wardy, Robert, *The Birth of Rhetoric: Gorgias, Plato and their Successors*, London and New York: Routledge, 1996.
Weiss, Roslyn. 'Oh Brother! The Fraternity of Rhetoric and Philosophy in Plato's *Gorgias*', *Interpretation* 30 (2002–2003), pp. 195–206.

Person and Spirit

FRAN O'ROURKE

Virginia Woolf intriguingly declared: 'Human character changed on or about December 1910.'[1] Richard Rorty perhaps clarified this remark when he suggested that 'the big change in the outlook of intellectuals – as opposed to a change in human nature – that happened around 1910 was that they began to be confident that human beings had only bodies, and no souls.'[2] A century later it is timely to assess this shift in outlook. For present purposes I am happy to adopt Ian Ramsey's wording of the popular understanding of 'soul' as 'an immaterial, indivisible reality of a non-spatio-temporal kind'.[3] The term 'spiritual' may be used interchangeably with soul to denote such immaterial, non-spatio-temporal reality. I will present some of the arguments that may be discerned in Aristotle, Proclus, the unknown author of the *Liber de Causis*, and Aquinas in favour of the view that, beyond the physical body, there is in the human person a spiritual element in virtue of which we perform those activities that are distinctly human.

Aristotle declared: 'There is no such thing as face (*prosopon*) or flesh without soul (*psyche*).'[4] A commonly held view throughout the history of philosophy, which has increased in popularity and is today widespread, maintains on the contrary that there is no place for the soul: psychic life is a product of the brain, humans are exclusively material. This position may rest upon the assumption that all reality is essentially material in nature. This supposition needs to be questioned. Friedrich Albert Lange famously began his 1866 study *The History of Materialism* with the statement: 'Materialism is as old as philosophy, but not older.'[5] The point of Lange's remark is that philosophy may sometimes be the source of its own problems. I will therefore raise briefly a methodic objection to the position which holds that human nature may be explained exclusively in terms of matter, or the more fundamental belief that all reality is material. This is a metaphysical claim of great magnitude, one which rests, I suggest, on a simple methodic error, namely that reality or existence may be identified with one of its particular modes or determinations, specifically its perceptible mode. It is true that material bodies are the first objects of human cognition and the proper realm of human knowledge. It is a gratuitous assertion, however, to conclude *a priori* that material bodies are all that exist. The notion of existence does not exclude in advance the possibility of reality of a different modality than that of matter.

If we examine the concept of existence or the concept of life, there is nothing to suggest that either of these basic perfections is restricted to a particular mode or limitation. It is conceivable that modes of existence, or modes of life, other than material or corporeal may exist. In its intrinsic meaning, being has no limitations; it is boundless in its connotation. It is a spurious assumption, therefore, that being is only the physical, just as it is unwarranted to believe that all that exists is either the mental or rational. Language can be misleading. 'To be *material*' is to *be*; 'to be *ideal*' is to *be*; 'to be *mental*' is to *be*. We cannot, however, invert these statements and conclude that 'to be' is simply 'to be *material*', or that 'to be' is nothing more than 'to be *ideal*' and so forth. Existence cannot be reduced to a particular manner of being, or equated with any single determination. The most obvious pitfall is to equate reality with the natural world, with what we physically touch and see here and now, and to say: 'This is all there is.' This is an error of method, namely that of interpreting existence exclusively in terms of what we observe. Method is crucial in determining what is real or not. A restrictive method distorts the scope of the inquiry and reduces the subject matter to its own measure: if all you have is a hammer, everything looks like a nail.

Can human nature be exhaustively explained in physical, material or biological terms? Human nature is manifestly corporeal and biological; is it exclusively so? It has been argued by many philosophers that a number of activities indicate that man is capable of processes which go beyond the limits of material reality, thereby indicating the presence of a non-material principle which cannot be explained in material terms.

According to Aristotle, all living things necessarily possess a principle distinguishing them from non-living beings. His predecessors attributed three properties to soul: movement, perception and incorporeality.[6] The latter is distinctive of human substances, and in particular of intellectual activity. Aristotle was greatly exercised by the question whether or not the intellect could operate independently of the body. The solution to this problem largely decides the question of the soul's immortality and Aristotle's position has given rise to much debate throughout the history of philosophy.

Emphasising the simplicity of the individual substance, and the unity of body and soul, Aristotle himself raises the greatest obstacle to the independence of the soul and its survival after death: 'One can no more ask if the body and the soul are one than if the wax and the impression it receives are one.'[7] We are confronted with two fundamental and related problems: the unity of body and soul, and the possible independence of soul. The soul is for Aristotle the actualising form of the body, i.e. the element which causes the body, in the first place, to be a body. The question is whether its full reality and activity are exhausted by that function, or whether it has autonomous independence beyond the role of actualising the body. Is it a real particular in itself (τόδε τι, hoc aliquid) as well as the form (εἶδος) of the body? Can it exist independently as an incorporeal reality? Immortality depends upon immateriality.

Early in *De Anima* Aristotle considers the possible survival of the soul and examines the difficulties of the soul acting in separation from the body. Intellectual thought is the most likely justification in its favour: 'If there is any way of acting or being acted upon proper to soul, soul will be capable of separate existence; if there is none, its separate existence is impossible.'[8] He tentatively proposes the immortality of the intellect: 'Νοῦς seems to be an independent substance implanted in us, which cannot be destroyed.'[9] He argues that if the intellect, like the sense organs, were subject to decay, this would inevitably occur with the debility of old age. Unlike sensation which usually declines with the ageing of the body's sense organs, the mind is unaffected since it has no special organ; it may of course be affected indirectly, because its activity belongs to the individual, whose body is clearly affected by the ageing process. The individual ceases to think only when the substance is corrupted at death, and the compound of body and soul dissolved. 'Thinking, loving and hating are not affections of the mind, but of the individual man who possesses the mind.'[10] For Aristotle it is neither the soul nor the body that thinks but the individual, just as it is the individual who perceives, loves and hates. The individual is a unity of body and soul. The dependence of intellect upon the body, however, is not the same as that of sensation. Aristotle makes an important distinction: memory and love terminate with the death of the individual, but thought and reflection (τὸ νοεῖν καὶ τὸ θεωρεῖν) are beyond destruction.[11]

Strict hylomorphism (unity of body and soul as matter and form) should dictate that the human soul perish on the individual's death. Intellect (νοῦς) may be an exception since it is not material, i.e. composed of parts, and cannot suffer disintegration. Aristotle's hylomorphism has been praised by some as best safeguarding the unity of the human individual;[12] for others it is intrinsically linked to an outmoded physics, hence no longer sustainable. The current orthodoxy regards Aristotle's views on the immateriality of νοῦς as an awkward inconsistency. H. M. Robinson remarks: 'More often than not nowadays the favoured opinion is that Aristotle is essentially or in spirit some sort of materialist. I say that the favoured opinion is that he is a materialist *essentially* or *in spirit* because few dare to say that he actually *is* a materialist, because few dare to deny that his doctrine of *nous* is immaterialist.'[13] Christopher Shields agrees that 'the majority of commentators have disregarded Aristotle's conception of an immaterial *nous*.'[14]

Before dealing with νοῦς, we should point out that, according to Aristotle, sensation is also an immaterial activity, since it is 'the reception of the form of sensible objects without the matter'.[15] Thus while physically external and distant, the objects of knowledge can be present immaterially through sense images (425b24-5). Aristotle distinguishes between the *organ* of sensation, which has spatial magnitude, and the (immaterial) *power* of sensation, which resides within the organ but is without magnitude (424a26-8). Aristotle notes the obvious parallels between intelligence and sensation (429a13-15). The fundamental difference is that sensation depends intrinsically upon a physical organ while intellect does not. The senses know individual things here and now, confined in time and space; intellect knows universal realities. These exist in some manner, he suggests, within the soul itself. A person may contemplate his thoughts at will, but cannot arbitrarily choose to sense a particular object: the object must itself be present, since sensation knows what is individual and external (417b22-8).

Borrowing from Anaxagoras, Aristotle states that, since the soul knows all things, it must be 'unmixed' (ἀμιγῆ).[16] The human soul must be unadulterated in order to know. There is good reason, he says, to affirm that it is not mixed with the body, but is non-corporeal or immaterial.[17] If it were corporeal, it would inevitably have a determinate quality (such as hot or cold), which would make cognition of its contrary impossible. It would also require a physical organ, similar to those of the senses (429a25-6). Were it material, it could not receive within itself the intelligible natures of all things; but since it is open to receive all reality intelligibly within itself, it is unrestricted to any material mode, and is therefore immaterial, simple and impassible.[18] The soul, Aristotle states, has been well described as the 'place of forms' (429a27-

8: τόπος εἰδῶν); this applies, he explains, not to the soul as a whole, but to its thinking element; and the forms are contained not actually, but potentially. He also defines it as the 'form of forms' (432a2: εἶδος εἰδῶν), since it assimilates the forms, i.e. intelligible natures, of all things.

The immateriality of the intellect is established in the first place by its universality; the clearest proof is its unlimited openness to every possible object. The sense faculties function, each infallibly in a particular domain, because they have a clearly limited range, determined by the receptivity of the sense organ. Sensation is directed towards a particular material object here and now, located narrowly in time and space. The intellect is open to the totality because it has no such organ. Its universality is a consequence of its immaterial capacity. Its target is universal reality – the unrestricted totality of beings in general (τα πάντα), as well as the universal concepts of those essences which are instantiated in countless substances (τα καθόλου). There is nothing that exists whose essence cannot be the object of intellect; universality is the mark of the immaterial psyche. While the senses grasp particular individuals, the intellect knows universal essences according to their immaterial intelligibility.[19] The universality of intellect is best summed up in Aristotle's phrase that 'The soul is in a sense all things.'[20] According to the Arab philosopher Avicenna (980–1037), the ultimate perfection which the soul can attain is to have delineated in it the entire order and causes of the universe. Cognitively or intentionally (in the order of knowledge) the ultimate horizon of reflection is the totality of the real, of all-which-is: human being has through spirit a unique relation to the totality. In Plato's words, he is 'spectator of all time and all existence'. Man is finite in his being; he is not the whole of being, nevertheless through cognition he embraces the totality of the real. This is expressed by Blaise Pascal (1623–62): 'By space the universe contains me as a speck; by thinking I contain it.' Evidence of the universality of human cognition is our unrestricted desire to know the totality: we do not set bounds to the range of human inquiry.

Aristotle states in his *De Anima* that thinking as such does not involve an organ, whereas each of the senses does. This independence from a physical organ, i.e. the non-material character of intellect, is further evidenced by its impassibility: it cannot be damaged by its object. Sense organs can be destroyed by violent stimulation, the ear by deafening sounds, the eye by excessive light (429a30–429b5, 435b7–16). The intellect is not impaired by intense thought; on the contrary, having struggled with difficult matters,

Aristotle remarks that it reflects more easily upon simpler matters. This allows him conclude that 'the faculty of sense is not apart from the body, whereas the mind is separable'.[21] Aristotle of course stresses that without initial sense activity, the intellect is empty of content. He emphasises the unity of the human individual; the question is how both poles of human cognition, sensible and intellective, can belong to a single being.

Of its nature immaterial, and independent of a physical organ, the intellect has neither magnitude nor parts: these would be a hindrance to the process of thinking. The mind is one and simple; it is not a magnitude.[22] 'For, if it is a magnitude, how will it think with any one of its parts?' (407a6–11, Hett trans.). The mind must be single and complete, as are its thoughts which are simple and indivisible. Mind grasps thoughts once and entirely, not successively piece by piece, one part after another. If the mind were a material magnitude, it would have to know its object through its divisible parts.

Much debate and controversy would have been spared if Aristotle had explained more carefully what he meant by 'separate'. Aquinas for one has no doubts about its meaning and expresses surprise at the controversy it provoked:

> Indeed it is astonishing how easily some have let themselves be deceived by his calling the intellect 'separate'; for the text itself makes it perfectly clear what he means – namely that, unlike the senses, the intellect has no bodily organ. For the nobility of the human soul transcends the scope and limits of bodily matter. Hence it enjoys a certain activity in which bodily matter has no share; the potentiality to which activity is without a bodily organ; and in this sense only is it a 'separate' intellect.[23]

Aristotle's view on the immortality of the soul is far from definitive. Martin Luther pronounced harshly: 'Why, this wretched man, in his best book, *On the Soul*, teaches that the soul dies with the body, although many have tried with vain words to save his reputation.'[24] Luther is here referring to apparent difficulties in Aristotle's view that only the thinking function of the soul is immortal; this poses an obstacle for the unity of the individual and threatens the unity of the soul itself. I will return to Aquinas' solution to this question which, far from 'vain words', brings to Aristotle's psychology a metaphysical depth that was unavailable to the Greek master and which allows him resolve the problems of intellect associated with hylomorphism. First, however, a brief word on self-knowledge, as interpreted by Aristotle, Aquinas and others. The soul's capacity for self-reflection, along with its universality of scope, has also been traditionally invoked as proof of the spiritual character of human nature.

One of the most elusive questions in philosophical psychology is: 'How do we know that we know?' Aristotle states that when the soul has 'become each of its objects' (429b5–6: ὅταν δ' οὕτως ἕκαστα γένηται), then the mind is also capable of thinking itself (429b5–6: αὐτὸς δὲ αὑτὸν τότε δύναται νοεῖν). The explanation may be found, I suggest, in the fact that the soul is 'somehow' (πώς) all that is. The power of self-reflection is thus a consequence of the soul's universality. Because of its universal scope, the intellect may introspectively and concomitantly know every cognitive act of the individual, whether sensible or intellectual. The intellect knows itself, Aristotle suggests, as it does any other immaterial object: 'It is itself an object of thought, just as its objects are. For, in the case of those things which have no matter, that which thinks and that which is thought are the same; for contemplative knowledge and that which is known in that way are the same' (430a2–5, Hamlyn trans.).

Drawing extensively on Aristotle for his psychology, Aquinas identifies three arguments for the spirituality of the soul:

> First, because this operation covers all corporeal forms as its objects; therefore, it is necessary that the principle of this operation be free from all material forms. Second, because understanding concerns universals, whereas in a corporeal organ only individuated intentions can be received. Third, because the intellect understands itself; but this does not occur in a power whose operation is performed by means of a corporeal organ.[25]

In support of the latter argument Aquinas appeals to Avicenna, but especially to the unknown author of the work known as the *Liber de Causis*. This work may be dated to the ninth or tenth century, probably from the area of Baghdad; the treatise was transmitted to the West via a translation from Arabic, but may have been written in Syriac. It was long taken as Aristotle's lost theology, but is in fact a distillation of Proclus' *Elements of Theology*. In proposition 15 of that work, Proclus asserts: 'All that is capable of reverting upon itself is incorporeal (ἀσώματον).' Proposition 171 states: 'Intellect is indeed truly incorporeal, which its reversion upon itself makes clear, for bodies are incapable of such reversion.' In his commentary on the *Liber de Causis* Aquinas quotes with approval Proclus' reason for the immateriality of intellect:

> No body is naturally suited to turn toward itself. For if that which turns toward something is in contact with that toward which it turns, then it is clear that all the parts of the body that turns toward itself will be in contact with all [the rest of its parts]. This is not possible for anything that has parts, because of the separation of the parts, each of which lies in a different place.[26]

In simple terms, what these authors have in mind is the inability of material reality, defined by mutual exteriority of parts, *partes extra partes*, to reflect back upon itself. Put simply, parts get in the way.

Self-knowledge is for Aristotle an evidence of experience. It is a concomitant awareness that accompanies our knowledge of the object: we know ourselves as subject in knowing the reality of the object. Aquinas is more emphatic:

> Knowledge about the soul is most certain in this, that each one experiences within himself that he has a soul and that acts of the soul are within him. But it is very difficult to know what the soul is. Hence the Philosopher adds that it is very difficult to gain clear knowledge about it.[27]

Blaise Pascal conveys the elusive nature of self-knowledge, and the difficulty of understanding human nature:

> Who would not think, seeing us compose all things of mind and body, but that this mixture would be quite intelligible to us? Yet it is the very thing we least understand. Man is to himself the most wonderful object in nature; for he cannot conceive what the body is, still less what the mind is, and least of all how a body should be united to a mind. This is the consummation of his difficulties, and yet it is his very being.

Pascal then quotes St Augustine: 'The manner in which the spirit is united to the body can not be understood by man; and yet it is man.'[28]

Pascal's point is that, while it is difficult to comprehend how the spiritual and physical are intertwined, their unity is the undeniable and inescapable starting point from which to investigate human nature. Both matter and spirit are essential to lived experience and neither may be surrendered for methodic simplicity. There is visceral evidence for the intimate bond of soul and body. One might refer to the difficulty of intellectual effort when one is exhausted, afflicted by pain, or affected by alcohol: the intimacy of body and soul in such conditions is crudely obvious. More subtly, but equally empirically, the psychosomatic unity is illustrated by the manner in which we commonly react physically to non-physical influences, such as feelings, insights and memories. But once the nature and meaning of these empirical events is appreciated, it is also apparent that the spiritual and physical are distinct. I can be moved to tears by feelings of either joy or sorrow. In each case the physical process is the same: my lacrimal canals dilate and a hydrous liquid is secreted. But the meaning of my tears is different if caused by joy at the experience of beautiful music, evoked by a well-dramatised romantic scene on stage or screen, or by the receipt of sad news. If I become emotionally affected on learning of a tragic event, my throat contracts and eyes moisten. The real meaning of this physiological occurrence is not the tautness of muscles or discharge from ducts and glands. When I burst into tears on hearing of my friend's death, it is not because I am hardwired to release some physical tension. While my emotion has a physical side-effect, it is more properly an intentional state embracing in sympathy the lives of others across time and distance, far outstretching the material conditions of the here and now.

I blush if someone accuses me of something shameful. This event is not simply a surge of blood to my cheeks, but an involuntary response to the intellectual understanding of the sounds uttered and a spontaneous moral evaluation of my self-esteem *vis-à-vis* another. Beyond the physiological manifestation lies a spiritual meaning. I perspire and tremble when informed of a pending danger: this is more than a physiological reaction – the secretion of saline moisture through my epidermis is provoked by the conscious evaluation of an event that has not yet occurred but is only anticipated. The memory of a horrific incident perturbs my physical equilibrium: a weakness wells within my stomach and a shiver runs down my spine. Such physical expressions of reanimated horror engage countless physiological processes, electric charges, neural surges and synaptic links. The force of the memory, however, cannot be equated with these physical processes alone.

Such everyday experiences may indeed be described at the biological or physiological level, but these accounts do not reveal their meaning. Description in terms of anatomic rhythm and bodily equilibrium is no explanation. Socrates offered alternative accounts of why, having been condemned to die, he remained seated in prison; one was in terms of muscles and ligaments that enabled his seated posture, but the real explanation was his respect for the laws of Athens. If asked why the the kettle is boiling, I might refer to gas combustion, heat transfer and air pressure; more meaningfully I would respond that I want a hot whiskey.

Despite the challenge of establishing their common ground, the perspectives of the physical and metaphysical are together essential to the integrity of human nature. The complementary need for metaphysical explanation was recognised by Albert Einstein, who lamented the one-sided positivism of his day. He traces this to David Hume who, he suggests, 'created a danger for philosophy in that, following his critique, a fateful "fear of metaphysics" arose which has come to be a malady of contemporary empiricist philosophising; this malady is the counterpart to that earlier philosophising in the clouds, which thought it could neglect and dispense with what was given by the senses … It finally turns out that one can, after all, not get along without metaphysics.'[29] While Einstein points to the irrelevance of those philosophies that in the past ignored the physical and empirical, he warned his contemporaries against the other extreme. The metaphysical is also required.

The question whether or not human nature is spiritual is of the greatest consequence for our ultimate destiny. It must be answered in the affirmative before we can even raise the most important of all personal questions, namely that of personal survival beyond death. Without spirit, the human adventure, exciting and fulfilling while it lasts, comes to an end; if I am solely an aggregate of chemicals, the 'self' necessarily ceases at the dissolution that is death. The alternative opens up a different perspective. To affirm the deep reality of spirit within human nature is to reject that the universe is ruled by blind physical forces, dominated by pitiless indifference.[30]

It remains in conclusion to briefly outline the solution offered by Aquinas for the autonomous existence of the soul. As we saw, the strict logic of Aristotle's hylomorphism requires that on the dissolution of the individual at death, along with the disintegration of the body (matter), the soul (form) should also cease to exist. The soul is for Aristotle the highest principle of actuality within the individual, but its function is to constitute and perfect the body, which of itself has only the potential for life. Body and soul are co-principles of the single individual and are reciprocally related: neither exists without the other. Aquinas fundamentally remoulds Aristotle's metaphysics of act and potency with his deeper understanding of existence as radical act, the first perfection and actualising energy of every nature or essence. For Aquinas the form or essence is what determines the individual to be *what* it is; it determines essence, but does not confer existence. There is within the substance a deeper principle of actuality, namely the primary perfection of being: the act of existence, which is aptly denoted by the active verbal form of the infinitive *esse* (to be). It is this theory of being which enables him to resolve the question of the independence of soul, which was an obstacle for Aristotelian hylomorphism.

According to Aquinas, the soul has its own autonomous act of existence: actualising the body, determining it to be a human body and nothing else, it communicates its being to the body within the unity of a single substance. While it depends initially upon the body for the exercise of its activities, once its intellectual capacities have been actualised it can perform the immaterial acts of intellection and reflection without recourse to a particular physical organ. While these operations clearly depend on the individual human substance, they do not involve the exercise of a material organ. They proceed from the whole person as an intellectual being. But not only does the soul not depend upon a corporeal organ to exercise its capacities, much more significantly it does not depend upon the body for its existence. It has rather its own subsistent being; otherwise it could not perform those activities that are not bound by the conditions of space and time that define bodily sense knowledge.

Unlike Aristotelian form, the soul is for Aquinas not *forma immersa*, but *forma emergens*.[31] If it were immersed or inherent in the body, it could not perform activities independently of bodily organs. The activities of eating, breathing and seeing are inherent in the soul–body composite; the power of intellect and the activity of thinking are inherent in the soul, and therefore intrinsically non-corporeal. Aquinas' radical metaphysics of existential being explains how the soul, while performing its work as actualising principle of the body, is not absorbed in that function but has a deeper activity, namely that of existence. As suggested at the outset, existence is not confined to a particular modality, but is the all-pervasive, ubiquitous, unrestricted and universal, dynamic energy; in the natural world, existence finds its highest expression in the human soul which, for its part, is most compellingly discerned in the openness of spirit to universal being, and the ability to revert back upon its own knowledge in an act of personal reflection. To be a person is to self-reflectingly take possession of one's individual being within the universe and to freely shape one's destiny.

NOTES
1. Virginia Woolf, *The Essays of Virginia Woolf*, Vol. III (London: Hogarth, 1995), p. 421.
2. Richard Rorty, *Philosophy and Social Hope* (London: Penguin, 1999), p. 168.
3. Ian Ramsey, 'Biology and Personality: Some Philosophical Reflections', *Biology and Personality*, I. T. Ramsey, ed. (Oxford: Basil Blackwell, 1965), p. 177.
4. *Gen. An.* 734b25. *Prosopon* is also the word for 'person'.
5. Friedrich Albert Lange, *Geschichte des Materialismus und Kritik seiner Bedeutung in der Gegenwart* (1887), Iserlohn: Baedeker, p. 3: 'Der Materialismus ist so alt als die Philosophie, aber nicht älter.'
6. *De An.* I, 2, 405b10–12: ὁρίζονται δὲ πάντες τὴν ψυχὴν τρισὶν ὡς εἰπεῖν, κινήσει, αἰσθήσει, τῷ ἀσωμάτῳ.
7. *De An.* II, 1, 412b6–8, W. S. Hett, trans. (Cambridge, MA: Harvard University Press (Loeb), 1986), p. 68.
8. *De An.* I, 1, 403a7–12, J. A. Smith, trans., *The Complete Works of Aristotle*, Jonathan Barnes, ed. (Princeton: Princeton University Press, 1991), p. 642.
9. *De An.* I, 3, 408b18–19: ὁ δὲ νοῦς ἔοικεν ἐγγίνεσθαι οὐσία τις οὖσα, καὶ οὐ φθείρεσθαι.
10. *De An.* I, 4, 408b25–7: τὸ δὲ διανοεῖσθαι καὶ φιλεῖν ἢ μισεῖν οὐκ ἔστιν ἐκείνου πάθη, ἀλλὰ τουδὶ τοῦ ἔχοντος ἐκεῖνο.
11. *De An.* I, 4, 408b24, 408b27–8.
12. Enrico Berti, 'Aristote était-il un penseur dualiste?', *Thêta-Pi* 2 (1973), p. 97.
13. H. M. Robinson, 'Aristotelian Dualism', *Oxford Studies in Ancient Philosophy* 1 (1983), p. 123.
14. Christopher Shields, 'Some Recent Approaches to Aristotle's *De Anima*', Aristotle, *De Anima* Books II and III, D. W. Hamlyn trans., Christopher Shields, rev. ed. (Oxford: Clarendon Press, 1993), p. 165.
15. *De An.* II, 12, 424a17–19, Hett, trans., p. 137; see also 425b23–4.
16. *De An.* III, 4, 429a18: ἀνάγκη ἄρα, ἐπεὶ πάντα νοεῖ, ἀμιγῆ εἶναι.
17. *De An.* III, 4, 429a24–5: διὸ οὐδὲ μεμῖχθαι εὔλογον αὐτὸν τῷ σώματι.
18. *De An.* III, 4, 429b23: ὁ νοῦς ἁπλοῦν ἐστὶ καὶ ἀπαθές.
19. *De An.* II, 5, 417b22–3: τῶν καθ' ἕκαστον ἡ κατ' ἐνέργειαν αἴσθησις, ἡ δ' ἐπιστήμη τῶν καθόλου.
20. *De An.* III, 8, 431b21: ἡ ψυχὴ τὰ ὄντα πώς ἐστι πάντα.
21. *De An.* III, 4, 429b4–5: τὸ μὲν γὰρ αἰσθητικὸν οὐκ ἄνευ σώματος, ὁ δὲ χωριστός. Trans. Hett, p. 167.
22. *De An.* I, 3, 407a2–3: οὐ καλῶς τὸ λέγειν τὴν ψυχὴν μέγεθος εἶναι.
23. *In De An.* III, 7, 699: 'Mirum est autem quomodo tam leviter erraverunt, ex hoc quod dicit quod intellectus est separatus, cum ex litera sua huius rei habeatur intellectus,

dicit enim separatus intellectus, quia non habet organum, sicut sensus. Et hoc contingit propter hoc, quia anima humana propter suam nobilitatem supergreditur facultatem materiae corporalis, et non potest totaliter includi ab ea. Unde remanet ei aliqua actio, in qua materia corporalis non communicat. Et propter hoc potentia eius ad hanc actionem non habet organum corporale, et sic est intellectus separatus.' Kenelm Foster OP and Sylvester Humphries OP, trans. *Commentary on Aristotle's De Anima* (London: Routledge & Kegan Paul, 1951), p. 410.

24. *Works of Martin Luther* II (Philadelphia: A. J. Holman, 1915), p. 25.
25. *In II Sent.*, 19, 1, 1: Primo, quia haec operatio est omnium formarum corporalium sicut objectorum; unde oportet illud principium cujus est haec operatio, ab omni forma corporali absolutum esse. Secundo, quia intelligere est universalium; in organo autem corporali recipi non possunt nisi intentiones individuatae. Tertio, quia intellectus intelligit se; quod non contingit in aliqua virtute cujus operatio sit per organum corporale.
26. Proclus, *Elements of Theology* XV, Robert Pasnau, trans., *On Human Nature* (Cambridge: Cambridge University Press, 2002), p. 194.
27. *De Ver* 10, 8 ad 8: Secundum hoc scientia de anima est certissima, quod unusquisque in seipso experitur se animam habere, et actus animae sibi inesse; sed cognoscere quid sit anima, difficillimum est; unde Philosophus ibidem subiungit, quod omnino difficillimum est accipere aliquam finem de ipsa. As he remarks, to know the soul 'requires a diligent and subtle investigation' (ST I, 87, 1: *Requiritur diligens et subtilis inquisitio*).
28. *Pensées* 72. See St Augustine, *De Civ. Dei*, xxi, 10: Modus quo corporibus adhaerent spiritus comprehendi ab hominibus non potest, et hoc tamen homo est.
29. Albert Einstein, *Ideas and Opinions* (London: Souvenir Press, 2005), p. 24.
30. See Richard Dawkins, *A River Out of Eden* (New York: Basic Books, 1995), p. 133.
31. ST I, 76, 1 ad 4: Humana anima non est forma in materia corporali immersa, vel ab ea totaliter comprehensa, propter suam perfectionem. Et ideo nihil prohibet aliquam eius virtutem non esse corporis actum; quamvis anima secundum suam essentiam sit corporis forma.

Existence and Will: The Political Inheritance of William of Ockham

JAMES GREENAWAY

Political theory and practice, before they even begin, have already assumed much about man in his personal, social and historical dimensions. One force that pervades this existential field is symbolised as the will; and it is this will of man which is probably one of the most thorny and perennial problems in politics, in both theory and practice. William of Ockham (1287–1347) presents a philosophical consideration of the will that is sometimes theoretical and sometimes practical. His theoretical treatment of the will belongs largely to the first half of his career as a speculative philosopher, but after embarking on a dangerous dispute with Pope John XXII over the problem of property, his concerns tend more toward the political where he treats the will in a more obviously political manner. For him, the stakes were high. Charging the pope with heresy over the claim to a plenitude of power, Ockham is a character who engaged wholeheartedly in responding to the challenges of his day. He was clearly driven by a fierce will of his own, but never at the expense of his own calling as a philosopher. He is a boundary figure who was more than medieval, but less than modern. As such, he brings to the table a most unique perspective. There are themes in his work, as well as possibilities to be mined, that provide an always timely reminder of where will fits into the scope of political theory and practice. Here, I aim to present some aspects of Ockham's philosophical consideration of the will and see what he has to say to contemporary political thought. I will do so by considering two ironies in his work.

WILL IN THE PROBLEM OF NOMINALISM AND RADICAL CONTINGENCY
Let's begin with a brief discussion of Ockham's earlier speculative thought to see it in its philosophic-historical context. Nominalism is probably the philosophical position most associated with him. He denied the real existence of universals such as redness, dog-ness, humanity, etc. embedded in, or existing separately in some other sphere of reality from, concrete actual

things. He claimed that universals are merely conceptual and linguistic signs we use to refer to mental entities.[1] This attitude seems to fit with one of his other great concerns: to secure the contents of Christian faith from the adventitious wiles of speculation, such as Averroist thought.

In the recent encounter with the intellectual world of high Islamic culture, its Aristotelian commentaries, and its osmotic transfer to the West through thinkers like Siger de Brabant, there appeared the conceptualisation of ultimate reality as a universal intellect correlated with an elitist brigade of self-appointed intellectuals.

Nominalism, as much as the success of Averroism in the late medieval West, signifies the breakdown of the Christian synthesis of faith and reason. The rejection of universals seems to suggest not merely a late scholastic preference or academic adherence to a school of Nominalism, but a loss of confidence in an overarching framework of meaning that Christendom had evoked. Christendom itself had functioned as a civil theology[2] for roughly a millennium, meaning that it had given purpose to existence and presented a philosophical coherence that tied the things of the world together – that is, temporal existence could bear spiritual meaning. In this way, it symbolised a civilisational confidence regarding the existence and essence of things. The crisis of meaning that ensued from the breakdown of medieval Christendom in Ockham's day seems to result, among other things, in a new philosophical emphasis on contingency. The world is not the manifestation of the divine intellect in the *ratio aeterna*, as Thomas would have it, but is the world that God willed from an infinite variety of worlds. Note the emphasis on the primacy of will. For Ockham, God created the world by an act of divine will but he could have created it differently. Similarly, the world continues to exist as it does by divine ordination (*de potentia Dei ordinata*), but the sequence of secondary causes and effects could change by the absolute power of God's will (*de potentia Dei absoluta*). Unlike Thomas' conception of a rational Creator and a creation that reveals the rational quality of the divine mind, the world lacks an essentially meaningful structure because there are no real universals. The world is a manifestation not of reason but of will. Causality in the order of nature is not denied by Ockham, but is entirely dependent on the will of God who may change it.

In speaking of causality and the order of being, we do well to distinguish between primary and secondary causation. Divine will is of course an absolute power and has necessity. Created being, or existence itself, rests upon a primary cause (or what Bernard Lonergan calls 'external causation'.) Being thus bears the hallmark of contingency. Brendan Purcell writes that, 'In the Judeo-Christian experience there was a strong awareness of the world's createdness. So the world did not necessarily exist, but as a matter of fact, had come into existence.'[3] The contingency of being is related to external causation, that is, to be anchored in what is not contingent but necessary. However, the order of secondary causes (Lonergan's 'internal causation') is an ordained order whose radical contingency can admit of no essential universality according to Ockham. Purcell goes on to note that, with regard to secondary or internal causation

> ... there could be no natural science without that awareness of a contingent world [as opposed to a necessary, eternal world]. It's a contingent world whose laws – unlike those of mathematics or logic, which are necessary and universal – are not necessary, yet when they're discovered they're found to be universal. Still, as Walsh has noted, contingency itself can only be understood in terms of what is not contingent, or it is itself without meaning.[4]

Ockham's radical contingency, that does not countenance universals at the level of secondary causes, manifests precisely the crisis of meaning of his day and that he, as a sensitive thinker of his time, responded to with an emphasis upon the will. In this apparently bleak situation, Ockham clings to the content of faith, deposited in the mind by the will of God. The workings of God are not subject to rational inquiry. That is, revelation is an initiative on the part of God and its miraculous nature cannot be investigated fruitfully by any rational critique, but only accepted by the further miracle of faith that is worked in man by God. Faith is literally infused in man by God's absolute power and its contents compel the sacrifice of intellect.[5] Ockham gives the first western construction of a strictly fideistic religious position, accepting the rationally impenetrable dogma by an act of faith that is worked in man by a miracle of God.

So we come to the first irony in the thought of William of Ockham: while seeking to avoid the spiritual breakdown of his day, he nevertheless played into that very breakdown by actively divesting faith of its carefully wrought Christian synthesis with rationality. The career of faith must now bear the burden of the charge that later thinkers, unimpressed by the claims of religion, will bring: the charge of irrationality and absurdity. David Walsh points out that 'His nominalistic philosophical mode, with its reduction of all substantive questions to methodological and power relational issues, announces the end of the medieval confidence in the unity of all things.'[6] Wanting to preserve the integrity of faith, Ockham seems to participate in the very process of unravelling the spiritual and civilisational conditions that led to that very integrity.

WILL, EXISTENTIAL AUTHORITY AND THE DENOUEMENT OF CHRISTENDOM

In the early formation of Christendom, Pope Gelasius I famously articulated the traditional meaning of medieval society in his Two Swords formula. In a letter to Emperor Anastasius (494), he insisted on the separation of imperial-political power from priestly-spiritual power.[7] He was reminding the emperor of what was already, at the end of the fifth century, an old truth about Christianity: that Christ had differentiated between the giving to God what is God's and the giving to Caesar what is Caesar's (Mt 22:21, Mk 12:17, Lk 20:25). In other words, this fundamental and specifically Christian differentiation of authority divested the political of the ancient burden of securing eternal beatitude. The separation of authorities in the Gospels – the political from the spiritual – was of profound epochal importance and to be found nowhere else in as decisive a manner. In the separation of one from the other, the autonomous dignity of each was established, but it was not an autonomy that bore no reference to the other. The political and spiritual could, in principle, be differentiated from each other, but never isolated. Both the political and the spiritual remained linked, not necessarily to each other, but to a third sphere of autonomy; this third sphere we can call the 'existential' for the purposes of argument. Existential autonomy is essentially a zone of individual authority exercised over the things of one's own or things that pertain to one's own being.

It is this existential sphere of autonomy that Gelasius missed in his dualistic formula and of which William of Ockham became an early champion. However, some century and a half before him, in the 1180s according to Brian Tierney, English glossators on Gratian's *Decretum* articulated for the first time a zone of right which was somehow embedded in the natural existence of the individual: '*Ius Naturale* [from which proceed actions which are], licit and approved, neither commanded nor forbidden by the Lord or by any statute.'[8] It is a third centre of authority that is valid and competent in its own right.

It is a personal authority that is derived from the soul or consciousness of concrete individuals and as such emerges from an existential tension toward the ground of being.[9] It is this existential authority that the finest medieval thinkers were sensitive to and addressed in their own way so that in their works we can chart the eruption of this dynamic and characteristic factor in western society.

The pragmatic process of differentiating a triad of authorities – the political, the spiritual and the existential – in the history of society is messy; and it is inevitable that the messiness, the umbrage and the jurisdictional spats among the three centres began within that medieval cosmion when each began to assert itself against the others for the first time. The various struggles between the papacy and the imperial and/or royal heads are more familiar but the struggle of the existential against encroachments by institutional powers was more subtle (failing to appear comprehensively on the radar of political philosophy until later) although its consequences were seismic.

The thought of William of Ockham fits into this struggle for a uniquely western order that seeks to establish an equilibrium among the three forms of authority. What Ockham definitively opened up was this existential 'zone of human autonomy',[10] the enormous influence of which has prompted modern thinkers to see in Ockham the beginnings of the rights of man.[11] The differentiation of existential authority was a process already unfolding in the Christian West, but it took the philosophical workmanship of Ockham to take the insights of the glossators and canonists who preceded him, combine them with the anxiety of his own life as a Franciscan of the time, in order to finally establish the existential authority of the individual as a legitimate pillar of authority alongside the political and spiritual pillars.

Ockham's nominalistic-fideistic symbolism of the breakdown of his day is his method of dealing with the problem presented by the crisis of meaning in the late medieval denouement of Christendom. When Ockham asserted that men knew Christian faith only because God had willed it, and not because it could be reconciled with, or understood by, natural reason he was asserting the primacy of will over intellect. It is this concentration on the will that pushes Ockham's thought into an entirely new field of thought that surpasses the conventional categories assigned to him of nominalism and fideism. It is his theory of the will in his political thought that trumps the importance of those categories. Joseph Strayer writes that, from the perspective of his political thought,

... it meant that action rather than reflection, success rather than abstract justice were the qualities which were going to be honoured for the next two centuries. Ockham was also a strong nominalist ... According to this reasoning, the individual Christian is far more important than the artificial and unreal idea of Christendom.[12]

Nominalism and fideism are undoubtedly significant dimensions of Ockham's work but it is this focus on non-universalism and non-necessity that allows Ockham to relativise that very nominalism and fideism. In a theory of knowledge, Ockham is a nominalist, in theology he advocates fideism predominantly, but in political thought it is the will that is primary; it is the existential basis of human will that constitutes Ockham's contribution to political thought. His importance lies not only in the ironic emphasis he gives to the divergence of the spiritual from the political spheres, but also on the assertion of the will as an authoritative force embedded in the existence of individual persons.

NATURAL LAW: WILL AND REASON

The nominalist tendency toward investigating the parts within the whole of society, rather than that whole itself, bends Ockham's thought toward the element of justice inhering within the right relations among those parts; and it is the treatment of justice that first belies his reputation as a strict nominalist.[13] There is in his thought a theory of conditional natural law that he does not extensively develop. The Stoics and Cicero, the early Church Fathers, Augustine and, closer to Ockham's time, Gratian and Thomas *inter alia* had developed theories of natural law that had become topical as such within the focus of their work. In the economy of Ockham's writings, a theory of natural law indeed drives the trajectory of his thought, but he lacks any interest in extensively unpacking it. Instead, he took the facticity of human life by itself and both observed and accepted the just order of natural law as already embedded in existence itself – that is, in the movement of human relations, interpersonal and sociopolitical – even though the nominalist temperament seemed to weigh against the notion of a universal substance of law. Ockham's mind was simply too sharp to circumscribe itself within the boundaries of what is permissible within nominalism; and furthermore, his nominalist temperament directs him to the raw existence of things, persons, relations, etc. and not the whole in which they subsist. Ockham acts upon what he finds, which is, in this instance, a natural equity already being lived among individuals.

Let us take a brief look at Ockham's notion of natural equity or natural law. In the *Dialogue* III, the master answers the probing questions of the pupil regarding natural law, indicating that its meaning is three-fold:

> In one sense natural law is said to be that law which is in conformity with natural reason that in no case fails – as, for example, 'Thou shalt not commit adultery' ... In another sense, natural law is that law which is to be observed by those who go on natural equity alone, without any human custom or constitution, and which is natural because it is [not] contrary to the state of nature ... In a third sense, natural law is said to be that which may be deduced by *evident reason* from the law of nations or from some human deed ... and this can be called 'conditional natural law'.[14]

The first mode of natural law refers to laws which are immutable, such as the Decalogue. The second mode refers to laws which derive from the state of innocence before the Fall, but are laws which are mutable. These laws are subject to change. For example, in the dispensation of fallen man, an order of common property is no longer adequate. It is from man's fallen-ness that his need for the regulation of private property arises. The third mode of *ius naturale* refers to laws of evident reason that are observable in a living community. According to Brian Tierney, Ockham 'does seem to introduce a new kind of natural law [in his third mode], unstable, changeable according to the will of the people involved. ... Ockham's argument was shifting here from natural law to natural rights.'[15] Takashi Shogimen accepts that he discusses this third form of natural law in terms of natural right, and suggests further that this shows Ockham's view that both will and reason constitute a *potestas* or power that arises by natural right:

> The will of those concerned [e.g., a community or nation] translates a right into a power ... the volition that follows the dictate of evident reason (namely natural right) constitutes power – non-institutional power that is cognitively legitimate.[16]

In Ockham's thought, the notion of a natural right precedes positive law. Individuals are rightly subject to institutional ecclesiastical or temporal authority, but are also constituted by an existential authority that becomes a power when exercised. So long as it is 'evidently reasonable', existential authority as an assertive will is sufficiently legitimate to counter the political or spiritual claims of emperors or popes when they overreach their competence and infringe coercively upon the sphere of the individual. Will then is always treated by Ockham as legitimate when exercised reasonably. Ockham's outlining of a zone of human autonomy is the existential jurisdiction of the individual person; the person whose existence was naturally vested with rights-as-powers and a responsibility to exercise such in a rational manner. Reason is understood not in an instrumental sense, but in its classic Christian sense as *noesis* or *ratio* moved by spirit in the direction of the ground of being. Both will and reason are dynamic factors in consciousness and its existential authority; that is, will and reason both emerge from man's participation in the ground of existence. Ockham's importance for us lies in the reminder his work suggests of their political codependence. In other words, the assertion of will without reason – hereafter referred to as ratio, to underscore its existential depth in tension toward the ground – amounts to a deformation of existence that, in its political dimension, is potentially murderous and always disintegrative of the body politic.

WILL AND LIBERTY

The *de facto* exercise of temporal *potestas* by the papacy was also a feature of the political landscape in Ockham's day. The dispute over the Franciscan ideal of poverty involved more than a mere doctrinal detail over the life of Christ; it involved the jurisdictional remit of the church which was by then equivalent to a transnational state with immense material resources at its disposal, eventually pitted against the resources of the empire.[17] The assertion of a fierce papal will in the claim to a plenitude of power had met with plenty of theoretical and pragmatic opposition and now Ockham weighs in too, convinced that such an assertion amounts to heresy. For him, the power of the pope cannot have the character of a heretical *plenitudo potestatis*, even in spiritual matters: he writes, 'the pope does not possess a plenary power in spiritual matters, for he cannot prescribe to anyone those things that are works of supererogation – such as virginity, fasting on bread and water, entering a religious order, and so forth'.[18] Note the component of individual authority over matters of personal spiritual discernment, evincing a sphere of personal autonomy over which not even the pope cannot legitimately claim a final authority or a power to act. Shogimen shows the existential context of Ockham's concerns over papal and ecclesiastical power:

> Modern scholarship has already highlighted that Ockham's definition of both ecclesiastical and secular power is largely and primarily 'negative': he is concerned not so much with what ruling powers can do, as with what they *cannot* do ... Neither ecclesiastical nor temporal power can provide more than an environment in which men can freely live out their moral lives. In Ockham's vision, individuals *qua* individuals are morally and spiritually autonomous. The impending problem that faces him, namely the papacy's heretical claim to universal dominion, however, deprives Christians of opportunities to be virtuous.[19]

For Ockham, right reason morally requires service to the common good, and if an individual wills the dictate of right reason simply because it is the dictate of right reason, he becomes virtuous. But if he wills the dictate of right reason not because it is right, but because he is compelled to do so by an institutional authority such as the papacy or the king, he cannot be virtuous. The papal claim to a plenitude of power violates the rights and liberties granted by God and nature, and deprives Christians of the possibility of being virtuous. The mature Christian should not be compelled even to do good and an individual can never be virtuous as long as he is coerced; freedom of the will is necessary in order to be virtuous.[20]

So for Ockham, human liberty is identified with will: '*libertas et spontaneitas videntur non posse distingui*'.[21] Annabel S. Brett points out that for him, 'Human freedom is at base nothing other than the capacity for willed action, hence identical with the human will itself.'[22]

Ockham held that institutional power, both ecclesiastical and temporal, existed for the good of individual free men:

> Since, therefore, it is agreed that the pope, to whom in the person of Saint Peter Christ said 'Feed my sheep', is bound to exercise an anxious care for the faithful, and ... has no power to take away the rights, liberties and possessions of his subjects without fault

on their part nor reasonable and manifest cause ([except] insofar as he may be able to exact his necessary expenses from them), we are left with the conclusion that papal principate was instituted for the utility of its subjects and not for its own utility or honour, and, in consequence, is worthy to be called not 'of lordship' but 'of service'.[23]

With regard to temporal rather than ecclesiastical power, McGrade notes that there is a similar minimalising of jurisdiction and function:

> Instead of viewing law and government as the animating force in society, the source of all order and value, Ockham regarded them as purely instrumental. The political element in human affairs becomes for him a means to the social existence of free men, but not the basis of the community or its end.[24]

Like Aquinas, Ockham maintains that government and positive law can only regulate the external aspects of sociopolitical existence, but have no jurisdiction over internal principles of action. More important is the living community of individual persons whose very existence in likemindedness engenders social meaning or civil theology. Following the dictate of right reason for its own sake, the individual wills to act virtuously, responsibly and morally for the common good in conjunction with others. The ruling institutions provide the means and occasionally the encouragement to do so. The picture that clearly builds up in Ockham's political thought is that of a three-fold universe of powers, the most immediate and fundamental of which is that of the existential: a personal field of legitimate wilfulness coupled with rationality. Ockham did not jettison Christendom so much as concentrate it in the existence of the individual. In other words, Christendom for Ockham is not an imperial realisation of the Kingdom of God, but a personal one.

We have seen how he sought to preserve the integrity of Christian dogma, but succumbed to a bifurcation of faith from reason, thus playing into the very process of spiritual disintegration that marked the crisis of meaning in his day. This was the first of Ockham's ironies. The second irony is that, in spite of this, he unwittingly participated in the process of authority's differentiation and thus secured Christendom, if under a different guise, for the early modern dispensation. This double irony results in an identification of the individual as an inviolable and inexhaustible centre of meaning, whose very existence anchors the Christian truth of society in the first place. The institutionalisation of that Christendom occurs, or does not occur, secondarily.

WILL-RATIO AS A POLITICAL COMPLEX

So how does this double irony play out? The loss of meaningful experience in the coupling of faith and reason led Ockham to make explicit a tension that had been germinating through the course of later medieval thought: the tension between will and ratio.[25] The unravelling of the Christian project of finding an adequate synthesis between faith and reason – and in this, the undoing of the work of Augustine, Scotus Eriugena, Anselm, Thomas, etc. – is indeed the ebbing away of Christendom as a civil theology or civilisational consensus as to the meaning of a Christian in the world. But the resulting fragmentation that divorces reason from an ever-privatising faith does not yield an apparent monopoly of the public square for reason and its offspring in the natural sciences. Rather, public or political rationality is seen to move in a newly excavated tension with the will that was largely eclipsed by the high scholastic focus on faith. In other words, the will becomes increasingly topical in the rise of political philosophy. In the anxiety of his own life as a Franciscan-on-the-run, Ockham brings will to a more than speculative level in his concerns over individual autonomy. We have already seen above that he claims that liberty and will cannot be distinguished, so that a meaningful claim to liberty always involves the will and vice versa. Existential authority then is a complex we can characterise as will-ratio. In the formulation of a will-ratio complex, the primacy of will is maintained as individuals do not cease to be wilful when they have ceased to be rational; but maintained also is the insight that both will and reason emerge as a complex from the participatory existence of the individual subject and not in isolation from each other. What Ockham's work seems to suggest, again without becoming thematic, is that will and reason in the human mind, as much as in the divine mind, not only complement each other but that their complementarity ought not to be severed. Will is only authentically will when rational.

This has enduring political implications. In his *Hitler and the Germans* lectures of 1964, Voegelin reminded his audience of the existential derailment or stupidity that occurs in the collapse of tension between will and reason:

And now I would like to treat the matter systematically, particularly the problem of the higher stupidity ... We started from the loss of reality through dehumanisation. There a sector of reality – that is, of man's relation to God, his presence under divine being – is lost and replaced, deliberately ... by his will.

Now here one encounters a problem, that again we just do not have in modern German – in other languages we do – the expressions to differentiate between what 'will' in the classical and Christian sense is, and what 'will' in revolt against God is. In the classical and Christian sense, the will, the *voluntas*, is always and only the rationally ordered will. This means that wherever the power of existence (*Existenzmacht*) joins forces with reason and spirit, there is the 'will'. Where power of existence separates itself from reason and spirit, we do not speak of will, in the classic Christian vocabulary, but of *concupiscientia* or of *libido*. The expression 'libido' has become very popular through psychoanalysis. But it is the general expression for existence-powerful desire that is not ordered by reason or spirit.[26]

Brendan Purcell comments on the problem in his editorial introduction to the lectures:

One must ask: Whence this systematic regression from the rationality of common sense? Voegelin's answer is that the fundamental stupidity is to put one's own will, libido, at the centre of the universe, and that such dedivinisation leads all too quickly to a dehumanisation.[27]

Libidinous 'power of existence' in its radical isolation from reason in its classic Christian sense of ratio is a symptom of a spiritual sickness or pneumopathology, which Voegelin uses to diagnose the disorder of the National Socialist era in Germany.[28] Voegelin here was treating the phenomenon as it manifested itself to massively murderous effect in a specific time and place. However, such pneumopathological rottenness is an existential corruption that is a general human possibility at all times, individually and politically. The civilisational schism that followed from the bifurcation of faith from reason provided a philosophical environment in which a thinker like Ockham could relocate the Christianity of Christendom in the interiority of the individual first and foremost, thus maintaining the civilisational substance. However, it would appear that the civilisational schism was not exhausted, extending as it did to the divorce of will from reason. Brett highlights that for Ockham, 'It is the rectitude of the act of volition which is the condition for the moral righteousness of the external act, although ... right reasoning must also be present.'[29] However, certainly from the time of Hobbes onward, it is the libidinously denatured will, sundered from ratio, that is recognised as the orientating force in man. An Ockhamite will-ratio complex therefore is sufficiently post-medieval to capture the significance of the new civilisational assertion of existential authority, but not quite modern enough to indulge in the exuberance of the will unbound.

Of course, it would be folly to think that the naked libido, as an existentially corrupt force, has run its course politically in the totalitarian nightmare of the twentieth century. What of the politics of liberty? The classical liberal tradition is, in many ways, grounded in a concern for the individual that has largely inoculated itself from the magical power politics of totalitarian ideology. The 'Great Idea' of pure race, of a transfigurative and communistic equality, of a myth of the state, etc. is simply not compelling in contemporary liberal democracies.[30] However, we do well to remember that existential deformation is not primarily a political problem, but emerges from the consciousness of an individual first – even if it is a deformation evident on a mass social scale. Liberal democracies are not therefore inured against the disintegration of the Ockhamite will-ratio complex. While not suffering from the extremes of a libidinous indulgence in mass murder and the reimagination of reality according to some Great Idea, liberal democracies nonetheless are subject to a more subtle fracturing of the tension in the will-reason complex.

Rawls writes in *Political Liberalism*:

> Being reasonable is not an epistemological idea (though it has epistemological elements). Rather, it is part of a political ideal of democratic citizenship that includes the idea of public reason. The content of this ideal includes what free and equal citizens as reasonable can require of each other with respect to their reasonable comprehensive views.[31]

The liberty of liberalism rests upon the wilfulness of man, which itself rests upon the rationality of man. It is the rationality of man that is the essential condition for a genuine public reason. The concept of citizenship is thus a concept of life in society that is both wilful and rational. On the Ockhamite complex of will-ratio, Martin Buber suggests a rationality that can penetrate to an existential depth but that remains the condition of genuine citizenship:

> The principle of human life is not simple but twofold, being built up in a twofold movement which is of such a kind that the one movement is the presupposition of the other. I propose to call the first movement 'the primal setting at a distance' and the second 'entering into relation' ... Man, as man, sets man at a distance and makes him independent; he lets the life of men like himself go on round about him, and so he, and he alone, is able to enter into relation ... with those like himself.[32]

Buber's two movements of 'primal setting at a distance' and 'entering into relation' are both actions that involve to some degree the will-ratio of each citizen; while Rawls' 'being reasonable' requires that the specifically *political* recognition of reason be not epistemological but rather recognise the wilfulness of citizens as a legitimate existential authority that generates civil theology.

Citizenship in liberal democracy is a public political good that means more than officially recognised membership in a state. It is an umbrella term that intends a social entitlement to a gamut of political goods such as order, justice, liberty, equality and so on, which themselves reflexively flow from the likemindedness of individuals. If we look at the individuals who comprise a society, both statistically and substantially, through an Ockhamite lens, we might see the will-ratio complex in the generation of civil theology (understood as public consensus). If Ockham assumed the connection of will and ratio cannot be rightfully severed, then the political goods that flow from their public reason cannot be meaningfully severed one from the other either. For example, one may not rightfully assert one's liberty at the expense of public order, or dispense with liberty in the maximum achievement of equality. Each political good became a political good because it was first an existential good whose provenance is in the participatory tension of consciousness toward the ground. To emphasise one political good too exclusively can lead to an oblivion where other political goods are wilfully forgotten. Of course, political goods can be enumerated, one from the next, but the danger is that, in the listing of each, one may forget that they comprise something of a complex themselves.[33] (Though the list of political goods is by far not exhausted, the complex could look like this: order-liberty-justice-equality.) Thus there is always a danger in liberalism, in its strong emphasis upon liberty, that a forgetfulness of other political goods can occur; because what is truly forgotten is that liberty belongs with other political goods in a community of goods in a deeper way than its political formulation suggests.

Where the tradition of liberalism has maintained its major focus on liberty through its discourse about rights, civic republicanism is another tradition that has accompanied it, emphasising instead the historicity of society through its public rationality of traditions and virtues. The one has concentrated on liberty by politically maximising the assertion of wilfulness of the individual, while the other has insisted upon the rationality of political consensus that emerges from a civil theology. These broad traditions overlap and enrich the other because they emerge together from the same existential substrate, just as their political goods do, and just as will and ratio do.

Liberalism and civic republicanism can lead to healthy dichotomies, but the oblivion that results from the willed rejection of the other can lead to debilitating derailments. For example, there are well-known dichotomies that are healthy, challenging and mutually tempering that are driven by the traditions of left and right; dichotomies between the positive and negative liberties, between the statism of social democracies and some brands of libertarianism, between the rule of law and the morality of society, and so forth. There are also the derailments that can occur in extreme partisanship that can involve the rejection of Rawls' public reason in the sense of political traditions and their political goods, as well as the deeper philosophical bed of civil theology in its sense of public consensus and the field of meaning that is spontaneously generated by the sentiment of likemindedness.

Liberal thought has been accused by some in contemporary political philosophy of accentuating liberty to the detriment of other political goods. Liberalism by itself has been criticised as too narrow a theory that omits important social dimensions of political existence.[34] In liberalism, forgetfulness of the complex of goods within which liberty flourishes becomes a possibility with the result that that very liberty can become something of a fetish. Charles Taylor writes that

Primacy-of-right theories [which he calls 'Atomism', referring mostly to the notion of liberty proposed by Robert Nozick] ... accept a principle ascribing rights to men as binding unconditionally, binding, that is, on men as such. But they do not accept as similarly unconditional a principle of belonging or obligation.[35]

Taylor emphasises the social conditions that make possible 'primacy-of-right' theories like that of Nozick.[36] He goes on to say that the social conditions of freedom, or of theories that dwell solely upon the maximisation of liberty as wilfulness, are

> based on the notion, first, that developed freedom requires a certain understanding of the self, one in which the aspirations to autonomy and self-direction become conceivable; and second, that this self-understanding is not something we can sustain on our own, but that our identity is always partly defined in conversation with others or through the common understanding which underlies the practices of our society.[37]

Taylor is pointing toward the insufficiency of political thought that emphasises liberty-as-will over the rationality of civil theology.

To suggest that civil theology is public rationality is also to underscore that civil theology is historical. The people who give us a 'public' are concrete persons in concrete societies in time and place, cognisant of ancestors and concerned for bequeathing an inheritance to their successors. To ignore, negate, or attempt to destroy a civil theology through the immediacy of will is to wilfully eclipse the historicity of existence. In 1790, Edmund Burke exhorted Englishmen not to be seduced by the oblivion of a will unshackled from civil theology:

> A politic caution, a guarded circumspection, a moral rather than a complexional timidity, were among the ruling principles of our forefathers in their most decided conduct. Not being illuminated with the light of which the gentlemen of France tell us they have got so abundant a share, they acted under a strong impression of the ignorance and fallibility of mankind ... Let us imitate their caution

if we wish to deserve their fortune or to retain their bequests. Let us add, if we please, but let us preserve what they have left; and standing on the firm ground of the British constitution, let us be satisfied to admire, rather than attempt to follow in their desperate flights, the aeronauts of France ...[38]

In a similar if less dramatic way, Robert Bork suggests that the landmark 1965 US Supreme Court decision in *Griswold* v. *Connecticut* that found a right to privacy was an assertion of will whose other outcome was a judicial device that could trump the historicity of public reason. The statutes in place in Connecticut that were challenged successfully had criminalised the use of, and the being accessory to the use of, contraceptives since 1879. He argues that these statutes functioned only as a precatory law. Precatory laws in general affirm a moral or political principle. In this case, the statutes themselves were never enforced, nor were they likely to ever be enforced, but embodied an official attitude toward premarital and extramarital sexual relations.[39] Of course, this may be an improper use of law – even 'an uncommonly silly' use of law that Ockham too may well have ridiculed – and, if ever enforced, could be self-defeating; such statutes could then be declared void through desuetude.[40] However, Bork claims the existence of precatory laws was never the issue in *Griswold*, nor even was the protection of marriage against state intrusion. The issue, he claims, was the enlistment of the 'Court on one side of one issue in a cultural struggle.'[41] The finding of an unenumerated right to privacy could now surpass the historically grounded constitution. 'The creation of a new device for judicial power to remake the Constitution was the point.'[42] Through the employment of what become known as substantive due process – itself not uncontroversial – the court found an extraconstitutional, penumbral sphere of foundational meaning that maximises the meaning of the constitutionally enumerated rights. Without a foundational right to privacy, it was argued, there is no meaning in the constitutional right to liberty. Aside from the more obvious legal problems associated with unenumerated rights – for example, what is the legal status of foundational meaning that lies outside an already fundamental law? – and specifically with a general right to privacy, there is a more philosophic and political problem that arises in this context: to lay claim to and commandeer such an undefined and extralegal sphere is certainly a wilful act but may also be a libidinous indulgence devoid of ratio. Bork remarks:

The Court majority said there was now a right of privacy but did not even intimate an answer to the question, 'Privacy to do what?' ... The truth is that 'privacy' will turn out to protect those activities that enough Justices to form a majority think ought to be protected and not activities with which they have little sympathy.[43]

Furthermore, the finding of unenumerated rights may not always resonate well with the political reasonableness of a historically derived morality embodied by a constitution and animated by a citizenry.[44] If, as Bork suggests, the *Griswold* ruling replaced the earlier precatory law with a new one that reflected a different cultural perspective, it did so by creating an undefined right to privacy as a judicial device to wilfully close the possibility of public consensus. The original statutes that were struck down, as precatory, articulated a moral principle that a liberal state may or may not have any business articulating. That is an old bone of contention that goes back to Locke in the liberal tradition and arguably further to Plato. However, if Bork is correct, the finding of a right to privacy amounts to a legal infringement upon a civil theology that Ockham would probably have found deeply distasteful. The existential process of public rationality is inevitably fraught and restless. We disagree, debate, joust – and not without some name-calling – but in the absence of an explicit injustice, foreclosing on public reason by legal means only adds bitterness to the culture wars which nevertheless rage on.

CONCLUSION

Ockham's own treatment of will in conjunction with reason is more often assumed then made thematic. However, that man can recognise and exercise reason and that human and divine will are emphatic realities, is sufficiently clear. The assumption in Ockham that will and reason ought not to be uncoupled is more than a bland piece of commonsense. First, when will and reason are uncoupled, personal or social disorder can occur; and to monumentally disastrous effect. Second, the existential field of concerns in which the will-ratio complex of experience becomes topical is a very rich one indeed: where will and reason are discussed, Ockham is securing the autonomy and authority of the individual against the power-play of largely libidinous institutional wills that he witnessed in his own day.

Ockham is rightly recognised as one of the first great champions of individual liberties, and as such, indicates the trajectory of the unfolding western arrangement that prioritised the dignity of man among the triad of authorities. Ockham was not overly concerned about finding an institutional solution to abuses of temporal or ecclesiastical powers, but with the extra-institutional authority of individual human beings to live unmolested by such abuses and to exercise a governance over the things of one's own such as life, liberty and property. Existential authority becomes the theme of his political thought in his concern to shore up the jurisdiction of the individual: that is, the zone of inviolable autonomy embedded in the existence of each person that accords with natural equity. He reaches down to the raw existence of individuals and, by extension, communities in order to grasp and elevate that living body of meaning, the civil theology of a society, which is spontaneously generated by the existential authority of individual likeminded human beings. This allowed him to turn to the existential questions of liberty and moral responsibility that mark the assertion of existential authority. Ockham has taken these concerns and rearticulated them in the midst of the crisis of meaning of his day when Christendom, as a civil theology, was no longer the integrating force in society. The results of Ockham's work do not involve the loss of society's Christian moorings and the casting adrift of the animating principles of the West, but present the individual's will and reason as a zone of legitimate authority; and more broadly, place that existential authority into an uneasy equilibrium with the institutions of political and spiritual authorities. Liberal democracies rest upon this equilibrium, precariously maintaining themselves and only to the extent that they maintain the integrity of existence in will-ratio.

NOTES

1. Or 'Terms of Second Intention'. See William of Ockham, *Ordinatio* I, dist.ii, qu.3 and *Quodlibet* IV, qu. 35 in Bosely and Tweedale, *Basic Issues in Medieval Philosophy* (Peterborough, ON: Broadview Press, 1997), pp. 387–95.
2. *Theologia civilis* is Augustine's term for meaning in political society. See *City of God*, Bk VI, Chapter 5. According to Bruce Douglass, civil theology is the entirety of beliefs 'through which the members of a political society relate their political experience to the ultimate conditions of human existence'. Bruce Douglass, *Thought* 55 (June 1980), p. 169. For a survey of writings on civil theology, see Jeffrey C. Herndon, *Eric Voegelin and the Problem of Christian Political Order* (Columbia MA: University of Missouri, 2007), pp. 19–27.
3. Brendan Purcell, *From Big Bang to Big Mystery: Human Origins in the Light of Creation and Evolution*, (Dublin: Veritas, 2011), p. 89.
4. Ibid.
5. See Voegelin's discussion of fideism and *sacrificium intellectus* in *History of Political Ideas 3*, pp. 107–110 (part of *The Collected Works of Eric Voegelin* series, volume 21

specifically. Hereafter the reference to the various volumes will be *Collected Works* 1, 2, etc.)
6. Walsh, 'Editor's Introduction', ibid, p. 8.
7. The text goes: 'Two there are, august emperor, by which this world is chiefly ruled, the sacred authority of the priesthood and the royal power.' *Medieval Europe: A Short Sourcebook,* Hollister et al. (New York: Alfred A. Knopf, 1982), p. 40.
8. Brian Tierney, *The Idea of Natural Rights: Studies on Natural Rights, Natural Law, and Church Law* (Grand Rapids, MI: W. B. Eerdmans, 1997), pp. 1150–625, p. 67 (hereafter referred to as *The Idea of Natural Rights*).
9. The ground of being is Eric Voegelin's adaptation from Aristotle of the ultimate divine reality in which man participates as his very nature. On the link between the ground of being and political philosophy, Voegelin writes, 'The problems of human order in society and history originate in the order of consciousness … [C]onsciousness is not a given to be deduced from outside but an experience of participation in the ground of being whose logos has to be brought to clarity through the meditative exegesis of itself.' Voegelin, 'Foreword', *Anamnesis,* in *Collected Works* 6, p. 33.
10. Georges de Lagarde, quoted by Brian Tierney, *The Idea of Natural Rights,* pp. 44–5.
11. See Brian Tierney's discussion of this, ibid., p. 14.
12. Joseph Strayer, *Middle Ages, 1395–1500* (New York: D. Appleton-Century Co., 1948), pp. 395–1500, p. 424.
13. Nominalism is something of an umbrella term. It comprises Terminism and Conceptualism as variations on a Nominalist theme. See especially William J. Courtenay, *Ockham and Ockhamism: Studies in the Dissemination and Impact of his Thoughts* (Leiden: Koninklijke Brill NV, 2008).
14. William of Ockham, *Dialogue* III, II, 3, *Medieval Political Philosophy,* pp. 500–01. My emphasis.
15. Tierney, *The Idea of Natural Rights,* p. 180.
16. Takashi Shogimen, *Ockham and Political Discourse in the Late Middle Ages,* (Cambridge: Cambridge University Press, 2007), pp. 245–46.
17. For an excellent commentary on Ockham's involvement with the Franciscan poverty controversy, see Shogimen, *Ockham and Political Discourse in the Late Middle Ages,* pp. 36–74. Also, John Kilcullen, 'The Political Writings', *The Cambridge Companion to Ockham* (Cambrdige: Cambrdige University Press, 1999), pp. 302–25.
18. William of Ockham, *Dialogue* III, II, 2, *Medieval Political Philosophy,* p. 496.
19. Shogimen, *Ockham and Political Discourse in the Late Middle Ages,* p. 234.
20. Ibid., pp. 246–7. See especially Shogimen's footnote on p. 247 for sources on Ockham's ethics.
21. William of Ockham, *I Sentences,* X, 2. Shogimen discusses the meaning of liberty in *Ockham and Political Discourse in the Late Middle Ages,* p. 247ff.
22. Brett, 'Introduction', *Ockham, On the Power of Emperors and Popes* (Bristol: Thoemmes Press, 1998), p. 32
23. Ockham, ibid., pp. 87–8.
24. McGrade, *The Political Thought of William of Ockham* (Cambridge: Cambridge University Press, 2002), p. 85.
25. The problem of the primacy of either intellect over will, or will over intellect, in the thought of Thomas and Duns Scotus respectively is mediated somewhat by the assertion by Scotus and Ockham of the will as a rational appetite. If the intellect and the will can possess rational qualities, then it would seem that ratio constitutes a deeper existential bed that gives rise to both. See Mary Beth Ingham and Mechthild

Dreyer, 'The Rational Will and Freedom', *The Philosophical Vision of John Duns Scotus: An Introduction* (Cambridge: Cambridge University Press, 1999), pp. 146–52; and Marilyn McCord Adams, 'Ockham on Will, Nature, and Morality', *The Cambridge Companion to Ockham* (Cambridge: Cambridge University Press, 1999), pp. 254–5.

26. Voegelin, *Hitler and the Germans*, in *Collected Works 31*, p. 107.
27. Purcell, 'Editor's Introduction', ibid., p. 27.
28. See Voegelin's comments, ibid., pp. 101–2.
29. Brett, 'Introduction' in Ockham, *On the Power of Emperors and Popes*, p. 32.
30. See Walsh, 'The Politics of Liberty', *Guarded by Mystery: Meaning in a Post-Modern Age*, Washington DC: The Catholic University of America Press, 1999, pp. 123–46.
31. Rawls, *Political Liberalism*, (New York: Columbia University Press), 1993, p. 62.
32. Martin Buber, *The Knowledge of Man: Selected Essays*, M. S. Friedman, trans. (New York: Harper & Row, 1965), p. 60, p. 67.
33. One problem that arises from the enumeration of political goods and rights is that, when other unenumerated goods or rights are newly experienced and asserted, they seek their place in the enumeration. Where this involves a fundamental law such as a constitution, the reconciliation of legal and political problems has the potential to become deeply damaging to the polity. See my comments on Robert Bork below.
34. For example, see Jürgen Habermas's treatment of liberalism's insufficiency, as well as republicanism's 'ethical overload' in his proposal of Discourse Theory. In Habermas, 'Three Normative Models of Democracy', *The Inclusion of the Other: Studies in Political Theory* (Cambridge, MA: MIT Press, 1998).
35. Taylor, 'Atomism', *Philosophy and the Human Sciences: Philosophical Papers, Vol. 2*, (Cambridge: Cambridge University Press, 1985), p. 188.
36. Taylor's reference is to Nozick, *Anarchy, State and Utopia* (New York: Basic Books, 1974).
37. Taylor, *Philosophy and the Human Sciences*, p. 209.
38. Edmund Burke, *Select Works: Reflections on the Revolution in France*, E. J. Payne, ed. (London: Clarendon Press, 1898), p. 293.
39. Bork, *The Tempting of America: The Political Seduction of the Law* (New York: Touchstone, 1991), p. 96.
40. Justice Stewart stated in his dissent in *Griswold* v. *Connecticut* that, although the statutes were 'uncommonly silly', they were perfectly constitutional. Asininity does not equate with unconstitutionality.
41. Bork, *The Tempting of America*, p. 96.
42. Ibid., pp. 96–7.
43. Ibid., p. 99. The ruling in *Griswold* v. *Connecticut* found only a right to marital privacy, but both the majority and dissenting opinions focused on privacy in general, and in the 1972 ruling, *Eisenstadt* v. *Baird*, the right to privacy was extended beyond married couples.
44. Of course, a society's set of values being historically derived does not of itself make it just or moral. The point has to do with the best manner of bringing about a greater common good; and in this, whether regulation and substantive due process are to be preferred to persuasion, consensus and an authentic 'changing of hearts and minds'.

BIBLIOGRAPHY

Boseley, Richard N. and Martin M. Tweedale, *Basic Issues in Medieval Philosophy*, Peterborough, Ontario: Broadview, 2006.

Augustine, St, *City of God*, David Knowles, ed., Harmondsworth: Penguin Books, 1981.

Bork, Robert, *The Tempting of America: The Political Seduction of the Law*, New York: Touchstone, 1991.

Brett, Annabel S., introduction to *On the Power of Emperors and Popes*, by William of Ockham, Bristol: Thoemmes Press, 1998.

Burke, Edward, *Select Works: Reflections on the Revolution in France*, E. J. Payne. ed., London: Clarendon Press, 1898.

Courtenay, William J., *Ockham and Ockhamism: Studies in the Dissemination and Impact of his Thought*, Leiden: Koninklijke Brill NV, 2008.

Buber, Martin, *The Knowledge of Man: Selected Essays*, M. S. Friedman, trans., New York: Harper & Row, 1965.

Douglass, R. Bruce, 'Civil Religion and western Christianity', *Thought* 55 (June 1980), p. 169.

Habermas, Jürgen, *The Inclusion of the Other: Studies in Political Theory*, Cambridge, MA: MIT Press, 1998.

Hollister, C. Warren, Joe W. Leedom, Marc A. Meyer, and David S. Spear, eds., *Medieval Europe: A Short Sourcebook*, New York: Alfred A. Knopf, 1982.

Ingham, Mary Beth and Mechthild Dreyer, 'The Rational Will and Freedom', *The Philosophical Vision of John Duns Scotus: An Introduction*, Cambridge: Cambridge University Press, 1999, pp. 146–52.

Kilcullen, John, 'The Political Writings', *The Cambridge Companion to Ockham*, Paul Vincent Spade, ed., Cambridge: Cambridge University Press, 1999, pp. 302–25.

Lerner, Ralph, and Muhsin Mahdi, eds., *Medieval Political Philosophy*, Ithaca, NY: Cornell University Press, 1972.

McCord Adams, Marilyn, 'Ockham on Will, Nature, and Morality', *The Cambridge Companion to Ockham*, Paul Vincent Spade, ed., Cambridge: Cambridge University Press, 1999, pp. 245–72.

McGrade, Arthur Stephen, *The Political Thought of William of Ockham*, Cambridge: Cambridge University Press, 2002.

Nozick, Robert, *Anarchy, State and Utopia*, New York: Basic Books, 1974.

Brendan Purcell, *From Big Bang to Big Mystery: Human Origins in the Light of Creation and Evolution*, Dublin: Veritas, 2011.

_____, 'Introduction', *The Collected Works of Eric Voegelin, Vol. 31: Hitler and the Germans*, by Eric Voegelin, Columbia, MO: University of Missouri Press, 1999, pp. 21–40.

Rawls, John, *Political Liberalism*, New York: Columbia University Press, 1993.

Shogimen, Takashi, *Ockham and Political Discourse in the Late Middle Ages*, Cambridge: Cambridge University Press, 2007.

Strayer, Joseph, *Middle Ages, 395–1500*, New York: D. Appleton-Century Co., 1942.

Taylor, Charles, *Philosophy and the Human Sciences: Philosophical Papers, Vol. 2*, Cambridge: Cambridge University Press, 1985.

Tierney, Brian, *The Idea of Natural Rights: Studies on Natural Rights, Natural Law, and Church Law, 1150–1625*, Grand Rapids, MI: W. B. Eerdmans, 1997.

Eric Voegelin, *The Collected Works of Eric Voegelin, Vol. 6: Anamnesis: On the Theory of History and Politics*, Columbia, MO: University of Missouri Press, 1998.

———, *The Collected Works of Eric Voegelin, Vol. 20: History of Political Ideas, Volume 2: The Middle Ages to Aquinas*, Columbia, MO: University of Missouri Press, 1997.

———, *The Collected Works of Eric Voegelin, Vol. 21: History of Political Ideas, Volume 3: The Later Middle Ages*, Columbia, MO: University of Missouri Press, 1998.

———, *The Collected Works of Eric Voegelin, Vol. 31: Hitler and the Germans*, Columbia, MO: University of Missouri Press, 1999.

David Walsh, *Guarded by Mystery: Meaning in a Postmodern Age*, Washington, DC: The Catholic University of America Press, 1999.

———, 'Introduction', *The Collected Works of Eric Voegelin, Vol. 21: History of Political Ideas, Volume 3: The Later Middle Ages*, by Eric Voegelin, Columbia, MO: University of Missouri Press, 1998, pp. 1–26.

Why Chickens Have No Myths: Walker Percy on Language and Man

GERARD CASEY

IT'S LIFE, JIM, BUT NOT AS WE KNOW IT ... [1]

Gregor Samsa awoke one morning from his troubled dreams and found that while he had not been metamorphosed into a giant insect – what a story that would have made! – he had been transplanted from his comfortable bed to the floor of what looked like a rain forest. All around him were trees, or what looked like trees, with strange shapes and unrecognisable foliage. The tree-like things stretched up to the sky – and what a sky! Purple instead of the normal blue and, as Gregor saw when he reached a clearing, with not one but what looked like two suns! Wherever Gregor was, it wasn't Earth; it wasn't even Prague. The forest was raucous with sounds – an Amazonian cacophony of whistles, shrieks and jabberings. Suspended between terror and exhilaration, Gregor began to explore his new environment. First things first – what would he eat and drink? Was he in danger from attack by plants or animals? How would he know what *was* a plant or an animal? Were there human beings on this planet or, if not human beings, then rational beings of some kind or other? *How would he know if there were any such beings on this planet?*

From our regrettable familiarity with sci-fi movies and TV series, it seems that if there were to be alien rational beings they would look just like us except that they would have lumpy foreheads or funny ears, like the Vulcans, the Catullans, the Iotians, the Xyrillians or the J'naii in *Star Trek*. But is it necessary that alien rational beings have to look humanoid or is this just a function of the financial limitations of the producers and the imaginative limitations of the scriptwriters? Even in *Star Trek*, alien beings were sometimes non-humanoid in form, like the glutinous liquid-like Nacene, the hermaphroditic crystalloid Tholians, the quasi-divine Q and the silicon-based fibrous Horta. *How were the crews of the various Starships Enterprise supposed to know if any of the entities they encountered were rational?*

Returning from the exotic atmosphere of imaginary planets to our own real planet at an earlier stage of our history, the question of whether or not to recognise other entities as human beings arose when the Spanish explorers reached South America. Were the entities they encountered here which looked as if they might be human *really* human or were they merely some as yet undiscovered form of primate? *How were our Spanish explorers supposed to tell?*

'ALL THE KING'S HORSES ...'

In his *From Big Bang to Big Mystery*, Brendan Purcell several times refers to writings of the American philosopher-novelist Walker Percy,[2] remarking in particular on Percy's claim that there is a greater difference between animals and man than there is between an animal and a planet[3] and quoting Percy's question at the start of his *Lost in the Cosmos*, 'Why is it that of all the billions and billions of strange objects in the Cosmos ... you are beyond doubt the strangest?'[4]

Percy believes that, in its attempts to understand man, modern science becomes incoherent and that this incoherence is not an incidental but remediable failure but a failure that has its roots in the very nature of science itself.[5] For Percy, the root of the incoherence lies in the fact that in the human sciences two very different kinds of things are jumbled together; things that can be measured, such as electrical impulses in the brain, and things that cannot be measured, such as states of consciousness. He remarks, 'no amount of effort by "brain" scientists and "mind" scientists can ever narrow the gap'.[6] Some people are of the impression that with the passage of time and with increasingly sophisticated neurological monitoring equipment the gap can be traversed. However, the problem is not a merely technical one but rather one of principle and is one, moreover, that has been around for quite some time. In the nineteenth century, John Tyndall, physicist, scientific materialist and free-thinker, wrote:

> But the passage from the physics of the brain to the corresponding facts of consciousness is unthinkable. Granted that a definite thought, and a definite molecular action in the brain occur simultaneously; we do not possess the intellectual organ, nor apparently any rudiment of the organ, which would enable us to pass, by a process of reasoning, from the one to the other. They

appear together, but we do not know why. Were our minds and senses so expanded, strengthened, and illuminated, as to enable us to see and feel the very molecules of the brain; were we capable of following all their motions, all their groupings, all their electric discharges, if such there be; and were we intimately acquainted with the corresponding states of though and feeling, we should be as far as ever from the solution to the problem, 'How are these physical processes connected with the facts of consciousness?' The chasm between the two classes of phenomena would still remain intellectually impassable. Let the consciousness of *love*, for example, be associated with a right-handed spiral motion of the molecules of the brain, and the consciousness of *hate* with a left-handed spiral motion. We should then know when we love, that the motion is in one direction, and when we hate that the motion is in the other; but the 'Why?' would remain as unanswerable as before.[7]

The rift which Tyndall identifies between the mental and the physical in man and which finds contemporary expression in the so-called mysterianism in respect of consciousness of such as Colin McGinn,[8] Percy echoes in a linguistic mode: 'the one way to get at ... the great modern rift between mind and matter ... [is] ... the only place where they intersect, language'.[9]

There is something fundamentally odd, even unsettling, about reductionist theories of man, given the specific identity of the investigator and the object under investigation. As much as Percy believes modern science to be incoherent, so too he takes Darwin and Freud to be incoherent inasmuch as

> neither can account for his own activity by his own theory. For how does Darwin account for the 'variation' which is his own species and its peculiar behaviour – in his case, sitting in his study in Kent and writing the truth as he saw it about evolution? And if Freud's psyche is like ours, a dynamism of contending forces, how did it ever arrive at the truth about psyches, including his own?[10]

I have made more or less the same point on occasion, arguing that philosophers and the explanations they give must be serious[11] by which I don't mean that philosophers have to be solemn or portentous but rather that a condition of their holding a belief, *really* holding that belief rather than just notionally adhering to it, is that their actions should, as far as possible, conform, and be able to conform, to it. I have tried to express this point in the form of a maxim: no theory can be seriously maintained such that, if it were to be true, its very maintenance would become impossible, meaningless, contradictory or self-refuting. Apart from the formal constraints on theories of the necessity for consistency and coherence, and the material constraints of explanatory adequacy and coverage, there is, I contend, also a self-referential constraint on theories, namely, that such theories must not render impossible the conditions of their own statement or the conditions of their being maintained. If they do so, they are theoretically self-stultifying. Articles are written and lectures delivered by and to language-users and, from an anthropological point of view, language (and the activity dependent upon it) is a, if not the, most salient empirical characteristic of man. Once again, Percy:

> Behaviourists not only study responses; they write articles and deliver lectures setting forth what they take to be the truth about responses, and would be offended if anyone suggested that their writings and lectures were nothing more than responses and therefore no more true or false than a dog's salivation.[12]

LANGUAGE, ANIMAL AND MAN

Speaking of our capacity for language, Percy remarks, 'This capacity for language seems to be, in the evolutionary scale, a relatively recent, sudden, and explosive development ... it appears to have occurred in Neanderthal man as recently as ... 75,000 to 35,000 years ago.'[13] This capacity is, in evolutionary terms, relatively recent. More importantly, the capacity for language appears to be unique to man and, since its mist-shrouded origin, uniquely constitutive of what man is.

Taking his cue from the American philosopher, C. S. Peirce, Percy divides events into two kinds, dyadic and triadic. In dyadic events, an event A affects event B and event B affects event C and, no matter how complex the result, the whole series is ultimately reducible to units of A affecting units of B and vice versa. But language events, which are just as much a part of the world of our experience as are dyadic events, cannot be explained dyadically, not least because the effort to do so is self-stultifying. Animals can relate words to things as signal event to action event. 'Ball', uttered by a dog's master, can induce a dog to expect to fetch a ball. Now, consider the position of a child born into the booming, buzzing confusion of our workaday world. When a child begins to interact verbally with its mother, on the child's side we are dealing first with mere random or imitative noises and then, very quickly, with at most a rudimentary kind of signalling that, considered just as such, is not very different in kind from animal communication. On the mother's side, however, the child's actions, movements, sounds, noises, are all interpreted as being the actions of a communicative human being. The child's initial verbal activity is dyadic yet it is interpreted triadically. Eventually, the word 'ball' uttered by a child's mother doesn't just induce a physical orientation to a ball but produces meaning: '… this event cannot be explained by a dyadic model, however complex'.[14]

Let us take the triad of child, the word 'balloon' and the balloon object. In speaking of this triad, Percy notes that, in the end, each element is an instance of a type. The world 'balloon' as spoken is a token of the universal 'balloon'; the balloon itself is a token of the type balloon, and the one who couples the word 'balloon' with the balloon is not just the mass of flesh and energy interchanges but something else.

> Who, what is the coupler? Do you mean some part of his brain does the coupling? I could not say whether it is his brain which couples, his 'mind', his 'self', his 'I'. All one can say for certain is that if two things which are otherwise connected are coupled, there must be a coupler … The boy in Delta is not the organism boy. The balloon in Delta is not the balloon in the world. The *balloon* in Delta is not the sound *balloon*.[15]

He goes on to note that

> Peirce's insistence on both the reality and the nonmateriality of the third element – whatever one chooses to call it, interpretant, mind, coupler – is of critical importance to natural science because its claim to reality is grounded not on this or that theology or metaphysic but on empirical observation and the necessities of scientific logic.[16]

'Why,' asks Percy, 'is it that men speak and animals don't?'[17] Is it just that animals do not have the requisite physiological equipment? If so, perhaps we could devise some technological way of surmounting this obstacle.[18] This is not a new idea. Over two hundred years ago, impressed by the ability of vocally incapacitated human beings to communicate with others by means of signs, Julien de la Mettrie wondered if

> it be impossible to teach this animal [the ape] a language? I do not think so ... Why then should the education of monkeys be impossible? Why might not the monkey, by dint of great pains, at last imitate after the manner of deaf mutes, the motions necessary for pronunciation?[19]

When the idea of investigating the possibility of an animal's speaking was rediscovered in the twentieth century, attempts were made to get chimpanzees to vocalise. The result was a miserable failure.[20] De la Mettrie's alternative research strategy was rediscovered by Beatrix T. Gardner, R. Allen Gardner, David Premack and D. M. Rumbaugh in the 1960s. Various sub-strategies were devised. The chimpanzee Washoe was allegedly taught a version of American Sign Language (Ameslan); another chimpanzee, Lana, was taught to enter sequences at a console and another, Sarah, was taught to manipulate items on a visual display. The early reports were astounding; it seemed as if the chimps were able to manifest a linguistic ability comparable to that of children. However, as time passed and the initial flurry of excitement subsided, significant differences emerged in the interpretation accorded to the chimpanzees' activities. For example, some researchers began to modify their original claims regarding the chimpanzee's linguistic ability. In 1977, Rumbaugh was claiming for chimpanzees not language but what he called the requisites of linguistic competence[21] and in 1976 Premack began to replace talk of language with talk of the cognitive preconditions of language.[22] Other researchers continued to produce enthusiastic reports. Some critics, while they were prepared to grant that the apes manifested some linguistic skills, nevertheless considered them to be trivial. Other critics questioned the validity of the data on the chimpanzee's performances. According to some, the experiments were not accurately described although this was perhaps more the case with earlier reports than with later ones.[23] One major line of criticism alleged that the methodological inadequacies of these experiments (for example, the problem of cueing) were either insuperable or else sufficiently endemic to invalidate many of the reports.[24] Inadequate or partial reporting of experimental circumstances was a very serious problem with the sign-language projects. According to Seidenberg, the reports on Washoe and Koko are anecdotal and unsystematic.[25] Another line of criticism alleged that there were conceptual inadequacies of various kinds operating in the research. An example of one such problem was the very peculiar practices of scoring Washoe correct in her answers if they were in the correct *category*. For example, if she were asked to select, say, a banana, and she actually selected an apple, this response counted as correct, because bananas and apples were taken to belong to the same category!

The attempts of researchers to demonstrate that animals are more intelligent than humans at some stage of their development seem never to end. As I was completing this paper, a story appeared on the news media claiming that African grey parrots were smarter than your average two-year-old.[26] The popular account of the experiment is altogether unnuanced while the scientific report is significantly more reticent in its findings:

> Taken together, our findings demonstrate for the first time that a non-ape species is able to solve an auditory 'inference by exclusion' task instantaneously. The strong first-trial performance as well as the performance in the control tasks *suggest* that the parrots *may* indeed be capable of causal reasoning, which is in line with findings obtained in another reasoning task. Yet, their *performance is error-prone and may be influenced by interferences through stimulus–response processes.*[27]

It seems to be the case, then, despite all the efforts to prove the contrary, that animals cannot use language. They may come agonisingly close to doing so, as the chimpanzee appears to do, but close wins no cigar. We can witness a sophisticated degree of signal-response in the chimpanzees' behaviour but no unambiguous evidence of the sign-signifier relation. That relationship is evidenced by the presence of concepts. Animals, it seems, *cannot* form concepts whereas man *must* form concepts if he is to know in his distinctively human way.

CONCEPTS AND LANGUAGE

Language, which on one level is an obviously natural and unremarkable phenomenon has, on another level, the astonishing property of transcending the push-pull dyadic interactions of the natural world. So commonplace is language that it is scarcely possible for us to recognise its astonishing peculiarity:

> Man's capacity for symbol-mongering in general and language in particular is so intimately part and parcel of his being human, of his perceiving and knowing, of his very consciousness itself, that it is all but impossible for him to focus on the magic prism through which he sees everything else.[28]

All our knowledge has its roots in our contact with the world through our senses. The original sensory matrix produced by our senses is transformed in time into a perceptual matrix that is prolonged in us beyond the point of actual contact with the world by means of what are called the interior senses – memory, imagination, the cogitative sense (estimative sense in animals) and the common sense. The cogitative sense is sometimes called 'particular reason' as in man it mimics the purely rational capacities. The estimative sense is that quasi-rational sensory capacity that grounds cognition in the higher animals, particularly the primates (and, it would seem, some species of parrot), allowing them to perceive significant objects in their environment and to relate to them in ways conducive to their welfare. Latent in these sensory/perceptual matrices are concepts, the primary purpose of which, after their abstraction, is their reapplication to the matrices from which they emerged. The key point to note here is that concepts are only latent in the sensory matrices. It requires activity to educe them from that context and the only animal on this earth that appears to have that capacity is man.

It must be clearly understood that concepts, though educed from sensory matrices, are not any form of sensory knowledge, however refined that sensory knowledge may be. Conception and perception are easily confused but with a little thought can just as easily be disentangled. For example, in a lecture ask your students to 'think of a triangle'. Use the ambiguous word 'think' deliberately. Then say, 'Now think of a square'. When they have had some time to do what you have asked them to do, ask them if they can distinguish clearly between their thoughts of the triangle and their thoughts of the square. The answer to this question will usually be yes. Now ask them to think of a chiliagon (a thousand-sided figure) and, when they have done that, ask them to think of a chiliagon + 1. Can they distinguish clearly between the two? The answer now is usually no. In saying this, of course, what the students are trying to do is to see a difference between the two figures in their imaginations and when it comes down to it, one lumpy circle looks much like another whereas a triangle and a square are imaginatively quite distinct. While it might be impossible to imagine a perceptual difference between a chiliagon and a chiliagon + 1, the conceptual difference between the two is as clear and distinct as the conceptual difference between a triangle and a square and is essentially expressed in language. Concepts are inextricably linked to language; no language, no concepts; no concepts, no language.

Sensation/perception is related to our needs, desires and interests, and therefore is only fragmentarily related to the world around us as its organismic environment. Conception, on the other hand, the blood brother of language, leaves (in principle, at least) no gaps at all. Through conception, we live in a world, not just an environment. 'The signal-using organism has an environment. The sign-user has an environment, but it also has a *world*.'[29] Conception can bring into our world things that do not exist as part of our organic environment at all: fictional entities, mythic entities and the like.

Although concepts are made and are thus artificial, they are nonetheless based on and related to a pre-cognitive reality even though it may be that no immediate direct correlate for any particular concept can be found in the real world. If empiricism, in all its forms, has a tendency to regard conceptual knowledge as a refined or effete form of sensory knowledge, rationalism exhibits the opposed tendency to regard sensory knowledge as a crude and diffused form of conception. In its extreme form, rationalism tends towards idealism, towards understanding the world to be metaphysically dependent upon the cognitive activity of man.

Concepts emerge from the nexus of experience and are primarily designed to organise our experience to further our continued existence and our flourishing.[30] The most basic task of every organism, including man, is to maintain itself in existence. Organisms can do many things other than survive but they cannot do any of them unless they survive; survival is the *sine qua non* of human flourishing. We have senses not so that we can take aesthetic delight in sunsets but so that we can orient ourselves in the world, avoid danger and find food, shelter and mates. Try crossing a busy street with your eyes closed and ear plugs in and you will immediately see how essential our senses are to our survival.

But the senses are limited to the here and now, to what is immediately present and perceivable. Our survival chances are enhanced if we have some way to anticipate and avoid non-present dangers and threats and diminished if we do not. This is where the formation of beliefs comes into play. Beliefs function, as it were, to extend our sensory systems beyond the here and now and so improve, for the most part, our chances of survival. Not only do beliefs contribute to our survival; they also contribute to our flourishing by permitting us to develop concepts that bear on abstract entities such as reasons and causes which, despite being abstract, nonetheless allow us to organise our actions coherently and productively.

KNOWLEDGE OF THE TREE OF GOOD AND EVIL[31]
Once we have acquired language, it is almost impossible to return to what our pristine pre-linguistic experience must have been like. Because concepts are formed via abstraction – by our attending to some aspects of our experience while leaving others to one side – there is an ever-present danger that our conceptual life may become detached from the sensory nexus within which it originates. Some systems of thought see this as a major and irredeemable defect of any form of conceptualisation. The General Semanticists (Alfred Korzybski et al.) are particularly emphatic in denying that the word 'balloon' is a balloon and in this they would seem to be at one with Zen Buddhists who think of language as a finger pointing at the moon. It must be conceded that language can sometimes become a substitute for reality so that flesh and blood reality is drained from our thought, much as some tourists never see the places they visit until they look at the photographs they have taken. The word 'just' is often a symptom of this onset of bloodlessness as in a sentence such as 'That's just a magpie', where the 'just' functions to absorb the living, strutting bird into what Percy calls 'the sarcophagus of its sign'.[32]

Man has developed techniques for reconnecting with reality, not least the practice and appreciation of various forms of art, one of whose functions (not the only one) is a process of defamiliarisation. Why would anyone buy a painting of a tree when he can look out the window and see an actual tree? If the artist does his job well, the viewer can be re-introduced to the concrete and unassimilable reality of real things and can, through the painting, actually re-learn to look at real trees again as if it were the dawn of creation and he had just opened his eyes. Defamiliarisation, however, does not last forever and the medicine has to be repeated in different ways in different modes.

Human beings are fascinated with themselves. We talk to and about ourselves all the time. Percy suggests that if Martians were to drop in to see us, what would be most obvious about us is that we 'spend most of [our] time in one kind of symbolic transaction or other, talking or listening, gossiping, reading books, writing books, making reports, listening to lectures, delivering lectures, telling jokes, looking at paintings, watching TV, going to movies'.[33] Apart from the entertainment value of such activities (and it is not negligible) they allow us to escape, even if momentarily, from the quotidian routine and to re-establish contact with the individual reality which is the very stuff of our world.

Sometimes we do not need art – life itself does the job for us. Who feels as alive as the man who has just escaped death! Imagine you get up on a Monday morning, have the same skimpy and inadequate breakfast you always have, go to work to the same place where you have worked for the last fifteen years to face the same tasks you have faced since what seems like the beginning of time. At work, you collapse and are rushed to hospital. They run some tests on you and inform you that you are in the advanced stages of pancreatic cancer with just two months to live. Later that afternoon, an embarrassed house doctor comes back to tell you that the hospital confused your records with those of another man with the same name and that there is nothing really wrong with you that eating a regular breakfast and taking a good holiday won't cure. How do you feel? As if reprieved at the last minute from the firing squad. How does the world look to you now? Suddenly, everything is alive, vibrant, coloured. Martin Bell, one-time war correspondent of the BBC agrees: 'I'm the happiest that I've ever been. The turning point was nearly getting killed in a war zone. After that, every day has been like the first day of the rest of my life. I am living not on borrowed time, but on donated time. Every day I wake up happy to be alive.'[34]

Language and thought bring us into a new world, a brave new world, but a world that has both heights and depths. We are in a world filled with meaning – or not – as the case may be. Despair, ecstasy and boredom become possible to creatures such as us but you will search high and low to find a jealous pig or a parrot suffering from existential angst. Dogs don't get bored and cats just go to sleep when there's nothing to do, but 'a man in the world has the unique capacity for being delighted with the world and himself and his place in the world, or being bored with it, anxious about it, or depressed about it'.[35] More significantly, our world is also a world of 'ought' where before there was no ought – it is a normative world not just a world of brute facts. We have eaten of the tree – and once we have acquired knowledge of good and evil there can be no return to Eden. For if there is an 'I' – namely, me – there are other 'I's' and they cannot be treated as merely things in the world. 'Man knows he is something more than an organism in an environment, because for one thing he acts like anything but an organism in an environment. Yet he no longer has the means of understanding the traditional Judeo-Christian teaching that the 'something more' is a soul somehow locked in the organism like a ghost in a machine. What is he then? He has not the faintest idea.'[36]

Human language is not only through and through conceptual; it is also essentially social in origin and in function. Wittgenstein showed definitively in *Philosophical Investigations* that there could be no such thing as a language that could only in principle be known to only one person. On intersubjectivity, Percy notes that I and Thou are connected via symbolic interaction. More to the point:

> The second person is required as an element not merely in the genetic event of learning language but as the *indispensable and enduring conditions of all symbolic behaviour*. The very act of symbolic formulation, whether it be language, logic, art, or even thinking, is of its very nature a formulation for a *someone else*.[37]

The word 'conscious' is derived from the Latin words for 'to know' and 'with'. To be conscious is 'to know with'. Consciousness, human consciousness, is a mode of knowing through or by means of the concept and the concept is what is given by the phenomenon of naming (at least in a rudimentary form): 'not only are we always conscious of something; we are also conscious of it as something we conceive under the symbol assigned to it. And, without the symbol, I suggest we would not be conscious of it at all.'[38] Percy goes on to say, 'Is not consciousness nothing more or less than the act or transaction by which I communicate with you or with myself a symbol, sentence, line or poetry, map, whatever, through which we both look at and perceive what the thing, the symbol, is about?'[39] To be conscious is to pay attention to something under the auspices of its sign, a sign that is social in origin.

Language is strange but you, another human being, are even stranger. As Percy puts it, the word 'apple' as uttered by you

> ... is part of my world but it is not a singular thing like an individual apple. It is in fact understandable only insofar as it conforms to a rule for uttering apples. But the oddest thing of all is your status in my world. You – Betty, Dick – are like other items in my world – cats, dogs, and apples. But you have a unique property. You are also co-namer, co-discoverer, co-sustainer of my world ...[40]

Not only are you strange but I am even stranger, strange even to myself. The subject, the coupler, the third actor in the language triad is not itself caught in the net of language, like the movie camera that sees but is not itself seen. 'The fateful flaw of human semiotics is this: that of all the objects in the entire Cosmos which the sign-user can apprehend through the conjoining of signifier and signified (word uttered and thing beheld), there is one which forever escapes his comprehension—and this is the sign-user himself. Semiotically, the self is literally unspeakable to itself.'[41]

The self can (and often does) get rid of itself through distraction – through drink, drugs, sex, shopping, football matches, partying and the like. On a slightly higher level, the same objective of getting rid of the self can be attained through immersion in art, music, literature, or science. But all things good or bad come to an end and the self is inevitably left face to face with itself when the party is over, the music stops, the game grinds to a halt or the research project concludes. What now?

No visitor from another planet to earth could fail to observe and be puzzled by our propensity to kill one another. What is wrong with human beings? Is it the case that man, Arthur Koestler asked, is 'an aberrant biological species, an evolutionary misfit, afflicted by an endemic disorder which sets it apart from all other animal species'?[42] Koestler believes that it is a problem with the serendipitous development of the human brain, with the later neo-cortex sitting on top of the older brain but not being insufficiently integrated with it. He thinks that evolution blundered in what he describes as 'the rapid, quasi-brutal *superimposition* (instead of *transformation*) of the neocortex on the ancestral structures and the resulting *insufficient coordination* between the new brain and the old, and *inadequate control* of the former over the latter.'[43] We have, as it were, a penthouse brain, with rickety staircases and a lift that works intermittently thus ensuring less than perfect coordination with the penthouse and the other floors of the building.

Human violence is often attributed to some inbuilt tendency on the part of the individual human being to be aggressive. However, Koestler believes, and in this I think he is correct, that the human problem is not individual aggression, which accounts for only a tiny amount of the damage we do to one another, but rather our very sociability which, wrongly placed, leads to fanaticism.

> The trouble with our species is not an excess of *aggression*, but an excess capacity for fanatical *devotion*. Even a cursory glance at history should convince one that individual crimes committed for selfish motives play a quite insignificant part in the human tragedy, compared to the numbers massacred in unselfish loyalty to one's tribe, nation, dynasty, church, or political ideology, *ad majorem gloriam dei* … Homicide committed for personal reasons is a statistical rarity in all cultures, including our own. Homicide for *un*selfish reasons, at the risk of one's own life, is the dominant phenomenon in history.[44]

Appearances to the contrary notwithstanding, and *pace* Hobbes, we have been quite successful in keeping individual deviant behaviour under control. For a social group to exist at all implies that the modes of social control, formal or informal, are effective. If not, the group would cease to exist. It is commonplace that persons are prepared to do things as part of a group that they would never contemplate acting alone and this degree of cooperation is possible only because of man's possession of language. Language and ritual is what constitutes a group as a group. You have to be identified as X or Y, and that requires the telling and the believing of a story. Koestler notes that 'man's deadliest weapon is *language*'.[45] Without language, man would not be man. There would be no literature, no social life as we know it – but also, no war.

So, it is not self-assertion that is responsible for man's inhumanity to man. Paradoxically, it is precisely the same attribute (what Koestler calls the integrative tendency) or what I would call self-transcendence through the social that is responsible both for social cohesion and is also responsible for large-scale human destruction. The paradox is that 'the act of identification with the group is a *self-transcending* act, yet it reinforces the *self-assertive* tendencies of the group'.[46]

If there were to be other rational beings in our universe, would they necessarily be subject to the darker side of human sociability? If, as Koestler suggests, the dark side of being human derives from the specific peculiarities of human evolution, then perhaps not;[47] however, if individual self-transcendence leading to social self-assertion is a defining characteristic of language just as such, then we might need to keep a close eye on any future visitors from another planet.

BACK TO GREGOR

Returning to our latter-day Gregor Samsa (and Captain Kirk and the Spanish explorers) and the questions we left suspended in mid-air like the smile of the Cheshire cat – in his new and exotic environment, how will Gregor know if any of the entities he encounters are rational? What of our Spanish explorers and their problem? How did Captain Kirk and his crew manage? How *do* you tell whether another being is or is not rational?

Well, not by the physical appearance of such entities. There is no obvious reason why another rational being has to look humanoid. And not by their bio-chemical composition, for it seems possible to have non-carbon-based forms of life. And not by whether such entities are self-moving rather than merely blown in the wind, for whether locomotion be a necessary condition of rationality or not, it is certainly not a sufficient condition. It comes to this: if you want to know what something is and you don't have some kind of metaphysical microscope that will allow you to peer into its ontological interior, there is one and only one way to come to know what something is and that is by discerning its characteristic re-activities or characteristic activities and inferring the conditions which make such re-activities and activities possible.

This is what typically seemed to happen in the case of *Star Trek*. The crew of the Starship Enterprise would inadvertently injure or offend one of these entities and suffer retaliation as a result. The crew would then conclude that any entity that could resent ill-treatment was either sentient or rational. If the entity were in some way rational, this was established by means of some form of rational communication when the crew of the Enterprise and the aliens eventually manage to speak to one another. So it was with our Spanish explorers and the apparently humanoid but actually human creatures they encountered. So too will it be with Gregor Samsa and any entities he might encounter. Language and rationality go hand in hand – to be rational is to have language; to have language is to be rational.

NOTES

1. Before any irate Trekkies start to protest, I know that, like 'Play it again, Sam' in *Casablanca* and 'Elementary, my dear Watson' in the Sherlock Holmes stories, 'It's life, Jim, but not as we know it' wasn't actually said in the original *Star Trek* series but comes from the novelty song 'Star Trekkin'' released in 1987.
2. Percy's relevant publications are *The Message in the Bottle: How Queer Man is, How Queer Language is, and what One has to do with the Other* (New York: Farrer, Straus and Giroux, 1975; now published by Picador) – this book is a collection of articles written between 1954 and 1975, most published in philosophical journals such as *The New Scholasticism, The Modern Schoolman, The Journal of Philosophy* and *Philosophy and Phenomenological Research*; *Lost in the Cosmos: The Last Self-Help Book* (New York: Picador, 1983); a collection of miscellaneous Percy pieces collected and edited by Patrick Samway, *Signposts in a Strange Land* (New York: Picador, 1991).
3. Brendan Purcell, *From Big Bang to Big Mystery: Human Origins in the Light of Creation and Evolution* (Dublin: Veritas, 2011), p. 16
4. Ibid., p. 173.
5. Percy, 'The Fateful Rift', *Signposts in a Strange Land*, p. 271. Percy is not recommending recourse to extra-scientific solutions but is proposing instead a rethinking of science.
6. Ibid., pp. 275–6.
7. John Tyndall, *Fragments of Science* (London: Longmans, Green and Co., 1871), p. 121.
8. Colin McGinn, *The Problem of Consciousness* (Oxford: Blackwell, 1990).
9. Percy, 'The Fateful Rift', *Signposts in a Strange Land*, p. 279.
10. Ibid., p. 277.
11. See Gerard Casey, *Libertarian Anarchy: Against the State* (London: Continuum, 2012), pp. 48–57.
12. Percy, 'The Delta Factor', *The Message in the Bottle*, p. 17.
13. Percy, 'Is a Theory of Man Possible?', *Signposts in a Strange Land*, p. 118.
14. Percy, 'The Fateful Rift', *Signposts in a Strange Land*, p. 280. Coming from a very different philosophical approach, Wittgenstein seems to be thinking along the same lines as Percy when he remarks that 'The child, I should like to say, learns to react in such-and-such a way; and in so reacting it doesn't so far know anything. Knowing only begins at a later level.' Ludwig Wittgenstein, *On Certainty* (Oxford: Blackwell, 1969), §538.
15. Percy, 'The Delta Factor', *The Message in the Bottle*, p. 44.
16. Percy, 'The Fateful Rift', *Signposts in a Strange Land*, p. 287.
17. Percy, 'The Delta Factor', *The Message in the Bottle*, p. 8.
18. Some of the following material on animal speech first appeared in Gerard Casey, 'Minds and Machines', *American Catholic Philosophical Quarterly* 66.1 (1992), pp. 57–80.
19. Julien Offray de la Mettrie, *Man a Machine* (Leyden, 1748; Open Court French-English edition, 1912), pp. 100–1.
20. K. J. Hayes and C. Hayes, 'The Intellectual Development of a Home-Raised Chimpanzee', *Proceedings of the American Philosophical Society* 95 (1951), pp. 105–9. A useful anthology of articles in this area is Thomas A. Sebeok and Jean Umiker-Sebeok, eds., *Speaking of Apes: A Critical Anthology of Two-Way Communication with Man* (New York and London: Plenum Press, 1980). This collection contains articles by Kellogg, Lenneberg, Brown, Bronowski & Bellugi, McNeill, Mounin, Terrace & Bever, Limber, Rumbaugh, Fouts & Rigby, Gardner & Gardner, Chomsky and others. See also Martin

Gardner, 'How Well Can Animals Converse?', *Semiotica* 38 (1982), pp. 357–67; Robert J. McLaughlin, 'Language and Man: Aristotle Meets Koko', *The Thomist* 45 (1981), pp. 541–70; and Mark S. Seidenberg, 'Aping Language', *Semiotica* 44 (1983), pp. 177–94.

21. D. M. Rumbaugh, ed., *Language Learning by a Chimpanzee: The Lana Project* (New York: Academic Press, 1977).
22. David Premack, *Intelligence in Ape and Man* (Hillsdale, NJ.: Lawrence Erlbaum Associates, 1976).
23. C. A. Risteau and D. Robbins, 'A Threat to Man's Uniqueness? Language and Communication in the Chimpanzee', *Journal of Psycholinguistic Research* 8 (1979), pp. 267–300; H. S. Terrace, 'Is Problem-Solving Language?', *Journal of the Experimental Analysis of Behaviour* 31 (1979), pp. 161–75; M. S. Seidenberg and L. A. Petitto, 'Signing Behaviour in Apes: A Critical Review', *Cognition* 7 (1979), pp. 177–215.
24. Sebeok and Umiker-Sebeok, eds., *Speaking of Apes*.
25. Seidenberg, 'Signing Behaviour in Apes', pp. 183–4.
26. For a popular account of the results of the experiment see http://news.sky.com/story/970006/brainy-parrots-are-smarter-than-children. The scientific account can be found at Christian Schloegl, Judith Schmidt, Markus Boeckle, Brigitte M. Weiß and Kurt Kotrschal, 'Grey Parrots use inferential reasoning based on acoustic cues alone', *Proceedings of the Royal Society of London, Series B, Containing papers of a biological character* (published online 8 August 2012), http://rspb.royalsocietypublishing.org/content/suppl/2012/07/31/rspb.2012.1292.DC1
27. Schloegl et al., 'Grey Parrots', p. 7. My emphasis.
28. Percy, 'The Delta Factor', *The Message in the Bottle*, p. 29.
29. Percy, *Lost in the Cosmos*, p. 100.
30. Some of this material in the following paragraphs first appeared in another form in 'Thinking Critically about Critical Thinking', *Critical Thinking and Higher Order Thinking: A Current Perspective,* Michael Shaughnessy, ed. (New York: Nova Science Publishers, 2012), pp. 23–39.
31. Genesis 2:17.
32. Percy, *Lost in the Cosmos*, p. 105.
33. Percy, 'Is a Theory of Man Possible?', *Signposts in a Strange Land*, p. 119.
34. Martin Bell, 'Agony can be ecstasy', *The Times* (20 September 2005).
35. Percy, 'Is a Theory of Man Possible?', *Signposts in a Strange Land*, p. 127
36. Percy, 'The Delta Factor', *The Message in the Bottle*, p. 9.
37. Percy, 'The Symbolic Structure of Interpersonal Process', *The Message in the Bottle*, p. 200.
38. Percy, 'Is a Theory of Man Possible?', *Signposts in a Strange Land*, p. 124.
39. Ibid., p. 125.
40. Percy, *Lost in the Cosmos*, p. 102.
41. Ibid., p. 107.
42. Arthur Koestler, *Janus: A Summing Up* (London: Picador, 1979), p. 5.
43. Koestler, *Janus*, p. 11.
44. Ibid., p. 14.
45. Ibid., p. 15.
46. Ibid., p. 82.
47. See C. S. Lewis's *Perelandra* (London: The Bodley Head, 1943), for a fictional treatment of this topic.

Refugee Fideists: Teaching Religion in a Scientific Culture

EOIN G. CASSIDY

INTRODUCTION

> Love gives us our being. We do not exist only because of love, we exist because we love. If we do not love – and in all the moments in which we do not love we no longer are – we do not exist.
>
> Chiara Lubich[1]

Human consciousness: a lot on language and free will but very little on friendship and love. Interestingly, as I now observe, this was the only phrase highlighted in the notes taken by me as I and many others sat enthralled, listening to a first class debate in Oxford in February 2012 on the credibility of theism in light of a discussion of the nature of human beings and the question of their ultimate origins.[2]

Given the legacy of the Enlightenment and more specifically John Locke's espousal of individualism, which still permeates contemporary English language discourse on the person, perhaps one should not be too surprised at this turn of events. And yet, at another level, the absence of any systematic treatment of love or friendship in a debate of this kind is a pity. This is especially the case given the crucial importance of these two closely related themes in any coherent Judaeo-Christian theological map of the cosmos.[3] In addition, the omission of any systematic treatment of love and friendship from the debate is surprising, in that the debate brought together two worthy protagonists, Rowan Williams and Richard Dawkins, both of whom have attained a high level of public recognition for their very different stances on the coherence of a theistic anthropology in a scientific culture. Rowan Williams is not only a leading theologian in the Anglican tradition; more importantly, he was, at the time of the debate, the Archbishop of Canterbury. Widely regarded as a highly skilled and effective communicator, Richard Dawkins is probably best described as an ultra-Darwinian because he is committed to highlighting what he believes to be the atheistic message that lies at the heart of evolutionary theory.[4]

What do we mean by human nature? If one is a theist, who is the God in whom one trusts? The importance of this issue becomes apparent if one is prepared to argue, as I am, that not only is there a societal tendency today to presume that these questions are unproblematic, but also that the loss of confidence in the credibility of theism, which in turn gives rise to refugee fideism, is in no small manner caused by an inadequate answers to these questions, which seek to inform us as to who we are and who we believe God to be. Clearly this is no trivial matter and is an issue which faces everyone concerned to hold fast to the coherence of a Christian theodicy in the context of how the problem of evil appears to us in the science/religion debate – what is sometimes called existential or natural evil. Issues that readily come to mind include those raised by the suffering caused by illness, particularly in young people, and the effects of the so-called natural disasters caused by earthquakes, volcanoes and so on. Therefore the reference to the Oxford debate above is designed a) to highlight the importance of working with appropriate images of God and of human nature,[5] and b) to foster a greater awareness that given the cultural legacy of empiricism and scientific/logical positivism, which still permeates much of contemporary philosophical discourse, achieving this methodological goal is easier said than done.

Whilst acknowledging the transcendence of God and therefore that the divine nature can never be captured in and through the imagery of human language, there are nevertheless some images which can point us in the direction of God, such as those that are depicted by 'love and friendship'. For Christians, the decisive significance of these related images is expressed in two remarkable doctrines: one which proclaims Jesus as the Word or Revelation of God, thus amongst other things reveals God on the cross to be both compassionate and forgiving; and another, that equally remarkable doctrine of the 'Blessed Trinity', which testifies to the inclusive character of God's love – a love that is generous rather than the corruption of love that is obsessive.[6]

To say that both of these doctrines baffle logic is to understate the very real problems that early Christians encountered as they defended and argued for the intelligibility of these two foundational dogmas of the Christian faith. In this context, it is striking to observe that almost without exception, every major theological dispute in the first four centuries of Christianity had its roots either in a rejection of one or other of the core Christian Christological and Trinitarian doctrines. Furthermore, the fact that the early Christian emphasis on love being extended to enemies was not only novel but also decidedly countercultural in the context of the dominant Graeco-Roman ethos of the time, emphasises the importance early Christians attached to proclaiming the radically inclusive character of God's love. For very obvious reasons, this love of enemies was perceived by the Romans to be profoundly shocking and destructive of the good of society. Consequently, it is hardly surprising to observe that the Romans made life particularly difficult for those early Christians who insisted on holding steadfast to the literal and clearly passivist interpretation of this injunction.[7]

THE COMPLEMENTARY PERSPECTIVES OF A PHILOSOPHER AND A SCIENTIST

In 2011, just before the Oxford debate, Irish philosopher Brendan Purcell published a book with an almost identical focus on human nature and human origins. Entitled *From Big Bang to Big Mystery: Human Origins in the Light of Creation and Evolution*, both the scope and ambition of the book are impressive, in that the author shows not only an awareness of but also engages with the findings of those sciences whose remit, however tangentially, touch on areas relevant to his study – subjects as diverse as palaeontology, archaeology and zoology. Nevertheless, what makes this book refreshingly different is the manner in which Purcell unambiguously places love and friendship centre stage of his study. The importance of this should not be underestimated, particularly in:

- a scientific cultural milieu, which in its scientific/logical positivist guise shows a marked reluctance to admit the validity of any transcendent/spiritual dimension to the boundaries of sense perception, thus effectively conspiring to airbrush out of the human equation any supposed experience of love or friendship.

- a secular cultural milieu, which in its reluctance to admit the validity of any transcendent dimension to human nature, also conspires to airbrush the experience of interpersonal relationships, such as love or friendship, out of the human equation.

In the cultural legacy of scientific or logical positivism, a spiritual or non-material/non-sense dimension to reality is described as literally 'nonsense'. Add to this the parameters of a secular and largely capitalist societal worldview and one is faced with the very real temptation to reduce all relationships to the pragmatic Heideggerian 'world of my concerns', which Martin Buber would describe as the pragmatic I-It relationship, as distinct from the I-You relationship of love or friendship. Just imagine attempting to reinterpret the parable of the Good Samaritan in the light of a 'world of my concerns'.

Some books have big ambitions, and such is the case with *From Big Bang to Big Mystery*, and some small books have even bigger ambitions, and *Quarks, Chaos and Christianity: Questions to Science and Religion* is one of those.[8] First published in 1994, John Polkinghorne (Church of England priest and physicist) attempts, in a summary fashion, to re-imagine the contours of a philosophy of religion for the modern, largely western cultural milieu, shaped as it is by the achievements of modern science. In Brendan Purcell's book, the focus is the no less challenging one of showing that a Christian anthropology is not only defensible in today's scientific and secular cultural milieu, but is in fact the only one that truly accords with the evidence as presented by the wide range of disciplines that constitute the world of science.

Although written from two very different perspectives and with two very different styles, it is my view that these two books provide a basis for an internal dialogue from the perspective of theism, on the relationship between religion and science. The contention here is that they are thus an invaluable resource for religion teachers, as they negotiate the many obstacles in the path of effective religion teaching in the scientific cultural milieu that is the school environment of today.

From the experience of over twenty years of teaching in the area of science and religion, it is interesting to observe how little has actually changed in terms of asking the big questions; and that is despite the huge advances in the many related scientific disciplines during that period. They appear to us who are of a certain age as well-worn issues, but there is nothing of the old chestnut about these issues to students in their early twenties. So let's look at the following four issues through the complementary lens of a scientist and a philosopher, with a view to meeting the challenges posed in what I describe as refugee fideism:

1. Under the heading, 'There is No Room for Dialogue: Understanding Refugee Fideism', the effect of the conflict model on the relationship between religion and science and faith and reason is acknowledged. It will be suggested that this conflict model is based on an uncritical cultural acceptance of the reductionist logic of empiricism or scientific/logical positivism on what counts as evidence.

2. Under the heading of 'The Bible and Science', the importance of the historical legacy of the Galileo and Darwin debacles that pitted Church authorities against the scientific community will be acknowledged. This is a topic which leads on to a more widespread treatment of the difficulties facing those who wish to argue for the truth of the Bible in the scientific cultural environment of today.

3. Under the heading of 'Evolutionary Theory and Ultra-Darwinism', the manner in which evolutionary theory remains at the cutting edge of the contemporary religion/science dialogue will be acknowledged. This leads on to a broader reflection on the difficulties facing theists in arguing for a coherent Christian anthropology in the light of the atheistic claims of ultra Darwinism

4. Under the heading 'Evolution and the Problem of Evil', the manner in which the problem of evil impacts upon the science/religion debate is acknowledged. The question asked is how a God who is omnipotent and omniscient can be excused from the suffering caused by so-called natural disasters, not to speak of the suffering caused by the many illnesses which blight the lives of so many children and young adults.

1. THERE IS NO ROOM FOR DIALOGUE: UNDERSTANDING REFUGEE FIDEISM

Fideism is a broad church where faith perspective is accorded the status of an ultimate, where truth is perceived to be a consequence of belief rather than as a reason for belief. Karl Barth's theological sensitivity to the radical otherness of God comes to mind, as does Kierkegaard's unease with an all-too comfortable interpretation of the belief that what is real is rational. Different again is the fideism associated with the later writings of Wittgenstein, whose rejection of the ontological limitations of logical positivism led him to contextualise all truth claims within communities of belief.

While allowing for the wider cultural influence of relativism reflected in Wittgenstein's references to forms of life and language games and so pervasive today, nevertheless there are many who do not fall into any of these categories. They are what might be described as refugee fideists – seeking the sanctuary or the security offered by fideism because of a perception that reason will not give them the means to offer credible grounds for the faith which sustains them. What is just as interesting to observe is that they do not seem to be particularly ill at ease wearing this fideist garb. For those who have grown up in a culture which places the highest premium on the ideals of tolerance and respect for diversity of opinion, this comfortable fideism is not at all surprising. Nevertheless, there is something incongruous about a culture which can go against the logical principle of non-contradiction and cherish conflicting positions on the one subject – for theists there is a God, and for atheists there is no God. Both cannot be cherished equally, in that only one of those propositions is true. Both cannot be true at the same time. This topic is one that goes far beyond the frontiers of any epistemological debate on the limits to human knowledge, and raises issues which impact not only on the way one approaches the subject of philosophy of religion but also on the value placed on the discipline itself. If taken to extremes, the embrace of cultural relativism/fideism or pluralism without any qualifications can lead to a cultural questioning of the very value of the search for truth, something that is at the core of any genuine science/religion dialogue.

I am confident that most teachers of religion would welcome the opportunity offered in the school environment to stress the importance and value of religious belief. If however, the discourse was to be pursued, and grounds sought, as to the basis for their theism, I suspect that there would be some who would respond with the proverbial shrug of the shoulders – a stance which could reflect sensitivity to the personal dimension to religious belief. However, this attitude could also reflect a lack of confidence or a fear of not being able to offer a coherent answer. One thing is sure, if this reluctance to reflect on the credibility of religious belief were to be continued into their professional career as secondary school teachers of religion, their career path in this domain would have a rather short trajectory. Hence, the indispensability of some form of philosophy of religion, which alone will give religion teachers the wherewithal to argue convincingly for the credibility of theism in the scientific cultural milieu that is today's school.

CONFRONTING THE CONFLICT MODEL

> It seems to me that many educated people in the western world ... would like some sort of faith [religious belief], but feel that it is only to be had on terms which amount to intellectual suicide. (Polkinghorne, Gifford Lectures, 1990, 5)

There is a cultural current operative today which adopts a conflict model to describe the relationship between religion and science, and is in consequence inimical to the possibility of any dialogue between them. My experience leads me to suggest that the extent to which this model has become a cultural frame of reference for young adults today should not be underestimated. In essence, the conflict model holds that the observable world of science leaves no space for the truth claims of religion. The reasons given for this stance are extremely varied but are often expressed in the following terms: science and religion are based upon the radically contrasting and indeed conflicting methodologies suggested by the words 'fact' and 'faith'. Science reveals an observable world – a world explained by reference to facts rather than opinions, a world where only scientific evidence matters. Religion, on the contrary, reveals a private world perceived through the lens of faith, for which not only is there no evidential support, but which is, for the most part, proclaimed in the teeth of all available scientific evidence. Polkinghorne offers the following short summary of this expression of the conflict model:

> Science is based on facts and leads to real knowledge. Religion is just based on opinion. It may help you or me to live our lives – religion may be 'true for me' or 'true for you' – but it's not just plain 'true', pure and simple. (Polkinghorne, 1994, 12)

Of course, this is a viewpoint that is not shared by Polkinghorne. Why? Because we don't live in parallel universes – we inhabit one world and something is either true or false, fact or fiction. Truth matters, or at least it does if one wishes one's beliefs to be taken seriously. All of Polkinghorne's writings reflect an acute sensitivity to the importance of this issue, arguing consistently that religion can only be of real value if it is actually true. As he puts it, 'religion is not a technique for whistling in the dark to keep our spirits up' (Polkinghorne, 1994, 20).

If, as Polkinghorne correctly insists, religion cannot be immune from issues of evidence, he also insists that science is not immune from issues of faith. The relationship between fact and faith cannot ignore the foundational assumptions/faith positions that are a necessary presupposition for the very possibility of science – such as, first, the belief that the world is a cosmos, an ordered and law governed universe; and, second, the belief that the world is intelligible, that the laws which govern its existence are capable of being uncovered by the human mind. As Polkinghorne is wont to say, 'These are non-trivial facts'.

In terms of our understanding of the relationship between religion and science, Polkinghorne is not only questioning the validity of the conflict model, but also what has been described as the separation model. Unlike the conflict model, the separation model suggests that neither science and religion can be used to criticise the other because they have really nothing in common – they ask very different questions about the universe: science asks the 'how' questions whereas Christianity asks the 'why' questions. While agreeing that the focus of their respective questioning differs, Polkinghorne is in profound disagreement with the separation as well as the conflict models. As he sees it, science and religion are actually intellectual cousins under the skin – both science and religion are trying to understand the varied and indeed surprising way the world actually is:

> *Both are searching for motivated belief.* Neither can claim certain knowledge, for each must base its conclusions on interplay between interpretation and experience. In consequence, both must be open to the possibility of correction. Neither deals simply with pure fact or with mere opinion. They are both part of the great human endeavour to understand. (Polkinghorne, 1994, 22)

WHAT COUNTS AS EVIDENCE IN A WORLD OF PERSONAL EXPERIENCE?
If Polkinghorne is right, then, the truth claims of religion, and not just those of science, must be subjected to evidential scrutiny. And again, he has no problem in acknowledging this. As he says, 'The fundamental question to be asked of any theological statement is, "What is the evidence that makes you think that this might be true?"' (Polkinghorne 1994, 3–4). And yet, it is never quite that simple: there are numerous examples from the world of everyday personal experience, of people who continue to believe despite the lack of corroborative evidence. And finally, there is the even more fundamental question of what counts as evidence. For example, can the world of everyday personal experience be drawn on as evidence of the existence of a loving God, a good person, a beautiful painting, or indeed to adjudicate on the validity of a statement that one ought or ought not follow a particular course of action? I think so, especially since this world of personal experience includes us, I who am writing this article and you who are reading and critiquing it. To quote Polkinghorne:

> Personal experience – aesthetics, ethics and religious belief are not mere froth on the surface of matter and conscious life cannot be explained as an effect of patterns of energy. (Polkinghorne, 1994, 77)

The desire to search for meaning and the confidence that we are capable of finding answers to the foundational questions of meaning and value suggests that this is also a world of insightful experience, one which uncovers the wonders of mathematical modelling of the universe, and even greater wonder as experiments are designed which prove the accuracy of the modelling – as was the case with the recent discovery of the existence of a key particle, one of the building blocks of the universe, which has been named the Higgs Boson particle in honour of the mathematician who predicted its existence many years ago. What is utterly remarkable about all of this is, first, the fact that the world inside the mind, i.e. maths, seems to correspond with that which is outside of the mind. Second, and equally remarkable is the fact that we, as human beings, have the capability to discover such a convergence.

All of this rich tapestry of life is part of the world of personal experience and it is not something that can be brushed aside as being of no import as would be suggested by those ultra-Darwinians who for ideological, as distinct from scientific reasons, seek to interpret evolutionary theory in a manner that rejects, before the evidence has been sifted, any possibility that there may be a qualitative as well as a quantitative difference between ourselves and our nearest biological cousins amongst the higher primates. Granted that, unlike the hard sciences in the empirical world of sense perception, it can be difficult to measure the evidence for a world of personal experience which includes ethics, aesthetics, love/friendship and belief in God in a manner that offers proof of its objectivity. Nevertheless, the arbitrary ruling out of the equation any consideration of dimensions of human nature that reveal a spiritual/transcendent dimension to human existence suggests an agenda which is not that of science, which correctly prides itself as being evidenced-based.

This issue as to what counts as evidence is from a philosophical point of view – arguably the key one determining the stances of two radically opposing positions on the science/religion debate. There are many, including myself, who would hold that it is those who ignore the rich world of personal experience that are in an intellectual cul de sac – one which cannot even begin to account for the way in which we as humans understand ourselves, and where the materialist vision of the person is rendered inevitable in and thorough an exclusively materialist/empiricist methodology.

THE CULTURAL LEGACY OF EMPIRICISM

It is here that attention is drawn to what I would describe as the cultural effects of the legacy of empiricism, positivism and indeed the scientific/logical positivism on the accessibility or otherwise of religion in today's world. The deleterious effects on the credibility of theism of the cultural embrace of a pseudo-scientific materialist reductionism are very obvious. One only has to look at the successful effort made by writers such as Dawkins and Dennett to ground their espousal of atheism under the guise of a common sense/no nonsense epistemology, whose sceptical and indeed nihilistic undertones belies its common sense designation.

It is a long time since Wittgenstein, in the final pages of the *Tractatus*, first raised serious questions about the intellectual coherence of a worldview shaped by the contours of logical positivism. Nevertheless, it has to be frankly acknowledged that the contemporary cultural environment in the 'west' is one which is hospitable to the belief that the boundary between sense and nonsense is coterminous with that which determines the limit of scientific discourse – a world that is observable and measurable. This is a cultural milieu which makes it extremely difficult to explain belief in a transcendent/spiritual dimension to reality, and gives support to those who would like to insist that the publicly observable world of science leaves no space for the truth claims of religion.

Faced with this cultural backdrop, I am continually conscious of the need to offer publicly accessible responses, which challenge the assumed normative status of an empiricist epistemology and/or materialist ontology. Interestingly, one need go no further than *From Big Bang to Big Mystery* to find evidence of such a publicly accessible response. In unashamedly using the evidence of personal experience alongside the evidence of the hard sciences to provide evidence in support of his thesis, Purcell has refused to be straitjacketed into the reductionist methodology that refuses to acknowledge the realm of value, purpose and personal experience which lies beyond the reach of scientific positivism. Yet this realm is as real as the bricks and mortar of science and must be incorporated into any adequate account of the nature of reality. Proof of the correctness of this stance comes from an unlikely set of sources, from the mouths of Richard Dawkins and Stephen Hawking. Both are quoted as admitting a reluctance to dismiss the experience of love as of no consequence, Dawkins is also quoted as freely acknowledging that the evidence for his fatherly love for his daughter was quite different to that demanded by the natural science.[9]

2. THE BIBLE AND SCIENCE

THE EXPONENTIAL GROWTH OF A SCIENTIFIC CULTURE: HISTORICAL BAGGAGE

In terms of the larger issue – the barriers that prevent or hinder a healthy dialogue between religion and science, the nature of biblical truth and the extent to which the Bible is believable in the face of scientific advances is still the number one issue, at least in the public imagination. Given the importance of the Bible as a source of inspiration for over one billion Christians, it is not an issue that can be ignored. Given the increased public awareness of the nature of literary genres and the remarkable progress in biblical exegesis over the past half century and more, it is hard to see how the advances in science could still be perceived to threaten people's belief in the truth claims in the Bible, and yet the fact is that they do, or perhaps, as I have argued throughout this article, it is not so much the advances in science but the advances in the scientific culture in the 'West' which challenges people's faith in the credibility of the Bible. If that is in fact the case, it raises issues that go beyond scientific literacy and focuses attention upon societal cultural memory or more accurately societies' culturally received historical memory, which may or may not reflect historical reality.

Unfortunately, for many who may know little or nothing about history or indeed about science, the belief is that the historical baggage of the Galilean and Darwinian controversies has so poisoned the relationship between science and religion in the popular imagination that it is very difficult to avoid the conflict model, not to speak about marrying the two in what Ian Barbour liked to describe as the consonance model. In the course of the past half century there has been an exponential growth in the influence that is exercised by the scientific ethos of contemporary society. The benefits to society in general and for the younger generation in particular of this development have been hugely positive. It is all the more important, therefore, that those professionally engaged in religious education address honestly the legacy issues of the historical controversies that pitted Church authorities against the scientific community. For example, science is an evidence-based enquiry, and unfortunately the perceived reluctance or inability on the part of Church authorities to submit the truth claims of the Bible to scientific scrutiny (Galileo and Darwin) raises the cultural perception amongst a vocal and growing minority today that the Bible is scientifically incoherent, and that those who place their faith in it as the Word of God are credulous or simply ridiculous.

There is no disputing that these are difficult issues to address and yet support for one's endeavours can come from the most unlikely source. Paradoxically, the historical encounter with Galileo and Darwin can tell us a lot about the dialogue between science and religion that transcends the historical particularities of his time, and it can also alert us to the dangers of an over-simplistic reading of history which, in this case, would assume that both Galileo and Darwin were opposed to religion in general, and specifically to the idea of biblical truth. Interestingly, neither assumption is accurate. In fact Galileo explicitly warned against reading the Bible as if it were a scientific treatise. This point finds expression in that celebrated quotation, 'The Bible teaches how to go to heaven and not how the heavens move.' Furthermore, his high esteem for the truth of the Bible is to be seen in his espousal of the 'two books' metaphor first proposed by Francis Bacon – the idea that God's self-revelation is contained in two great books, the book of nature and the book of the Bible. Galileo used this metaphor to emphasise not just the complementary nature of the relation between science and religion but also the legitimate differences in both the methodology and the object of their search. As for Darwin, while acknowledging the effect of the tragic death of his daughter on his religious practice, nevertheless it does not take away from the remarkable beauty of the concluding sentence of *The Origin of the Species* that give expression to a religious sensibility that cannot be gainsaid.

> There is a grandeur in this view of life, with its several powers having been originally breathed by the Creator into a few forms or into one; and that, whilst this planet has gone cycling on according to the fixed laws of gravity, from so simple a beginning endless forms most beautiful and most wonderful have been, and are being evolved.

BELIEF IN THE BIBLE: TRUTH MATTERS

Under the heading *Truth Matters*, it is of the first importance that one is able to argue credibly for the truth of the Bible, especially if one wishes to teach religion to secondary school students in the scientific culture of today's school. Faced by the perception that the truth claims of the Bible are fatally undermined by the advances of science, there can be a temptation to retreat from truth claims into the comforting world of story-telling – the Bible as story or myth – but are these stories to be catalogued under fiction or non-fiction? The issue of truth cannot be avoided. If it is fiction, then its status is no more exalted than stories told about any fictional character. The failure to understand the nature of biblical truth is not without its cost, because it effectively closes the door to the possibility of any meaningful dialogue between religion and science.

The temptation to retreat from the truth claims of the Bible or to hold that the truth claims of the Bible are immune from criticisms of science, it is this which defines the stance of the second classical model of the relation between religion and science, which is called the separation model. Based upon the view that since a very different set of questions are asked of the world by science (the 'how' questions) and religion (the 'why' questions), both should be immune from criticism from the other side.

The separation model is often proposed as a means of protecting the Bible from the criticisms of science. However, I would want to argue that it fails in this endeavour, because the idea that the Bible inhabits some parallel universe of faith that is somehow immune from the truth claims of science is simply not true We all inhabit one world, and discourse that purports to add to our store of knowledge is governed by that most fundamental of all the laws of logic, namely the law of non-contradiction. For example, I can respect the Hindu belief in re-incarnation and I can also respect that Christians do not accept this doctrine. But I am not prepared to admit that both doctrines can be true because to do so would be to go against this fundamental law of logic.

One would imagine that this foundational law of logic would be incontestable. Well, one would be wrong, because there is increasing evidence that in the pluralist and emotivist culture of today, culture has trumped logic. The cultural parameters of the 'west' provide ample evidence of the extent to which we have embraced the idea of pluralism as a cultural and perhaps even as a moral imperative. In many respects, this emotivist facet of contemporary culture could not be further removed from that of science, because in a pluralist and emotivist cultural milieu, respect for diversity will always trump respect for the truth, sincerity will be regarded as the ultimate human accolade and in terms of the hierarchy of virtues tolerance will reign supreme.

Whilst acknowledging the sobering reality of religious conflict that provides the historical context for a society that today welcomes cultural and religious diversity, we must also embrace the many positive values associated with the acceptance of a more tolerant and pluralist worldview. However, there is also a shadow side to a pluralist culture, in that the attempt to embrace all beliefs and values can lead to the trivialising of all beliefs. Yes, in this scenario, the Bible and indeed the sacred texts from other religions are protected from all criticism from outside of their own faith community. But there is a huge cost: the radical privatisation of religion and the abandonment of all universal truth claims. Truth matters because all religions are in the business of making universal truth claims. Religion teachers and other such professionals, if they are to be taken seriously, must be able to account for their beliefs and offer some credible evidence for the fact that one holds them and is willing to teach sacred texts in a public forum.

TRUTH MATTERS BUT SO DOES MEANING

Are the stories about Noah or about Jonah or about Adam and Eve true or false? These questions are posed as if they could and should be answered with relative ease. And yet to state the obvious, in the way this question is framed, there is very little, if any, attention given to reflecting on the meaning of stories. Rather, there is the largely unquestioned assumption that their meaning is unproblematic, and therefore that the only relevant question has to do with whether the stories are true or not. However, this is a highly dubious assumption to make – something that could be testified by anyone with the smallest sensitivity to the nature of mythic story-telling and to the way that it functions in ancient literature.

Understanding the meaning of a biblical text can be an extremely complicated task that involves a whole range of exegetical skills. And there are no shortcuts, because if one does not know the meaning of a text one is hardly in a position to adjudicate on its truth or otherwise. What has bedevilled the science and religion debate in the past, and still does unfortunately today, is that we still take shortcuts. All too quickly we rush to ask questions about the truth of a biblical text before attending properly to its meaning. The results have been nothing short of disastrous, leading as it did to an exponential growth of ideologically entrenched fundamentalists of all hues, with only one thing in common: a refusal to engage in the critically important dialogue between religion and science in society as well as in the classroom. In this context, if we wish to have religiously literate young adults leaving school or college, attending to this issue of biblical education in the classroom must remain a top priority.

3. EVOLUTIONARY THEORY AND ULTRA-DARWINISM

If the contrast between fact and faith offers an intellectual home for the proponents of the conflict and the separation models, it is nevertheless only in the context of a series of reflections on the implications of evolutionary theory that the truly scientific character of the debate comes to the fore. Although even here, at least in part, the result of the bitter legacy of conflict with various church authorities, it is hard even today to find the cultural space to engage in an informed and rational debate on the issues. The absence of a non-polemical public space makes it difficult to counter a cultural rather than scientific assumption that acceptance of any form of evolutionary hypothesis is incompatible with a theistic worldview. Two of the more well-known exponents of ultra-Darwinian atheism, namely Dawkins and Dennett, proclaim that belief in the creator God of classical theism as reflected in the Judaeo-Christian creation story in the book of Genesis not only flies in the face of all scientific evidence but is also unnecessary and illogical. It is unnecessary because evolutionary theory provides a perfectly good alternative to the God hypothesis of classical theism, as well as those traditions surrounding the idea of a special creation to account for the existence of the human soul. It is also utterly illogical, given that accepted theories of evolution reveal a world founded not on divine purposeful action but on blind random chance, the out-workings of which are written in tooth and claw.

DEFENDING THEISM AS A SCIENTIST

As one would expect from someone from a scientific background, Polkinghorne's response is shaped by his love of physics and in particular by the insights of quantum mechanics. In fact, if there is one scientific constant that straddles a lifetime's dedication to promoting a dialogue between religion and science, it is Polkinghorne's appreciation of the significance of quantum physics. From his perspective, not only is it a theory which goes some distance to explaining the behaviour of atomic and sub-atomic particles but also one which has the potential to revolutionise our views about the structure of the whole physical universe that we inhabit. Quantum physics reveals a complex world – a non-mechanical, fitful world where everything is shaped by an intrinsic interconnectedness. This is a world which will never be fully understood if one's scientific horizon is limited to the existence of invariable mechanical laws, understood and analysed atomistically (a bottom-up understanding of causality).

To what extent quantum theory is open to an interpretation hospitable to a theistic worldview that can offer a coherent response to the key points listed above is, however, another matter. Whilst it is obvious I have great admiration for Polkinghorne, I do nevertheless have a word of caution about leaving the religion/science dialogue increasingly in the hands of those professionally versed in science. This is particularly the case in today's cultural milieu, where there is always the danger of attempting to canonise science, or at least the latest scientific theory. Science does not and indeed cannot explain everything; rather it explains what it explains, and nothing more. For example, in his discussion on the person which follows, I don't think that

Polkinghorne shows enough awareness of the discontinuities that separate us from all other living organisms. If one is to do justice to the facts as they have been placed before us with such lucidity by Purcell, it is simply not possible to avoid serious consideration being given to the discussion of the idea of a special creation, however that might be envisaged.

Clearly it is a grave misuse of science to use it as an ideological tool to undermine the beliefs of others. In this context, it is important that scientists maintain a certain modesty of ambition unlike contemporary scientific positivists of the ultra-Darwinian variety, who I suggest are primarily engaged in promoting an atheistic ideology rather than in promoting scientific research. There are facts about us humans that science must adapt to, rather than the other way round, facts such as the almost universal belief in free will, and that we are, to that extent, responsible for the course of our moral life, facts such as the widespread belief, which crosses both generational and cultural boundaries, that those who have died are not parted from us forever more.

Evolutionary theory has undoubtedly immensely enriched our understanding of the manner in which all living creatures are related, but it cannot answer all questions. It is not a type of meta-theory which provides the context for the development not only of the hard sciences – physics, genetics, etc., but also the behavioural sciences and which includes all the various branches of social psychology and sociology. Furthermore, it is simply bad science to use evolutionary theory as if it were possible to explain the God hypothesis and religion in general exclusively in terms of the exigencies of a successful biological evolutionary process. To my mind's eye, there is not just one big bang (the origin of the universe) but two other 'big bangs' metaphorically speaking, to explain the origins of life, and the origins of human species. I would want to argue that all three lie outside the explanatory power of this theory. It is to Purcell's great credit to have highlighted those 'messy bits' – those clear indices of discontinuity with any other species that the ultra-Darwinians seek to downplay.

In what follows, we shall explore with Polkinghorne the possibilities thrown up by the recent developments in quantum physics with a view to the pursuit of a mutually fruitful dialogue between religion and science.

WHO AM I? EVOLUTION AND THE HUMAN SOUL

The challenges put forward by evolutionary theory to the way in which we understand the person are many and complicated, but for the purposes of this article, the focus is on whether evolutionary theory is compatible with a Christian anthropology. For example, the idea of a special creation seems to go against a core tenet of evolution, namely gradualism; there are also difficulties over the extent to which, if at all, evolutionary theory is compatible with the idea of immortality and/or the idea of a spiritual substance.

In the context of a detailed reflection on human nature to which he devotes a chapter under the heading of 'Who Are We?', Polkinghorne once again adopts an approach marked by a refreshing candour which acknowledges the nature of the challenge posed by evolutionary theory to those who would argue that there is uniqueness to human experience. As one would expect of a theist, he rejects all hints of materialist/biological reductionism. As he says, 'Biology is not just large-scale physics' (Polkinghorne, 1994, 76). However, clearly no fan of either Aristotle or Aquinas, and fearing a type of Cartesian dualism, he is not at all comfortable with the only real alternative, namely that there is a transcendent/spiritual dimension to human existence. Similarly, he is not at all comfortable with the idea of a special creation which he describes as 'the addition of some sort of extra magic ingredient'. In company with mainstream scientific opinion, Polkinghorne believes, wrongly in my opinion, that we overturn the logic that gives rise to the idea of a special creation, in favour of the belief that creation is one continuous process is irrefutable and that one day we will even understand the process by which life and conscious life evolved. As he says:

> There seems to be a continuous story from the chemically rich shallow pools of early Earth, to the first elementary replicating and living systems, and then on through biological evolution to you and me. (Polkinghorne, 1994, 66)

Drawing upon his knowledge of and interest in quantum physics, what Polkinghorne has to do is to reconcile a belief in the uniqueness of the human being within the interrelationship of everything in the universe – not an easy task. In this context, he proposes that science could and should make room for a more holistic approach – a top-down type of causality. It is his opinion that issues surrounding a belief in the uniqueness of the human person – a belief traditionally expressed in a belief in the human soul – will never be resolved unless one accepts the validity of a more holistic approach associated with a top-down causal relationship. What he is referring to here is the influence of the whole on the parts, where the whole really is greater than the parts, is not reducible to its parts, and most importantly would seem to be radically different to the parts.

While acknowledging the force of this insight, it is not without some very substantial problems which seem to overturn the whole logical foundations of classical scientific reasoning that has stood the test of time for over two and a half thousand years. Specifically, it would seem to call into question a core principle of Aristotelian logic/metaphysics that finds expression in and through the distinction between Act and Potency (often expressed rather simply as 'you cannot give what you haven't got'). Perhaps there needs to be a fuller development of the insight that is to be found in the following, an 'evolutionary world is … one that makes itself to a large degree. Yet this self-making takes place in a setting of finely tuned potentiality' (Polkinghorne 1994, 56).

The reference here to 'finely tuned potentiality' suggests that even in the micro-cosmic world of quarks or strings (as in string theory), there is a God-given potentiality for life and even conscious life, no matter how slight. It is not an explanation which should be rejected out of hand, rather it is clearly one that merits further reflection. However, just how one could imagine the evolution of life from inert matter and conscious life from non-conscious life or subjects from objects is nevertheless far from clear. Furthermore, it is a matter of the highest significance if one is to make sense of an evolutionary vision of creation as 'a continuous story from the chemically rich shallow pools of early Earth … to you and me' (see above). The complex nature of the problems outlined above raise questions about the precise status, if any, that should be accorded human beings designated as *imago Dei*. This in turn has given rise to a belief in what has been described as a special creation.

However the issues outlined above are resolved, recent discoveries in the area of quantum physics make it increasingly difficult to accept that mechanical discoveries provide a template for all knowledge. If validated, this insight would undoubtedly raise questions about the lack of evidential support for a core premise upon which ultra-Darwinian evolutionary materialism is constructed.

4. EVOLUTION AND THE PROBLEM OF EVIL

Many of the issues encompassed by that vast canvas that falls under the heading of moral evil is outside the remit of this essay. Consequently in this section, we will for the most part restrict ourselves to a brief reflection upon what is sometimes called existential or natural evil. Issues that readily come to mind include those raised by the suffering caused by illness particularly in young people, and the effects of the so-called natural disasters that are caused by earthquakes, volcanoes etc. To what extent can God as the omnipotent creator be exempt from all blame? Into this very complex mix, one cannot avoid questions that are raised by images of God, which make it difficult to argue for the credibility of a Christian theism. For example, there are many who are of the opinion that, in the light of the serious issues raised by the problem of evil, the seeming widespread acceptance of a Deist image of God in the popular scientific culture of today has a very deleterious effect on the credibility of a theistic worldview.

CONFRONTING DEISM

Deism which is most closely associated with the English philosopher/theologian William Paley was first devised in the early eighteenth century, partly as a reaction to authority figures in the various Churches who would abuse people's credulous belief in miracles, and partly out of a desire to believe in a non-interventionist God who would be worthy of the new age of scientific enlightenment – a God who has created the world according to fixed Newtonian scientific laws and now leaves to its own devices to progress according to these same immutable laws of nature. This is a God who treats us as adults and feels no need to intervene in the world to fix things that may be broken.

Perhaps because it is a God for our scientific culture today, which buys into a cultural scepticism about the existence of miracles, or perhaps it is the idea of a non-interfering God that treats us as adults, anyway, for whatever reason, there is little doubt but that most people today when asked to describe God will in fact describe this deist God. This omnipotent and omniscient God is often pictured as sitting up in heaven looking with equanimity on the world he has created – an all-powerful and all-seeing God looking with benign indifference on the holocaust, or a child suffering from cancer, or on a tsunami as it drowns all in its wake, old men and young children alike. One can understand the sense of outrage at the idea of believing in such a God who is so distant/impersonal, and so lacking in any concern for those creatures, who are destined to live miserable lives in a world that is his creation – and his alone.

The most celebrated Deist image of God is of a divine watchmaker, which was proposed by William Paley, and which, perhaps surprisingly, continues even to this day to have a considerable hold on the public imagination. The persistence of this image in the popular imagination is no doubt helped by Richard Dawkins who in the light of the obvious difficulties outlined above, alters the name of this God to read, *The Blind Watch-Maker*.

However one reacts to the criticism by Dawkins of this deist God, it should not be confused intentionally or unintentionally with the God of Christianity. To take a small but significant example, in complete opposition to the distant and non-interventionist God of Deism is the belief that the Christian God does intervene in human history and that it is a decisive intervention from the side of love rather than an interfering or manipulative intervention. What Christians believe is that the divine intervention in human history is one which offers healing, whilst always respecting the freedom to refuse the offer – a freedom which was respected even though it led to Christ's death on a cross.

The Deist image of God is one that is far removed from any idea that we may have of a God of love – the compassionate face of the Christian God that is revealed on the cross. In fact, it would be difficult to conceive of a distant and/or an impersonal God dying on the cross for anybody. Furthermore, to the extent that Deism suggests a God who is indifferent to the vicissitudes of life as it is lived, it is an image which is singularly inappropriate to addressing the problems posed by the problem of evil. Whilst I would be the first to acknowledge that attending to an appropriate image of God is not going to solve the problem of evil, what is certain is that an inappropriate image will block any attempt at some sort of reconciliation with God before such a project could even get started.

ORDER AND DISORDER: NECESSITY AND CHANCE

The growing realisation, particularly in the area of genetics as well as quantum physics, of the crucial role played by chance in the evolutionary process needs no introduction. Similarly, what needs no introduction is the challenge posed to the idea of a purposeful creation by the interpretation of this characteristic of evolution as blind random chance. Over the course of nearly half a century Polkinghorne, along with a growing band of like-minded thinkers whose names include Arthur Peacocke, Keith Ward, Ian Barbour and Paul Davies, amongst many others – has dedicated himself to offering a coherent theistic response to the question or cluster of questions which suggest that the role played by chance in evolution renders unviable, and indeed inappropriate, belief in a creator God – a loving, purposeful and intelligently designed creation. These include those which have been traditionally grouped under the heading of the problem of evil.

In a chapter from his 1994 publication, 'What's Been Going On', Polkinghorne attempts to address some of the seemingly intractable issues raised here. Interestingly, the chapter commences with a refusal to take refuge in a quasi Deist God of origins. With customary frankness, he acknowledges that the problem of evil cannot be so easily sidestepped and that if there is a creator, then, as he says, 'God is a God of the whole show' (Polkinghorne, 1994, 51). Having acknowledged the nature and the scale of the issues involved, he proposes a response which, as we saw above, is firmly rooted in an analysis of the significance of the developments in Quantum physics. It is one which acknowledges that both quantum theory (Heisenberg's Uncertainty Principle) and evolutionary theory (random genetic mutation) reveal a world very different from that which would have been described by Isaac Newton in the seventeenth century.

What separates Polkinghorne and others of a like mind, and here I include myself, from those that interpret chaos theory as an atheist's blueprint, is his belief that Indeterminacy/chance is hospitable to a theist world view. And not only that, by making room for an open future, it reveals at a whole series of levels a vision of creation much more in keeping with a loving God than ever was possible under the rubric of classical science. What the advances in quantum physics and evolutionary science are uncovering is a world that is hospitable to the idea that we are not mere spectators in an already completed project but active partners, co-creators with God in the 'becoming' of the world. As he says:

> I believe that the God who both loves and is faithful has given to creation the twin gifts of independence and reliability. These find their interplay in the fruitful interplay of chance and necessity in the evolving cosmic history. (Polkinghorne, 1994, 55)

ARGUING FOR AN EVOLUTIONARY MODEL OF CREATION

Whilst not wishing to exaggerate the significance of this approach, there is no doubting the potential of an evolutionary model of creation to address some of the more intractable problems posed by the problem of evil.

Because evolution allows room for freedom, for the fact that there are things that come about by chance, this model of creation has the potential to reveal a God who has no wish to control or to micro-manage the universe. Furthermore, to believe in a world that has not yet reached perfection but is literally still evolving means that inevitably it appears to us at present as a world with rough edges. Finally, to believe in a loving God who has given to us the priceless gift of freedom to be co-creators of this universe means that we should never underestimate the significance of actions that contribute to its destruction and go a long way to explaining the existence of evil in the world. Whilst freely acknowledging that the existence of evil in the world will always pose very real difficulties for those who would believe in a loving God, nevertheless, it is an insight such as the above that allows Polkinghorne to conclude this all too brief reflection with the following inspirational thought.

> I don't believe that God directly wills either the act of a murderer or the incidence of a cancer. I believe God allows both to happen in a creation that has been given the gift of being itself. (Polkinghorne, 1994, 62)

In the final section of this article, the focus has shifted to a brief treatment of how, in the context of a brief reflection on the problem of evil, the scientific theory of evolution does not confirm the mismatch between science and religion that is so commonly presumed to be the case today. The problem/mystery of evil is also an issue which reminds us of the importance of ensuring that, in so far as possible, one works with an appropriate image of God, such as those proposed by the related motifs of love and friendship. In drawing on the insights of Martin Buber and Chiara Lubich, Purcell offers a sensitive portrayal of a God of love. If this portrayal is accurate, it suggests that it is only something like the belief that God's providential interaction with its history allows room for freedom which is capable of providing the all-important counterbalance to an over-emphasis on the omnipotence (all-powerful) and omniscience (all-knowing) God. This is the case because it literally means that God does not have the power to do an unloving act or indeed to look with anything like the benign indifference on the effects of evil that is suggested by the God of deism. In that context, the possibility of meeting the challenge of refugee fideism is dependent in no small measure on successfully critiquing the image of the deist God, an impersonal and distant

God that so permeated the scientific discourse of Modernity, and even today continues to have such a significant hold on the public imagination.

CONCLUSION

Given the limits of a short article, all that was possible here was to offer an outline sketch of core issues thrown up by our contemporary scientific culture which create substantial barriers that prevent the possibility of any meaningful dialogue between religion and science. If anything, it highlights the importance of a more substantial analysis of the issues involved. Amongst these, one could include the following questions that interrogate experience from an explicitly theist or perhaps even a theological background:

- If we are to love and be a friend and be befriended, we cannot be just material, merely measurable and measuring. Or can we?

- The truth of the Bible is to be received within the context of friendship with God and in community with God's people and God's salvation history. If this is accurate, to what extent can an atheist understand, let alone critique the Bible?

- Quantum physics reveals a world which is hospitable to novelty and choice and mystery – and thus love and friendship?

- A world that allows human love, freedom and evil, is also a world that calls for salvation and redemption and thus true hope. Or does it?

In this context, both Brendan Purcell and John Polkinghorne are to be commended, not only on the scale of their ambition, but more importantly for the confidence they both have in the innate power of reason to vindicate their religious faith. Neither could be accused of being refugee fideists and neither could ever be accused of being afraid of the advances of science as reflected in the well-worn phrase 'the God of the Gaps'. Furthermore, in the context the challenges suggested in the title of this article, both show a willingness and an ability not only to negotiate the complex world of contemporary science, but also to hear the questions raised in today's scientific and secular cultural milieu – questions that can hinder as well as facilitate the dialogue between religion and science which must be at the core of any credible philosophy of religion for today.

NOTES

1. Brendan Purcell, *From Big Bang To Big Mystery: Human Origins in the Light of Creation and Evolution* (Dublin: Veritas, 2011), p. 62.
2. The debate which was introduced by vice chancellor of the university Lord Chris Patton and chaired by Prof. Antony Kenny can be accessed on YouTube at http://www.youtube.com/watch?v=Hb4aanpsx6Q
3. In this context, it is hardly surprising that two of the most celebrated twentieth century philosophers, Martin Buber and Emmanuel Levinas, both of whom were Jewish, dedicated their professional lives to espousing the importance of a relational anthropology.
4. My use of the designation ultra-Darwinian rather than the more usual title of Neo-Darwinian is designed to highlight the fact that developments in evolutionary theory, thus Neo-Darwinian, made possible by genetics are not inherently atheistic, as is suggested by ultra-Darwinians such as Richard Dawkins. See Cunningham Conor, *Darwin's Pious Idea: Why the Ultra-Darwinists and Creationists Both Get it Wrong*, (Cambridge: Eerdmans, 2010), p. xv–xvii.
5. This is an issue to which I return to in the final section of this paper.
6. St Augustine spent over twenty years writing his seminal work on the Trinity – twenty years attempting to clarify, with only limited success, what is undoubtedly well described as the mystery of the Blessed Trinity. However, in book eight of *De Trinitate* he left us with a memorable image of the Trinitarian character of true love, an image that like so many in his writings is grounded in his own experience recounted by him in book four of the *Confessions*.
7. See St Augustine as he acknowledges the force of this criticism of the Christian Church even in the fifth century, which in turn gave rise to that remarkable *tour de force* that is *The City of God*.
8. John Polkinghorne, *Quarks, Chaos and Christianity: Questions to Science and Religion* (New York: The Crossroad Publishing Company, 1994). Hereafter referenced in the text as Polkinghorne, 1994.
9. See Brendan Purcell, pp. 294–5.

Merleau-Ponty on Sensibility, Alterity and Trace

TIMOTHY MOONEY

As is by now widely appreciated, the starting point of Emmanuel Levinas' philosophy is that my responsibility for the Other does not proceed from any initiative of myself as thinking and willing subject. Put another way, it is not the consequence of a decision based on the weighing of reasons simultaneously present to a rational and synchronous awareness. It is always already there, commanding me before any decision or deliberation.[1] Such an original responsibility is founded in sensibility. In the very nudity and vulnerability of the visage and living body facing me is first signified the transcendence of the Other. The face is in its originary factuality and before any principle transcendence *par excellence*. Within the world, it points to an infinity beyond the world, to the irreplaceable singularity and inexhaustible richness of an existent to which no 'I' and no science can ever be adequate. The presence of the Other calls my spontaneity into question, and is called ethics.[2]

Close attention to the expressive flesh of sensibility in the Other and in oneself – if not yet to the originary ethical relationship established in sensibility – characterises the thought of Maurice Merleau-Ponty, with which Levinas displays an explicit familiarity in *Totality and Infinity* (1961). In his later years, Levinas composed two essays on the earlier thinker, 'On Intersubjectivity: Notes on Merleau-Ponty' (1983) and 'Sensibility' (1984).[3] All three of his treatments are congruent with each other, and all show a marked sensitivity to certain ways in which Merleau-Ponty's analyses foreshadow and inspire his own. It is also argued by Levinas, however, that these analyses are oriented towards an epistemic account of experiencing the Other that hinders them from the outset. In finding the level of sensibility insufficient, Merleau-Ponty passes over one's own original passivity in relation to him or her. At every level he neglects his or her singularity and vulnerability, and he does so at every stage in his work from *The Structure of*

Behavior and *Phenomenology of Perception* through to his last and unfinished work *The Visible and the Invisible*.

In this essay I hope to bring out what Levinas sees as of enduring worth in Merleau-Ponty's work (and in the Husserl who anticipates him). I also wish to bring out the character of his critique of Merleau-Ponty, and show that it does seem to have purchase on the latter's work, since his account of the originary passivity in early human life is indeed oriented towards the active and epistemic levels of which it is the precondition. Yet the orientation of early and anonymous life to stages beyond itself does not lead Merleau-Ponty to pass over its singular character as Levinas thinks he does. And the necessity of reaching the cognitive stage to recognise the transcendence of both a singular and vulnerable Other – a stage that Levinas initially underplays – does not entail that a precondition of this stage can become the proper object of knowledge, or an object of cognition at all. The originary trace of the Other in Merleau-Ponty is a past that was never a present. Whilst it is Levinas' claim to have drawn out the significance of this past immemorial, Merleau-Ponty can accommodate such a view with an account of reflection that is cognisant of its structural limitations. He does not thereby foreshadow the Levinasian notion, though he does begin to point towards conditions of possibility of responding ethically that will be made explicit by Paul Ricoeur.

I

Merleau-Ponty's phenomenology of human embodiment makes extensive use of Husserl's distinction between the body as *Körper* and as *Leib*. The former refers to it as an extended something subject to causal laws, that is, to the body as reflectively objectified from outside, whether in everyday cognitive life or in natural scientific study. The latter refers to my body as it is lived. It is not experienced as an object or thing, for it is the locus of experience that both precedes and underpins thematic and representational performances.[4] Merleau-Ponty will sketch a further notion of the body that can be entitled 'the body itself' or 'one's own body' (*le corps propre*). The body itself includes my skill schema, that is, my anonymous, sub-representational system of acquired skills that practically constitutes the surrounding world for me. When I imagine something that I can attain immediately, my body itself has anonymously projected an action solution for that outcome, and in so doing has articulated the environment into affordances and directions to be taken towards them, with them and beyond them. I encounter my equipment already organised into routes to realisation.[5]

This notion of the body is formulated in order to bridge the *Körper* and the *Leib*. The contribution of the lived body to the constitution of space was opened up by Husserl, for in its seeings and in its movements it has attendant sensations of movement or kinaestheses – for example, in eye, neck, torso and limb muscles – that are integral to the sense that something in the world possesses.[6] Thus the presence of leg as well as eye kinaestheses in concert with a coloured shape expanding to fill ever more of my visual field informs me that I am approaching a stationary car, as distinct from a moving car approaching a stationary me. Husserl's focus is nonetheless on bodily experiences that can be brought to conscious presence, however inadequately, whereas the action projections or motor intentionalities of the body's skill schema are sub-reflective, incapable of being taken up in reflection. Such anonymous performances are hidden beneath the world that they constitute. It is ultimately impossible to uncover or articulate them in their nudity.[7]

In Merleau-Ponty's words, the body itself 'is something between transcendent Nature, naturalism's being in-itself, and the immanence of mind, its acts, and its noemata', something towards which Husserl was pointing. Levinas agrees, and adds that Merleau-Ponty does not understand his projective body in foundational terms.[8] The latter is quite clear that the body itself goes beyond its skill-schema, and has indeed been gifted certain senses prior to building up its repertoire of capacities. One's own body is always already a body for Others, who have never appeared as objects exhibiting movements that required me to infer governing psyches within them, as putatively ethereal insides of mechanical outsides.[9] The expressive instrument that we call a face carries a whole existence in and through it, with the Other's living body lighting up and transforming the objects around it. He or she is the theatre of a certain process of elaboration and of a certain view of the world.[10]

Already for Husserl, the Other's living body is permeated with soul through and through. Each of its movements 'is full of soul, the coming and going, the standing and sitting, the walking and dancing etc.'[11] Merleau-Ponty's contribution is precisely to flag our bodies as processes of expressive elaboration. Just as in a painting or a melody the meaning is inseparable from the swirls of colours or the tones, so too the meanings that we express in our gestures cannot be sundered from our modes of expression. Hence the living body can best be compared with a work of art.[12] It is not a question, moreover, of a culturally marked expressivity overlying bare biological being. We are naturally conventional in our practical and creative doings, and though we are intrinsically dependent on our biology, there is no form of human behaviour 'that does not elude the simplicity of animal life', and that is devoid of the distinctive 'genius for ambiguity which might serve to define man.'[13]

In language Merleau-Ponty finds a fundamental feature of our naturally cultural being. It does not translate pre-given cognitions, but accomplishes them. The denomination of objects – amongst them what is mine and what is yours, what is own and alien – does not follow upon explicit recognition, but is itself such recognition. Language is our common, open-ended and mutually illuminating fabric. It provides me with more detailed articulations of meanings that originate in human gestures, expressing the nuances of emotional life as well as the more abstract theoretical cognitions of the sciences. Originally interwoven with and enriching my understanding of bodily expressions, it is a fundamental ground of empathic awareness. Language constitutes the consummate reciprocity between oneself and others – thus I find speech opening me up to thoughts and points of view that are not my own and beyond my initiative. When my views are contested, furthermore, thoughts are drawn out of me that I had no idea I possessed, and which I did not in fact possess before and outside of my discursive relationship with the Other. Without reciprocity there could be no alter ego, since the world of the one would swallow up the world of others.[14]

The Other that is revealed prior to discourse still reveals his or her unsurpassable alterity within discourse, in Levinas' rendering, contesting further any typologies I might use to capture him or her. Language gives me what I have never known, revealing the Other as my teacher. Levinas adds that none have shown better than Merleau-Ponty the incarnate and revelatory character of speech, whose significations commence with no antecedent representations.[15] Yet this is just one instance of Merleau-Ponty's acuity:

> It is difficult for me to find terms adequate to express my admiration for the subtle beauty of the analyses in Merleau-Ponty's work of that original incarnation of spirit in which Nature reveals its meaning in movements of the human body that are essentially signifying, i.e. expressive, i.e. cultural; from gesture to language,

to art, to poetry and science: that original incarnation in which Nature reveals its meaning (or its soul?) in Culture. The French philosopher's own quest doubtless permitted him to say the non-said (or at least the non-published) of Husserl's thought, a thought whose 'possibilities' require an attentive ear throughout, despite the apparent immobility or repetition of the main theses.[16]

And it is within the very flesh of the sensibility that expresses itself, continues Levinas, that the ambiguity of body and of consciousness is first manifested for Merleau-Ponty. We find an originary articulation of the inner and the outer that is prior and irreducible to the noetic and noematic structure of intentional, cognitive awareness (in which the noesis comprises those moments of a conscious act referring it to its object, and the noema the object in its being intended).[17] This is one of the ways in which Merleau-Ponty builds on the Husserl of *Ideas II*, a text that is itself praised by Levinas for its richness and precision, notably in its account of the tactile life that goes towards founding empathic experience.[18]

Touch is radically different to vision and all the other senses in that it involves a double sensation. For Husserl, this double sensation constitutes my living body's permanent presence with me, and is also essential to constitute my outer body, to recognise it as mine. If I touch my left hand with my right, I touch on something that is soft and hard and smooth and warm. These qualities are tacitly taken as belonging to the left hand, and can quite correctly be objectified as properties of an extended something, of the body as *Körper*. Yet these qualities are caught or felt by way of the right and active hand. In this touching hand, there is a localised correspondence between what is felt and the feeling of it. Through all of this, the left hand also has localised tactile sensations. These are passive ones of being touched or of being felt. It is experienced as the living flesh or *Leib* being impinged upon. But this double sensation and double relationship is reversible. Without having to make much or in fact any further movement, I can alternate the roles, so that the left hand becomes the active touching one, and the right hand the passive one being touched.[19]

Just as remarkably, such reversibility extends to the entire body. In tacit terms, I know what it feels like for every part of my body to be touched by some other part, and what it feels like to do the touching. Through touch, my body is constituted as both an exterior and as an interior. It is felt on from the outside, and felt in from the inside. Yet I do not even have to touch one of my body parts with another. If I move one of my hands over an exterior thing, I feel its outer qualities in my hand, from within me. There are not two experiences, rather two aspects of one experience.[20] Together they comprise a reflexivity that is peculiar to the body. Conscious reflexivity is the consciousness of being conscious, whereas bodily reflexivity is the feeling of feeling, of being touched in touching. Touching is the living body's own self-appearance in its apprehension of things. Furthermore, it is because it is felt from within that I recognise the body that I see from outside as mine. The extended thing is only seen as belonging to me because it is simultaneously being felt from the inside.[21]

On foot of this aesthetic unity of seeing oneself touching and being-touched, claims Husserl, one can immediately recognise another body as the living body of the Other and on this basis empathise with him or her, without having to engage in inferences or reasoning by analogy.[22] Merleau-Ponty discovers an ambiguity or lack of coincidence in the experience of touching and being-touched, since one cannot explicitly register the reversible touching and being touched in one blow. One can only alternate between the two experiences, giving the one or the other my attention. The body has its outer-inner relation constituting it as mine, but I cannot objectify it even after I have learned about it. I am always too late to catch the overall experience, which is structurally in the background of awareness.[23] But he agrees that it founds the apprehension of the Other. Just as my one hand was present at the advent of the other one touching it, so the Other's body is animate before me when I shake his hand, or even when I look at it. He appears through an extension of my own non-coincident bodily reflexivity, each of us participating in a single anonymous intercorporeality.[24]

Levinas finds it interesting that the aesthetic or 'esthesiological' community taken as founding empathy and intersubjectivity and intellectual communication is not directly given, only being produced by reconstruction. This is not taken as a deficiency in one's perception of others, but as a positive characteristic of that perception. For Merleau-Ponty, 'I borrow myself from the other; I make him out of my own thoughts: that is not a failure in the perception of others, it is the perception of others.'[25] But anterior to our interdependent thoughts, observes Levinas, Merleau-Ponty is clearly discerning – with the help of Husserl – a relation to others that depends on the carnal structure of sensibility. Flesh understood as the explicitly recognised body of oneself or of the Other turns out to be constituted by conscious capacities that are already indebted to the body of sensibility. As Levinas expresses it, recognitive consciousness 'turns out to have already called upon what it is supposed to be constituting'.[26] Such a strange anachronism already indicates the diachronic relation to the Other that underpins rational and synchronous awareness.

For all of these insights, Merleau-Ponty nonetheless ends up with a view that underplays my originary passivity towards the Other, and his or her singular and irreplaceable transcendence and vulnerability. In the touching and being touched, claims Levinas, the human existence is only a moment of an event of intelligibility, or better of proto-intelligibility, the heart of which is no longer enveloped or situated within specifically human existence. We should take note 'of this anti-humanist or non-humanist tendency to link the human to an ontology of anonymous being. It is a tendency characterising an entire era that, while reflecting upon anthropology, is suspicious of the human'. In that era, this view would seem all the more defensible for being indifferent to the drama of persons, who, precisely as singular and irreplaceable, are never the tokens of universal types.[27]

Beyond impersonal anonymity, the premise of a new relationship between others and myself that is rooted in sensibility is understood finally as a deficient knowledge of them. The reason is that the event of proto-intelligibility found in the body's reflexive relationship to itself and to the Other is oriented towards the cognitive or epistemic domain. Despite the originality of the tactile structure brought out by Husserl and developed by Merleau-Ponty, it is precisely in its pre-theoretical character 'already related to the theoretical and already, as it were, the shadow of that to which it is related'.[28] It is a form of knowledge, even if a knowing in a different and peculiar mode. The idea that sensibility could reach the Other *otherwise* that by the 'gnosis' of touching or seeing (in other words epistemic touching and seeing) appears foreign to the analyses of the phenomenologists. In their account it is always the knowledge of an alter ego that breaks an originally egological isolation.[29]

The orientation of Merleau-Ponty's account of existence towards the cognitive domain also deforms his account of linguistic signification, granting that it can reveal the Other as my teacher, and that it is not taken to translate antecedent representations. What is perceived still requires a name to become a signification in the full and proper sense, signification always having been constituted as an intentional object. In Levinas' eyes, the structure of intentional, constitutive consciousness recovers all its rights for Merleau-Ponty, despite the mediation of the body that speaks or inscribes. He fails to appreciate that all recourse to words presupposes a surplus of signification over representation, whether in fact or in principle. The originary or primary signification that is the face of the Other is presupposed in discourse. It is the Other that puts me in question and under obligation, already commanding me before the appearance of the symbol. The latter marks the inevitable inadequacy of what is given to consciousness with regard to the being it symbolises, an inexhaustible surplus of infinity.[30]

My originary passivity in relation to the Other of sensibility is obscured yet further by the body itself, which is at once upright, elevated and able. Through its skill schema, as noted above, the body itself articulates the environment into affordances and the directions to be taken towards them, with them and beyond them to attain its chosen outcomes. One's skilled and sub-representational motor awareness lies at the disposal of the 'I can', of the consciousness that apprehends Others and things in the light of its own projects. The very 'gait' (*démarche*) of the mental is that of a being that approaches, orbits and manipulates everything outside itself with its presumptive spontaneity.[31] What such an account covers over, according to Levinas, is one's dependence on Others and on the world, and the fragility of the 'I can' through which so many actions are envisaged as immediate possibilities for oneself. The putative body-master bears the ongoing possibility of body-slavery, of passing from the freedom of health to the encumbrance of sickness.[32]

In the end, what we find perpetuated is philosophy's abiding concern with the general or universal in the human. In 'Philosophy as Rigorous Science', Husserl had set out phenomenology's ambition to be a pure science of essences. To give an essence a place in the world of individual being, he says, 'is something that … a mere subsumption under essential concepts cannot accomplish. For phenomenology, the singular is eternally the *apeiron*'.[33] For Merleau-Ponty also there is no science except that of the neutral or the general.[34] But even in the universal investiture of cognitively seeing the Other, states Levinas, 'there lies coiled the dispossession of disinterestedness beneath the concreteness of responsibility, of non-in-difference, of love'.[35] My responsibility is to a unique being naked in his or her exposure to death. Par excellence, the sociality of love is not the integration of parts into a whole, since it maintains separation in proximity by not absorbing the strangeness in difference.[36]

II

I believe that it would be wrongheaded to endeavour to unearth in the texts of Merleau-Ponty a Levinas *avant la lettre*, as if one could pass over the latter's originality or discover in these earlier texts leading clues to an account that could have been framed without first having read Levinas himself. Keeping this in mind, we are not prevented from finding in these texts some explicit statements exceeded by their expressive power and by their implicit respect for the Other, albeit without the primal responsibility indicated by the later thinker. To paraphrase Merleau-Ponty's words on Husserl, we can try to evoke some neglected and unthought-of elements in the margin of some of his pages.[37] And in so doing, we can find him consistent in the view that to perceive the Other is to aim beyond perception 'at an inexhaustible ground which may one day shatter the image that I have formed of him'.[38]

It is true that for Merleau-Ponty our early lives are characterised by a sensibility that is pre-theoretical without being alien to the theoretical. In the touching and being-touched, we are exemplars of an event of proto-intelligibility. Here Levinas' critique seems to bear on his work, at least if one accepts the latter's suspicions about the cognitive stage of development. Merleau-Ponty is adamant that our earliest experiences are specifically human, and are oriented towards stages beyond themselves. In developing into personhood, one is never a body 'surmounted with a mind which would unfold its proper acts over this infrastructure'. Human existence is integrated in its development as well as its outcome. For each of us, he continues, 'the somatic processes do not unfold in isolation, but are integrated into a cycle of more extensive action. It is not a question of two *de facto* orders external to each other, but of two types of relations, the second of which integrates the first.'[39]

Significantly, nothing in this account confines the value of human existence to an advanced stage of development or the ability to call one's lived experiences one's own. From its earliest stages the human being is a vector beyond itself whose possibilities are inseparable from his or her actuality. Early anonymous life is already integrated in its becoming, and is prefiguring that stage of publicity that ostensibly signifies an irreducible and irreplaceable existence, with the baby already being predisposed to engage in linguistic activity. Early awareness should not be compared with a plastic material that receives its developed structure from outside, solely by way of a sociological causality or the human world that surrounds the infant. If the adult's gestural use of language did not interface with an existing predisposition for the act of speech in the child, 'it would have no power over the mosaic of sensations possessed by infantile consciousness', and it would not be possible to understand how it could play its guiding role in building up the perceived world.[40]

It is not merely the orientation of early life to intentional and cognitive experience that concerns Levinas, but its anonymity. We have been read as common, indifferent exemplars of an event of proto-intelligibility. Yet there is another way of understanding our earliest and most anonymous life in Merleau-Ponty, and it need not involve that indifference to the drama of the personal or potentially personal in the human. Within an integrated existence, the sensibility of touching and being-touched is not just specifically human, but internally related to other experiences characterising a life that is never the universality of a constituting subject or of a pre-intentional proto-subject. We always encounter an embodied being particularised by its body, internally related to nature without being reducible to it, and comprising an individual manner of dealing in the world. Only for the Cartesian or mechanistic materialist could the structures of sensibility be indifferent to this or that body.[41]

Merleau-Ponty makes it clear, furthermore, that one's singular humanity exceeds biological individuation, and in the same vein, that early anonymous existence cannot be equated with impersonal life. If pre-personal existence were common to all, then the moments of an individual's experience would cease 'to be an integrated and strictly unique totality, in which details exist only in virtue of the whole'.[42] As one grows up one gains new experiences and skills from just this unique perspective, and as noted above, some skills become so familiar that their execution no longer require memorial and imaginative representation. They make up the anonymity of what Aristotle would call second nature. In developed human life, our repertoire of experiences and capacities is such that 'there appears around our personal existence a margin of *almost* impersonal existence, which can practically be taken for granted, and which I rely on to keep me alive'.[43] Even later experiences undergone passively – as against active and volitional experiences and deployed capacities – are in one and the same blow a sublimation of biological into personal existence, and as they grow up in the world, each person comes to exist for me 'as an incontestable style or milieu of co-existence'.[44] In this regard 'even reflexes have a meaning, and each individual's style is still visible in them, just as the beating of the heart is felt as far away as the body's periphery'.[45]

In the course of a life an individual usually maintains his or her peculiar manner of living. Merleau-Ponty stresses that this style of the Other is not something that can be known and sought after outside of all contact with the world, as if it were a means or the end of some human art. Rather it is integral to the lived perception of each human person. To say that perception already stylises is to say that the Other is apprehended as a once-off manner of being flesh, as a particular and noticeable variation of the general norm of walking, looking, touching and speaking that I hold within my self-awareness by dint of being incarnate. If I am capable of painting someone in their expressivity, contends Merleau-Ponty, what I transmit to canvas first and foremost will be more than a corporeal contour, and more again than a vital or sensual value. It will be the emblem of a certain way of inhabiting the world, of handling it and interpreting it 'by a face as by clothing, by agility of gesture as by inertia of body – in short, the emblem of a certain relationship to being'.[46]

Merleau-Ponty is as attuned to the fragility and vulnerability of the Other as to his or her irreplaceable singularity. Whilst his explication of the skill schema is without doubt that of a being who appropriates its environment towards its own projects with a presumptive spontaneity, the occlusion of dependence on Others again and on the world is apparent rather than real. It is always the injured Other, the particular pathological case, who is needed to foreground the hidden constitutive achievements of the healthy 'I can' and to remind the latter of its somatic good fortune. The thrust of intellectualist or cognitivist accounts of human intentionality, by contrast, has been to obscure the sheer contingency of its meaningful contents, contents founded on and clinging to somatic functions that are ever vulnerable to disease and destruction.[47] These are the reasons why Merleau-Ponty will focus on human persons who try to hold up their conscious superstructures when their foundations have given way, seeking to realise everyday outcomes 'without being able to conceal the particular deficiency which robs them of their complete significance'.[48]

In such elucidations a certain pathos runs in tandem with fragility and loss. This is witnessed in the reference to the amputee who is solicited by certain objects, though they are no longer genuine affordances for him. Through his habitual orientation towards the world the pen and paper and piano still invoke his earlier projects of writing and of playing. Present intentional awareness retains the mark of the body that secretly nourished it.[49] It is found too in the discussion of Johann Schneider, a patient who has maintained almost full practical motility, and with it a world of practical means and ends, but who cannot readily move in novel ways or escape his concrete milieu. He cannot ask his children anything more than the stereotypical questions expected of someone in the general role of being a father. No longer supporting new or abstract projection or an appreciation of singular lives, his remaining structures of sensibility do not allow him 'to breathe, speak and, if need be, weep in the realm of imagination'.[50] With more radical injuries again, the openness to otherness recedes completely, such that bodily events become the events of the day.[51]

Each of these studies is of course an explicit, reflective characterisation of another's somatic condition and its internal relationship to his or her world. Merleau-Ponty can allow that the Other (who has passively affected oneself prior to reflective regard) maintains an irreplaceable singularity beyond that of bodily expressivity, whilst emphasising that his or her point of view must be an intentional object, that is, something thematised. That the child is always already affected by singular Others does not entail that he or she has an appreciation of this. Only at a certain age do we come to realise that there are different points of view, so that Others will no longer be 'empty heads turned towards one single, self-evident world where everything takes place'.[52] Such objectifying seeing is systematised in philosophical and phenomenological reflection. Levinas would retort that this misses the original character of the experience of the Other, confusing it with an empirical facticity consequent on epistemic structures that have passed over alterity (without even grasping it partially or inadequately, since it is not potentially knowable even in part), and forgetting that originary responsibility has already affected the damaged life become forced in on itself.

For Levinas, the recognition of the Other as an alter ego is of its essence a violent and totalising act, since self and other are taken as indifferent instances of a cognising type.[53] Wayne Froman remarks that the violence in question is taken to involve the negation of what is intrinsic to the Other person and resistant to subsumption into the eidetic or essential universality of the 'ego in general' each of us instantiates.[54] The critique of this position is associated more famously with Derrida. The breakthrough accomplished by the Husserlian phenomenology of the Other, in Derrida's view, is to recognise that the Other is not just another point of view of the world, but as a transcendental alter ego, the origin of the world, that is, of the world as constitutively revealed from that point of view and as the correlate of that point of view, which is not something in the world. This alterity is recognisable by way of the first alterity of the lived body as expressively full of soul.[55]

Violence is intrinsic to such recognition, states Derrida, but it is a necessary and transcendental violence, realising that the Other can only appear in and through the same, as an alterity within the same. Without egoity in general (and, one could argue, without already constitutive proto-egoity in general) the empirical violence of which Levinas speaks would be violence without a human victim, and if one were not an ego, violence without an author.[56] As Froman points out, this necessity is already comprehended by Merleau-Ponty, and emerges in his critique of Sartre.[57] The Other as the For Itself who becomes known in bringing me under its gaze appears to offer an escape from solipsism, whereas for Merleau-Ponty:

> [T]his agnosticism with regard to the other's being for himself, which appeared to guarantee his security, suddenly appears as the worst of infringements upon it. For he who states it implies that it is applicable to all those who hear him. He does not speak only of himself, of his own perspective, and for himself; he speaks for all. He says: *the For Itself* (in general) is alone ... or: *the being for another* is the death of the For Itself, or things of this kind – without specifying whether this concerns the being for itself such as he lives it or the being for itself such as those who hear him live it, the being for another such as he experiences it or the being for another such as the others experience it. This singular that he permits himself – the For Itself, the For the Other – indicates that he means to speak in the name of all, that in his description he implies the power to speak for all, whereas the description contests this power. Hence I only apparently confine myself to my own experience – to my being for myself and to my being for another – and only apparently respect the radical originality of the for itself of another and his being for me.[58]

The necessary and transcendental violence, furthermore, does not entail that the Other's point of view is inaccessible because of my finitude. In a Levinasian register, this would involve the category mistake of treating it as a potential object of knowledge. But it is just this mistake that Husserl is careful to avoid, and Merleau-Ponty and Derrida after him. According to Husserl, the alter ego is essentially inaccessible, that is, inaccessible in itself and in principle (as distinct from inaccessible because of my finitude). If anything in his or her being were directly or originally accessible, then 'it would merely be a moment of my own essence, and he himself and I myself would be the same'.[59] Separation is the first and essential condition of Otherness, rather than a primary misfortune to be overcome.

For this reason the ego as intentional object has a paradoxical character. I encounter the Other as a living and expressive being, but his or her point of view is indicated by a mediate intentionality, and can never become a direct intentional object, let alone one of knowledge. What is grasped originally is the body of a psyche essentially inaccessible to me originally, even if they comprise one psychophysical unity.[60] In Derrida's interpretation, I am faced by a transcendence of infinity, not of totality. The Other is infinite because the face of his experience as he has lived it will never be given to me. I can only thematise in fact and principle the phenomenon of a non-phenomenality.[61] For the same reason Merleau-Ponty refers to the Other as an inexhaustible ground incapable of being experienced first hand, an Other who 'may one day shatter the image that I have formed of him'.[62] There are difficulties in perceiving Others, he remarks, that cannot be attributed to objective thought, and that are not dissolved with the discovery of the expressivity in behaviour.[63]

Merleau-Ponty will in this vein consider some remarks of Pascal, who claims that one need not love someone for her beauty, which is perishable, but for her mind. But the mind too can be lost, which leads Pascal to conclude that one loves only qualities.[64] Merleau-Ponty states that we can weigh the love that promises to be eternal when perhaps an illness or an accident will destroy it. It is true at the moment of the promise, he adds, that the love extends beyond qualities, the body and time, though I could not love beyond qualities, body and time. But this is no guarantee that I ever reached the substance of the person.[65] The price of 'knowing' another is that they can shatter one's illusions about oneself as well as about them. It can transpire that 'I loved only qualities (that smile which is so like another smile, that beauty which asserts itself like a fact, that youthfulness of gesture and behaviour) and not the singular manner of existence which is that person herself.'[66] Yet even where the familiar style of the Other has lost its charm, his or her voice can respond all too well to what I thought without saying it, and I glimpse briefly my being as it is known from another perspective, and 'I am no more than the respondent for the interpellation that is made to me.'[67]

III

Levinas subsequently gives much attention to the necessity of recognising the Other's Otherness by elaborating the distinction – already made very briefly in *Totality and Infinity* – between the saying and the said. Although the saying is indicated in the communicative intent and meaning content of the propositional said, it can only be thematised as a trace of the absolutely bygone, which is not an actual or a possible representation.[68] Yet Levinas reiterates that one's being originally affected by and made responsible to the Other is an experience both chronologically *and* logically prior to anything that can be thematised as an intentional object, despite all the qualifications that can be adduced in favour of the recognition thesis (if one pursues the line of argument beginning with Husserl and taken up by Merleau-Ponty and Derrida). In signifying a past that was never a present, the trace reports a past of which the respondent was not and could not have been aware, and which the Other did not intend or mean in any way, whether in thematic or volitional terms.[69]

It is worth noting that Merleau-Ponty's account is capable of accommodating this idea. At its lower level it already allows for the Levinasian notion of the trace, anterior to an observed or observable style of bodily expressivity. I remarked above that, in Merleau-Ponty's view, early anonymous existence transcends the universal structure of touching and being-touched, and cannot be equated with impersonal life, comprising an integrated, strictly unique totality. The experience of such existence does not disappear in adulthood. It retains its priority and endows subsequent perception with its significance. The contribution of the original bodily experience of the Other to reportably personal and volitional life is 'more ancient than thought' and 'impenetrable to reflection'.[70] When I perceive other people, on this account 'I have only the trace of a consciousness which evades me in its actuality', since it is rooted in sensibility prior to all comparison and identification.[71]

The trace of the Other in Merleau-Ponty hinges on the difference between pre-reflective and sub-reflective experience. What he first calls 'radical reflection' is reflection that is conscious of itself in its operation, grasping its structural limitations.[72] Beneath the experiences it focuses on as intending objects inadequately or mediately, there lie experiences that cannot be thematised at all. Reflection in its full significance is indebted to a sub-reflective fund 'which it presupposes, upon which it draws, and which constitutes for it a kind of original past, a past which has never been a present'.[73] In his later work he gives the name 'hyper-reflection' to this operation that is aware of its own sway. It realises that the reflectively available relationship of thought to its object (as empirical phenomenon or as the phenomenon of a non-phenomenality) must be situated 'within a more muted relationship with the world, within an initiation into the world upon which it rests and which is always already accomplished when the reflective return intervenes'.[74] The world in this sense is the background with its originary presence of Others as well as things.

Keeping the difference between a sub-reflective and a pre-reflective singularity of the Other in mind, Merleau-Ponty does not initially allow that my responsibility is sourced in and commanded by him or her. When he comes to address the upper level of thematic experience, he appears at first to preclude the Levinasian notion of the trace altogether. In our own living presents of temporal awareness, according to Merleau-Ponty, the Other will never exist for us as we exist for ourselves. Though our temporalities are not mutually exclusive, he is always a lesser figure, for we are never present at the thrust of his temporalisation.[75] The dissymmetry of a reportable ethical relationship between us, moreover, is such that it is always I myself who am privileged. Even the Other who in discourse is revealed as my teacher seems to drop out of consideration. I may well resolve to act in a world in which I accord as much place to Others as to myself, but this 'interworld' is still a project of mine, 'and it would be hypocritical to pretend that I seek the welfare of another *as if it were mine*, since this very attachment to another's interest still has its source in me'.[76]

It goes without saying that a decision to act has to be mine, that my conscious response to the Other must be imputable to me. I have to freely commit myself to a certain course and in terms of somatic capacities have the power to begin.[77] But room is hardly left for my imputable response having as a condition of possibility a pre-cognitive command sourced in the Other (to whom it is a particular empirical response). Which is not to assert that the Levinasian injunction has to be concerned with *how* I should act. My being originally responsible to the Other and hence summoned by him or her is not yet a prescription as to the peculiar way to respond in the here and now. Levinas' whole account revolves around the transcendental claim *that* I have been summonsed in advance, so that my 'serenity of consciousness' has in the first place been disrupted by 'the extreme urgency of assignation'.[78] What remain to be filled out, nevertheless, are conditions that must hold on my side if I am to respond at all, conditions themselves anterior to how I should respond.

In this light Merleau-Ponty will in fact qualify his remark about the Other's interest having its source in me, and in so doing point obliquely towards certain conditions of responding ethically that will be identified by Paul Ricoeur. If we confine ourselves to the conception of a single constitutive consciousness, says Merleau-Ponty, then we can say that attachments and decisions have their source in us. But as soon as we place ourselves within being, we realise that we are involved in the world and with Others in an inextricable weave, and it is 'necessarily the case that our actions must have their origin outside us', so that there is no absolute freedom as the source of our commitments.[79] The example that he provides is of a man resisting torture to make him give up the names and addresses of his comrades and those he loves. He may feel himself still with them and their common struggle, and may for years before have staked his life on facing just this test. In such a case he has phantoms of the Others buttressing him. He probably evokes them daily in his prison, and does not wish to be found wanting under their imaginary gaze. It may even be his awareness of a proudly willed solitude – itself a mode of Being-with – that chiefly carries him through. He wants to prove that what he always said and thought about freedom was not empty.[80]

What is indicated and most significant in all this, I think, is that the man believes he can hold out. And Ricoeur would argue that we must find certain conditions holding on his side if he responds ethically in this manner. He agrees with Levinas that one is summoned by the Other and originally responsible to him or her.[81] He parts company with the latter in refusing to underdetermine the very possibility of responding, claiming that self-esteem is one of its indefeasible conditions of possibility. I have to assign a minimal worth as well as a minimal coherence to my life to be an existent 'who does not detest itself to the point of being unable to hear the injunction coming from the Other'.[82] And in addition to my having regard for him or her, I must believe that I am capable in moral and not merely somatic terms of doing something to respond, something that makes a difference. According to Ricoeur, any ethical response to the other will also demand a degree of constancy on my part. Responding cannot just be expressed by the accusative 'Here I am' – it must include the nominative 'Here I stand'.[83] The concept of responsibility carries the sense of 'being counted on' as well as 'being accountable for', since the Other who calls me implicitly counts on me not to kill or injure or abandon or break my word and so on.[84]

Ricoeur stresses that this constancy is quite different from the rigid self-consistency of Stoicism in being a response to an expectation, in the absence of which I might be incapable of maintaining myself so. This intimates that it would more often transcend Merleau-Ponty's proudly willed solitude. It can also be distinguished from the 'sameness' of one's present character in being a commitment to hold fast in the future amidst possible changes of character.[85] Such constancy would also be a commitment to hold fast amidst changes in the Other's character and health, a commitment that could not be weighed because in the full and proper sense it would not be something that an illness or an accident was capable of destroying. On this question, it strikes the present writer that on occasion Merleau-Ponty gives too much weight to the role of the body and to youthful aesthetic experience in his discussions of conscious life and commitments, failing to foreground the deep affection and loyalty in one older person's love of another. He does not assign sufficient importance to his remark that the bodily existence on which I depend, the possibility of my having a world, is for all that 'the barest outline of a genuine presence in the world'.[86]

This brings us to a characteristic found in some of Merleau-Ponty's thought and throughout the thought of Levinas, whatever about their respective contributions to the meanings of sensibility, alterity and the trace. The latter criticises what he sees as the anti-humanist or non-humanist tendency to link the human to an ontology of anonymous being, taking it to characterise an entire era that is suspicious of the human and indifferent to the drama of persons. Yet his philosophical work – and Merleau-Ponty's after *Phenomenology of Perception* – manifests a distinctive underprivileging of human activity in thought and deed, activity that in building up our second natures contributes to the ethical life of most of us. For Levinas in particular, there are good reasons for being hesitant about philosophies of action and will, but this leads all too easily to the neglect of agency, and besides this of the role of cognition in developing experience. It is Ricoeur who goes on to find a capacity for receptivity in the self that is 'the result of a reflexive structure, better defined by its power of reconsidering pre-existing objectifications than by an initial separation'.[87]

A philosophy of passivity is not the fate of a thinking founded in sensibility, and more philosophical work could have been done by Merleau-Ponty on ethical action. At the end of his *magnum opus*, he does acknowledge the role of human activity in spite of what he regards as the limitations of theory. There are finally no theoretical answers to the questions of making this or that promise, giving up liberty to save liberty, losing everything for what seems very little. Yet in and through all these questions we encounter those whom we love and those in slavery, all standing there irrefutably. What is required of the philosopher in his own view is silence, and he will leave the last words to Antoine de Saint-Exupéry:

> Your son is caught in the fire: you are the one who will save him ... If there is an obstacle, you would be ready to give your shoulder, provided only that you can charge down that obstacle. Your abode is your act itself. Your act is you ... You give yourself in exchange ... Your significance shows itself, effulgent. It is your duty, your hatred, your love, your steadfastness, your ingenuity ... Man is but a network of relationships, and these alone matter to him.[88]

NOTES

1. *Autrement qu'être ou au-delà de l'essence* (The Hague: Martinus Nijhoff, 1979), p. 196, p. 205, p. 211. *Otherwise than Being, or Beyond Essence*, Alphonso Lingis, trans. (Pittsburgh: Duquesne University Press, 1999), p. 154, p. 161, p. 166. Henceforth *AE*.
2. *Totalité et Infini: Essai sur l'extériorité* (The Hague: Martinus Nijhoff, 1961), p. 13, pp. 21–2, p. 188, pp. 238–40. *Totality and Infinity: An Essay on Exteriority*, Alphonso Lingis, trans. (Pittsburgh: Duquesne University Press, 1969), p. 43, pp. 50–1, p. 213, pp. 261–2. Henceforth *TI*.
3. Both essays are published together in Levinas' *Hors Sujet* (Saint Clément: Fata Morgana, 1987), pp. 133–40, pp. 147–56. *Outside of the Subject*, Michael B. Smith, trans. (London: Athlone Press, 1993), pp. 96–103, pp. 107–15. Henceforth *HS*. It should be added that the second essay is prefaced by a piece in memory of Alphonse de Waelhens, one of the first great Merleau-Ponty scholars.
4. *Husserliana IV. Ideen zu einer reinen Phänomenologie und phänomenologischen Philosophie: Zweites Buch*, Marly Biemel, ed. (The Hague: Martinus Nijhoff, 1952), p. 32ff. *Ideas Pertaining to a Pure Phenomenology and to a Phenomenological Philosophy, Second Book*, Richard Rojcewicz and André Schuwer, trans. (Dordrecht: Kluwer, 1989), p. 35ff. Henceforth *Hua IV*.
5. *Phénoménologie de la perception* (Paris: Éditions Gallimard, 1945), pp. 97–9, 117, 164–6. *Phenomenology of Perception*, Colin Smith, trans. (London: Routledge and Kegan Paul, 1962), pp. 82–4, pp. 100–1, 140–2. Henceforth *PP*.
6. *Hua IV*, 21–22, 56–57 (tr. pp. 23–4, pp. 61–2).
7. *PP*, p. 161n1 (tr. p. 138n2).
8. *Signes* (Paris: Gallimard, 1960), p. 209. *Signs*, Richard McCleary, trans. (Evanston: Northwestern University Press, 1964), p. 166. Henceforth *SNS*; *HS*, p. 135 (tr. p. 98).
9. *PP*, pp. 403–4 (tr. p. 351).

10. Ibid., p. 406 (tr. p. 353).
11. *Hua IV*, p. 240 (tr. p. 252).
12. *PP*, pp. 176–7 (tr. pp. 150–1).
13. Ibid., p. 221 (tr. p. 189).
14. Ibid., pp. 207–9, pp. 217–18, p. 407, p. 410 (tr. pp. 178–9, pp. 186–7, p. 354, p. 357).
15. *TI*, pp. 45–6, p. 169, pp. 180–1 (tr. p. 73, p. 195, pp. 205–6).
16. *HS*, pp. 135–6 (tr. p. 98, slightly emended).
17. Ibid., p. 136 (tr. pp. 98–9).
18. Ibid., p. 152 (tr. p. 112).
19. *Hua IV*, pp. 144–5 (tr. pp. 152–3).
20. Ibid., pp. 145–6 (tr. p. 153).
21. Ibid., pp. 150–1 (tr. pp. 158–9).
22. *Husserliana 1. Cartesianische Meditationen und Pariser Vorträge*, Stephen Strasser, ed. (The Hague: Martinus Nijhoff, 1963, 2nd ed.), pp. 129, pp. 140–1, pp. 148–9. *Cartesian Meditations*, Dorion Cairns, trans. (The Hague: Martinus Nijhoff, 1960), pp. 97, pp. 110–11, pp. 119–20.
23. *PP*, p. 109 (tr. p. 93).
24. *SNS*, pp. 212–13 (tr. p. 168).
25. *HS*, p. 137 (tr. p. 100); *SNS*, p. 201 (tr. p. 159).
26. *HS*, p. 134 (tr. p. 97, emended).
27. Ibid., p. 136 (tr. p. 99). A comprehensive critical overview of the anti-humanist tendency in the era of French philosophy referred to by Levinas can be found in Derrida's *Marges de la philosophie* (Paris: Éditions de Minuit, 1972), pp. 131–64. *Margins of Philosophy*, Alan Bass, trans. (Chicago: University of Chicago Press, 1982), pp. 111–36. The relevant piece is entitled 'The Ends of Man' and was first presented at a conference on philosophy and anthropology in New York in 1968.
28. *HS*, p. 138 (tr. p. 100, slightly emended).
29. Ibid., p. 138 (tr. p. 101).
30. *TI*, pp. 181–2 (tr. pp. 206–7).
31. *HS*, p. 148 (tr. p. 108).
32. *TI*, p. 138 (tr. p. 164).
33. *Philosophie als strenge Wissenschaft* (Frankfurt: Vittorio Klostermann, 1981), p. 43. 'Philosophy as a Rigorous Science', *Phenomenology and the Crisis of Philosophy*, Quentin Lauer, trans. (New York: Harper and Row, 1965), p. 116.
34. *HS*, p. 155 (tr. pp. 114–15).
35. Ibid., p. 155 (tr. p. 115).
36. Ibid., pp. 140 (tr. p. 103).
37. *SNS*, p. 202 (tr. p. 160).
38. *PP*, p. 415 (tr. p. 361).
39. *La Structure du comportement* (Paris: Presses Universitaires de France, 1942), p. 195. *The Structure of Behaviour*, Alden L. Fisher, trans. (Boston: The Beacon Press, 1963), pp. 180–1.
40. Ibid., pp. 183–4 (tr. pp. 169–70).
41. *PP*, pp. 67–9, 406 (tr. pp. 55–7, 354).
42. Ibid., p. 99 (tr. p. 83). If Merleau-Ponty is clear that early and anonymous existence cannot be equated with impersonal life, and need not involve an indifference to the drama of the personal or potentially personal in human life, Levinas would be within his rights in arguing that it should not. There is admittedly one place in *Phenomenology*

of Perception where the explication of the sensible structure of touching and being-touched reads *as if* Merleau-Ponty is indifferent to the aforementioned drama, since our bodies are 'two sides of one and the same phenomenon, and the anonymous existence of which my body is the ever-renewed trace henceforth inhabits both bodies simultaneously'. Ibid., p. 406 (tr. p. 354). Yet Merleau-Ponty immediately appends the remark that, of itself, the structure of sensibility makes only for another living being, not for an individually human life. He goes on to state that the Other and myself as beings in the world are concrete bearers of a double anonymity, anonymous as absolutely individual and as absolutely general. In his last and unfinished work he continues to hold that the anonymity of the flesh of sensibility is ineliminably singular in each instance, in addition to being a dimension and a universal. See *PP*, p. 512 (tr. p. 448) and *Le visible et l'invisible, suivi de notes de travail*, Claude Lefort, ed. (Paris: Éditions Gallimard, 1964), pp. 187–8. *The Visible and the Invisible, followed by Working Notes*, Alphonso Lingis, trans. (Evanston: Northwestern University Press, 1968), p. 142. Henceforth *VI*.

43. *PP*, p. 99 (tr. p. 84).
44. Ibid., p. 418 (tr. p. 364, emended).
45. Ibid., p. 100 (tr. p. 85).
46. *SNS*, pp. 67–8 (tr. p. 54).
47. *PP*, p. 172 (tr. p. 147).
48. Ibid., p. 160 (tr. p. 137).
49. Ibid., p. 97 (tr. p. 82).
50. Ibid., pp. 228, 121–2 (tr. pp. 196, 104–5).
51. Ibid., p. 101 (tr. p. 85).
52. Ibid., p. 407 (tr. p. 355).
53. *TI*, p. 39 (tr. p. 67).
54. 'Alterity and the Paradox of Being.' In Galen A. Johnson and Michael B. Smith, eds, *Ontology and Alterity in Merleau-Ponty* (Evanston; Northwestern University Press, 1990), pp. 103–4. Henceforth Froman.
55. Jacques Derrida, *L'écriture et la différence* (Paris: Seuil, 1967), pp. 183–4. *Writing and Difference*, Alan Bass, trans. (Chicago: University of Chicago Press, 1978), pp. 124–5. Henceforth Derrida.
56. Ibid., p. 185 (tr. p. 126).
57. Froman, p. 105.
58. *VI*, p. 111 (tr. p. 79).
59. *Husserliana 1. Cartesianische Meditationen und Pariser Vorträge*, Stephen Strasser, ed. (The Hague: Martinus Nijhoff, 1963, 2nd ed.), p. 139. Trans. Dorion Cairns, *Cartesian Meditations* (The Hague: Martinus Nijhoff, 1960), p. 109.
60. Ibid., p. 153 (tr. p. 124).
61. Derrida, p. 183 (tr. pp. 124–5).
62. *PP*, pp. vi–vii, 415 (tr. pp. xii, 361).
63. Ibid., p. 409 (tr. p. 356).
64. *Pensées*, 323 (Paris: Éditions Garnier Frères, 1964), pp. 157–8. *Thoughts*, J. M. Cohen, trans. (Westport: Greenwood Press, 1978), pp. 111–12.
65. *Le primat de la perception et ses conséquences philosophiques* (Lagrasse: Éditions Verdier, 1996), pp. 70–1, 90. *The Primacy of Perception and Other Essays*, James M. Edie, trans. (Evanston, I: Northwestern University Press, 1964), pp. 26–7, p. 35.
66. *PP*, p. 434 (tr. p. 378, emended).

67. *VI*, pp. 26-27 (tr. pp. 10–11).
68. *AE*, pp. 64–7, 78–81 (tr. pp. 37–8, pp. 45–8). See also *TI*, pp. 237–8 (tr. p. 260). According to Michael Yeo, Merleau-Ponty's conception of the gestural and linguistic expressivity of the Other itself lays the ground for an ethics of Alterity. See 'Perceiving/Reading the Other: Ethical Dimensions' in Thomas W. Busch and Shaun Gallagher, eds., *Merleau-Ponty, Hermeneutics and Postmodernism* (Stony Brook, NY: State University of New York Press, 1992), pp. 37–52. It can be noted that Merleau-Ponty draws a distinction between 'speaking speech' (*parole parlante*) and 'spoken speech' (*parole parlée*) that not only reveals the Other as my teacher, but enriches the world of shared as well as shareable meanings that manifest human creativity. *PP*, p. 214, p. 226, p. 229 (tr. p. 184, p. 194, pp. 196–7).
69. 'La trace de l'autre' in *En découvrant l'existence avec Husserl et Heidegger* (Paris: Librairie Vrin, 1967, 2nd ed.), pp. 199–200. 'The Trace of the Other', Mark C. Taylor, ed., Alphonso Lingis, trans. *Deconstruction in Context: Literature and Philosophy* (Chicago: University of Chicago Press, 1986), pp. 356–7. It should be noted that Levinas locates this trace in the very structure of temporal awareness, anterior to and behind the living present of consciousness. Merleau-Ponty does so too, though his emphasis is on pre-linguistic experiences in early life in which self and Other have not yet been identified and by the same token distinguished.
70. *PP*, p. 294 (tr. p. 254).
71. Ibid., p. 404 (tr. p. 352).
72. Ibid., p. 253 (tr. p. 219).
73. Ibid., p. 280 (tr. p. 242).
74. *VI*, p. 57 (tr. p. 35).
75. *PP*, p. 495 (tr. p. 433).
76. Ibid., pp. 409–10 (tr. p. 357).
77. Ibid., pp. 500, 501 (tr. p. 438, p. 439).
78. *AE*, pp. 109–10, 115 (tr. p. 87, p. 90).
79. *PP*, p. 581 (tr. p. 454).
80. Ibid., pp. 517–18 (tr. pp. 453–4).
81. *Soi-même comme un autre* (Paris: Éditions du Seuil, 1990), p. 221, p. 409. *Oneself as Another*, Kathleen Blamey, trans. (Chicago and London: University of Chicago Press, 1992), p. 189, p. 355. Henceforth Ricoeur.
82. Ibid., pp. 221–2, 226 (tr. p. 189, p. 193).
83. *AE*, p. 190 (tr. p. 149); Ricoeur, p. 391 (tr. p. 339).
84. Ricoeur, p. 195, p. 391 (tr. p. 165, p. 339). It can be observed that Levinas is careful not to pass over the cognitive domain of ethics and politics completely, and this is seen in his notion of the third person, the Other of the Other to whom he or she as well as I myself am responsible. At this public level we have to deal with competing claims, and formulate principles of living together fairly whilst maximising the good. In such a domain I must also be concerned with what is good for me, since I am a further Other for Others. *AE*, pp. 164–5, 200–7 (tr. p. 128, pp. 157–62). What is not admitted, so far as I am aware, is the necessity of regard, self-esteem and constancy in responding to the originary call of the Other.
85. Ricoeur, p. 149, p. 198, p. 311, p. 393 (tr. p. 124, p. 168, p. 267, p. 341).
86. *PP*, p. 193 (tr. p. 165).
87. Ricoeur, p. 391 (tr. p. 339, slightly emended).
88. *Pilote de guerre* (Paris: Éditions Gallimard, 1942), p. 171, p. 174, p. 176. Quoted in *PP*, p. 520 (tr. p. 456, slightly emended).

Eric Voegelin's Use of Metaphor

GLENN HUGHES

> *Man be my metaphor.*
> Dylan Thomas

The importance of metaphors to Voegelin's philosophy of human existence and history may be appreciated by considering certain key symbols upon which his philosophy – especially his mature philosophy – relies. I am using the term 'symbol' here in the way that Voegelin himself does; and that usage requires its own preliminary comment.

The word 'symbol' is central to Voegelin's explication of human self-understanding, as it signifies for him all-important 'language phenomena' through which we represent our understanding of realities in which we existentially participate. Occasionally, to make his use of the term clear, Voegelin contrasts the terms 'symbol' and 'concept'. 'I distinguish concepts,' he writes, 'as definitional formulations referring to objects that have existence in space and time'.[1] 'Symbols', on the other hand, in his usage are formulations referring to all elements, aspects, structures, or dimensions of reality in which humans are subjectively or existentially *involved*. This makes symbols, of course, an extremely broad category. There are symbols pertaining to interpersonal relations, such as *love* and *justice*; to social institutional order, such as *democracy* and *autocracy*; to modes of self-interpretation, such as *myth* and *philosophy*; and to the encompassing processes or movements in which we find ourselves ontologically involved, such as *history*, or *being*, or *the whole*. Symbols in Voegelin's sense embrace both the earliest petroglyphs expressing the basic structure of the cosmos and the most recent articulations of the 'mathematical form of the universe'.[2] To put it simply: symbols for Voegelin are any images, signs, words, phrases, or stories that articulate elements in the human experience of *participation* in reality. 'Symbols,' as he writes, 'are the language phenomena engendered by the process of participatory experience.'[3]

In Voegelin's philosophy, many of the most important symbols are those expressing insights into the basic structure of human consciousness, into the nature of history, and into the character of reality as a whole. In Voegelin's mature work, with respect to the structure of human consciousness, we find his analyses relying heavily on such symbols as *participation, questioning unrest,* the *tension toward the ground of being,* the *flux of presence, intentionality* and *luminosity,* and, of course, the *in-between* (or *metaxy*). With respect to the nature of history, we encounter such key symbols as the *leaps in being* and *lines of meaning* in history. And with regard to reality as a whole, crucial symbols include the *cosmos, immanence* and *transcendence,* the *primordial community of being* (with its four 'partners'), *the ground of being,* and *the Beyond* – not to mention the symbols *reality* and *being* themselves. The referential meaning of each of these major symbols is intimately connected with that of all the others, since consciousness, existence, history and being can only be explicated in terms of their interrelations; and one of Voegelin's principal philosophical aims has been to develop a sophisticated network, or web, or constellation, of evocative symbols that would both be internally coherent and occasion in the reader helpful, perhaps therapeutic, insights into fundamental truths about the human situation.

Many commentators on Voegelin have discussed his use of the term 'symbol', and much has been written about the important symbols listed above, as well as about others central to his work such as *cosmion, linguistic indices,* the *poles of existential tension, thing-reality* and *It-reality, reflective distance* and *meditative exegesis*. But as far as I know, no one has written about the metaphoric character of some of his key philosophical symbols. This is not too surprising, because most of Voegelin's key philosophical symbols do not have a predominantly metaphorical function – symbols such as *participation, reality* and *being*, while intrinsically ambiguous or analogical in character,[4] are not metaphors – and also because Voegelin himself lays no stress on the meaning and importance of metaphor in philosophical explication, mentioning the topic only a few times. Those few times, though, are telling – as when he refers to the 'spatial metaphor' of the symbol of the 'between', a symbol that becomes all-important for his mature philosophy of existence.[5] It will be worthwhile, I believe, to consider Voegelin's reliance on metaphor for a few of his work's most important symbols, as doing so will illuminate some elementary truths about both existence and philosophy, while clarifying an important feature of Voegelin's philosophical language.

METAPHOR

It will be best to begin by clarifying what a metaphor is.

A metaphor is a species of analogy. *Analogy*, though originating as a term denoting an equality of ratio in ancient Greek mathematics, in the wide connotations of contemporary usage refers quite generally to a *similarity of characteristics or structural relationships* between different things, situations, persons, attitudes, actions, language or themes. Resemblance, or parallelism, is the core meaning of analogy, whether the context of analogical thinking is mathematical, scientific, linguistic, rhetorical, literary or theological. Mathematically, an analogy of ratio could be expressed in the form: as the numerical value of c is to d, so the numerical value of x is to y. In the world of literary criticism, one can state that the roles of Leopold Bloom, Stephen Dedalus and Molly Bloom in James Joyce's *Ulysses* are analogous to those of Ulysses, Telemachus and Penelope in *The Odyssey* of Homer. In Christian theology, the idea of the analogy of being (*analogia entis*) serves to affirm an indirect understanding of divine reality through the identification of likenesses of proportionality (or attribution) between imperfect, finite beings, on the one hand, and transcendent, perfect being, on the other. In the commonsense realm of dramatic living, one could say that one person's struggle to resist overeating is analogous to another's struggle to resist being captious or contradictory in discussion. Finally, in the very broadest sense of the term's application, analogies include both synonyms and precise translations between languages: *catastrophe* and *disaster* are thus analogues, as are the English word *dog* and the French word *chien*.

The term *metaphor* refers to a distinctive type of analogy, one that goes beyond mere parallelism. A metaphor is a figure of speech that illuminates or expands the meaning of something by *transferring or applying to it* the properties of something else that, literally understood, has an ontological form different from it.[6] It is the result of a certain type of 'focused analogical thinking' that issues in a claim – stated, implied or insinuated – that 'x is y,' while it yet remains clearly understood that 'x is not y', for the principal purpose of augmenting the connotative meanings of 'x'.[7] No claim is metaphorical unless it is true both that 'x is not y' and that the explicit or implicit claim that 'x is y' clarifies our understanding of 'x' through greater or lesser suggestive power. Frequently, both of the two terms of a metaphor, the 'x' and the 'y' – the 'subject' and the 'modifier' (or, in the terminology made common by I. A. Richards, the 'tenor' and the 'vehicle') – belong to the world of sense-perception or sense-based experience ('your eyes are jewels'). Not infrequently, though, the subject of a metaphor is something abstract or spiritual, and the modifier is imaginatively concrete ('despair is a whirlpool'), which allows something not easily explained to be clarified by its identification with a readily apprehensible image. Finally, less commonly, the subject is a concrete reality that is clarified by its identification with an abstract reality ('your eyes are despair'). The result, in all cases, is the creation of a composite 'focal object', a 'meta-image', grasped 'in an instant of time', whose power to reveal or augment a subject's meaning or implications derives from the grammatical and imaginative 'erasure' of the difference, or distance, between the two parts of the metaphor.[8]

To illustrate, let us consider four very simple metaphorical figures, all taken from the world of poetry:

> The music is a house of glass standing on a slope
> Tomas Tranströmer, 'Allegro'[9]

> ROMEO: ... what light through yonder window breaks?
> It is the east, and Juliet is the sun.
> Shakespeare, *Romeo and Juliet*, II, 2

> ... the mill of the mind
> Consuming its rag and bone.
> W. B. Yeats, 'An Acre of Grass'[10]

> Time is the fire in which we burn.
> Delmore Schwartz, 'Calmly We Walk Through This April's Day'[11]

In the first two examples, sensorily perceived objects are identified with other sensorily perceived objects. A specific piece of music is, surprisingly, identified with a house of glass standing on a slope, which to the metaphorically inclined mind clarifies in a peculiar but highly evocative way some aspects of the nature and meaning of this musical piece. It also – and this is an important point to which we will return – identifies or unites two distinct ontological forms in such a way that we are startled with recognition of how the 'patterns of meaning in the world intersect and echo one another'.[12] In the second example, familiar to everyone, the beloved Juliet, seen at her lit bedroom window at night, is identified by Romeo with the sun rising in the east. Romeo identifies the form of Juliet's person and presence with the central object of brilliance in the celestial universe, and her appearance with the emergence of day from night. The metaphor – if we can appreciate it despite overfamiliarity with these lines of poetry – entails a wonderfully hyperbolical expansion of Juliet's meaning for Romeo through the imaginative fusing of her being with the most magnificent and important object in nature.

The third and fourth metaphors use as modifiers experiences of concretely imaginable objects to reveal meaningful aspects of two intrinsically abstract subjects: 'mind' and 'time'. Yeats identifies the mind with a mill that, as it turns, grinds and consumes the base materials of rags and bones so as to produce a finer, usable substance – which suggests a range of significant insights into, and questions about, mental activity. Delmore Schwartz's metaphor pushes our thought in a yet more richly existential direction by using the concrete image of a fire that burns, consuming, to enlarge our understanding and feelings about the nature of time and our participation in it. Both of these latter two metaphors manifest the suggestive power of – and the human need for – figurative imagery drawn from sense-based experiences of objects in the world to augment and refine our understanding of realities that are 1) intrinsically abstract or spiritual, 2) central to human existence, and 3) not fully knowable (what *is* 'mind?' what *is* 'time?'). This point will be central to our later, most important, observations.

Two general features of metaphor ought to be discussed before we turn attention to the varieties of metaphor pertinent to our focus on some of Voegelin's key symbols.

The first of these concerns the syntax and semantics of metaphor – its form of linguistic construction, and the type of meaning it radiates. A metaphor, in stating or implying that 'x is y' while taking it as given that 'x is not y', has the structure of paradox. This is a form of paradox we readily embrace, although we know perfectly well that a piece of music is not a glass house and that Juliet is not the sun. We embrace it because it does not offend our sense of the overall structure of meaning in reality, which includes an awareness of two facts: first, that of the harmonious correspondence, and interpenetration, of significant forms in the world; and second, more profoundly, of the *ultimate oneness* of all distinct participants in reality. Unlike a purely logical paradox – such as the statement 'an apple is not an apple' – the paradox of metaphor always hints at the truth of the inescapable *ontological* paradox that, on the one hand, there is a vast multiplicity of objects, persons, events, times, places and acts in reality and that, on the other hand, as all these are parts of the one Being, or Is-ness, of reality, everything *is* finally one with everything else. Recognition of this ontological paradox of the 'identity of identity and difference', as Hegel called it, is a first principle of a sound philosophical understanding of the structure of reality, so is best described, not as illogical, but (to use a term of Northrop Frye) 'counterlogical' – or, perhaps, supralogical.[13] And since all metaphors echo this supralogical truth, we embrace them not only for their often-surprising disclosure of formal and emotional correspondences, and for their revelatory expansion of our awareness of the meaning of the metaphor's subject, the 'x', but for their implicit affirmation and reminder of the consubstantiality of all things – of the fact that we live in a *cosmos* whose underlying oneness is so easily forgotten.

Second, the power of a metaphor to move and enlighten us grows in the measure to which its subject and modifier (or, in complex or extended metaphors, the combinations of these) refer to or touch on existentially significant experiences – objects or events or components in our lives that are especially charged with meaningfulness. Romeo's ecstatic metaphor arising from romantic love, '... and Juliet is the sun', can call up in us – assuming we are in the mood, and sympathetically taking part in Romeo's state of mind – a host of feelings that pertain to crucial experiences in the drama of human living, feelings both recognisable and inchoate that reach back into childhood and are associated with wonder, love, beauty and self-transcendence, in such a way that the metaphor *as an integrated image* 'carries us away, embodies us in itself, and moves us deeply as we surrender ourselves to it'.[14] The more the integrated image of a metaphor enables us to undergo our own emotional and intellectual integration of diffuse experiences of profound existential importance, the more psychic resonance it will have, and the more illumination it will throw on (1) internal relations in reality; (2) existential truths and possibilities; and (3) the paradox-inflected ways in which language can express the otherwise inexpressible.

EXISTENTIAL METAPHORS

Among the most compelling and illuminating metaphors are those in which the 'subject' is either the nature of human existence as a whole, or some aspect of reality belonging to existence as a whole. I will call these 'existential metaphors'.[15]

Of the four metaphors quoted above, 'Time is the fire in which we burn' is an obvious existential metaphor, since its subject concerns the very nature of existence as an immersion in temporality. The metaphor's modifier, identifying time as a fire constantly consuming us, directs our attention to an essential fact of our being in a way that heightens our emotional and intellectual apprehension of it. Although conscious existence is not merely bodily-based being in time, it *is* bodily-based being, and this bodily-founded existence will exist in time (burning with desire, longing, inquiry, boredom, suffering, joy, hope, despair) until it is consumed away. The metaphor invites us to pay close attention to what existence is and entails – as it also evokes the existential paradox of participation, in that we remain separate individuals even as we are all identical in both our universal involvement in temporality and in our universal participation in the ground of temporality. Indirectly, it also invites us to reflect on whether there is more to existence than existence in time; whether there is a reality beyond time, a transcendent reality, in which we also participate; but that question remains in the background, mute.

Let us look at a more familiar example of existential metaphor, one that has often been used by dramatists, poets, novelists, historians, theologians and philosophers: the identification of conscious existence with being an actor in a drama. Shakespeare's is the most famous articulation:

> All the world's a stage,
> And all the men and women merely players;
> They have their exits and their entrances,
> And one man in his time plays many parts ...
> *As You Like It*, II, vii

Voegelin, of course, employs this metaphor with careful deliberateness at the start of his Introduction to his five-volume magnum opus *Order and History*. He argues for the appropriateness of the metaphor by elaborating how a number of the elements involved in playing a part in a drama onstage are illuminative of what it is, and what it feels like, to exist as a human being. But he also cautions that the metaphor of acting in a play (a metaphor not only 'justified', he explains, but 'perhaps even *necessary*', since what it reveals about existence is so important to philosophical self-understanding) 'may lead astray' if it is taken too literally. For, in acting a part in a written drama, one knows who one is as a character, what one is going to say and choose to do, what the outcome will be, and what the play as a whole is about. But in human existence, '[b]oth the play and the role are unknown ... [so that] the actor does not know with certainty who he himself is.' Furthermore, in a play, an actor's performance is temporary; it is a partial and brief engagement of the self within a larger life. But in the drama of humanity every person is necessarily 'engaged with the whole of his existence', and must remain at every moment an actor 'playing a part in the drama of being and, through the brute fact of his existence, committed to play it without knowing what it is'.[16]

Both the full meaning of the human drama and the precise meaning of one's own role in it cannot be known with any certainty for a number of reasons. One is that the future development of both personal life and history must remain unknown because of the unknowable future uses of freedom. Another is that human existence is a participation *within* reality, and enjoys only a 'perspective of participation', with no access to a 'vantage point outside existence from which its meaning [as a whole, and thus the meaning of one's role in it] can be viewed'. And finally – as Voegelin explains repeatedly in his writings – there is the fact that the human drama originates in, and unfolds as a story only as ontologically involved in, a *transcendent* realm of reality whose nature and purposes are mysterious to us. For all of these reasons, there is a permanent 'blind spot at the centre of all human knowledge about man'. However much we may learn, we will remain ignorant about 'the decisive core of existence' – that is, about why, exactly, we exist, and what *ultimate* purposes our individual or communal struggles, inquiries, passions and achievements serve.[17]

Use of existential metaphors, as indicated in the examples from Schwartz and Shakespeare above, need not address the topic of the transcendent basis of the human drama. But if an existential metaphor is meant to help in the elucidation of an overarching philosophy of human existence – or if, in the literary realm, a poet or novelist uses existential metaphors with the aim of illuminating the larger, *spiritual* meaning of existence – then the effort will be successful only if such metaphors contain imagery suggestive of, or are contextualised by acknowledgment of, the mystery of transcendent reality.

Literary examples manifesting recognition of this fact from the world of poetry, both western and Eastern, are easy to come by. In English letters, the poems of John Donne, George Herbert, Emily Dickinson and Gerard Manley Hopkins, to name just a few obvious figures, are rich in existential metaphors whose imagery guides attention to the supervening transcendent context of life in the world. Emily Dickinson writes:

> The Infinite a sudden Guest
> Has been assumed to be –
> But how can that stupendous come
> Which never went away?[18]

In Chinese and Japanese poetry influenced by Buddhism, we find a long tradition of the use of metaphors to illuminate both (1) the nature of existence as a quest for the eternal and (2) the transcendent realm of meaning as the true essence of all consciousness and reality. Here is an example from the T'ang poet Han Shan (ca. eighth–ninth century AD), whose name, which literally translates as 'Cold Mountain', both refers to the hard-to-reach mountain retreat of his retirement and serves as a metaphor for his spiritual quest and its attainments:

> I climb the road to Cold Mountain,
> The road to Cold Mountain that never ends ...
> Moss is slippery, though no rain has fallen;
> Pines sigh, but it isn't the wind.
> Who can break from the snares of the world
> And sit with me among the white clouds?[19]

Existential metaphors that focus our attention on the *full meaning* of existence, then, cannot dispense with reference to, or evocation of, transcendence. And one consequence of this is that when a person is obtuse or resistant to the fact of transcendent mystery, it may reveal itself in an obtuseness or resistance to the use of existential metaphors in a manner meant to enhance awareness of the transcendent context of the human situation – whether such metaphors are encountered in literature, philosophy, religious symbols, theology, or art. Let me illustrate this point with a personal anecdote.

I own a large, sumi-style ink painting of a Japanese ink pot, made and sold to me many years ago by a poet-painter friend. Calligraphed near the ink-pot, in two short lines, is the text: 'Two poets –/One ink bottle.' The piece was framed and hanging on a wall of my home some thirty years ago when a middle-aged screenwriter with whom I was working briefly stopped by on an errand. He looked at the painting and, after a reflective moment, said in reference to its text: 'What the hell is that supposed to mean?' He was genuinely puzzled, though not really seeking an explanation.

The problem for my acquaintance was that the short poem of the text with its ink-bottle illustration presented an existential metaphor, and he was not accustomed to recognising or responding to existential metaphors. To a philosophical or literary mind – especially one familiar with the Zen Buddhist tradition from which the ink painting with its text is derived – the gist of the metaphor is obvious: just as two poets draw ink for their writing from the same ink-bottle, so they both draw inspiration, poetry, and – most fundamentally – existence itself from a single ontological origin, the common source of persons and things. The phrase 'Two poets–/One ink bottle' metaphorically articulates an essential truth about human existence: that all conscious and creative existences are a *participation* in the one, shared ground of being, and that all commonalities of feeling and insight, activity and vocation, are rooted in an even more elemental ontological identity. And what exactly is this shared ground of being for which the ink bottle (or ink) is a metaphor? It is a subject that is, in itself, an unnameable mystery, beyond direct knowledge or expression – it is the mystery of transcendent reality. What the text actually gives us, in fact, is only the multi-part modifier (or 'vehicle') of the metaphor; the subject as such, which is the mutual participation of all persons in 'transcendence' or 'the mystery of origins', is only *alluded to* by means of a compound image drawn from the world of familiar objects, persons, actions and ideas. Such poetic allusion hints at the facts that both 1) the mystery of transcendence and 2) the precise nature of human participation in the mystery of transcendence lie beyond direct understanding or expression.

PRIMAL METAPHORS AND PHILOSOPHY

Existential metaphors that intentionally symbolise either *the ultimate basis of reality*, or *existence as participating in ultimate reality* – such as the metaphor of 'Cold Mountain' in the text above – would seem to warrant their own special term, so I will call them 'primal existential metaphors', or 'primal metaphors' for short. Given that the ultimate basis of reality is a transcendent dimension of meaning, and that existence takes its essential meaning from its conscious participation in transcendent reality, it is the proper task of primal metaphors to direct our attention to, and to guide our quest to understand our lives in relation to, the transcendence that is the common ground of all persons and things. Primal metaphors that do this (or attempt to) are common enough in poetry and other literature, and necessarily ubiquitous in the religious language of myth and scripture, commentary and theology, devotion and prayer. But philosophical writing, too, cannot do without the use of such primal metaphors, insofar as a philosopher is open to the fullness of reality as grounded in a transcendent realm of meaning, and is engaged in the attempt to explicate the elementary facts of the human situation and the most far-reaching questions and challenges with which conscious existence is faced.

One example of such a primal metaphor in philosophy would be Karl Jaspers' image of 'the Encompassing', a metaphor taken from the realm of spatial experience which he uses to enable or enhance our apprehension of that 'which never appears as an *object* in experience' but of which we are aware as 'the most extreme, self-supporting ground of Being, whether it is Being in itself, or Being as it is for us'.[20] As Jaspers' definition indicates, the metaphor of 'the Encompassing' is meant to assist us in appreciating the inescapably present and yet non-contingent character of transcendence: 'the most extreme, self-supporting ground of Being'. Embedded in this definition we may notice a *second* metaphor for transcendent reality, whose character as a metaphor could slip past us if we are habituated to a certain style of philosophical language: the image of the 'ground' of Being. 'Ground' is an image taken from our experience of the physical world; and a philosopher such as Max Scheler, who also employs it, is perfectly aware of the metaphorical status of the term when he writes that 'the centre' from which a human being is able to understand the realities of body, psyche and spatiotemporal world cannot *itself* 'be located in space or in time: it can only be located in the highest Ground of Being itself'.[21] And Voegelin, too, of course, relies consistently on the metaphor of 'the ground of being' to refer to the transcendent basis of existence and world (perhaps with Scheler's work as a major influence).

All three philosophers – Jaspers, Scheler and Voegelin – understand that the primal metaphors they use to signify transcendent reality may be misconstrued by being taken literally. Voegelin is continually warning his readers that 'the ground' is not to be taken as 'a spatially distant thing' or as a 'datum of experience ... given in the manner of an object of the external world', but is merely an image helpfully suggestive of a transcendent reality 'that incomprehensibly lies beyond all that we experience of it in [existential] participation.'[22] All three are satisfied to rely on such metaphors, nevertheless, because they agree that their semantic paradoxicality (transcendence is an 'encompassing' reality/transcendence has no kind of spatially encompassing quality; transcendence is a 'ground'/transcendence is nothing like a spatial ground) is appropriate, and *seemly*, since it reflects two facts: (1) consciousness's awareness of the oneness of the *cosmos* and the ontological paradox of participatory existence (each existence is consubstantial with all reality in its identity with transcendent Being/each existence is a distinct, individual 'partner' in Being, founded in a body located in space and time), and (2) the usefulness, for a philosophy that explicates with sufficient probity and completeness the truth of the human situation, to signify the unknown of ultimate, transcendent reality through the metaphorical use of images and symbols drawn from familiar experiences.

Not all philosophers are in agreement about such use of metaphors. We find in the works of some philosophers, as with Hegel's references to transcendent reality as 'Absolute Idea', or with Martin Buber's description of transcendent being as 'the eternal Thou', terms used to signify the transcendent mystery that are indeed *analogical* but not, strictly speaking, metaphorical: that is, there is no *transfer* to the subject (i.e. transcendence) of the properties of something *formally* different from it, but rather an affirmation that there is an analogical correspondence of form between transcendence (Absolute Idea, or Absolute Act of Understanding; eternal Thou) and an ontological form familiar from everyday experience (a human idea, or act of understanding; a human Thou). Again, other philosophers – such as Schopenhauer and (the early) Wittgenstein – although they would not deny the reality of the mystery of transcendence or the ground of being, have claimed that philosophy simply has no business attempting to signify it, since to ask the question of what it is cannot be answered in any manner that is adequate to the communication of its ontological content – and 'whereof one cannot [adequately] speak, thereof one must be silent.'[23] And finally, there are philosophers (Holbach, Marx, Sartre) who, in their ontological accounts of human existence, deny outright that there is a transcendent dimension of reality, and would reject primal metaphors such as 'the Encompassing' or 'the Ground of Being' (in Scheler's and Voegelin's sense) as invalid and delusory.

In Voegelin's view, of course, thinkers included in this last group share a profound deficiency as philosophers insofar as they are 'closed' to the recognition and affirmation of transcendent reality, for whatever reasons. A properly responsible philosophy of existence, he would argue, must acknowledge and illuminate as far as it is possible both the structure and the significance of human existential involvement in transcendent being, and can only use either analogical symbolisms or primal metaphors to do so. Now, Voegelin's own comfortableness with the use of primal metaphors – the use of imagery drawn from experiences of spatiotemporal objects to signify transcendent reality and our human involvement in it – is noteworthy. What, we may ask, is the basis of his tolerance of, and readiness as a philosopher to rely on, primal metaphors? Before attempting to answer this, let us mention a few primal metaphors central to his mature philosophical work.

VOEGELIN AND METAPHOR

We have already mentioned that the metaphor of 'the ground of being' is Voegelin's preferred way of referring to ultimate, transcendent reality. He also consistently uses the term 'the Beyond' to signify the realm of transcendence – another spatial metaphor that, he cautions upon occasion, must not be taken in the literal sense of spatial distance: 'the Beyond is not a thing beyond the things [of the world]', but is the non-spatiotemporal origin and basis of all things, which is discovered and encountered only as an 'experienced presence' in consciousness in the course of its search for the ultimate (divine) reality 'which constitutes consciousness by reaching into it'.[24] Again, in order to symbolise the fact that human consciousness, though bodily founded in space and time, is in fact co-constituted by the transcendent reality that is the ultimate goal of its quest for meaning, and must be philosophically explicated as such, Voegelin relies on primal metaphors, including 'luminosity' and (most importantly) 'the In-Between' (or 'metaxy'). He uses the light-metaphor of 'luminosity' to signify that 'structural aspect' of consciousness in which it experiences itself, not as the subject and originating centre of its own intending operations, but as a 'predicative event' within reality, an 'event of participatory illumination', whose existence and intentional activities have been *given to it* by the 'subject' that is reality itself – whose basis and origin is the transcendent ground of being.[25] Finally, Voegelin's later philosophy may almost be said to revolve around his description of human consciousness as an 'In-Between' of immanence and transcendence. Though the term 'In-Between' is a spatial metaphor, what is intended by Voegelin is obviously not a spatial description: the term signifies 'not an empty space between immanent and transcendent objects' but consciousness's experience and understanding of itself as a (non-imaginable) reality *co-constituted* by participation in both temporal and eternal meaning, in world and divine transcendence.[26]

The question is: why is Voegelin convinced of the philosophical appropriateness and heuristic advantage of the use of such metaphors at the centre of his explication of existence and reality, while many (or most) philosophers would eschew them? What accounts for Voegelin's ease with metaphorical language in speaking of ultimate and non-imaginable realities, and his confidence that, despite the ever-present danger that readers or listeners will literalise and hypostatise such metaphoric symbols (a danger he is constantly warning about), they have an evocative precision that, in his view, cannot be bettered, and so belong at the very heart of a philosophical exegesis of the human condition?

As briefly as possible, I would like to suggest five interrelated reasons that, taken together, help to explain this feature of Voegelin's outlook and work.

First there is the fact, about which his writings and reflections leave no doubt, that from his earliest years Voegelin's development as a person was characterised by a fascination with the mysterious, the inexplicable, the 'sphere of the ulterior unknown, of the unexplored and strange, of the undefined surplus of significance and momentousness', to use a phrasing of Bernard Lonergan.[27] The roots of this fascination in character-orienting childhood memories centred on evocative images are poignantly explored in Voegelin's 'anamnetic experiments' of 1943.[28] Its mature issue was an adult mind permanently open to the recognition of transcendent mystery; intrigued by and drawn to the study of religious and philosophical expressions (both western and Eastern) of the quest for, and the experience of participation in, a mystery of transcendent ultimacy; an appreciation of the history of mysticism; and, from early in his career, a conviction that 'the philosophical problem of transcendence [is] the decisive problem of philosophy'.[29] The attraction to metaphors pertaining to transcendence, then, first of all reflects a lifelong responsiveness to all kinds of symbols capable of quickening the imagination of both child and adult to apprehensions of an ineffable but real mystery 'beyond' both experienceable world and human comprehension.

Second, Voegelin had a poet's sensitivity – not so common among philosophers – to the power of metaphorical imagery. He understood keenly its capacity to move and inspire the psyche in searching engagement with the complexities of existence, and to evoke feeling-laden recognitions of the layered depths of significance both in the drama of everyday life and in the cosmos as a whole. This sensitivity showed itself, and was nourished by, Voegelin's lifelong love of literature, about which we have plenty of biographical information, as well as the nuanced studies of or references to, in his writings and letters, works by Shakespeare, Baudelaire, Henry James, T. S. Eliot, von Doderer, Musil, Broch, Goethe, Proust, Joyce, Valéry, Wedekind, Beckett and Thomas Mann, among many others, not to mention ancient Egyptian poetry, classical Greek tragedy, and the poetry of the Bible. Literary criticism, he once said, was one of his 'permanent occupations'; and his appreciation of excellent literary style and well-turned figures of speech is reflected in the most impressive rhetorical passages of his own writing, which at their best have an equal among philosophers in the work of only a few, including Plato, Kierkegaard and Nietzsche.[30] These passages often rely, not surprisingly, on metaphorical flourishes: his description of the contemporary unification of mankind 'into a global madhouse bursting with stupendous vitality', of the 'grotesque rubble into which the image of God is broken today', of the 'intellectual mud that covers the public scene', of 'activist dreamers who want to liberate us from our imperfections by locking us up in the perfect prison of their phantasy'.[31] The power of such metaphors derive from a lifetime's study of the rhetorical modes and effects of great literature.

Third, Voegelin's readiness to rely on metaphor to express ultimacies of meaning is connected with his recognition of what he refers to as the 'equivalency of symbolisations'.[32] This is the recognition that a diversity of language symbols (and sometimes other types of symbols) can signify the same or similar experiences and insights, constituting an 'equivalency' of formulations that can be verified through the reader or listener successfully penetrating to the 'engendering experiences' from which the diverging symbolic expressions have arisen, and recognising the identity or equivalence of these experiences through allowing the symbols to 'reconstitute' these experiences in his or her own soul.[33] Appreciation of the equivalence of key symbolisations across the range of human cultures and within the world's religious and philosophical traditions became one of the foundational principles of Voegelin's philosophy of consciousness, and of his method of both interpretative exegesis and philosophical exposition. It was an appreciation that allowed Voegelin to accept such metaphors for transcendent reality as 'the Ground' and 'the Beyond' as the functional equivalents – given appropriate conditions of intention in use and interpretative reception – of such abstract symbols as 'Absolute Spirit,' 'Pure Act,' or 'That than which no greater can be thought'. It also enabled Voegelin to avoid, throughout his career, the all-too-common philosophical mistake of assuming that only one philosophical language can claim to be the 'correct' linguistic vehicle for exploring and communicating insights into the most profound realities. The issue is not whether this or that key symbol is imaginatively metaphorical or conceptually abstract, but whether or not it has the potential to communicate a sufficiently sophisticated, or differentiated, insight into the relevant truth.

Fourth, Voegelin's awareness of the evocative power and importance of metaphorical figures reflects his attention to, and deep interest in, the *developmental* aspect of consciousness, both in personal life and in human history. Both in individual consciousness and in the drama of history there is a 'primary experience of the cosmos', where the experiential emphasis falls on a sense of the oneness of reality, on the felt interwovenness of all being including mysteriously powerful ultimate or divine being.[34] In this primary experience, before the emergence of any later development of 'differentiated' experience, a mystery of transcendent (or world-incommensurable) meaning is *present* and is *felt*, but any interpretation or elucidation of it relies (and is felt to satisfactorily rely) on the resources of spatiotemporal imagination. When, however, personally or historically, a 'differentiation of consciousness' augments the primary experience through introducing conceptual recognition that ultimate reality has a world-transcendent character, symbolisations of the transcendent mystery are no longer restricted to images drawn from sense-based experiences of concrete objects.[35] But – and this is the crucial point – the 'primary experience of the cosmos' does not 'go away'; our sense of the oneness and completeness of reality remains always our *foundational* apprehension of it, underlying and making possible any 'differentiation' of its immanent and transcendent dimensions. Because this is so, and also because it is only through the power of emotionally evocative concrete images, including metaphors, that we *feel immediately and massively* our engagement with reality and the significance of our actions in the drama of our lives, 'differentiation' does not annul the appropriateness of the use of properly orientating concrete images for expressing the truth of transcendence and of existential participation in transcendence. As Bernard Lonergan has put it: The abstract terms expressing the differentiated insights of scientific or metaphysical or theological understanding will be effective in our 'concrete living' only if those insights 'can be embodied in images that release feeling and emotion and flow spontaneously into deeds no less than words'.[36] Primal metaphors such as 'the Beyond' and 'the In-Between' invite the reader to experience *a felt completeness of existential attunement* with the basic realities of our human situation, speaking as they do simultaneously to (1) our primary experience *and* (2) our differentiated experience of the wholeness of reality.

A fifth and final reason helping to explain Voegelin's use of primal metaphors is his conviction that a sound philosophy of existence must explicate the fact, and must urge the reader to remember, that human consciousness, while co-constituted by transcendence, is at all times a 'concretely embodied consciousness' incapable of transcending its immersion in the world and the limited perspective of incarnate participation.[37] Because of our ability to understand the spiritual dimension of our natures and to discover and use abstract concepts to refer to spiritual realities, including both the mind and transcendent reality itself, philosophers (and others) can be tempted to presume that such concepts give them a direct, substantive understanding of the reality conceived. In fact, transcendence – and so the nature of our participation in it – remains a mystery inaccessible to direct or substantive insight; it is a reality that we experience *only* in a 'tension' of participatory relatedness toward it, with transcendence itself '[lying] incomprehensibly beyond all that we experience of it in participation'.[38] Primal metaphors such as 'the Beyond' and 'the In-Between' (1) explicitly acknowledge transcendent reality, while (2) implicitly acknowledging, through the use of metaphor, that all understanding we have of it is both indirect and reliant upon language that is inadequate *in any form* to represent the mystery of transcendence, and so (3) work against the temptation to suppose that we can eliminate the 'blind spot' at the centre of our understanding of self and reality – reminding us, through the paradoxical 'is' and 'is not' of metaphor, that both ultimate reality and the essential meaning of existential participation in it are both known (as facts) and unknown (as to content or substance).

REALITY AND METAPHOR

There is one further facet of Voegelin's understanding of the useful place of existential and primal metaphors in philosophy that must be treated, even in so cursory an examination of the topic as this one. This is Voegelin's recognition and exposition of the fact that symbols, analogies or metaphors used by a philosopher to explicate elemental truths about reality and existence are not simply the product of the philosopher's creative imagination, since that imagination itself is a 'predicative event' within, and primordially belongs to, the comprehending reality within which it has emerged. This means that, on the one hand, the metaphor of, say, 'the Beyond' is the result of Voegelin's effort to find a true and persuasive image to signify and evoke the true nature of ultimate reality and of our human relationship to it. On the other hand, it means also that 'the Beyond' is a metaphoric symbol belonging to, and arising from, 'the reality that comprehends bodily located man' and his imagination. The metaphor, paradoxically, both 'does begin in time' (in human imagination) and 'does not begin in time' (as its ultimate origin is divine transcendence), and reflects the paradoxicality of existential participation itself, that is, the fact that it is both a separateness within and a oneness with the cosmos and its transcendent ground.[39] So, as a primal metaphor emerging from Voegelin's quest to tell an essential truth about reality, it must be seen also as, simultaneously, a product of reality's (and the transcendent ground of being's) 'movement' toward the illumination of its own truth. In Voegelin's words: the metaphor (along with other existential and primal metaphors in Voegelin's work) 'participates in the paradox of a quest that lets reality become luminous for its truth by pursuing truth as a thing intended.'[40]

This does not mean, however, that every existential or primal metaphor issuing from the creative imagination of a philosopher is appropriate and reliable – is a *true* metaphor. An existential metaphor such as that expressed by the title of the French *philosophe* La Mettrie's book, *L'Homme machine* (*Man a Machine*) (1747), or a primal metaphor that ignores transcendence and figuratively suggests that ultimate reality is something intrinsically conditioned by space and time (through the use, perhaps, of an organic metaphor, or a mechanical metaphor), distorts and misrepresents both human existence and ultimate reality. A thinker of immanentist or materialist persuasion can invent 'substitute images' to replace true images of reality, 'counterimages' or 'dream images', that imaginatively eclipse transcendence and immanentise existence.[41] In such cases, Voegelin states, the 'creatively formative force' of human imagination will have become subject to 'deformative perversion' as it relegates transcendence to 'imaginative oblivion.'[42]

But one might ask whether such 'deformed' images, since they also arise from and 'belong to' the comprehending reality in which human existence and imagination is a 'predicative event', don't equally carry the index of reality's 'self-illumination'? The answer requires making an important distinction. The deformed images or metaphors certainly emerge within reality, and can have significant personal and cultural impact; but they are *not* part of the 'movement of reality' that, through the human questing movement, 'becomes luminous *for its truth*', since their 'dream' imagery does *not* illuminate, but rather obscures, what ultimate reality truly is and what existential participation in ultimate reality truly entails. The fact is that, through the free creative use of his imagination, a person can deformatively 'out-imagine himself and out-comprehend the comprehending reality' – enacting, to a greater or lesser extent, a sort of imaginative self-excommunication from existential attunement with being. This is a phenomenon encountered all too frequently in modern philosophy, where we often find the human partner in the creative process imagining himself or herself to be 'the sole creator of truth', while the mystery of transcendence is eclipsed through imagining the ground of reality to be some kind of immanent reality that is in principle fully knowable.[43] A *true* philosophical quest, by contrast, will always enable both (1) the comprehending reality with its transcendent ground and (2) existence as a participation in the in-between of immanence and transcendence, to become articulate in appropriately truthful symbols, analogies and metaphors – or myths.

It is appropriate, as we have just done, to mention the topic of myth at the conclusion of this meditation on Voegelin's use of existential and primal metaphors. It is, after all, in the figurations of myth – as Voegelin frequently explains – that human efforts to articulate the awareness of transcendence, and of the surmised meanings or purposes of existential involvement in transcendence, inevitably find their most full and satisfying expression. Primal metaphors such as 'the Beyond' and 'the In-Between' are still only metaphors, but they are, we might say, 'proto-mythical' insofar as their imagery opens up these 'areas of reality' to the further filling in of the meaning of the 'story' of existence and reality by mythical imagination.[44] Understanding that story to have its ultimate origin in a transcendent ground of being, human discernment and imagination will express through mythic symbolisations its best surmises about why 'the Beyond' has initiated a story at all, and what purposes 'the In-Between' of existential participation in world and Beyond might have. As Voegelin writes: if we remain faithful to the human quest for meaning as far as seeking some kind of apprehension and articulation of ultimate meanings, then '[t]here is no alternative to the symbolisation of the In-Between of existence and its divine Beyond by mythical imagination.'[45]

This is to touch on a major topic in Voegelin's philosophy: his analysis of myth, both cosmological and post-cosmological, and his analyses of various myth – notably from Plato and from biblical texts – in which he discerns the movement of reality to have become most profoundly and provocatively 'luminous for its truth'. But since our concern here is restricted to Voegelin's use of existential and primal metaphors, we will conclude simply by emphasising that Voegelin's decision to employ primal metaphors at the core of his philosophy is consonant with his recognition of the unchanging human need for 'true myths' that orientate human consciousness as it attempts to understand its situation within, and to live in attunement with, the cosmos. And so we can recognise that, not unimportantly, his use of such metaphors functions as a rhetorical and ontological corrective to a widespread cultural attitude that imagines it possible to adequately describe and explicate human existence and reality without the use of either metaphorical *or* mythical language, because reality is imagined to be wholly immanent or material. It is thus not going too far to say that Voegelin's use of primal metaphors constitutes, at the scholarly level, 'a profoundly political act', since through its influence on his readers it contributes to therapeutic resistance against certain existential and social disorders emanating from 'a culture that believes truth' – including the most important truths – to be 'the exclusive property of non-metaphorical sentences'.[46]

NOTES

1. Eric Voegelin, 'Responses at the Panel Discussion of "The Beginning of the Beginning"', in Voegelin, *The Drama of Humanity and Other Miscellaneous Writings, 1939–1985*, William Petropulos and Gilbert Weiss, eds., Vol. 33 of *The Collected Works of Eric Voegelin* (Columbia: University of Missouri Press, 2004), p. 415.
2. Voegelin, 'Responses', p. 415.
3. Eric Voegelin, *Autobiographical Reflections: Revised Edition, with a Voegelin Glossary and Cumulative Index*, Ellis Sandoz, ed., Vol. 34 of *The Collected Works of Eric Voegelin* (Columbia: University of Missouri Press, 2006), p. 99.
4. See Eugene Webb, *Eric Voegelin: Philosopher of History* (Seattle: University of Washington Press, 1980), pp. 73–6.
5. Eric Voegelin, *Order and History, Volume V: In Search of Order*, Ellis Sandoz, ed., Vol. 18 of *The Collected Works of Eric Voegelin* (Columbia: University of Missouri Press, 2000), p. 30.
6. The original Greek term *metaphora* means 'transference'. See Willard R. Espy, *The Garden of Eloquence: A Rhetorical Bestiary* (New York: Harper & Row, 1983), p. 108.
7. Jan Zwicky, *Wisdom & Metaphor* (Kentville, Nova Scotia: Gaspereau Press, 2008), §5 (A). [This text has no page numbers, only section numbers that are the same on each set of facing pages. Numbers on the left-facing pages apply to text entries by the author; those on the right-facing pages mark 'corresponding' quotations from various poets, philosophers, etc. I will use the notation (A) to designate left-facing page entries and (B) to designate right-facing page entries.]
8. Michael Polanyi and Harry Prosch, *Meaning* (Chicago and London: University of Chicago Press, 1975), p. 79; Zwicky, *Wisdom & Metaphor*, §4 (A). The phrase, 'in an instant of time,' quoted without attribution by Zwicky, comes from Ezra Pound, who described the type of meta-image presented by a metaphor (though he used simply the term 'Image,' capitalised) as 'that which presents an intellectual and emotional complex in an instant of time'. Ezra Pound, 'A Few Don'ts' (1913), included in 'A Retrospect' (1918), *Literary Essays of Ezra Pound*, T. S. Eliot, ed. (London: Faber and Faber, 1954), p. 4.
9. Robert Bly, trans. and ed., *Friends, You Drank Some Darkness: Three Swedish Poets: Martinson, Ekelöf, and Tranströmer* (Boston: Beacon Press, 1975), p. 193.
10. W. B. Yeats, *Selected Poems and Two Plays*, M. L. Rosenthal, ed. (New York: Collier Books, 1966), p. 166.
11. Delmore Schwartz, *Selected Poems: Summer Knowledge* (New York: New Directions, 1967), pp. 66–7.
12. Zwicky, *Wisdom & Metaphor*, §6 (A).
13. Northrop Frye, *Myth and Metaphor: Selected Essays, 1974–1988*, Robert D. Denham, ed. (Charlottesville and London: University Press of Virginia, 1990), p. 254.
14. Polanyi and Prosch, *Meaning*, p. 79.
15. Northrop Frye uses this phrase in a somewhat different way; see *Myth and Metaphor*, p. 84, p. 226.
16. Eric Voegelin, *Order and History, Volume I: Israel and Revelation*, Maurice P. Hogan, ed., Vol. 14 of *The Collected Works of Eric Voegelin* (Columbia: University of Missouri Press, 2001), pp. 39–40 (my emphasis). Voegelin employs the metaphor elsewhere, most notably as the underlying trope of his Walter Turner Candler Lectures of 1967, 'The Drama of Humanity.' See Voegelin, 'The Drama of Humanity', *The Drama of Humanity and Other Miscellaneous Papers, 1939–1985*, pp. 174–242.

17. Ibid., p. 39, p. 40.
18. R. W. Franklin, ed., *The Poems of Emily Dickinson: Reading Edition*, (Cambridge, MA: The Belknap Press of Harvard University Press, 1999), p. 517 (poem #1344).
19. Burton Watson, trans., *Cold Mountain: 100 Poems by the T'ang poet Han-shan*, (New York: Columbia University Press, 1970), p. 58 (poem #40).
20. Karl Jaspers, *Reason and Existenz*, William Earle, trans., (New York: The Noonday Press, 1955), p. 52; for exposition of the notion, see pp. 51–76.
21. Max Scheler, *Man's Place in Nature*, Hans Meyerhoff, trans. (Boston: Beacon Press, 1961), p. 47.
22. Eric Voegelin, 'Reason: The Classic Experience', *Published Essays, 1966–1985*, Ellis Sandoz, ed., Vol. 12 of *The Collected Works of Eric Voegelin* (Baton Rouge: Louisiana State University Press, 1990), p. 271; *Israel and Revelation*, p. 39; 'What Is Political Reality?' *Anamnesis: On the Theory of History and Politics*, M. J. Hanak, trans., based on the abbreviated version originally translated by Gerhart Niemeyer, David Walsh, ed., Vol. 6 of *The Collected Works of Eric Voegelin* (Columbia: University of Missouri Press, 2002), p. 396.
23. Ludwig Wittgenstein, *Tractatus Logico-Philosophicus* (New York: Harcourt, Brace & Company, Inc., 1922), p. 189.
24. Voegelin, *In Search of Order*, p. 44; 'The Gospel and Culture', *Published Essays, 1966–1985*, p. 188.
25. Voegelin, *In Search of Order*, p. 30.
26. Voegelin, 'What Is Political Reality?', *Anamnesis*, p. 375. The conscious communion, or interpenetration, of immanence and transcendence is what Voegelin is commonly referring to when he describes consciousness or human existence as an 'in-between' (or *metaxy*, the Greek term he draws from Plato). He often expands its application to other aspects of the human situation, explaining that existence also has the 'structure of a tension' in-between imperfection and perfection, ignorance and knowledge, untruth and truth, disorder and order, and other existential 'poles' or 'indices'. The 'in-between' of immanence and transcendence remains, however, the elementary referent of the metaphor, and founds its other meanings, since 'perfection', 'knowledge', 'truth', 'order' and other positive 'poles' of the existential in-between identified by Voegelin (such as 'immortality', 'life', 'joy') point toward what is only unqualifiedly realised, or complete, or absolute, in divinely transcendent being.
27. Bernard Lonergan, *Insight: A Study of Human Understanding*, Vol. 3 of *Collected Works of Bernard Lonergan*, Frederick E. Crowe and Robert M. Doran, eds. (Toronto: University of Toronto Press, 1992), p. 556.
28. Eric Voegelin, 'Anamnesis', *Anamnesis*, pp. 84–98.
29. Eric Voegelin, from a letter to Alfred Schütz of September 17–20, 1943; published as 'Appendix to Letter 10', *Faith and Political Philosophy: The Correspondence Between Leo Strauss and Eric Voegelin, 1934–1964*, Peter Emberley and Barry Cooper, trans. and eds (University Park, PA: The Pennsylvania State University Press, 1993), p. 34.
30. Eric Voegelin, letter to Robert B. Heilman (19 December 1955), *Robert B. Heilman and Eric Voegelin: A Friendship in Letters, 1944–1984*, Charles R. Embry, ed. (Columbia: University of Missouri Press, 2004), p. 142 (Letter 57). For expansion, see Charles R. Embry, *The Philosopher and the Storyteller: Eric Voegelin and Twentieth-Century Literature* (Columbia: University of Missouri Press, 2008), pp. 13–33.
31. Eric Voegelin, 'Immortality: Experience and Symbol', *Published Essays, 1966–1985*, p. 55, p. 56; 'The Gospel and Culture', p. 178; 'Wisdom and the Magic of the Extreme: A Meditation', *Published Essays, 1966–1985*, p. 315.

32. See especially Eric Voegelin, 'Equivalences of Experience and Symbolization in History', *Published Essays, 1966–1985*, pp. 115–33.
33. Voegelin, 'Immortality', pp. 52–3.
34. On the 'primary experience of the cosmos', see Eric Voegelin, *Order and History, Volume IV: The Ecumenic Age*, Michael Franz, ed., Vol. 17 of *The Collected Works of Eric Voegelin* (Columbia: University of Missouri Press, 2000), pp. 118–28, and *Israel and Revelation*, pp. 40–50.
35. On the 'differentiation' of reality into immanent and transcendent realms, see (for one of many accounts) Voegelin, *The Ecumenic Age*, pp. 52–4.
36. Lonergan, *Insight*, p. 570.
37. Voegelin, *In Search of Order*, p. 29.
38. Voegelin, 'What Is Political Reality?', *Anamnesis*, p. 396.
39. Voegelin, *In Search of Order*, p. 42.
40. Ibid., p. 31. This *Collected Works* edition of *In Search of Order* contains a typographical error in the last word of this sentence – substituting 'tended' for 'intended' – as may be seen by comparing it with the original edition of the volume (Louisiana State University Press, 1987, p. 17) and by the expository context.
41. Voegelin, 'What Is Political Reality?', *Anamnesis*, p. 368; 'Wisdom and the Magic of the Extreme', p. 318, p. 319.
42. Voegelin, *In Search of Order*, p. 53, p. 55.
43. Ibid., p. 53; 'What is Political Realty?', *Anamnesis*, p. 369.
44. Voegelin, 'The Gospel and Culture', p. 188.
45. Ibid. Brendan Purcell, inspired by long study of Voegelin's work, extends the status of 'mythic symbolisation' as far as Paleolithic cave painting and the earliest human symbolisations of participation in the cosmos, since these evidence an awareness that 'existence isn't exhaustively and exclusively contained within the limits of time'. See Brendan Purcell, *From Big Bang to Big Mystery: Human Origins in the Light of Creation and Evolution* (Dublin: Veritas, 2011), pp. 273–75 (p. 275).
46. Zwicky, *Wisdom & Metaphor*, §84 (A).

'Leafy-with-love': Patrick Kavanagh's 'Canal Bank Walk'

JOSEPH MCCARROLL

INTRODUCTION

'Canal Bank Walk'

[1] Leafy-with-love banks and the green waters of the canal
[2] Pouring redemption for me, that I do
[3] The will of God, wallow in the habitual, the banal,
[4] Grow with nature again as before I grew.
[5] The bright stick trapped, the breeze adding a third
[6] Party to the couple kissing on an old seat,
[7] And a bird gathering materials for the nest for the Word,
[8] Eloquently new and abandoned to its delirious beat.
[9] O unworn world enrapture me, encapture me in a web
[10] Of fabulous grass and eternal voices by a beech,
[11] Feed the gaping need of my senses, give me ad lib
[12] To pray unselfconsciously with overflowing speech,
[13] For this soul needs to be honoured with a new dress woven
[14] From green and blue things and arguments that cannot be proven.

In the introduction to his anthology of Patrick Kavanagh's religious poems, Tom Stack comments:

> It is noteworthy that in Patrick Kavanagh's extant work of published poems, which numbers 253, no fewer than 138 of these include explicitly religious themes, images or allusions. This means that references to Christian faith, in one way or another, make their appearances in more than half of all his poetic writing.

The religious content of his poetry is, therefore, extensive and of considerable weight. It represents a large, remarkable and even something of a self-contained segment of Kavanagh's creative work with its own particular substance and strain.[1]

On 31 March 1955, Kavanagh was operated on for cancer and had a lung removed. During the warm days of that summer as he rested and recovered, he spent time along the banks of the Grand Canal. Two years later, from late June to October 1957, after a six-month stay in New York, he wrote eighteen poems in what he described as 'a new style'. 'Canal Bank Walk' was one of them.

In her introduction to his *Collected Poems*, Antoinette Quinn describes the new poems as follows:

> Though this poetry does not make a complete thematic or stylistic break with his previous verse, the outlook and mood are different. His 'noo pomes', as he called them, are more colourful and sensuous than usual and are utterly celebratory. Most are love poems to canal or street, country lane or cutaway bog. They are present-tense salutations, rapturously greeting the here and now or hailing the future with optimism. The style is vernacular, drawing on speech rhythms yet capable of modulating into prayer or rhapsody.[2]

THE INTERWEAVING OF KEY SOUNDS HELPS EXPRESS THE MEANING

The analysis presented here grew out of repeated reciting aloud of the poem, noticing the repetitions of different sounds and how they join together its constitutive meanings. The limited space allotted to contributions to the present volume precludes my setting out in full the cross-analysis of each sound and the way the interweaving of sounds helps knit the different meanings together, but the main sounds examined were *aw* (as in 'odd'), *ih* (as in 'will'), *ay* (as in 'say'), *er* (as in 'bird'), *oh* (as in 'flow'), *ir* (as in 'ear'), *ee* (as in 'green'), *awe* (as in 'saw'), *eh* (as in 'nest') and *oo* (as in 'blue').

THE ENCOUNTER ENGENDERING THE POEM

The poem is Kavanagh's expression of an understanding that came to him, charged with an awareness that had been 'given to him', during his time relaxing on the canal bank and remembering, reliving and reflecting on it afterwards. It is an understanding that the source of his best poetry is an encounter which has two dimensions, a horizontal dimension in time, and a vertical dimension outside time. The horizontal encounter is with a new unique moment of nature as it happens to him – which, he is aware, has never happened to anyone before and will never happen to anyone again, including him. The vertical encounter, he is aware, is also the gift of an understanding that this fresh moment of nature he is encountering is also an encounter with the Word speaking this moment of nature into being.

The self-opening required on his part to enter into this double encounter *with* the new moment of nature *and with* the Word uttering it is a receptivity, a letting-go, a simplicity, a self-immersion in the present moment, and the word Kavanagh selects to express this is 'wallow'. The will of God for him is to wallow in the habitual, that is, in these ordinary moments of nature.

The repetition of the *aw* sound in 'God' and 'wallow' suggest that the way he attunes himself to the will of God is by wallowing in the present moment with as much self-abandonment as he can, thereby leaving himself open to receiving the sense of this moment of nature as the coming forth of a new word from the Word.

The *aw* sound occurs again in the second part of the poem in the lovely flowing line that shows by its liquidity that he has been given the easy tumbling out from his heart of the words that catch what he is trying to describe.

Line 12: To pray un*consc*iously with overflowing speech

Kavanagh is trying to articulate the self-opening he has strained for and which has been given to him to enter the double encounter with the new moment of nature and with the Word singing it into being.

As the word 'wallow' expressed what he has to let himself do, simply to *be* in the present moment of nature, so now the word 'unself*consc*iously' expresses what he has achieved and been given at the end of the poem. The very thing he prays for is, in the same line, given to him, in a wondrous sound echo of what is sought, 'To pray unselfconsciously with overflowing speech'. The fluency asked for pours out in his words. This line embodies the poetic gift he has been praying for, an unforced spontaneity of expression falls from his lips as fluidly as the water flows over the lip of the lock. The recurrence of the same sound in the second syllable of 'un*consc*iously' echoes the *wall*owing that is at once a presence in the present moment of nature and an attunement to the will of *G*o*d*.[3] Kavanagh's encounter in the present moment is primarily with the Word uttering each new moment of nature perceived by him as unique, never having happened before, never to be repeated, and beheld in a unique manner by him alone. Sister Una Agnew, in her broader study of mystical elements in Kavanagh's life and work as a whole, calls those whose encounter has this quality 'nature mystics'.[4]

LINES 4 AND 12, DESIRE AND FULFILMENT, GIFT SOUGHT AND GIVEN

Line 4   G*r*ow with n*a*ture ag*ai*n as before I *g*rew.

The perfect balance of this line, a 3 + 2 beat hinged around 'ag*ai*n', marks it out, together with line 12, as the key to the poem's meaning and purpose, setting out the purpose, prayer and hope that animate 'Canal Bank Walk'. It is a line that grows on you with repetition.

The first part of the line expresses the longing for what he had before while the second part recalls it. The *gr* in 'grow' at the start of the line is balanced by the *gr* in 'grew', the last word, and they balance on the midpoint of the *g* in 'again'. This suggests what the lines say – he is asking for the heightened poetic gift he had before. This is further emphasised by the repetition of the *ay* sound in 'n*a*ture' and in 'ag*ai*n' immediately after it. In the poem itself, the grace of growing is granted.

The *ay* sound joins the g*a*ping need of the senses in line 11 to the resolution to grow with n*a*ture ag*ai*n in line 4 and the desire to '*pray* unselfconsciously with overflowing speech in line 12. As his senses' thrill to the beauty of the world, his soul bursts into the 'ad lib' 'unselfconscious' 'overflowing speech' that as a poet is his characteristic vision, spirituality and gift, and his special attunement with 'the Word'.

Line 4 pairs with line 12 as desire and fulfilment, as gift sought and given. Line 4 has a short clipped feel about it, perhaps suggestive of his anxiety about the recurring difficulty and unflowing quality of his poetry and his poetic sensibility when the gift is not being given, while in contrast line 12 has an expansive serene super-abundant quality suggestive of the very qualities he is praying for.

Line 4 expresses Kavanagh's hope that he will recover the poetic flow that he had before, but even more, that he will recover the experience that was the source of this poetic inspiration, namely, the gift of perceiving the present moment of nature he is beholding as a new word being uttered by the transcendent Word. This is the intuition he previously had, and he recognises that it has been and continues to be the source of his finest poetry.

The programmatic statement in line 3, that the way to achieve this intuition is to wallow in the habitual, the banal, has two aspects to it. The *first*, I'd guess, is an ascetic disengagement from other poetic personae he may have been tempted towards, or encouraged to pursue, by the climate of opinion he perceived in the cultural elite around him. The *second* is a discipline of striving for receptivity to that dimension of the present moment in nature as he beholds it as a word-just-now-being-uttered-by-the-Word.

But this quality of openness to the moment of nature as a word-being-spoken-in-his-presence-by-the-Word is itself a gift from the Word to the poet, not to be taken for granted, incapable of being summoned or forced or caused to be there by the poet's efforts or longing alone. This is the meaning of the poem as a whole: Kavanagh is at once seeking and achieving, requesting and being granted, a recovery of the highest form of spiritual growth and poetic experience he has ever known, the augmentation of the soul that comes when he opens himself to exercise his highest gift as a poet, his sensibility or sensitivity to the uniqueness of each moment in nature as the coming forth of a new word of breathtaking beauty from the very creating Word itself – supercharged with significance *precisely because* it is being uttered once and for all by the Word in the presence of the poet.

Patrick Kavanagh had a gift, at once poetic and spiritual – a receptivity to the transfinite Ground of the world creating and sustaining moments of nature: Kavanagh beholds these moments with awe and this inspires and calls forth from him poems in which he sees these moments of nature as new words being breathed forth from the very creating Word which he is graced to recognise and celebrate.

'Canal Bank Walk' centres on his awareness that this receptivity is on the one hand a gift to be requested, and on the other hand something he must keep himself prepared to receive. It needs to be protected and honed and cultivated by an ascetic discipline of withdrawal from the busyness of life and social interaction so as to regain the interior calm within which this gift of openness is re-given, repaired or augmented, or reawakens and regains its acuteness of 'hearing'.

Kavanagh is receptive to 'seeing' a moment of nature as a word being uttered by the Word and beheld by the poet. But also there is the longing, the hope, the prayer that perhaps some echo or resonance or imitation of his participation in the moment may be given or inspired or crafted by him in a poem that 'catches' or 'reflects' or 'embodies' the poet's parallel exclamatory delight – 'behold-the-beauty-of-this-unique-new-word-from-the-Word' in the poet's own new word.

This is the key element of Kavanagh's poetic vision in poems like 'Ploughman', 'A Prayer for Faith', 'March', 'Primrose', 'Advent', 'Is', 'The One', 'October', 'Our Lady's Tumbler' and 'Question to Life'.

POURING

The pouring image refers to the water pouring 'Niagarously' over the canal lock, as he puts it in another canal bank poem, 'Lines Written on a Seat on the Grand Canal, Dublin'. The locks are the only places water pours dramatically on the canal, between the locks it moves sedately. The pouring at this part of the Grand Canal can be heard from Baggot Street Bridge even against the street traffic noise.

Kavanagh was a Catholic, so the pouring of water may be associated in some way with baptism, but if it is, I'd say it is only obliquely. The waters at the lock pour more vigorously and massively than the ritual pouring in Catholic Baptism.

The redemption he is referring to is the recovery of his characteristic poetic gift from the blunting or blurring of it brought about by his turning to other forms of poetry less related to this gift, such as social commentary or criticism. The image of the lock and the water powerfully gushing down from it is an image of his twofold spiritual receptivity; on the one hand, sometimes standing before an ordinary moment of nature an intuitive perception comes to him that he is beholding the gushing-forth of that moment of nature from the Unseen source; on the other hand, when this glimpse of the transparence of a moment of nature for its issuing forth from the creating Word is given to him, he experiences an exuberant, thrilling aliveness awakened in him by this very intuition of the gushing-forth of the never-before-this-moment-seen coming into being of that moment of nature from the Word. This vision is what inspires the poem.

LINE 12 – 'TO PRAY UNSELFCONSCIOUSLY WITH OVERFLOWING SPEECH'

This is an exquisitely balanced line, and together with line 3, represents the fulfilment of the poet's hope – the easy flowing perfection of the line is itself the fulfilment of his prayer for spiritual and linguistic spontaneity. The line has two phrases, 'To *pray* unself*cons*ciously' and 'with *overflowing speech*'. The main emphasis in each phrase falls on the double *ch* sound in '*unselfconsciously*' and '*speech*'. The free-flowing pouring out of language he seeks, and has now been granted, is onomatopoeically expressed in the repetition of the *oh* sound in '*overflowing*'.

The pouring of the water through the locks is also suggestive of the freedom from Beyond of the outpouring of the grace of receptivity to the quality of a moment of nature as the uttering of a new word by the Word.

The long *oh* sound is also the poet's cry of the soul to the world and the Word that utters it into being and holds it in being, an 'O' of longing of the '*soul*' that it might '*grow*' again with nature as it grew before, which is answered and fulfilled in the '*overflowing* speech' out of which the poem itself, the new dress the soul needs, is *woven*.

' ... FOR THE WORD'

The centre of the poem is the phrase '... for the Word'. It is startling. It refers back to the three habitual and banal things, the stick in the canal, the breeze ruffling the courting couple and a bird building a nest. All three, Kavanagh is saying, are doing whatever it is they are doing 'for the Word' – they are the latest phrases in the song the Word is composing and singing, and, once sung into existence, they prepare the way for the Word to sing into being the next phrases of the song which will also have the Word's characteristic qualities, 'Eloquently new and abandoned to its delirious beat.'

At the same time they are 'pouring redemption for me', for Kavanagh, and he opens himself to receive this redemption by wallowing in this outpouring of ordinary moments of nature. His redemption takes the form of a gift from the Word of a poetic participation in the Word's creative singing. His immersion in this moment of nature pouring into existence before him brings him alive in a heightened personal and poetic way, and inspires a new poem.

It is a moment of attunement of the poet's wordsong to the Word's. In that moment he is no longer 'the bright stick trapped', but 'a bird gathering materials for the nest for the Word' because the new poem, the fruit of this flow of inspiration, is also a nest for the Word. The materials he has gathered for his nest of words were the ordinary things around him, rendered incandescent for their status as words sung or spoken by the Word, and indeed the Word has come to roost in the very centre of the poem.

The phrase, 'for the Word', coming directly after the similarly structured phrase, 'for the nest', is arresting and not immediately clear in its meaning, but it is the fulcrum on which the meaning of the whole poem turns.

A BINDING THREAD OF GREEN AND BLUE WEAVING ...

The poem is a cosmion, a little world bound together by a thread of green – the leafy-with-love-banks, the green waters of the canal, the fabulous grass on the banks of the canal and the eternal voices of the wind in the green leaves of the beech trees. In this it mirrors the little world of the canal bank walk itself. The leaves overhead in summer turn the canal bank into a living canopy making the canal bank walk a thin linear world of its own, a world in miniature with its own characteristic colours – green, blue and white light coming through the trees and reflected on the sometimes peaty brown, sometimes murky green waters flickering under the wind, and its own characteristic sound, the shushing and sussing of the wind in the leaves and reeds and the lapping of the waters.

This green thread is woven together with others to yield the final image of the poem, the new garment for the soul woven of green and blue things. The foundation for the garment image is the experience we have when we become familiar with an area of nature and spend time in it on a regular basis, especially time set aside to walk, stand or sit at ease. We find ourselves relaxing and in some sense 'putting on' that little world as our senses and perception, released from practical concerns, gradually attune us to its characteristic dimensions and features, and this is experienced by us as a refreshing expansion of consciousness. To evoke the effect on us of this participation in the world, in nature, at once engaging our senses and the soul, Kavanagh chooses the image of weaving a new garment for the soul. It is a baptismal and Pauline symbol though I do not know how familiar Kavanagh was with its use in Paul (Rm 13:12 and 14, Gal 3:27, Eph 4:24 and 6:11-14, Col 3:10 and 3:12, 1 Th 5:8).

... A NEST FOR THE WORD WHICH IS AT THE SAME TIME A GARMENT FOR HIS SOUL

Kavanagh is conscious that in writing the poem he is doing the same kind of thing that the bird is doing when it is gathering the twigs to build its nest. The nest is for the bird to live in, but it is also a nest 'for the Word' as the middle phrase of the poem puts it – not only is the bird going to live in that nest, the

Word somehow is also present in it. As Kavanagh convalesces along the canal bank gathering memories, images and associations, he is already building a nest of words with them in which he himself will live in a heightened way, which will be a new garment for his soul. But, at the same time, like the bird, he is fashioning a poem in which the Word may somehow also be present. And the longing of Kavanagh's soul is that this may happen because he knows from past experience that this is the source of his most fully alive moments as a human being and his finest poetry.

The poem is at once his longing and prayer that it may be fulfilled, and also the fulfilment of the prayer. It is itself a reality, but not one whose existence is established by argument. What he has experienced and is articulating in the poem is that his openness to the gushing forth of nature from the Word in the present moment in which he is walking along the canal bank does enrapture him and flood his awareness and release a spontaneous flow of beautiful imagery that has grown into the poem itself. There is no proof for us of this other than the poem itself and the hope that our reciting of it may evoke some echo or spark of that engendering encounter.

The last line, and the poem as a whole, and indeed Kavanagh's poetic spirituality, echo Hebrews 11:1-3:

> Now faith is the assurance of things hoped for, the conviction of things not seen. For by it the men of old received divine approval. By faith we understand that the world was created by the word of God, so that what is seen was made out of things which do not appear.

'O UNWORN WORLD ENRAPTURE ME'

The word 'un*worn*' takes its more obvious meaning from the eloquent newness and delirious beat that radiate into the poem in both directions from the Word at its centre. *Backwards* from the bird building her nest, the breeze blowing around the couple on the old seat, the pouring waters, to the leafy-with-love banks, *and forwards* into the fabulous grass and eternal voices by a beech. The world is 'unworn', then, in the sense that it is fresh, never-before-seen at just this moment by anyone apart from the one who is present and paying attention – it is not yet worn out.

In a less obvious sense, the part of nature that is flowing past him at this unique moment is 'unworn' in the sense that it has never been 'put on' in the

Pauline sense by anyone because it has never happened until just now. And only he is present to experience it, to participate in it, to be moved and reborn by it, in Paul's symbol, to put it on. Kavanagh returns to this experience in the final couplet with the image of a new 'dress' that his soul needs in line 13, 'For this soul needs to be honoured with a new dress woven'. Why 'honoured'? Well, the soul is traditionally feminine. If a new dress were woven for the soul, it would be hitherto 'unworn' by her, but once put on would be 'on her'. The images of the canal waters 'pouring redemption' and the new garment woven out of green and blue things evoke Christian baptismal and nuptial resonances, and the word 'honoured' could be an echo of the promise to 'love, honour and obey' in the marriage vow.

THE LONG GREEN EE (AS IN 'GREEN') SOUND

The long *ee* sound seems to be the most important line of assonance in the poem. It is a green canal of sound that flows from the first line to the last, joining together the most passionate longing in the poem, the double prayer for inspiration for his senses and his soul in lines 9–11 and the delirious *beat* of the Word singing each new moment of nature into being in lines 7 and 8 constituting the proof without argument that these prayers have been answered.

The two '*me*'s in his prayer for delight in nature in line 9 flow into the sound of '*beech*' and on into the passionate double *ee* sound in the plea, '*Feed* the gaping *need* of my senses' in line 11, and on to the second prayer, for spontaneity of poetic utterance so he can pray with the 'overflowing *speech*' (line 12), and weave the new garment his soul '*needs*' (line 13).

And the '*leafy*' banks and '*green*' waters of the opening line, the green leaves of the '*beech*' tree that the winds *s*'s through in line 10, and the '*green*' things in the closing line, are part of the euphonic proof without argument that he has been given the gift of overflowing '*speech*' that he asked for in lines 9–12.

The whole effort of the poem is a straining by Kavanagh to 'catch' and attune himself to the beat of the creating Word, achieving thereby some measure of that attunement, as the poem itself shows, reminding me of the concluding paragraph of philosopher Eric Voegelin's monumental analysis of the work and thought of Plato:

> Plato dies at the age of eighty-one. On the evening of his death he had a Thracian girl play the flute to him. The girl could not find the

beat of the *nomos* [the eternal law that orders the cosmos]. With a movement of his finger, Plato indicated to her the Measure.[5]

KAVANAGH'S CANAL AND HERACLITUS' RIVER

One of the aphorisms of the Greek mystic philosopher Heraclitus was about rivers – we cannot step into the same river twice. Why? Because it is, and it isn't, the same river. The water we stepped into has flowed on and we cannot step into it again. And the water we step into the next time we have never stepped into before because it has only just now arrived. By the same token, we are, and we are not, the same. We also change, so in a sense it is not exactly the same person who steps into the river this time as stepped into it years earlier.[6] I see a point of similarity between this and Kavanagh's visionary intuition of each new moment of nature as a new word just freshly uttered by the Word.

Two of Heraclitus' other aphorisms express a breakthrough to a realisation of the eternal *Logos* behind the universe whose existence we intuit, without being able to understand it the way we understand things in the world; all things in the universe come to pass in accordance with this *Logos*; and there is in us a *logos* which is limitless in depth, which is the very heart of our humanity and which orients us towards the transcendent *Logos*.

> This *Logos* here, though it is eternal, men are unable to understand before they hear it as well as when they hear it first ... all things come to pass in accordance with this *Logos*. (B1)

> You could not find the limits of the soul even if you travelled every path so deep is its *logos*. (B45)

Where would Kavanagh have encountered an equivalently exalted understanding of the eternal *Logos* in accordance with which all things come to pass, and of an immeasurable depth in the human soul whose constitutive substance has some likeness to the eternal *Logos* that requires us to speak of it as a human *logos*? The answer is Sunday Mass. From the period after the Council of Trent until after the Second Vatican Council, the Prologue to the Gospel of John (Jn 1:1-5) was recited after the end of the Mass. Every regular attender at Sunday Mass would have known that the Latin word *Verbum*, translating the Greek word *Logos*, in English was the Word. The notion of the Divine Word as the one through whom all things were made would have been familiar to Kavanagh, and it is this Word that is literally at the centre of the poem.

THE EXCLAMATORY ORIGIN OF THE POEM

In getting to the heart of poems like 'Canal Bank Walk' it may be helpful to consider that such experiences sometimes find initial expression in an exclamatory way, like the 'O' that opens Line 9, and only reach final expression after a lengthy work of reflection and linguistic effort and creativity. The initial experience may overwhelm our ability to make sense of it, leaving us 'at a loss for words', prompting a lengthy and arduous struggle to stretch the words we have in new ways striving to catch, even partially, what has happened and what it may mean.

Eric Voegelin speaks of a 'pneumatic' core and a 'noetic' periphery in spiritual experiences.[7] 'Pneumatic' comes from *pneuma*, the Greek word for spirit. He says that core spiritual experiences may be ineffable, untranslatable into ordinary language, and so when we try to put them into ordinary language, we have to stretch it. 'Noetic' comes from the Greek *nous*, which means 'understanding' where the initial insight or intuition is meant, or 'reason' where the more descriptive, reflective, discursive, even argumentative, working out of the meaning of the experience is what is meant, often called *logos*. Between our participation in an encounter with the Word and our articulation of it, a development takes place from initial fumbling and faltering exclamation to considered expression.

Poems like 'Canal Bank Walk' have a participatory origin that provokes an exclamatory response from the poet. This spontaneously flows into description and reflection. Exclamation is the initial outburst of insight, wonder, amazement or appreciation. It may have all kinds of emotional tonalities depending on what has been encountered or gone through. This initial response often moves us to try to put into words what has happened and then to ponder its meaning. The poem is the poet's articulation of what has happened and of the meaning it had or has come to have for him.

The point here is not that there is some primary exclamation we can or have to work back to, but that the poem springs from an ineffable encounter and is the fruit of the poet's struggle to articulate that encounter and understand its meaning for him, and the more I explored this aspect of the poem the more equivalences from Psalms 1, 19 and 33 came to mind.

PSALMS 1, 19 AND 33 AND THE SPIRITUAL ENCOUNTER IN 'CANAL BANK WALK'

The opening word of Psalm 1 is *ashre*, an exclamatory term meaning 'O the blessings of ...' The psalm contrasts the man who listens for and lives from the words spoken by God and the men who do not. The second verse says such a man delights in the law of the Lord and meditates on it day and night. He seeks to attune himself to the words spoken by God as the law of his life and he does this by speaking these words softly to himself over and over again. The word used for 'meditates' includes not only 'remembers' and 'ponders' but also 'recites' or 'speaks quietly to himself'. Buber comments:

> Nor is it enough to learn it passively. We must again and again 'mutter' it, we must repeat its living word after it, with our speaking we must enter into the word's spokenness, so that it is spoken anew by us in our biographical situation of today – and so on in eternal actuality. He who in his own activity serves the God Who reveals Himself – even though he may by nature spring from a mean earthly realm – is transplanted by the streams of water of the Direction. Only now can his own being thrive, ripen and bring forth fruit, and the law by which seasons of greenness and seasons of withering succeed one another in the life of the living being, no longer hold for him – his sap circulates continually in undiminished freshness.[8]

I sense an equivalence between this and Kavanagh's poem with its longing for the heightened living and experience and sensitivity that comes to him when he beholds a moment of nature as a word being spoken by the Word.

In that moment, he comes alive, or rather, since this has happened to him before, he comes alive again, in a fuller way, as a poet and as a man. Like the tree in the psalm that draws life from the flowing water it has been transplanted beside, Kavanagh draws poetic experience and inspiration from the canal he spends time by. Apart from the running waters, the leaves of the tree in the psalm would wither and it would bear no fruit. Kavanagh needs to attend closely to each ordinary little moment of nature until it is given to him to behold it as a word being uttered by the Word – that is what brings him alive poetically until his playing aloud with words gradually bears fruit in a new poem.

And the assurance of leaves and fruit in due season provided by the tree's transplanted rootedness beside the running streams in the psalm reminded me of an anxiety underlying some of Kavanagh's work that he might lose his poetic gift of perceiving a moment of nature as a word issuing from the Word. There is a sense of relief in the poem that the vision and the poem expressing it has been given once again. All this is articulated in the symbol of the exuberant generosity of the Word that gives him such moments of inspiration – 'leafy-with-love'.

Kavanagh's characteristic spirituality, however, of a moment of nature grasped as the uttering of a word by the Word echoes something found in other psalms.

Psalm 19 is in two parts, the first about nature, the second about the revealed word of God. The opening four verses of the first part struck me as equivalent to Kavanagh's moment-of-nature as word of God spirituality. And Psalm 33:5-9 celebrate the way God brings the world of nature into existence by the words he speaks with the same love (*hesed*) with which he brought Israel into existence. These parallels convince me that the engendering spirituality in Kavanagh's 'Canal Bank Walk' and his similar poems is not something eccentric or outside the Judaeo-Christian experience of creation and revelation but rather a new fruit of it.

LEAFY-WITH-LOVE

'Canal Bank Walk' opens with a new symbol, 'Leafy-with-love'. It contains compactly the meaning unfolded throughout the rest of the poem. It is the only mention of love in the poem. It is not immediately obvious what love he is referring to. It is not a poem about a woman he loves. It is only peripherally about a courting couple. The meaning of the symbol is echoed in 'the breeze adding a third party' and the 'eternal voices', both phrases evocative of the Love which is the Holy Spirit.

The theme of the poem is Kavanagh's longing for the participation in new moments of nature that are rendered incandescent to him as personal encounters between him and the Word in the Word's singing them into being, a moment that brings him incomparably alive and sparks off his poetic imagination in a unique way yielding a new poem.

By opening with this new symbol Kavanagh infuses its significance throughout whole poem. The outburst of meaning that this phrase discharges into the poem has to do with superabundance, the superabundance characteristic of love, in particular of divine Love's dealings with us.

'Leafy-with-love' means that the encounters with the Word which quicken and refresh us are not few and far between but overwhelmingly many, 'plenteous', as the RSV translation of the De Profundis, the sixth psalm of repentance, Psalm 130:7, puts it. These breakthrough moments are not the exception but the divine rule.

How does the symbol suggest this? I see it as a poetic equivalent of the image of abundance in the word of the Lord that came to Abram:

> And behold the word of the Lord came to him … And he brought him outside and said, 'Look toward heaven, and number the stars, if you are able to number them.' Then he said to him, 'So shall your descendants be.' (Gn 15:5)

The universe is a symbol of God. It shows us something of what he is like. The dizzying dimensions of the universe, its size and age, and the unimaginably mighty forces at work in it, are an image of God's power. The dazzling depth of its details, like the innumerable numbers of grains of sand, flakes of snow, drops of rain, flowers and seeds, like the infinity of stars in the night sky in the word of God to Abram, are symbols of the infinite generosity and particularity of God's involvement in even the smallest aspects of the universe. 'Leafy-with-love' has the same meaning. It symbolises the intimacy of God's involvement with the world, down to the last sub-atomic particle.

In the summer the trees are luxuriant with an uncountable multitude of leaves. Any one of them could catch the eye of someone relaxing and spending time along the canal. Concentrating on any one of them could easily become participation in one of those moments of nature that opens into an encounter with the Word singing it into being. Leaves, thus, are a natural symbol of the showering multiplicity beyond number of the new and unique moments of nature which are not only spoken into existence by the Word, but also spoken uniquely to us, new words of love spoken uniquely to us by Love.

And Kavanagh writes here, I feel, with representative consciousness and authority. He is not describing some experience that *he* has but which *we* don't have or can't have. Rather, he is articulating the meaning of the present moments of any one of us as a human being, their dimension of being words addressed to us by Love, seeking to engage us in a lover's conversation.

'Leafy-with-love' means that at every moment each of us is in a thicket of love with as many words being spoken *just to us* by the Word as there are leaves around us when we are walking among trees in summer.

NOTES
1. Tom Stack, *No Earthly Estate, God and Patrick Kavanagh: An Anthology*, selected and introduced by Tom Stack (Dublin: Columba Press, 2002), p. 9.
2. Patrick Kavanagh, *Collected Poems*, Antoinette Quinn, ed. (London: Allen Lane, 2004), pp. xxvii.
3. Examples of divine human encounter in the present moment: Martin Buber's *I and Thou* (New York: Touchstone Book, Simon & Schuster, 1970); T. S. Eliot, *Four Quartets* (London: Faber and Faber), Chiara Lubich, *Here and Now: Meditations on Living in the Present* (New York: New City Press, 2005); Fr Tomás Morales, *Thoughts: An Anthology of Texts of Fr Tomás Morales SJ* (Rome: Libreria Editrice, 2004), Numbers 643 and 638, p. 125 'The present moment is the only real, direct connection between time and eternity.' and 'In the present moment, God and man meet.'; Jean-Pierre de Caussade, *Self-Abandonment to Divine Providence*, P. H. Ramière SJ, ed., Algar Thorold, trans. (London: Burns Oates & Washbourne Ltd., 1948), also as *The Sacrament of the Present Moment*, Kitty Muggeridge, trans. (Glasgow: HarperOne, 1989); and Brother Lawrence *The Practice of the Presence of God*, Hal M. Helms, ed. (Brewster, MA, Paraclete Press, 2011).
4. Una Agnew SSL, *The Mystical Imagination of Patrick Kavanagh: A Buttonhole in Heaven?* (Dublin: Columba Press, 1998), p. 23.
5. Eric Voegelin, *Order and History, Volume III, Plato and Aristotle* (Baton Rouge, Louisiana: State University Press, 1957), p. 268.
6. 'That B12 is genuine is suggested by the features it shares with Heraclitean fragments: syntactic ambiguity (toisin autoisin 'the same' [in the dative] can be construed either with 'rivers' ['the same river'] or with 'those stepping in' ['the same people'], with what comes before or after), chiasmus, sound-painting (the first phrase creates the sound of rushing water with its diphthongs and sibilants), rhyme and alliteration.' http://plato.stanford.edu/entries/heraclitus/ (accessed 17 January 2012).
7. Eric Voegelin, 'Vision and Reason', *Order and History, Volume IV, The Ecumenic Age*, (Louisiana: Louisiana State University Press, 1974), p. 244.
8. Martin Buber, *Good and Evil: Two Interpretations* (New York: Charles Scribner's Sons, 1953), p. 58.

Epic as the Saving Truth of History: Solzhenitsyn's *Red Wheel*[1]

DAVID WALSH

If we think of revolution as the force that has shaped and continues to shape our world, then the response of an artist of Solzhenitsyn's caliber to its cataclysmic effect is surely of the first importance. That is why *The Red Wheel* is a project of far more than Russian significance. Not only did the effects of the Russian Revolution wash over peoples far removed from it in space and time, but it remained the emblematic instance of apocalyptic transformation that has haunted politics in the modern era. If our politics perpetually begins in upheaval, then the Russian Revolution is its epitome. The French Revolution may have been the decisive destruction of the old aristocratic order, but the Russian Revolution is the point at which the messianic transformation of society and history is inaugurated. The titanic drive of modernity is sent forth in all its limitless ambition. How art can sit in judgement over such a shattering overwhelming event is one of the most interesting question raised by Solzhenitsyn's project. It can do so only by dint of the fairness of its comprehensive judgement.

Solzhenitsyn would have to show that he has pondered the sources, influences and emphases more deeply and sympathetically than all of the alternative accounts. Within that immersion in the pathos of revolution he would have to draw up the principles by which actions and events would be judged. Such principles must come from the participants themselves in all of their far-flung but inescapably shared responsibility. The artist cannot evoke an authority outside of his subject matter. This is what makes him, or her, such a formidable opponent, as Solzhenitsyn discovered in his own life. The calf carries no other weapon but the crunching impact of his own skull in butting the oak.[2] But what a power that turns out to be, for art contains the possibility of surpassing the reality on which it operates. Real revolution, it seems to say, is a largely inward event, for the artist has effected just such a transformation in our understanding of the convulsion that had seemed to overwhelm us. We see it all in a new light. And in that light we glimpse the only possibility of a new life, if there is to be a new life. It is widely recognised that Solzhenitsyn was one of the great prophetic voices of our time, but how he managed to exercise that role through his literary work is far less understood. In particular we must ask how his greatest project, *The Red Wheel*, functioned as the evocative epic of our age.

We begin by confronting the greatest challenge that any account of history must overcome. Can there be any stable account of what happened that is not itself overtaken by the continuing shifts of historical perspective? Is every account of history historically relative? Is truth accessible from within history? Here the contrast with Tolstoy brings out the greater philosophical awareness of Solzhenitsyn's project. Once that most fundamental question of historical truth is addressed we can explore, second, the literary heightening of truth that goes beyond a mere historiographic narrative. Solzhenitsyn's conception of historical knots is of particular importance in this regard but it will be considered within the wider development of a juxtapositional form throughout *The Red Wheel*. It is that form that makes possible, third, the realisation that the epic is the point at which history itself is transcended. Historical action attains its significance when it has emerged as of more than historical significance. It is in the light of eternity that history is illumined. Art is particularly well equipped to reveal that perspective because it aims at its own eternal truth. But historiography too partakes of the same framework of relevance as it reaches toward the historical epic. The account of history cannot be separated from responsibility for it. If the epic is written from the perspective of our continuity with the past then it imposes on us a responsibility for the future.

1. IS A TRUTH OF HISTORY POSSIBLE?

The construction of an historical narrative is in its very nature fraught with the question of its truth. By suggesting a perspective on events that was not available to the participants we already cast uncertainty on our own application of a perspective. What is it that makes our perspective so superior that it will not be overtaken by later events and subsequent historians? Is an account of history anything more than a subjective viewpoint destined to be succeeded by other equally partial accounts? Surely none of us escapes the limitations of our perspective within history that prevent us from comprehending its order as a whole. We cannot perceive the part we play within a grander plan.

This was the problem that so preoccupied Tolstoy in *War and Peace* that he felt compelled to append an epilogue on the philosophical conundrum of freedom and necessity. If there is a great historical purpose at work unknown to its participants, then this surely means that their conviction of acting freely is an illusion. Even framing an historical narrative serves to reinforce the conception of a pattern of causality within which individual freedom counts very little. Explanation is sought, Tolstoy insisted, in terms of forces larger than particular persons. History itself 'moves' from west to east and back again with an inexorability that individuals, even leaders, were incapable of resisting. How else could the narrative be framed? Conceived as a series of wholly free individual choices the account could scarcely hang together as anything more than a random concurrence. Particular actions are intelligible only when seen as part of a wider pattern that reduces individual variations to irrelevance. The problem is that once we depart from that individual perspective we have no means of comprehending the actions and events at all. Even the historian who imposes a putatively higher viewpoint on the events, who perceives a pattern where none was perceived before, has no certainty that the preferred configuration is itself ultimate. The provisionality of every historical perspective seems inescapable.

This was the great insight of Tolstoy who declared it impossible to reach any definitive grasp of historical significance. 'Only by renouncing the claim to knowledge of an ultimate aim immediately intelligible to us, and admitting the ultimate purpose to be beyond our comprehension, may we discern the logical consistency and expediency of the lives of historical personages.'[3] Inscrutable divine providence is the limit beyond which we cannot penetrate, even though we may be able to reach ever more comprehensive surmises as to the pattern of the whole. The ultimate whole remains beyond our reach. In this respect, modern historians have not surpassed their ancient predecessors who attributed to the gods the directive role in the affairs of men. But in another sense the moderns are inferior in thinking they have understood history as the outcome of leaders' intentions and abstract forces.

> Modern history has rejected the beliefs of the ancients without providing a new conception to replace them; and then the logic of the situation has obliged the historians … to come by another path to the same conclusion: the recognition (1) that nations are

guided by individual men, and (2) that a goal exists toward which humanity and those nations are moving.[4]

In essence the historians are no better off than the participants who are drawn by an inexorability they can neither discern nor resist. To underline the inevitability at work is hardly to comprehend it. It is indeed to submit to it, as the inevitable condition of developing a historiographic account.

The only difficulty with this familiar Tolstoyan elevation of fate is that it cannot be sustained, for its formulation undermines it. Once fate is acknowledged to be irresistible a beachhead of resistance has already been established. One cannot simultaneously declaim against our imprisonment within the unbreakable chain of causality, as Tolstoy does in his epilogue, and at the same time think that this thought itself is the one instance of pure liberation. The answer to the undergraduate objection of free will and determinism is to recognise that the question has already resolved it. Freedom is the only perspective of thought. It cannot therefore be put in question. When he enters upon his great literary exploration of war and peace this is precisely what Tolstoy demonstrates. Whatever 'history' is, there is no point at which the freedom of human beings has been completely eradicated. Even when circumstances have severely circumscribed the options remaining, human beings still retain the inextinguishable freedom of how they are to regard them. It is this enduring capacity for response that in many respects constitutes the enduring interest of history. We may be powerless to redirect the course of events but we never lose the power to accept or oppose them. As our interest is drawn toward that most decisive of all levels, the interior of the human soul, the source from which freedom springs, we begin to suspect that history is not about external events at all, or at least not ultimately. This is the conclusion reached by Tolstoy when he is guided by his art, rather than half-baked fragments of philosophy. When pressed to pierce the meaning of the events that overwhelm them, his heroes move inexorably toward the perspective that transcends history. Prince Andrei in the operating tent glances over at a man whose leg has just been amputated and recognises Anatol Kuragin. The encounter brings back a flood of memories through which Andrei sees clearly what is really real.

> Compassion, love for our brothers, for those who love us, and for those who hate us, love for our enemies – yes, that is the love

which God preached on earth, and which Princess Marya tried to teach me and I did not understand; that is what remained for me had I lived. But now it is too late. I know it.[5]

The truth of history, despite the determinism Tolstoy cannot quite shake off, bursts through as a truth beyond history. In that moment the whole of history is illumined by a perspective that rises definitively above it. What happens in history, and therefore the varying perspectives it presents depending on our vantage point within it, fades in significance compared to the one point toward which all of history strains. It turns out that the meaning of events and patterns is no more than provisional, for they may lead to consequences that remain unforeseen. Good can come from evil and evil from good. But what cannot change is the truth of good and evil as such. The judgement under which history exists does not await an apocalypse that brings it to an end. It is the revelation under which history is enacted in every moment. When we narrate the course of history we do so in the form of a series of intersections of the timeless with time. Despite the impression that we are describing a flow of events, we are really stepping outside of them to glance over the whole. Historiography is in this sense not historical. It is itself one of the timeless moments from which the course of things can be apprehended. The project appears self-defeating only if we immerse the narration of history within the sequence itself. Then it seems destined to be overtaken by later developments. But what even makes it possible to describe what has happened is that we can have recourse to a perspective that transcends history. At their core the actions of human beings are moral events; they are not simply the unconscious motions of automatons. We may not be able to embrace the ultimate ramification of the Czar's abdication, but we are able to recognise it as the moral failure that it was. Historiography is possible because neither we nor the participants exist wholly within history. It is rather the case that we make history and remember it by virtue of the inexorable judgement under which we all equally stand. Historical recollection breaks down only when we assume that it must lead toward a viewpoint definitively unavailable to those who made history.

Once the search for the meaning of history has been abandoned then the meaning of the events within history can be explored. The question of the truth of the historical narrative does not then depend on our reaching a comprehensive account of all that has happened. It turns on our recognition that there is no higher viewpoint than the perspective of eternity from which history is judged. What happens in history matters much less than what outweighs every historical outcome. It is the relationship to what is beyond history that marks the line of meaning within history. Of course the events that are memorable are the ones that produce enormous consequences within history, but their meaning is not exhausted by that long train of effects they set in motion. Nor can we disdain the largely minor incidents simply because the fruit they bear appears to be more modest on the world scene. History is composed of the great and the small events such that they mutually illumine one another. Selection of historical events is indeed the task of the historiographer and this entails a judgement of significance in light of what is known about the subsequent course of events. The Napoleonic wars and the Russian Revolution each constitute such meaningful units within history. But even the most comprehensive treatment can scarcely account for the profound moral impulses, for good and bad, that have shaped the historical pattern itself. Historical explanation stops at the level of causal factors but shies away from what renders them decisive in that particular instance. This was the difficulty Tolstoy sensed in the glib assignment of causes by modern historians. Yet he was unable to explicate the deeper intuition, which nevertheless guided his artistic construction, that no causal analysis could ever account for what lies beyond the control of causality. At issue in history is always how we are to stand in relation to causes or objective factors. Is history the impact of social forces, economic motives, the vainglory of leadership, or anything else without our ceding responsibility toward them? How indeed could the historian account for moral growth or decline when he or she is equally liable before the same imperatives? There is finally no historical perspective apart from the perspective from which history is made. The epic is the appropriate form of historical recollection because it eschews the distance of the professional historian to acknowledge what even the latter is compelled to concede. That is that the author and the community for which he or she writes belong to the same moral universe.

The artist is for this reason freed from the burden of explanation and can therefore turn to the illumination of the spiritual horizon within which all human beings enact their historical existence. The writing of history too does not escape the imperative of moral responsibility. The only difference is that the artist must include the warrant of truth within the work itself. Professional historians are validated by the confirmation echoed by their professional peers, and only secondarily by the consensual judgement of the society for which they write. Art never places itself above the material it explores but rather finds its voice within the work itself. When it succeeds art can therefore function as the representative account of the community itself. It is neither the voice of God nor of impersonal forces of reality, but remains the voice of a human being who has miraculously discovered a resonance with others, perhaps all others. Art is in this sense an ideal medium for moral exploration because it neither preaches nor teaches. Instead it radiates and it sings of what is memorable as such. It thereby furnishes the truth by which its own achievement is to be judged. There is no need of higher authority or external validation, besides they too would stand in need of authentication. Art in this way exemplifies the deepest meaning of history as the eternal presence, the timeless moment, in which we are all contemporaries, none with a superior insight than any others. Of course the later in time do have the benefit of a more extended contemplation of the course of historical consequences but this scarcely affords any advantage in respect to the moral fidelity or failure that is most deeply at issue. Virtue remains the measure of all human beings, just as Homer understood in elevating it to the central place in the epics. How men live counts for more than what they accomplish. In the end it is that acknowledgment, shared by the poet, that elevates the truth of the poem above a flatly historical account. The latter may aim at something similar but it is less surely guided by the moral principles that measure the historical reality it contemplates.

2. LITERARY HEIGHTENING OF TRUTH

If the role of art is to show the truth it cannot say, because it too is governed by the same truth, then the literary form must reflect this inescapable continuity. The author is no longer the undisputed master of the material presenting the definitive viewpoint from which it is all comprehended. Tolstoy understood that this was the fatal deficiency of the professional historian for whom history unfolded toward his own unique vantage point. Yet despite the polemic Tolstoy conducted against this specialist genre he never succeeded in finding the literary form that would disrupt it. Despite his best efforts, his own authorial voice drifted toward that imperious perspective. His fascination with the great men of history, Napoleon and Aleksandr, belied his denunciation of great men explanations. It was only when he allowed himself to enter the interior life of his characters that their transcendence of all historical forces comes into view. Each is irreducibly a centre of history in his or her enactment of responsibility for the course of events in which they are engaged. It is only indirectly therefore that we glimpse an account of history that Tolstoy is never fully able to admit to himself. That is, that history is the realm in which, for all of the powerful collective influences at work, individuals remain free to define their response to the challenges that confront them. No explanation for their decisions that seeks to aggregate them under some objective logic can surpass the inescapable moral responsibility by which they must explain them to themselves. How can anything within history interpret the exercise of responsibility that is greater than all of history? A very different literary form would be required to contemplate the historical sweep in which every human being is an irreplaceable centre of history. This realisation is what distinguishes Solzhenitsyn's *Red Wheel*.

The historical novel already contains within it the seeds of its own evolution into the historical epic in which author and characters occupy the same realm of truth. Once characters become the means of probing historical truth, of plumbing the moral depth from which historical events arise, then it is only a matter of time before such multiple individualities surpass the narrative movement. What can narrative add to the acceptance or betrayal of obligation? This diminished role of narrative is surely what accounts for the juxtapositional form that Solzhenitsyn favours in *The Red Wheel*. Narrative has not entirely disappeared but now it is confined within the respective episodes. It is no longer the voice that seems in control of the account as a whole, capable of guiding us because it has comprehended the unfolding from beginning to end. Now the narrative is itself embedded in the incidents by which the wheel rolls. We do not even have access to the movement in any continuous sense but are instead drawn into the knots in which its most intense self-revelations take place. What is the Russian Revolution as Solzhenitsyn conceives it? If we are to take seriously his original project of a work with up to twenty knots we realise that the Revolution is a series of events whose boundaries are not easily demarcated. Even the very scale of the work suggests something of the challenge it presented to the author. He was willing to risk the weariness of readers for the sake of remaining true to the upheaval that overflows all possibility of a narrative unity. But this is not to suggest that the sheer abundance of materials overwhelmed the author. Solzhenitsyn is far too deliberate in his approach to the defining enterprise of his life for this to be the case. The careful elaboration of incidents, along with the manifold variety of literary techniques, are too well considered for them to be the result of anything but a deep estimation of their significance. Besides we have the main structural device of knots to confirm that the principle is the self-interpretation of history. They are the culminating moments when all of the elements at work have come into view.

In essence, the knots are the narrative. Assimilating them to the homogeneity of a narrative would rob them of their irruptive effect. Solzhenitsyn evidently did not want them reduced to the uniform level of significance that is the inevitable smoothing effect of a narrative. All that occurs, such monotone expositions seem to say, has found its place within the omniscience of the narrator. In *The Red Wheel* both author and reader occupy the same level, as shaken witnesses of shattering events. No doubt the episodic heightening of the drama lends considerable interest to the account. But there is something more than a mere literary device at work. The knots are a fundamental structural form for the conception of history, or at least for the history of 'R-17'. History, they seem to say, is punctuated by irruptions in which the meaning of what is taking place bursts on the scene. Time continues at its ordinary pace but for the participants it intermittently seems to slow down in order to process the vast new developments it is bringing forth. Or it may seem suddenly accelerated in the multiplicity of events taking place that seem to far exceed the transactions of a more routine timeframe. At any rate the knots are those compressed periods in which the momentous transpires. What is happening in history becomes manifest. The connections between widely scattered fragments are unexpectedly revealed and the direction of the historical epoch aligns its focus. The truth of events is grasped. History has interpreted itself. This is why there is no need for a narrator for there is no curtain to be thrown back when history has performed its own denouement. The author recedes to the status of an observer, little different from the reader before whom the whole is unfolded. Yet the withdrawal of the author must not be mistaken for absence. He is the one who has assembled the dizzying succession of scenes. His judgement and skill has brought their components together, an achievement that is all the more impressive for the degree to which his creation can function without him. In letting history speak for itself he identifies with Kierkegaard's remark in the *Upbuilding Discourses*, that he has been as much the learner as the author.[6]

Authorial recession is a familiar means of establishing the truth of what is said. It is what underpins the polyphonic novel so favoured by Dostoevsky, by which the centre of action is carried forward not by one particular figure but instead by a succession of characters each presenting their own unique perspective. The result is a polyphony of voices in which the absence of a dominant presence precludes the possibility of identifying any one of them with that of the author. He is strangely absent from his own creation. Instead the author risks the defeat of his own cherished convictions by insisting that truth emerge from a clash of perspectives without any predetermined outcome. Dostoevsky notoriously worried about this juxtaposition in which his own conceptions might lose out. Yet it was a risk he thought worth taking for the sake of the authoritative establishment of truth. What emerged from the winnowing of positions would stand without need of authorial support. This notion of the truth of 'living life' is one that Solzhenitsyn readily embraced in his novels.[7] He knew and appreciated the polyphonic approach. One suspects that Solzhenitsyn understood that all writing is polyphonic, for the author's voice cannot be carried by any of the characters he creates. They are needed precisely because none of them can say what he aims at saying. Only the text as a whole comes close to what has been intended. Even then there remains the endless possibility of extending it, a prospect Solzhenitsyn seems to have contemplated in the voluminous projections of *The Red Wheel* he had considered. The finitude of the human life span and, possibly, a merciful regard for the overburdened reader, however, imposed a limit on the work. Yet the central idea of polyphony remains in the principle of the knots. History revolves around multiple epiphanies which it is the duty of the author to treat as comprehensively as possible. History is studded with apocalyptic outbursts.

The whole is contained in the part or, rather, in the moment that reflects the whole. But this is because the whole is nowhere present. No account, no matter how comprehensive, can do justice to history as a whole. We are left then with the moments when its innermost truth flashes forth and they are each indispensable, for none of them contains the whole. Our only access to the meaning of the whole is in those precious glimpses when it comes into view. Narrative which seems to parallel the stream of historical time somehow fails to capture what is decisive, for it reduces everything to the one homogeneous level. But that is not the time in which we live. It is not that of the calendar or the clock. Instead the time of existence and of its memory bursts ecstatically with what it contains, often with such intensity that the outburst cannot be confined within any of the forms toward which it radiates. Within the knots all of the forces at work have reached their highest intensity but in such a way that they can no longer be held together. They must fly apart. The knots are the moments when history has leapt outside of itself. Participants and observers have become contemporaries in that ecstatic leap by which they have left the steady beat of the narrative far behind. Now all that matters is inescapably laid bare. The way that things are has become inescapably clear because they stand revealed in the light of an eternal judgement. That is what fixes the knots as the moments of arrested time. They are the points at which we see plainly that history does not occur in time, despite our everyday impression to the contrary, but within the irrefutable light of moral truth. Above all the knots are the moral epiphanies of history, although not epiphanies the author has constructed. They are the flashes by which the author brings together the disparate threads that hold everything fast.

Everything works toward that leap of insight by which connections are grasped that scarcely exist at the level of chronology. This is why fictional characters must be invented to supplement what history has supplied. Such a man is Colonel Vorotyntsev, the energetic and brilliant staff officer who plays such a prominent but ineffectual role in the first knot, *August 1914*, and remains a recurrent presence throughout the cycle. We recall that the same Vorotyntsev was a character in the 1953 play, *The Prisoners*, set in 1945 when the Soviet Army captured Russians who had fought for liberation with the Germans. Vorotyntsev confirms that he had fought during the Civil War on the 'White' side. If we conceive this, as Klimoff and Ericson do, as an epilogue to *The Red Wheel*, we see that the whole work is conceived in light of what might have been.[8] It is history as seen from the perspective of a man who had no effect upon it but who represents its tantalising other possibility. What if the Russian officer corps had been composed of men like Vorotyntsev rather than time servers, sycophants and incompetents? Even in 1953 Solzhenitsyn's imagination had already crystallised around the character who would be among the most penetrating figures of *The Red Wheel*. Gradually such fictional characters are reduced in significance as the knots proceed, although Vorotyntsev does not disappear completely. He is still present at the end of the fourth knot to provide some musings on the future direction of Russia and of his own potential role within it. It has been noted that the later knots are more heavily and consistently historical, as if the author no longer needs the extra-historical perspectives to illuminate what has happened. The outcome has been decided and fewer options remain for altering it. History had provided its own Vorotyntsevs although now their range of action is far more severely limited. Often it consists simply of holding their station in the face of the cataclysm that engulfs them. This was all that was possible for Colonel Balkashin and the soldiers of the Wheeled Batalion who were beaten to death by a mob.[9] Yet that elemental steadfastness, perhaps most of all when it is powerless, is enough to establish the truth. Juxtaposition is the principle out of which the knots are constructed.

What has happened can never be contained in its factual report. Somehow it must be heightened to elicit its defining character. That is what juxtaposition accomplishes. It enables Solzhenitsyn to present what happened in relation to what might have been, but not as a purely imaginary alternative. To work, juxtaposition must invoke what really might have altered the situation. It must be a real possibility in the moment, not simply an impossible wish fulfilment. Vorotyntsev is not therefore a purely fictional character but the truth of a possibility that remained an option. Men of his caliber with the requisite skill and energy might well have been able to form themselves into a cohesive force sufficient to overcome the debility of the sclerotic regime. The failure of their emergence is however not simply accidental or personal. It is bound up with the forces of inertia posed against it, a general mood of passivity that eventually even reaches those most capable individuals. Solzhenitsyn allows his hero to slide into the distraction of a private passion, his affair, that is symptomatic of the wider lassitude that invades Russian society from the top down. Even Vorotyntsev succumbs to its enervating spirit. Where does Russia exist, Solzhenitsyn seems to ask, when its most devoted members have been overtaken by a paralysing drift into the world of private dissipation? Yet the question could not even be asked unless there existed that cadre of individuals for whom the possibility of heroic vitality had not vanished entirely. They may have been powerless to reverse the mounting forces arrayed against them, but they were not powerless to choose their response to them. They could still attest to the truth by which history, and they too, are judged. Judgement is juxtaposition, for art can invoke no criterion beyond the truth emergent within it. Verisimilitude, the touchstone of the writer's code, requires nothing less than refusal of the manufactured point of view. We are confident in the judgement rendered because we can behold the balancing of perspectives from which it has been drawn.

Juxtaposition, one is inclined to suggest, is Solzhenitsyn's principal literary technique. A comprehensive weighing of experiences and views is surely what renders *The Gulag Archipelago* such a powerful testament.[10] It becomes apparent in the smaller scale writings to which Solzhenitsyn returned after *The Red Wheel*, especially the miniatures and short stories. We begin to see that the author of one of the most extended literary works of the century is at heart a miniaturist, capable of seeing the whole in the smallest instances. This was after all the secret of *The Red Wheel*, not that it is composed as one long tale, but as an assemblage of many, many much shorter ones. Each of them is essentially 'binary', depending for their meaning on a relationship to a whole that is not fully adumbrated. The technique is amply displayed in the later collection of short stories Solzhenitsyn referred to as 'binary tales', *Apricot Jam and Other Stories*.[11] Many of the stories seem to deal with events and material that may have been left over from or were part of the larger projected version of *The Red Wheel*. In them the juxtapositional technique is developed as a structural device whereby the same event is viewed from two very different perspectives. The opening story, 'Apricot Jam', begins with a desperate emaciated peasant who writes a letter appealing to a famous writer for help, while the second half recounts a conversation between the famous writer and his neighbours in which the letter features as an outstanding example of raw Russian language that the writer intends to use. When asked if he will answer the man's plea for help the writer simply dismisses the suggestion as he cannot regard himself as having anything in common with a dispossessed Kulak. They live in such completely different worlds, the story seems to say, that their lives scarcely touch one another. Yet they inhabit the same world, the world that the story has laid before us. The truth that neither side can grasp about the other is contained in their juxtaposition. Indeed it is their juxtaposition that brings out a depth in the Kulak and the writer, whether it is of openness or closure, that would not have been apparent in their isolation. History, in this case a very minor episode within it, has effected an epiphany not so much of character, but of the human condition. Behind the multiplicity of perspectives that divide human beings there lies the common humanity that binds or fails to bind them. Juxtaposition is in the service of that common humanity. That is the source of its truth.

3. HISTORY IS TRANSCENDED IN TRUTH

Juxtaposition is elaborated, not only in the system of knots and such dialectical forms as the binary stories, but in the whole vast array of techniques from historical documents, to cinematic montages, to epigrammatic folk sayings that Solzhenitsyn uses in his vast work. Everything is designed to elicit that moment of epiphany in which what has happened in history is rendered luminous. What is worth remembering, he seems to say, is not so much the bare events and outcomes as the meaning through which they are grasped. Even to see it all as constituting one great convulsion, a rolling of the red wheel, is already to step back from the details to comprehend them. In that moment history is arrested for it is only then that the wheel is glimpsed apart from the blur of its movement. The wheel that moves so inexorably, crushing all that lies in its path, is held fast in the moment of its beholding. History itself is thereby transformed so that it is not simply the whirring, buzzing confusion experienced by the participants, as they are trampled to death by mobs or forced to flee from palaces they had occupied forever. It is not the immediacy of events that is recorded but their meaning within a wider drama of which they are a part. Even the participants themselves seek out that larger significance as they attempt to probe the meaning of what has happened. They too bear witness to the realisation that they are not simply in history but are also somehow always outside of it. It is in becoming clear, if only in part, on why and how all that has transpired in their lives has occurred that they gain a release from it. They gain, if not the perspective of eternity on the events of their lives, at least the distance afforded by that perspective. It is not simply the author, Solzhenitsyn, who has transmuted their suffering into something beautiful for they have already begun the process themselves. Even in losing the thread of meaning, in failing to break through to any ultimate significance, they have nevertheless preserved the imperative of that transcendent quest. History is in this sense a ceaseless quest for the moment in which history is transcended.

It is reached when what has happened is grasped in its universal significance. That is when it stands under the moral judgement that attempts to plumb the depths of good and evil that lie within it. How does it appear *sub specie eternitatis*? This does not mean that the question is ever fully answered for, in an important sense, no definitive judgement can be rendered while history continues to unfold. Yet the question must be posed and it must be posed of that sphere of responsibility within which each person acts. The treatment of General Samsonov, the figure responsible for the Second Army in August 1914, exemplifies this relentless self-examination. For Solzhenitsyn it was not enough to catalogue the unhappy general's military blunders. It was necessary to probe their source. Did it lie in ineptitude, a failure of diligence, or some deeper character flaw? To what extent was the catastrophe that resulted in the loss of the Second Army assignable to a more extensive collapse of responsibility within the Russian high command? Solzhenitsyn leaves us in no doubt that the contagion of feckless incompetence was widely shared, almost as if everything conspired to ensure the defeat and demoralisation of Russia that was in no sense inevitable. How differently it would have turned out, he seems to say, if only the Tsar had displayed more resolute judgement in his military appointments, if only the senior military ranks had been populated with fewer blockheads who cared only about saving their own precious hides, and if only the wider political circles had glimpsed something of their own precarious position in the ensuing collapse the disaster would visit upon them. To single out one individual for most of the blame, however pivotal his role, would seem to misread the constellation of forces at work. Yet Solzhenitsyn comes close to doing just that. He refuses the Tolstoyan invocation of historical necessity in insisting that Samsonov could have done otherwise. Indeed he preserves his responsibility by demonstrating the extent to which Samsonov sought to honestly fulfil his duty. He was not one of the cowardly incompetent flatterers that proliferated in the Tsar's headquarters. He was a soldier who knew that his first duty was to remain with his men, and he sought to do so. Nevertheless, he was drawn toward the disastrous decision by which he moved to the front himself and thereby lost communication with army group headquarters. When one of the colonels pointed out how such an action was contrary to all military rationality, that he was 'neglecting the army commander's duty to control the *whole* army', he would not be dissuaded. Yet even in that final imbecility Solzhenitsyn does not condemn the doomed general outright. Instead he probes deeper into the mood that could so possess Samsonov that he departed from the most elementary rule of command.

What had been a colossal blunder could still be viewed in the higher light that had already been vouchsafed to Samsonov in prayer. He had sought to 'lay the whole of his life and the present suffering, before God (275)'[12] in a way that made his prayer one offered on behalf of all of Russia. It was no longer for himself alone that he prayed for he had united himself with Russia as a whole, taking upon himself the burden of suffering it would have to endure as it descended into the maelstrom in which nothing could be known of its future. Everything was dark except for the certainty that somehow Russia would be redeemed. He had no basis for this but the assurance he had received that his own suffering would be united with the divine saving action by which sacrifice is the path toward resurrection. In surrendering everything Samsonov had gained his release from all that held him earthbound. The whole burden of the moment, in which the fate of Russia was dependent on this one man seemed, in Solzhenitsyn's account, to become bearable. Even his body became 'less cumbersome, his soul less dark: all the weight and darkness soundlessly and invisibly fell away from him, evaporated, was drawn heavenwards. God who could assume all burdens was taking this burden to Himself.' This is surely the meaning of the voice that Samsonov hears in a dream on the night before the crucial battle that intones 'Thou shalt be assumed', until he finally bolts upright with the realisation of what it means. To be 'taken up' on the Feast of the Assumption meant that he would die. It was under the influence of that shattering revelation that Samsonov undertook his last disastrous step of moving up to the front, thereby breaking off communication with army group headquarters. The contrast between what happens in history and the transcendence of history could not be greater.

What at the level of historical action appears as culpable ineptitude assumes a very different appearance when it is seen in the light of eternity. What matters in that transcendent perspective is not the worldly consequences of action but the spirit in which they are undertaken. How do they stand in relation to the standpoint of eternity in which all consequences have ceased to be? What in a mundane sense was simply a well-intentioned blunder now may be seen as an act of supreme generosity by a leader who sacrifices himself on behalf of all. It may not be the wisest course of action by any of the military principles that normally apply, but it could also be seen as guided by a deeper wisdom that mandated more than was possible on a purely human scale. Even sacrifice that in worldly terms seems senseless may serve a higher purpose when it is subsumed within the redemptive axis of history. That is surely the perspective within which Solzhenitsyn is thinking about the Russian Revolution. How else can one contemplate the past except to find the meaning of the catastrophe that has occurred? And when every last particle of blame has been meticulously assigned there still remains the challenge of surmounting the accumulation of evil. It is one thing to acknowledge the 'banality of evil', but has one really been anything more than a guilty bystander if this is all that has been accomplished? Can evil be acknowledged without overcoming it? That requires the unconditional love that sacrifices itself on behalf of all. Redemption as the truth of history is the still point around which *The Red Wheel* revolves. One might even regard Solzhenitsyn's life-long absorption with the project as itself one great act of redemptive self-giving.

No detail was too small, no episode too insignificant for inclusion within the ever-expanding cycle of knots that he sought to comprehend by way of untying them again. To be released from the deadly fatality unleashed by the Revolution required not only an analysis of the responsibility for evil but also the spirit of forgiveness that triumphs over it. Samsonov stands for the Russian depth of soul that, despite its evident insufficiency in the moment of its greatest trial, yet remains as the possibility of renewal at some future time. The loss has not been for nothing. This is what *The Red Wheel* proclaims as it dutifully remembers and thereby saves.

Some confirmation of this reading of Samsonov, who is the most consequential figure of *August 1914*, is surely provided by the author's alter ego, the ubiquitous Colonel Vorotyntsev. This is all the more notable given that Vorotyntsev is at this stage still brimming with confidence in his own capacity to turn things around. He is the impatient man of action in contrast to the ponderous general who, like his army, is about to be no more. Yet it is Vorotyntsev who recognises the changes that have taken place in the Army Commander, changes that left him incapable of receiving any further reports or issuing commands.

> It was too late, and no use. Samsonov was soaring at such a height that he had no more use for such things, he was no longer surrounded by terrestrial enemies, no longer threatened, he had outsoared all dangers. No, it was not guilt but a sense of unappreciated greatness that had shadowed the commander's brow: perhaps seen from the outside he had done things that contradicted ordinary earthly ideas on strategy and tactics, but from his new point of view every action of his had been profoundly correct.[13]

It is almost as if Vorotyntsev-Solzhenitsyn concedes that the redemptive significance of the General outweighs his military incapacity. His piety may have misled him but it underpins his sacrificial role. In submitting to inscrutable divine wisdom, including the premonition that Russian defeat will eventually lead to revolution, Samsonov ceases to play a role within any purely mundane ordering of purpose. On the retreat he removes the general's insignia from his uniform and, becoming again the common soldier, he slips away from the group so that he might encounter the death that is their inescapable fate. Only as a man who claims no special privileges for himself can he stand in place of other men. In such an act of expiation, however, he has also ceased to be a part of history, with all the particularities of his time and setting, but has assumed the place of all those who must follow after. History, we see, is not just about the actions and events that happen in it, but also about the actions and events that make it possible.

Whatever Russia is to be in the future it must arise from those individuals who beheld it inwardly in the supreme sacrifice they made on its behalf. By transcending their merely historical situations they make history possible. This is the meaning of all epic accounts for they do not so much record the past as transmit it into the future. The exemplars furnish the models that constitute a common way of life. Men and gods engage in the heroic struggle through which the measure of what counts is instituted. In *The Red Wheel* this struggle is largely transacted between those who seek to remake Russia in accordance with their own idea of it, and those who seek to submit to the idea of Russia as itself the guiding principle of their action. It is the difference between ideology and truth. The protagonists of ideology are driven by the conviction of the superiority of their conception to all that has existed. The servants of truth subordinate themselves to what is required to bring what is already there more fully into existence. At issue is where reality lies when we are responsible for bringing it about. Are we entirely free to impose our will on reality as Lenin sought to insist? His whole role and significance turns on a readiness to press this conviction to the limit. It was from his titanic drive, Solzhenitsyn seems to suggest, that his historical success derived. Is history then a field in which the resolute can remake reality at will? For all of his personal foibles and tactical ineptitude, Lenin exemplified the drive that ultimately came to direct the red wheel. What could a Samsonov or even a Stolypin do to oppose the diabolical ruthlessness that would rather destroy Russia than see it slip out of the grasp of Bolshevism? In the face of historical success what can be said on behalf of truth lost from history? Surely this is the question toward which *The Red Wheel* continually points ever since the original plan of a celebratory exposition was replaced with the mature assessment of its disastrous impact.

It is in this respect that an artistic treatment surpasses a purely historiographic one. Art is not limited to presenting the historically significant events and outcomes. It is free to picture what has not been realised along with what has. By entering more deeply into the reality it investigates, art is able to address what must remain silent in the perspective of historiography. Art can include the standpoint that is shared with historiography but which the latter cannot confess. That is that the subject, in this case the fate of Russia, matters. When every major institution and every level of society fails, when the disease of spiritual disintegration has become so extensive that the nation's fate is sealed, when Russia is doomed, there nevertheless remains a true Russia that is preserved even if only in the status of the irrevocably lost. But of course it is not lost. Even to write the history of Russia's descent into revolutionary madness is to write the history of what is not utterly unreal. The Russia about whom such an historical fate can be recounted remains its truth. The true idea of Russia as the community of those who are bound together within their common self-consciousness, not the antagonistic factions that have lost any connection to a common way of life, somehow endures. That endurance is the condition of the possibility of writing its history. At the deepest level there cannot be a history of Russia's revolutionary self-destruction. Disintegration is premised on integration, even if it exists only in the mind of the historian who, of necessity, must hold out the promise of what has not happened. Solzhenitsyn's *Red Wheel* is even more deliberately a work of national salvation, an act of imaginative restoration of what history has scattered. The historian too affirms a similar act of faith. Even if he or she no longer holds out hope of a whole to be regained, there is the affirmation that the Russia that has disappeared is worthy of such an effort. It is at least worthy of being remembered. History is in this sense inescapably preservative of what has been lost.

The historical epic, however, can go much further. It looks resolutely toward the future and indeed calls forth the future it makes possible. The epic constitutes a new social order, often explicitly so on the basis of the disintegrated past. *The Red Wheel* is thus not simply a book about the revolutionary upheaval in the Russian past. It is the definitive means of surmounting it in the creation of a Russian future. Just as it was not necessary for Homer to have a concrete picture of the kind of society that would succeed the fracture of Achaeans and Trojans, so it is not necessary for Solzhenitsyn to hold out a detailed conception of a post-Revolutionary Russia or, by extension, of a post-totalitarian modernity. What matters is that *The Red Wheel* carries within it the seeds of that other society. When and where they are capable of bearing fruit is not the decisive aspect. It is enough that they are there embedded within the account of a great disaster as the only perspective from which the true scale of the catastrophe can be contemplated. The other Russia that resists the descent into revolutionary madness is preserved. Perhaps it is nowhere else preserved but within the pages of *The Red Wheel*. That is enough, for it means that Russia remains in its truth. Whenever and wherever Russia regains its historical path, the virtues on which it will be rebuilt will have been made available. No other foundation is possible for a people that wishes to persevere as a community in history than to find within themselves the generosity of self-sacrifice, rather than self-absorption, that makes their life together possible. It is the slender thread of heroic action in the face of impossible circumstances that ultimately transfigures defeat into triumph. In remembering the irruption of goodness in the midst of evil, *The Red Wheel* itself goes beyond merely remembering. It undertakes the resistance to history by which history is constituted.

NOTES

1. This essay formed part of a long paper I prepared for a conference on 'The Life and Work of Aleksandr Solzhenitsyn: The Way to *The Red Wheel*', Moscow, December 7–9, 2011. It was a memorable meeting for many reasons, but especially for Brendan's own excellent contribution as well as the sheer good fun he always guarantees. It was the occasion on which we celebrated his seventieth birthday.
2. Aleksandr Solzhenitsyn, *The Oak and the Calf*, Harry Willets, trans. (New York: Harper and Row, 1979).
3. Leo Tolstoy, *War and Peace*, Ann Dunnigan, trans. (New York: Signet, 1968), p. 1355.
4. Ibid., p. 1413.
5. Ibid., p. 978.
6. Søren Kierkegaard, *Eighteen Upbuilding Discourses*, Howard V. Hong and Edna H. Hong, trans. (Princeton: Princeton University Press, 1992), p. xv.
7. Both *Cancer Ward* and *In the First Circle* demonstrate the same technique.
8. Edward Ericson and Alexis Klimoff, *The Soul and Barbed Wire: An Introduction to Solzhenitsyn* (Wilmington: Intercollegiate Studies Institute, 2008).
9. *March 1917*, Chapter 204. It is translated in *The Solzhenitsyn Reader*, Edward Ericson and Daniel Mahoney, eds. (Wilmington: Intercollegiate Studies Institute, 2006), pp. 415–18.
10. A powerful example is the conclusion to one of the most luminous chapters of *The Gulag Archipelago*, Vol. Two, Thomas P. Whitney, trans. (New York: Harper and Row, 1975), 'The Ascent', in which Solzhenitsyn recounts his reawakening to the spiritual truth of existence. He concludes the rapturous meditation with the words: '*Bless you, prison,* for having been in my life!' But he immediately follows with the counterbalancing: '(And from beyond the grave come replies: It is very well for you to say that – when you came out of it alive.)'
11. *Apricot Jam and Other Stories* (Berkeley: Counterpoint, 2011).
12. Aleksandr Solzhenitsyn, *The Red Wheel*, Knot I: August1914, H. T. Willetts, trans. (New York: Farrar, Strauss and Giroux, 1989), Chapter 31.
13. Ibid., Chapter 44.

Religious Freedom and Dialogue: The Prophesy of *Dignitatis Humanae*[1]

PIERO CODA

The dignity of each human being is an important theme in Christian faith. And how could it be otherwise, since Christian faith is rooted entirely in the Son of God made flesh (Jn 1:14) who raised human dignity to the level of the life of God? Nevertheless, while this is true, and it has been professed and experienced in countless ways throughout the centuries, it is also the case that we needed to wait until the Second Vatican Council to have it clearly declared and expressed in its deepest and most radical expression: religious freedom.

Pope John Paul II affirmed that the Second Vatican Council continues to be the guiding light for the Catholic Church at the beginning of the third millennium. In this article I want to emphasise and explore the relevance and the prophetic scope of the Council's Declaration on human dignity, *Dignitatis humanae*.

In a private audience with Bishop Emile-Joseph De Smedt of Bruges, shortly before he was due to present the text of the Declaration to the Council Fathers for their approval in the final vote, Pope Paul VI commented: 'This document is crucial. It sets the attitude of the Church for the next few centuries. The world is waiting for it…'[2] A few decades later and in the light of events that have marked the history of the world from the Council to today, the well-known Tübingen theologian, Peter Hünermann, commented that *Dignitatis humanae* is 'a decisive document for the history of humankind'.[3]

What is the core meaning of this Declaration and where does it come from? What is its enduring value and what heritage does it transmit to us today? First of all, it should be noted that in terms of the formal nature of its teaching, the value of this document is not the most significant. The Declaration is not a Constitution (a term used to define the most important Council documents, aimed at setting out doctrinal guidelines regarding key issues of the Christian faith, such as the identity and the mission of the

Church [*Lumen gentium*] or the meaning of liturgy [*Sacrosanctum concilium*] or Revelation [*Dei Verbum*]). Nor is it a Decree (a document setting out general doctrinal principles in relation to a specific field such as the vocation and mission of the laity [*Apostolicam actuositatem*] or the life and ministry of priests [*Presbyterorum ordinis*] or ecumenism [*Unitatis redintegratio*]). *Dignitatis humanae* is a mere Declaration, and a quite short one. With only fifteen paragraphs it was promulgated at the very end of the Council, at the conclusion of the fourth session of the Council on 7 December 1965, the eve of the solemn celebration of the conclusion of the whole Council on 8 December. Yet, though it is a Declaration, the process of its elaboration and approval was long, eventful and marked by dramatic crises and clashes, a clear sign of what was really at stake!

It's enough to mention that a first draft of the Declaration was presented to the Council on 18 November 1963, within the framework of the fourth chapter of the schema on ecumenism. This detail about its origin is already quite meaningful, since it highlights the fact that it was in the context of dialogue – ecumenical dialogue – that the need arose to reflect on the principle of religious freedom and on its basis in the dignity of the human person. Considering its relevance and sensitivity, the topic of religious freedom was removed from its original context, and so the first schema, *Declaratio de libertate religiosa*, dated 23 September 1964, came to life. But this schema died a death almost immediately after a thousand objections were raised, and a second schema was drawn up right away with major contributions from the American Jesuit John Courtney Murray and the Italian priest Pietro Pavan (who had helped John XXIII to write his two social encyclicals *Mater et Magister* and *Pacem in terris*). Monsignor Carlo Colombo (Paul VI's theologian) also contributed much during the debate in the Council hall.

This new schema dated 11 November 1964, when presented during the session of 19 November, drew the longest applause heard during the Council. But tension still ran high. The text was considered not yet mature and therefore approval was postponed to the following session, the fourth, which concluded a year later with the above-mentioned approval on 7 December 1965.

This troubled process bears witness to the strategic importance of *Dignitatis humanae* and the dramatic nature of the debate between the so-called 'majority' of Council Fathers, who were trying to find a way to respond to the need of 'aggiornamento' that Pope John XXIII had called for at the Council, and the 'minority', committed to an all-out defence of the doctrinal and institutional identity of the Catholic Church that had consolidated from the time of the Council of Trent to the First Vatican Council and up to then persistently re-proposed as part of the Magisterium.

But let us now come to the point at issue. For our convenience and focusing on our specific interest, i.e. the connection between religious freedom and human dignity, I will address the key ideas of the *Declaration* on five different levels: first, the specific subject of the right to religious freedom; second, its anthropological foundation; third, its intrinsic relationship with freedom which – according to Christian theology – defines the act of faith per se; fourth, the significance of its progressive affirmation in historical consciousness; and finally, its prophetic and practical importance in regard to the historical era we are called to live through today.

THE RIGHT TO RELIGIOUS FREEDOM
First of all, I want to focus on the content of the right to religious freedom. With concise solemnity, the Declaration describes it as follows:

> This Vatican Council declares that the human person has a right to religious freedom. This freedom means that all men are to be immune from coercion on the part of individuals or of social groups and of any human power, in such wise that no one is to be forced to act in a manner contrary to his own beliefs, whether privately or publicly, whether alone or in association with others, within due limits. (n. 2)

These words point out very clearly that the right to religious freedom is a right that falls within the sphere of civil and political society in which human existence is promoted and, as such, it must be sanctioned and respected in legal systems. In other words, every man and every woman, with no distinction whatsoever, is recognised as a subject having the right to express his or her personal choice of religious belief, based on his or her personal judgement. Obviously – as clarified in the Declaration – this must be done 'within due limits', that is to say, as clarified in n. 7, taking into account that

> the moral principle of personal and social responsibility is to be observed. In the exercise of their rights, individual men and social groups are bound by the moral law to have respect both for the

rights of others and for their own duties toward others and for the common welfare of all.

As described above, the right to religious freedom is proposed in a mainly negative form.[4] Since the function of government is 'to make provision for the common welfare' (see n. 3), it is not to interfere in the personal religious sphere, which resides intangibly in the conscience of each human person and neither in the public sphere where, given the social nature of human beings, conscience can and must necessarily be expressed in a communitarian form. Indeed, the government 'would clearly transgress the limits set to its power, were it to presume to command or inhibit acts that are religious' (ibid.). In language we might use today, it could be said that the government is 'secular' by nature, meaning that it should not be denominationally religious nor ideologically atheistic.

But then a question springs to mind. Why did a considerable number (though never the majority) of the Council Fathers view statements like this with great suspicion? To understand this, we should carefully consider the cultural and theological paradigm out of which some of the Council Fathers were reading the issue. They considered the right to religious freedom as irreparably undermined by subjectivism and relativism. For them it seemed as if the right to religious freedom was like stating that the religious option was exclusively, entirely and subjectively in the hands of the human person, thereby betraying – as they saw it – the rights of objective truth definitively incarnated by Catholic faith and defended and promoted by Church institutions.

Clearly, relying on an obsolete notion of the *societas christiana*, one that was fading due to secularisation and pluralism, they did not understand the difference between a socio-cultural and legal fact such as the right to religious freedom, and the ethical and religious imperative of conscience open to seeking the truth and, once discovered, adhering to it. On the other hand – as pointed out during the Council debate – it was not appropriate to talk about the rights of objective truth because these rights always pertain to a subject, be it human beings or God himself. Finally, it must be borne in mind that for these Church Fathers a clear consequence derived from the paradigm of thought they took for granted, namely, that State power per se is to recognise that only the Catholic religion is the *religio vera*, and therefore to be encouraged and promoted by all means, and that other religious denominations are simply to be 'tolerated'.

The Declaration *Dignitatis humanae* developed a paradigm that went in a totally different direction, one that up until then had not been explored nor taken up by the Catholic Magisterium, not even in *Pacem in terris* by John XXIII (1963), where the principle of religious freedom was clearly recognised.

THE ANTHROPOLOGICAL FOUNDATIONS OF THE RIGHT TO FREEDOM

The second point I want to explore is the universal anthropological foundation of the principle of religious freedom that we find in *Dignitatis humanae*. It is in illustrating this principle that one can observe the change in paradigm of which the Declaration itself is such a clear sign. The principle is transparently set out in paragraphs 2 and 3, where its implications are also described in detail.

First of all, paragraph 2 highlights certain things with the same solemnity and strength used in the text immediately prior to it when declaring the principle of religious freedom:

> [This Vatican Council] declares that the right to religious freedom has its foundation in the very dignity of the human person as this dignity is known through the revealed word of God and by reason itself. (n. 1)

According to the Council, the right to religious freedom is not something that is merely subjective, but rather stems from human nature and the deep and radical vocation whereby every human being becomes a person endowed with reason and freedom that enable a person to establish an existential relationship with the Good, Truth and Justice. In a word – in religious terms – with God himself as the horizon and ultimate decisive sense of each and every good, truth and justice both in history and in its transcendent fulfilment. The paths of reason and the paths of faith intersect as *Dignitatis humanae* affirms:

> It is in accordance with their dignity as persons – that is, beings endowed with reason and free will and therefore privileged to bear personal responsibility – that all men should be at once impelled by nature and also bound by a moral obligation to seek the truth, especially religious truth. They are also bound to

adhere to the truth, once it is known, and to order their whole lives in accord with the demands of truth. However, men cannot discharge these obligations in a manner in keeping with their own nature unless they enjoy immunity from external coercion as well as psychological freedom. Therefore the right to religious freedom has its foundation not in the subjective disposition of the person, but in his very nature. In consequence, the right to this immunity continues to exist even in those who do not live up to their obligation of seeking the truth and adhering to it and the exercise of this right is not to be impeded, provided that just public order be observed. (n. 2).

In this passage (as well as in others that are similar) the dignity of the human person, on which religious freedom is based as its key expression, is recognised in terms of the relational and responsive vocation that characterises human being. It is as such that it is called to be fulfilled. This means that the human person – to say it in classical terms – is per se *capax Dei*, that is to say, capable of knowing and recognising God, and therefore freely choosing him and, in him, choosing truth, good and justice. In the biblical and Christian tradition this is expressed in an extraordinary definition – starting from the book of Genesis – of men and women created 'in God's image and likeness' (cf. Gn 1:26). This means that the human person not only stands before God through a free gift with a distinct and reasonable, free, irreplaceable and original identity, but also that the human person expresses him/herself and is fulfilled by living in a just and good relationship – that is, one based on love – with God and other creatures.

Actually, the language regarding truth that is found in *Dignitatis humanae* oscillates significantly. On the one hand, truth is expressed in personalistic terms, but on the other hand, it is also defined in objective terms. This is further confirmed by the many changes and additions to the *Declaration* that, as we have already mentioned, tried to accommodate the remarks and objections made by critics, without, however, managing to obtain a harmonious and coherent synthesis. And yet the two languages do not cancel each other out, especially if understood in terms of the level of meaning in each case. The personalistic language is the one that best manages to translate the anthropological significance of the religious relationship between human freedom and the truth of God that calls human freedom and offers itself to it.

For example, as the philosopher and theologian Jonathan Sacks, Chief Rabbi of the Commonwealth, puts it:

> [T]he discovery of monotheism is ... a less significant discovery than its other great insight: that God is personal, that there is something at the heart of reality that responds to and affirms our existence as persons. The universe is more than a billion galaxies silently rotating in space. We are not mere cosmic dust on the surface of eternity. We are here because someone wanted us to be. God did not create the universe as a scientist in a laboratory, or as a technocrat setting in motion the big bang but rather as a parent giving birth to a child. The universe is neither indifferent nor hostile to our existence. That was the great leap of the biblical imagination.[5]

In this perspective, the dia-logic underlying personalistic language is unquestionably the one that most effectively and clearly expresses the dynamics and rhythm of the relationship between the human person, in his or her freedom, and the personal God as the ultimate instance of the enlightenment of our being and existence in accordance with truth and love. This dia-logic pervades some of the wonderful statements found in *Dignitatis humanae*, statements that aim to describe this decisive, albeit mysterious, relationship. So, in language that resonates strongly with Augustine, words like *quaerere, amplecti ac servare veritatem* (meaning 'to seek', 'to embrace and protect the truth') are used from the very beginning (n. 1) of the Declaration. Again with Augustinian overtones, there's a text that states that 'the truth cannot impose itself except by virtue of its own truth, as it makes its entrance into the mind at once quietly and with power' (ibid.). Truth is actually a proposal made to human freedom, and it is not imposed. This is so because, at the end of the day, truth is nothing other than the gift with which God communicates himself to humanity, inviting us in our turn to be open in freedom to realising the truth and the justice of our relationship with God and with all (other human beings and created things), in an orderly and harmonious way.

From what we have just said, we can understand the strong and clear statements made in regard to the intangibility of personal conscience as well as the communicative and dialogical nature of the search and experience of truth not only in relationship with God, but also in our relationship with others. If, as pointed out in the Council's Pastoral Constitution of the Church in the modern world, *Gaudium et spes*, conscience is 'the most secret core and sanctuary of a man. There he is alone with God, Whose voice echoes in his depths' (n. 16), it follows – as explained in *Dignitatis humanae* – that

> In all his activity a man is bound to follow his conscience in order that he may come to God, the end and purpose of life. It follows that he is not to be forced to act in a manner contrary to his conscience. Nor, on the other hand, is he to be restrained from acting in accordance with his conscience, especially in matters religious. The reason is that the exercise of religion, of its very nature, consists before all else in those internal, voluntary and free acts whereby man sets the course of his life directly toward God. No merely human power can either command or prohibit acts of this kind. (n. 3)

And – as clarified in the Declaration – it also follows that

> Truth, however, is to be sought after in a manner proper to the dignity of the human person and his social nature. The inquiry is to be free, carried on with the aid of teaching or instruction, communication and dialogue, in the course of which men explain to one another the truth they have discovered, or think they have discovered, in order thus to assist one another in the quest for truth. Moreover, as the truth is discovered, it is by a personal assent that men are to adhere to it. (ibid.)

I would like to stress that with this broad statement, the principle of religious freedom that is undoubtedly based on the dignity of the human person and the inviolability of personal conscience, is at the same time preserved from an individualistic interpretation. The connection between freedom and truth is actually not described abstractly in terms of some rarefied transcendental relation, but rather it is acknowledged that the relationship of freedom and truth is mediated. It is a process that takes into account historicity, described as tradition (in a socio-cultural sense even before a theological one), and social relations, as dimensions that express and realise personal being.

This explains why the Declaration reminds us that there needs to be a transmission of values through teaching, communication and dialogue about them in a spirit of mutual openness, in order to help one another to seek truth. The principle of religious freedom is organically and dynamically associated not only with the principle of truth but also with the principle of dialogue. Obviously this is to be understood in terms of the vertical line of dialogue with God. But also in terms of the horizontal line of dialogue among people; and therefore in the diachronic line of the transmission of tradition from generation to generation, as well as in the synchronic line of encounter, exchange, comparison, common search and verification.

RELIGIOUS FREEDOM, TRUTH AND FAITH

I want now to look at the second part of *Dignitatis humane* and what it tells us about religious freedom in the light of revelation. Following the analysis we have proposed, we are now getting into the third level of statements made in the Declaration. We are dealing with the response to the question that the critics never tired of asking during the heated debate: what is the relationship, in fact and in law, between the principle of religious freedom, unquestionably formulated by the Council in an innovative way compared with the recent past of Catholic Magisterium, and Christian revelation, that is 'yesterday, today and forever' (cf. Heb 13:8)?

The question was not marginal. Quite the contrary. From a theological viewpoint it was key. In rejecting the proposal put forward by the schema *De libertate religiosa*, the detractors were saying that there is no trace of such a doctrine in Revelation and Tradition. Manifesting a clear and courageous choice, the Declaration undertook to give reasons for the doctrine in paragraphs 9, 10 and 11, countering the objection and declaring in determined fashion that

> ... this doctrine of freedom has roots in divine revelation, and for this reason Christians are bound to respect it all the more conscientiously. Revelation does not indeed affirm in so many words the right of man to immunity from external coercion in matters religious. It does, however, disclose the dignity of the human person in its full dimensions. It gives evidence of the respect which Christ showed toward the freedom with which man is to fulfil his duty of belief in the word of God and it gives

us lessons in the spirit which disciples of such a Master ought to adopt and continually follow. Thus further light is cast upon the general principles upon which the doctrine of this declaration on religious freedom is based. In particular, religious freedom in society is entirely consonant with the freedom of the act of Christian faith. (n. 9)

There are two things worth noticing in this text. First, the fact that religious freedom – in its anthropological foundation and legal expression in the civil sphere – is not only consonant with biblical revelation in general and Christological revelation in particular, but is also led back to it as one of its specific roots.

Particularly effective in this regard is the short but fine description that *Dignitatis humanae* gives of the event of Jesus Christ, 'in whom God manifested Himself and His ways' (n. 11). As explained in the following passage,

> He refused to be a political messiah, ruling by force: He preferred to call Himself the Son of Man, who came 'to serve and to give his life as a ransom for the many' (Mk 10:45). He showed Himself the perfect servant of God (Is 42:1-4) who 'does not break the bruised reed nor extinguish the smoking flax' (Mt 12:20). (n. 11)

The extraordinary measure of freedom that Christ showed is expressed in two ways. First, by his self-giving in response to the self-giving of God who is Father, *Abba*. And, second, by seeking, in conformity with God's loving plan for them, the liberation of his brothers and sisters. Christ did this with a style that is paradigmatically expressed by compassion and tenderness towards the one erring – who is still the son of the Father, even if prodigal – so that a bruised *reed* he will not *break* and a dimly burning wick he will not extinguish. Therefore, only love and forgiveness, and not imposition, can give light also to those who 'sit in darkness and in the shadow of death' (cf. Lk 1:79). And here are the wonderful words with which *Dignitatis humanae* reproposes Jesus Christ's ministry of freedom in the history of humanity:

> (He) bore witness to the truth, (cf. Jn 18:37) but He refused to impose the truth by force on those who spoke against it. Not by force of blows does His rule assert its claims. It is established by

witnessing to the truth and by hearing the truth, and it extends its dominion by the love whereby Christ, lifted up on the cross, draws all men to Himself (cf. Jn 12:32). (n. 11)

Truth, then, which offers itself as such to human freedom, inviting it to its fulfilment as true freedom, is the 'crucified truth' or, better still, the truth personified in Christ Crucified.

The second point emerging here from the text concerns what *Dignitatis humanae* describes as the 'congruity' between religious freedom in society and the freedom of the Christian act of faith. Actually, even more could have been said: not only is freedom, which characterises the act of faith, congruous with acknowledgement of religious freedom in the civil sphere, but – in Christian theology – it can be understood as the carrying out of that freedom, in seeking and adhering to God, and it is in this that dignity and vocation of the person are expressed. In *Dei Verbum,* n. 5, the Constitution on divine revelation, promulgated almost at the same time as *Dignitatis humanae,* the Second Vatican Council successfully declares that:

> 'The obedience of faith' (Rm 13:26; cf. Rm 1:5; 2 Cor 10:5-6) is to be given to God who reveals, an obedience by which man commits his whole self freely to God, offering the full submission of intellect and will to God who reveals, and freely assenting to the truth revealed by Him.[6]

RELIGIOUS FREEDOM IN HISTORY

But at this point we can ask: what about the community of the disciples of the Crucified Christ who, precisely as Crucified is the Risen Christ contemporary in every place and time, the generous, humble and gentle bestower of the Spirit of freedom, justice and peace, has this community been faithful over the centuries to the new mandate of freedom and love entrusted to it by the Son of Man? And here we come to the fourth level – one barely mentioned but nonetheless important, indeed very important – in the affirmations contained in *Dignitatis humanae*: what happened to the history of freedom (the *Freiheitsgeschichte* of modern people) in the history of Christianity and the Church? The Declaration introduces somewhat carefully and timidly a theme that the Catholic Church will eventually face with courage in the lead-up to Jubilee Year 2000 celebration under the tenacious impulse of Pope John

Paul II, asking before God and the entire world for forgiveness for the sin of infidelity to the Gospel of Jesus Christ. The Declaration states:

> In faithfulness therefore to the truth of the Gospel, the Church is following the way of Christ and the apostles when she recognises and gives support to the principle of religious freedom as befitting the dignity of man and as being in accord with divine revelation. Throughout the ages the Church has kept safe and handed on the doctrine received from the Master and from the apostles. In the life of the People of God, as it has made its pilgrim way through the vicissitudes of human history, there has at times appeared a way of acting that was hardly in accord with the spirit of the Gospel or even opposed to it. Nevertheless, the doctrine of the Church that no one is to be coerced into faith has always stood firm. (n. 12)

From this we get the two statements that, if we think about it carefully, end up harmoniously intertwining in the text of *Dignitatis humanae*. On the one hand, the sincere recognition at the very beginning of the *Declaration*:

> A sense of the dignity of the human person has been impressing itself more and more deeply on the consciousness of contemporary man, and the demand is increasingly made that men should act on their own judgement, enjoying and making use of a responsible freedom, not driven by coercion but motivated by a sense of duty. (n. 1)

On the other, the clear awareness that:

> The leaven of the Gospel has long been about its quiet work in the minds of men, and to it is due in great measure the fact that in the course of time men have come more widely to recognise their dignity as persons, and the conviction has grown stronger that the person in society is to be kept free from all manner of coercion in matters religious. (n. 12)

Here again, the logic that is to shape the understanding and management of relationships between communities of the disciples of Christ and the wider community of the entire human family is the principle of dialogue mentioned above, since it is intrinsic to the very same nature of God's revelation in Jesus Christ. With great openness *Gaudium et spes* puts it as follows:

> Just as it is in the world's interest to acknowledge the Church as an historical reality, and to recognise her good influence, so the Church herself knows how richly she has profited by the history and development of humanity. The experience of past ages, the progress of the sciences, and the treasures hidden in the various forms of human culture, by all of which the nature of man himself is more clearly revealed and new roads to truth are opened, these profit the Church, too ... Moreover, she gratefully understands that in her community life no less than in her individual sons, she receives a variety of helps from men of every rank and condition ... Indeed, the Church admits that she has greatly profited and still profits from the antagonism of those who oppose or who persecute her. (n. 44)

PROPHETIC AND PRACTICAL IMPLICATIONS

The last level of meaning to be found in the statements contained in *Dignitatis humanae* has to do with the new (and therefore daunting and risky) task and challenge that we are faced with today to make sure that religious freedom does not remain simply limited to a principle, but rather transforms our experience deeply, interiorly and effectively.

The Declaration offers a mere hint in its conclusion. However, in deep harmony with the spirit and the teachings of the Council, it reveals a bright and prophetic line of commitment, as pointed out by Peter Hünermann:

> With *Dignitatis humanae* the Council Fathers clarified – without realising it – the public requirements for dialogue, which is so urgent, between religions and modernity. In order to proceed further, this dialogue very much needed public religious freedom and juridical support to get it going. Through the religious foundation of religious freedom, the Council Fathers have also shown to other religions the model of a possible approach – starting from their respective roots – to the idea and concept of religious freedom, without losing one's specific identity and mission.[7]

But let us re-read *Dignitatis humanae* itself:

> All nations are coming into even closer unity. Men of different cultures and religions are being brought together in closer relationships. There is a growing consciousness of the personal responsibility that every man has. All this is evident. Consequently, in order that relationships of peace and harmony be established and maintained within the whole of mankind, it is necessary that religious freedom be everywhere provided with an effective constitutional guarantee and that respect be shown for the high duty and right of man freely to lead his religious life in society. (n. 15)

And what does this mean? To paraphrase the title of Jonathan Sacks' important essay, it means that the recognition of religious freedom on the basis of the common and universal dignity of the human person implies the concrete recognition and promotion of the dignity of difference. This is the Rubicon that human civilisation is called to cross today. Sacks, faithful to the Jewish tradition to which he belongs, says it very clearly:

> There is nothing relativist about the idea of the dignity of difference. It is based on the radical transcendence of God from the created universe, with its astonishing diversity of life forms – all of which, as we now know through genetic research, derive from a single source – and from the multiple languages and cultures through which we, as meaning-seeking beings, have attempted to understand the totality of existence.[8]

And this is what we have seen coming true, in a surprising and tangible manner, in the Assisi meeting that was like an icon that would have been absolutely unforeseeable in human history until a few decades ago. The World Day of Prayer for Peace and Religions strongly advocated by Pope John Paul II was celebrated on 27 October 1986 in that region so much associated with St Francis who praised the Lord of heaven and earth 'with all his creatures'. To borrow from Pope John Paul's words, that day was

> ... a visible illustration, a concrete example, a catechesis, intelligible to all, of what is presupposed and signified by the commitment

to ecumenism and the interreligious dialogue which was recommended and promoted by the Second Vatican Council.[9]

For Christian faith it is the truth of the triune God revealed in Jesus Christ that sheds light on God's plan for freedom and the free recapitulation of differences. Within the light of faith, these differences are viewed in their positive and creative meaning within the unity of the Total Christ that humankind is called to become. A great mystic of our time, Chiara Lubich, has summed this up beautifully as follows:

> The Father says: 'Love' in infinite tones and generates the Word, which is love, inside Himself, the Son, and the Son as such, echo of the Father, says 'Love' and returns to the Father![10]

The history of humankind and of the world is nothing other than the free and amazing created illustration of this divine, Trinitarian love, a love that is infinitely rich in tones and colours in which our history finds its beginning and its end. The journey is not going to be simple nor easy. History itself, especially in its tormented and uncertain present, bears witness to that. But, as Václav Havel wrote in his essay 'The Art of the Impossible':

> We should recognise that something stands beyond the present time and space, that we are tied to the world fully and eternally. We should recognise that if we do not manage to reflect universal, superindividual and supertemporal interests, we will jeopardise our specific, local and immediate interests. Only those having a sense of responsibility for the world and in the world are truly responsible to and for themselves.[11]

CONCLUSION

I would like to conclude this brief re-reading of *Dignitatis humanae* by recalling two paradoxes that have always troubled my mind and soul when talking about the mystery of freedom that dwells in us and constitutes us thanks to the love of God.

The first one was formulated by my philosophy professor at the University of Turin, Luigi Pareyson, in the first pages of one of his early works, the excellent essay titled *Esistenza e persona*.[12] There is just one thing – he writes

– we are not free of, and this mysteriously manifests to us the basis of the freedom that we are, a freedom that is both gift and vocation: we are not free from ... being free!

The second paradox was put forward by Teresa of Avila.[13] At a point in her *Interior Castle* she asks: do you know when people really become spiritual? By that she means able to follow the freedom of the Spirit that 'blows where it pleases' (cf. Jn 3:8)? Her response is that it is when, with a supreme and at the same time simple and free act of freedom, we return our will to God: not to renounce it, but to receive it anew with the measure of freedom of God himself: the measureless measure of love. And ultimately that is our highest dignity.

NOTES

1. I am particularly glad to dedicate this paper to my friend Dr Brendan Purcell who, thanks to the creative and free intelligence of his teaching, has always been able to describe the unquestionable wealth of the story of Jesus Christ and its effective unfolding in the history of humankind with persuasive incisiveness in the light of the incarnated prophecy of 'a new heaven and a new earth'.
2. G. Routhier, 'Portare a termine l'opera iniziata: la faticosa esperienza del quarto periodo', *Storia del concilio Vaticano II*, vol. 5: *Concilio di transizione. Il quarto periodo e la conclusione del Concilio (1965)*, G. Alberigo, ed. (Bologna: Società Editrice il Mulino, 2001), pp. 73–195, p. 133.
3. P. Hünermann, 'Le ultime settimane del Concilio', *Storia del Concilio Vaticano II*, vol. 5, G. Alberigo, pp. 371–491, p. 459.
4. See P. Pavan, *La Dichiarazione conciliare* Dignitatis humanae *a 20 anni dalla pubblicazione*, (Casale Monferrato: Piemme, 1986).
5. J. Sacks, *The Dignity of Difference: How to Avoid the Clash of Civilizations* (London: Continuum, 2002), p. 180.
6. See further Piero Coda, 'De revelatione fide suscipienda. Sul significato e le prospettive di *Dei Verbum* 5', *La parola di Dio compia la sua corsa. I 'loci theologici' alla luce della 'Dei Verbum'*, G. Lorizio and I. Sanna, eds. (Rome: Lateran University Press, 2006), pp. 69–83.
7. P. Hünermann, 'Le ultime settimane del Concilio', p. 465.
8. J. Sacks, *The Dignity of Difference*, pp. 200–1.
9. See Pope John Paul II's Address to the Roman Curia 22 December, 1986, n. 7.
10. See P. Coda, *Dio che dice Amore. Lezioni di teologia* (Rome: Città Nuova, 2007).
11. V. Havel, *The Art of the Impossible* (New York: Fromm, 1998), quoted in J. Sacks, *The Dignity of Difference*, p. 179.
12. L. Pareyson, *Esistenza e persona. Saggi teorici* (Turin: Taylor, 1950).
13. Teresa of Avila, *Interior Castle*, E. Allison Peers, trans. (New York and London: Image Books Doubleday, 1989), VII, chap. IV, par. 8, p. 229: 'Do you know when people really become spiritual? It is when they become the slaves of God and are branded with His sign, which is the sign of the Cross, in token that they have given Him their freedom. Then He can sell them as slaves to the whole world, as He Himself was

sold, and if He does this He will be doing them no wrong but showing them no slight favour. Unless they resolve to do this, they need not expect to make great progress. For the foundation of this whole edifice, as I have said, is humility, and, if you have not true humility, the Lord will not wish it to reach any great height: in fact, it is for your own good that it should not; if it did, it would fall to the ground. Therefore, sisters, if you wish to lay good foundations, each of you must try to be the least of all, and the slave of God, and must seek a way and means to please and serve all your companions. If you do that, it will be of more value to you than to them and your foundation will be so firmly laid that your Castle will not fall.'

Chiara Lubich and The Science of the 'Why?'

BRENDAN LEAHY

The following contribution may initially surprise readers. It revolves around the life and thought of Chiara Lubich (1920–2008), an Italian woman who cannot be considered a professional philosopher.[1] As founder of the worldwide Focolare movement, she is better known for her spiritual doctrine, her promotion of dialogue at all levels, notably interfaith dialogue, and multiple social initiatives that she established. Yet if we allow that founders of new communities within Christian history have also spawned new pathways in intellectual insight and indicated new directions in what Charles Taylor calls the 'social imaginary', then it is legitimate to consider the thought of Chiara Lubich as a source for exploration in a volume dedicated to the subject of the human person.

There are several other specific reasons for doing so. First, she always loved philosophy and, in pursuit of Truth, wanted to read philosophy in the University of Venice. The Second World War destroyed those plans. In their place, she was to excavate for Truth in the midst of what Eric Voegelin has called 'the community of suffering' brought about by ideological 'power and revolution' in the twentieth century.[2] The movement she founded came to life precisely in the midst of the Second World War, a period of deep searching for cultural renewal. It is appropriate in this context to cite another comment by Eric Voegelin that invites us to consider the importance of a figure such as Chiara Lubich within the philosophical and cultural landscape of our times. In 1938, writing the preface to the second edition of his work, *The Political Religions*, Voegelin, then in Harvard, commented:

> There is no distinguished philosopher or thinker in the western world today who, firstly, is not aware – and has not also expressed this sentiment – that the world is experiencing a serious crisis, is undergoing a process of withering, which has its origins in the secularisation of the soul and in the ensuing severance of a

> consequently purely secular soul from its roots in religiousness, and, secondly, does not know that recovery can only be achieved through religious renewal, be it within the framework of the historical churches, be it outside this framework. Such renewal, to a large extent, can only be initiated by great religious personalities, but everyone can be ready and willing to do his share ... [3]

A review of history lends support to Voegelin' assertion in that there have been many waves of religious renewal that enflamed the soul of many a person with evident social consequences. It is not difficult to point to an array of prophetic individuals who contributed much at times of crisis within western culture. It is enough to mention Augustine of Hippo and Benedict of Nursia, Francis and Clare of Assisi and the Franciscan movement that produced Bonaventure and Duns Scotus; Dominic de Guzmán whose order of preachers gave us Thomas Aquinas; Ignatius of Loyola's company that included Francisco Suárez. Social, economic and political organisation as well as philosophy, the arts and scientific study of nature have all been influenced in some way by the mystical inspiration of charismatic figures.

Chiara Lubich's thought emerges from a charism that focuses on 'unity'. Its original view of Christian revelation and vision of the world casts a light on various levels of existence. Throughout her life, Lubich encouraged and inspired many engaged in cultural pursuits. Among those who have acknowledged her immediate influence in their own life and scholarship are the late German Bishop of Aachen, Klaus Hemmerle, formerly professor of philosophy of religion in Freiburg (succeeding Bernard Welte under whom he had studied) and the Italian philosopher-theologian, Piero Coda, whose work on negativity in Hegel is well recognised.[4] Moving beyond Europe, in the University in Mumbai, Prof. Kala Acharya of the Somaiya Sanskriti Peetham and Prof. Shubhada Joshi of the Department of Philosophy enjoyed fruitful contact with Chiara Lubich. In terms of this book, Brendan Purcell is also one who has been influenced in his research and writings by his contact with her and the spirituality she promoted.

Having spent decades in many parts of the world promoting various forms of community-living and social projects, in the early 1980s Chiara Lubich established the cultural review, *Nuova Umanità*.[5] In 1989 she established an international study centre within the Focolare Movement to explore the cultural and doctrinal implications of its spiritual doctrine. This centre adopts a transdisciplinary approach with academics and professionals from various disciplines (from philosophy to politics, theology to art, economics to social communications, science, psychology etc.) 'thinking together' in the light of a profound commitment to place their shared personal existence at the heart of their intellectual journey.[6] It has been an experience akin to what Plato wrote in his Seventh Letter – the Truth is like a flame set off from a long communion of life and conversation, leaping from one to another. Among other things, the members of this centre study intuitions and writings of Chiara Lubich from the summer of 1949, a particular period of light and insight, close to the beginning of the Movement.[7]

On 6 June 1997, Chiara Lubich was conferred with an honorary doctorate in philosophy at the Jean-Baptiste de La Salle University in Mexico City. On 7 December 2007, just months before she died, a long-held dream came true for her. She oversaw the establishment of a university institute, set up by a Pontifical decree of the Holy See.[8] The name she chose for the institute was 'Sophia', Wisdom for which Jesus thanked the Father for having hidden from the wise and intelligent and revealed to infants (cf. Mt 11:25).

LEARNING FROM LIFE

In order to outline some aspects of Chiara Lubich's thought, it is important to underline how much she emphasised *life* and *living* life. Interestingly, in a recent work David Walsh has contended that philosophy from Kant to the present has seen a shift from an account of entities and concepts 'to an existential meditation on the horizon within which it finds itself … The death of metaphysics in thought has meant the return of metaphysics in life … It is not that we in the modern world have lost faith, but that philosophy has come to understand the meaning of faith in a very different way.'[9]

In the earlier phase of the movement's development, Chiara Lubich would sometimes quote a phrase associated with the early Franciscans: 'Paris, Paris, you kill Assisi!', Paris representing an arid academic pursuit while Assisi meaning the fruitful living source of the Franciscan movement. While always recognising the value of cultural exploration and study, she nevertheless sensed the need to remind her followers of the primary need to *live* life as that is the basis of thought. She believed passionately that it is an authentic communion of life shared with others, engaging the whole person, that gives a permanent direction to existence. It is on that basis that study, rather than distancing us from true knowing, develops and clarifies what is being lived.

Chiara Lubich learned this from life. As the Second World War raged, and so many certainties crumbled, the 'why' questions loomed large – why life? why suffering? why love? why hatred? But then a light: 'Look, I am a soul passing through this world. I have seen many beautiful and good things and I have always been attracted only by them. One day (one indescribable day) I saw a light. It appeared to me as more beautiful than the other beautiful things, and I followed it. I realised it was the Truth.'[10] The world around her became the access point to the light of God hidden behind all circumstances, good and bad, ugly and beautiful, just and unjust. It was fascination with this light that she and those who followed her launched on an adventure of life that was to be an ever new discovery of truth. Now, other persons, events and all that was changing around them, became illuminated, as it were, within this light, the light of God who is Love. It was a matter of opening unreservedly to it.

Essentially her experience was a new perception of the One who said of himself: 'I am the Truth' (Jn 14:6). Her experience blossomed into a mysticism that shaped a new way of living out of the Gospel that Jesus proclaimed, a new way at a time when humanity was beginning to enter an accelerated technological drive towards becoming a single family. The specific sentence of the Gospel that was to inspire her most was from the Fourth Gospel: 'May they all be one' (Jn 17:21). If the Gospel message had opened up in countless ways throughout the previous two thousand years of Christian history, now it was presenting itself in terms of unity. She tells of the simplicity of the discovery as she and her companions read the Gospel in the darkness of an air raid shelter in the northern Italian city of Trent. It was as if, she wrote, the words of that chapter of the Gospel were lit up from within.

With unity a central goal in life, one paradoxical element of Jesus' life stood out – the most hidden and interior, the deepest and most tragic suffering, that of a radical aloneness, isolation and absurdity of the Cross. In the ninth hour, Jesus exclaimed: 'My God, my God, why have you forsaken me?' (Mt 27:46). He cried out his being forsaken by the One he had always called 'Abba, Father'. Chiara Lubich came to understand that if Jesus, in this cry, expressed love, feeling separation from God in order to make himself our neighbour and re-unite us to the Father, then this cry, this face of Jesus, the Forsaken One, would be the ideal of her life. The key to the fulfilment of the Gospel phrase 'may they all be one' was, then, to be found precisely in this cry of forsakenness.

Piero Coda describes what this discovery was to mean for these young girls in Trent during the war. Their dream of unity could easily have remained a romantic notion were it not for the fact that it was rooted in a real search for and discovery of the face of Jesus Forsaken in every darkness, division and suffering. And since he had transformed death into life, division into unity, they understood him as the key to history: 'Because of Jesus Forsaken, recognised and welcomed as the one good, unity is no longer a utopia: it becomes history, humanity's real history.'[11] This became a guiding principle for all other elements of the mystical and spiritual experience Chiara and her companions lived – the focus on going to God in love for one another, balancing contemplation and action, openness in dialogue with others.

With its emphasis on love for one another, mutual co-interest and co-responsibility, the lifestyle promoted by Chiara Lubich bears witness to a paradigm shift in the history of Christian spirituality 'by going from the primacy of the individual to a balance between persons and communion.'[12] With her underlining of the need to move from the primarily inward-shaped spirituality to one that sees relationship with the neighbour as constitutive of one's personal existence and fulfilment, what Chiara Lubich teaches 'lays down the kind of foundations needed for a significant cultural paradigm shift. In a troubled and sometimes even tragic way our era demands such a shift with urgency.'[13] Indeed, her doctrine indicates a kind of holiness that is still perhaps to be discovered as surprisingly suited to our times, a holiness of the people, shaped along a collective, communitarian journey.

In an insightful article, Piero Coda traces the history of Christian mystical experiences in relation to the Blessed Trinity from St Augustine to Chiara Lubich.[14] He notes that with Augustine, search for union with the triune God focused on the 'internal place' of the soul. Accordingly, mystics like Dionysius the Areopagite described the triune God as the mysterious fountain of being, found only by an inner ascetical journey through darkness, silence and 'unknowing' into what is utterly unspeakable. The school of thought that emerged with the mendicant orders indicated two other 'places' for finding the Trinity – creation (emphasised specially by Thomas Aquinas) and the Crucified Christ (emphasised by Francis of Assisi). In his exploration of John of the Cross, Coda contends that the Carmelite mysticism offers a kind of fulfilment of the interior spiritual journey to the centre of the soul by adding the two other places where the Trinity can be found, namely, creation and Jesus crucified.

Recalling, however, that Augustine had also glimpsed another 'place' that he had not pursued in his reflection, namely mutual love as 'the place' from which we can fly up to the contemplation of the Trinity, Coda proposes that in our time Chiara Lubich's mystical experiences of the Trinity pick up on this dimension of reciprocity. On the one hand, she too writes of an inner personal union with Jesus Forsaken seen as the apex of the kenotic love of Jesus crucified. But she also refers to a union with the Risen Christ experienced in the collective unity of mutual love between her and her companions. It was these two unions that enabled Lubich's companions to share in her experiences. The unity of mutual love, lived in reciprocal 'kenosis' before one another, with Jesus Forsaken as the measure of love for one another, and the presence of the Risen Christ among them when they were united in his name, became the collective place of love wherein Lubich and her companions communally experienced God and thereby also came to recognise a new awareness of the Trinity in creation.

PHILOSOPHY – THE SCIENCE OF THE 'WHY?'

So what can be said of Chiara Lubich's philosophy? She outlined some of its elements in her acceptance address at an honorary doctorate ceremony in Mexico in 1996.[15] In referring to philosophy as the 'science of the "whys"', she referred to the moment of Jesus' question 'why' uttered on the Cross as 'pregnant with answers to all our questions'.[16] Here was a scene of the 'most abysmal separation that can ever be imagined', Jesus, the Son of God, feeling abandoned by the One with whom he was and remained one. She comments,

> ... in seeing that in his abandonment, Jesus was 'cursed' (Gal 3:13) in order to make himself one with those who are far from God, he really seemed to be the God of our times: the divine answer to the poverty of millions of the underprivileged and to the question for meaning and ideals on the part of the disillusioned and confused new generations. Likewise, he is the answer to the depths of tribulation and suffering etched into the human heart by the atheism that pervades so much of modern culture.[17]

It was by placing Jesus Forsaken as the ideal of their life that Chiara and her followers found the courage to go where he is present and work to relieve sufferings and build unity. But Jesus Forsaken was not simply the answer to our personal questions. Rather,

> He – God who asks 'why', who asks the reason for a severed relationship which seems to touch the very unity of God! – is certainly *the* question, so to speak, carried to its deepest, its most radical expression, that to which no human question dares to go. Thus, he seems to be the one who best represents human intelligence in the face of mystery ... He asks his great 'why' precisely in order to give the answer to the many 'whys' which are more the object of philosophical reflection.[18]

One of the questions to which Chiara applies herself is the question of being. While recognising that there are many different cultural ways to define being, she starts from a fundamental statement of human thought that 'being is', the acknowledgement of 'that great ocean of existence in which human beings are immersed in communion with everyone and everything.'[19] Being is offered to us by all that is around us and within us.

> This being – which all things have in common and for which they are not simply a nothingness – reveals, in a natural manifestation, that Being which none of them is, but which they all announce. Their becoming, their limits, their very ceasing to exist is the language in which it is stated that the being of all that exists is rooted in a Being that simply and absolutely IS.[20]

Chiara sees this as an analogy for our inner life. From the very beginnings of philosophical reflection, the awareness that human beings have had of themselves has been itself an acknowledgement of being. She writes that 'for human beings to say "I" is equivalent to opening oneself to being able to say, in communion with the being of all things, that the Absolute Being is'. Nevertheless, as a writer in the twentieth century, she recognises that in the course of the twentieth century in the West, 'consciousness of self has been – and is – lived as negating the objectivity of being. And it has closed itself off from the Absolute Being.'[21] In asking, 'is it true that consciousness of self and being – as the affirmation of reality in itself to the point of acknowledging the Absolute Being – cannot co-exist?',[22] she offers her view that Christianity can be explored anew to discover the solution it might propose in re-examining both the concept of the conscious subject and that of being. She proposes her discovery: 'And precisely here Jesus Forsaken presents himself as the master of light, of thought, and – I would dare to say – of *philosophy*.'[23]

She outlines her anthrop-ontological vision. In terms of our relationships with others, the issue arises as to how to reconcile affirmation of self and all that is not self. The 'other' is perceived as limit, threat. Yet, in the terrible moment of his passion, Jesus Forsaken tells us that though the consciousness of his subjectivity appears to be diminishing as he is dying (becoming nothing, as it were), in that very moment it reaches its fullness:

> With his being reduced to nothing, accepted out of love for the Father to whom he re-abandons himself ... Jesus shows us that I am myself, not when I close myself off from the other, but rather when I give myself, when out of love I lose myself in the other. If, for example, I have a flower and I give it to someone, certainly I deprive myself of it, and in depriving myself, I am losing something of myself (non-being); in reality, precisely because I give that flower, love grows in me (i.e., being). Therefore my subjectivity is when it is not, out of love; that is, when out of love it is completely transferred into the other. Jesus Forsaken is the greatest revelation of consciousness, understood as self-affirmation, precisely when he gives himself to the other, to an otherness that, at its greatest extent, in fact, is being. Genuine consciousness of self is born from the communion with being; a communion in which consciousness seems to lose itself but, in reality, it finds itself, it is. Jesus Forsaken thus enlightens being, revealing it as love. And with this he reveals to us that the Absolute Being is itself love ...[24]

Chiara proceeds to explore this Love in its Trinitarian origin, 'precisely in the dynamic relationship that exists among the three divine Persons, One with the Other, One for the Other, One in the Other' and comments, 'In the relationship of the three divine Persons, each one is love, each one is completely, by not being; because each one is, 'perichoretically' (that is, mutually indwelling), in the other Person, in eternal self-giving'.[25] So she concludes:

In the light of the Trinity, being reveals itself, if we can say this, as guarding deep within itself the non-being that is gift of self; not the non-being that negates being, rather the non-being that reveals being as love: being that is the three divine Persons. In the light of Jesus Forsaken, the subject, the being of all created things and the Absolute Being itself, find a new explanation that can serve as the basis for a new philosophy of being. This was the hope of great thinkers of our times, like Maritain and Przywara, who foresaw the possibility of progressing in the search for the truth precisely on the basis of the understanding of being as love, as is revealed in the cross of Christ ...[26]

What we see here is that, re-reading the event of Christian revelation, at its culminating point (Jesus forsaken on the Cross while utterly in relationship to the Father and to humanity), Chiara Lubich offers a reflection on how *relative* 'non-being' opens to a notion of *relational* non-being. On the one hand, finite and created beings are defined in *relative* terms of one not being the other. One thing or being is *not* another. Indeed, even within Trinitarian theology, the distinction between the three divine Persons as outlined, for instance, by Augustine involves defining each of the three Persons relative to one another again in the sense that each of the three divine Persons is 'not' the Other (each being, however, the One God). And yet, within the Triune life of God, each of the three divine Persons *is* inasmuch as they *are not* (in themselves, independently of others), in that they are themselves in giving totally and in receiving themselves in return (cf Jn 10: 17-19). Lubich proposes we can understand what it is to be human as an echo of this non-being that is relational. It is in the 'dying with' and 'rising with' Christ, as St Paul puts it in Romans 6:4-5, that we participate in and reflect the inner-Trinitarian life where to be 'in-existent', in being a gift of yourself to others, and in receiving from others in return, is to be.

Another aspect that might be worth presenting here is Chiara Lubich's consideration of the significance of creation. In its classic sense, the doctrine of creation underlines how God and creation are distinct, 'other' to one another. According to this doctrine, creation has the imprint of the divine truth; God and humanity are in a relationship of personal freedom. The Christian doctrine of the Incarnation is ontological in its implications as indicated in John's Prologue: 'in the beginning was the Word and the Word was God' (Jn

1:1) (otherness and relationship in God) and 'the Word became flesh' (Jn 1:14) (God's 'becoming' and the 'new' relationship, in the Word made flesh, between God, humanity and the world).

Chiara Lubich knows that in the history of western society, in gradually replacing the mythological view of the world, the Christian concept has sought to explain how the world is filled with the presence of God in his Word, through the Spirit, without falling into mythic interpretation. Yet, for many today, the question has become: how can God fill the world with himself? The world has gradually become empty of meaning. The current situation can be read as a dangerously negative one in terms of ecology at all levels. Lubich proposes, however, that the confusion experienced today is perhaps the slow coming to birth of a new world. As she observes:

> [G]one is the intelligence of love capable of grasping the truth and beauty of creation *from its origins*, from God who contains it and nourishes it with himself. Instead, it has been replaced by a sceptical and cold rationality that moves *among* things without penetrating into their deepest roots. The groaning of creation, of which St Paul speaks (Rm 8:22), seems no longer to be heard. It has been covered by what Heideggar called the 'idle chatter of existence', and therefore of an 'inauthentic' culture. Are we up against an irreversible crisis? Or rather the slow coming to birth of a new world?[27]

How can it be seen as a coming to birth of a new world? Here again she proposes Jesus Forsaken. He took onto himself the non-being of all who are separated from the source of being. Out of love, he made his own this 'negative' non-being and transformed it into himself, into the positive non-being that is love, as revealed in the resurrection. As she puts it, 'Jesus Forsaken made the Holy Spirit overflow into creation, thus becoming 'mother' of the new creation.'[28] It is an event still in the process of developing but, in its deepest identity, the Church, the Mystical Body of Christ understood as a community of mutual love, can be viewed as the realm where this is already a reality, the seed of its future accomplishment.

> If we live in mutual love, which brings Christ among us, and we are nourished by the Eucharist, which makes us become Christ

as a community and as individuals, and therefore Church, we can perceive the penetration of the Spirit of God into the heart of all beings, into each and into the entire cosmos. And through the Holy Spirit we intuit the existence of a nuptial relationship between the Uncreated and created because in becoming incarnate, the Word aligned himself with creation thereby divinising it and recapitulating it in himself. This wide and majestic vision makes us think of the entrance of all creation one day into the bosom of the Father … This sheds a new light upon and opens up the relationship between people and the world, of which the capacity to transform things through work and technology is just one aspect.[29]

TRINITARIAN ONTOLOGY AND PERSONHOOD

What we have sketched so far is a few points that emerge from Chiara Lubich's spiritual doctrine in its more philosophical tones. It is open to development. For his part, the philosopher pope, Blessed John Paul II, in proposing greater reflection on the relationship of faith and reason suggested that philosophical exploration on being can find much inspiration from the Trinitarian mystery revealed in the historical event of Jesus Christ.[30] In his work, *Introduction to Christianity*, Joseph Ratzinger, referring to Augustine's *De Trinitate*, commented on how much benefit might be derived from philosophical exploration of the implications of the Christ event. Noting how Augustine had attempted to re-read the themes of substance, accident and relation in terms of the God who has revealed himself in Jesus Christ, Ratzinger affirms:

> Therein lies concealed a revolution in man's view of the world: the sole dominion of thinking in terms of substance is ended; relation is discovered as an equally valid primordial mode of reality. It becomes possible to surmount what we call today 'objectifying thought'; a new plane of being comes into view. It is probably true to say that the task imposed on philosophy as a result of these facts is far from being completed – so much does modern thought depend on the possibilities thus disclosed, without which it would be inconceivable.[31]

Both Klaus Hemmerle and Piero Coda, mentioned above, have offered valid contributions to thinking through a dynamic philosophy and theology in the light of Christian revelation, not least influenced by Chiara Lubich.

In 1976 Klaus Hemmerle wrote a short work, *Thesen zu einer trinitarischen Ontologie* (*Theses of a Trinitarian Ontology*) that set the scene for the development in recent times of what is called 'Trinitarian ontology'.[32] Admittedly, traces of this notion were already to be found in writers such as Hans Urs von Balthasar (to whom Hemmerle dedicated his work), Theodor Haecker, Clemens Kaliba, Erich Przywara as well as Antonio Rosmini's 'metaphysics of charity'. Reading the work, it is clear that Hemmerle is reflecting something of his own intellectual biography. His doctoral thesis was on Franz von Baader's philosophy of creation and his post-doctoral thesis on God and thought in the later philosophy of Schelling.[33] He was particularly attracted to the writings of Bonaventure.[34] But it is also evident that he is very much influenced by Chiara Lubich's doctrine, especially her reading of 'kenosis' in Jesus Forsaken, linked by her to the dynamic relationality intrinsic in being.

In regard to the cultural interpretation and explanation of Christian revelation, Hemmerle notes that historically it didn't find or generate thought forms that were sufficient to express its specific newness: 'in the symbiosis between what is specifically Christian and ontology, the form, almost inadvertently, continued to be a sort of guest in multiple philosophical projects and systems that were heterogenous to it.'[35] Von Balthasar made a similar comment to the effect that 'inter-subjectivity, upon which the ethics of the gospel is based, failed to find an adequate philosophical foundation in the classical period' with the result that it is a largely Neoplatonic (and therefore undialogical) metaphysics which provides the conceptual underpinning for the newness of *agape*.[36]

In the *Thesen*, Hemmerle proposes the time has come to be more explicit in disclosing the horizon of interpretation of reality that comes from the revelation in Jesus Christ of the Triune God. This needs to be done mindful of the interpretative perspectives of the real offered both by the history of thought (such as the Greek metaphysical notion of substance [Aristotle's *ousia*]; the Medieval notion of the action of being [Aquinas' *actus essendi*]; and the modern focus on subjectivity [from Descartes' *cogito* onwards]) as well as by the contemporary natural and human sciences where the paradigm of relationality has come to the fore in various ways. He is not proposing that we drop a notion such as substance in order to give primacy to relationship, but rather that we recognise the dynamic of relationship in the very determination of being in itself. His re-thinking of ontology takes place in the light of an existential and intersubjective phenomenology developed on the basis of the mystery of Triune life of God revealed in Jesus Christ.

> Since God is Triune, and as such has his history in our history, our fundamental situation as human beings, our thinking and our being, indeed all being, experiences a turning point. This turning point surpasses all measure of 'traditional' human thought about God, about oneself, about the world, about being. The pure and simple re-reading of ontological pre-comprehension, traditionally characteristic of faith, does not obtain what is here disclosed and communicated to human being and intellect. The need for a 'new ontology', a 'Trinitarian ontology' is a consequence of faith itself.[37]

In the Trinitarian ontology, as outlined by Hemmerle, everything realises its essence precisely as 'event', 'self-possession in self-giving', 'being directed towards and for one another':[38] what distinguishes this Trinitarian ontology from other ontologies based on love and dialogue is that its deepest point is to be found in Christ's self-emptying, *kenosis*.

> The deepest point of a Trinitarian ontology is the fact that in the Son's kenosis every finitude and contradiction is assumed in the event of God who gives himself. In the 'why' cried out on the Cross and in the silence of Sheol to which the Son descends, all is integrated and nevertheless nothing is swallowed up.

In the Christ event, we discover love is not just solidarity, sharing or philanthropy. It is much more. The 'non-being in order to be love' that we see on the Cross is the root of all being and of all inter-relating. The Cross explains that love and being coincide. Indeed, in Christ we see how Love ontologically fills nothingness, making it full of being and the very expression of God's being. On the basis of the Christ event, we can say there is an 'ontological circle of a permanent Easter' written into being.

Hemmerle traces examples of Trinitarian ontology in the rhythm of language, art and in terms of epistemology. And so, for instance, he re-reads the philosophical axiom that *anima fit quodommodo omnia* (the soul is in some way all) in terms of the logic of the *agape* expressed in the first Letter of St John: 'everyone who loves is born of God and knows God. Whoever does not love does not know God, for God is love' (1 Jn 4:7-8). Our knowing is fulfilled if it enters into the rhythm that characterises being in its 'event', self-giving and receiving quality that is lived out in communion with others.

The Italian theologian, Piero Coda, explores what Trinitarian ontology means in terms of our notion of creation and of the person.[39] Far from being a remote or useless doctrine as Kant – along with many others – thought, the Trinity is today being rediscovered for its many social, personal, political and cultural implications. Coda develops his reflection on the basis that Christian revelation presents the Trinity as the 'realm' opened up for us in Jesus Christ that grounds a dynamic theology of history and the horizon of how to find our way to one another.

He reflects on the Christ event, especially the moment of the Cross. In that event, in his feeling abandoned by the Father and by his followers, Jesus reached us in the extreme condition of human individualism, isolation and utter unconditioned freedom. It is in this experience that by continuing to love 'to the end', he became most fully himself, Son of the Father, totally given to others. This is confirmed in and through his resurrection and outpouring of the Spirit. Now risen, Christ continues to bear the wounds of his crucifixion. They are a sign that he who has inhabited the most distant point from God, experiencing both humanity and creation's distance from God and the distance of members of the human family from one another, is now the all-embracing universal point where true interpersonal communion begins.

Without being able to expand on the point here, Coda sees articulated and explained in the Fourth Gospel the realm of reciprocity that envelops creation and humanity because of Jesus Christ. In emptying himself, divesting himself of all claims to be 'something', Jesus becomes the zero-point where encounter occurs between God and humanity, between God and creation; between members of the human family: 'As you, Father, are in me and I in you, may they too be in us ... I in them and you in me, so that they may become perfectly one' (Jn 17:21, 23).[40]

Recuperating the ontological insights of the Patristic and Medieval era as well as the positive contribution of the modern philosophy of intersubjectivity, Coda writes that 'the relationship between the Trinitarian dynamic of the life of the divine Persons and the relationship, in Christ, of and between created persons, is no longer merely one of analogy but of mutual interiority made freely available by the incarnation of the Son of God and the Easter gift of the Spirit'.[41]

Coda makes three points about what this means for us in terms of becoming fully human.

First, human nature is fully 'person-ated' in the incarnate Son of God in a unique and exemplary manner. Nevertheless, through the gift of grace men and women can reach their full personal being in-Christ, realising their identity and distinction, by freely participating in and imitating Christ's being-person, and having access through him to the filial relationship disclosed in him *vis-à-vis* the Father in the Spirit.

Second, in the Letter to the Ephesians we read that Christ created 'in himself one new humanity in place of the two' (the many) (2:14-16). In other words, human personhood is not simply fulfilled in terms of an individual vertical relationship to God in Christ. In the Christ event an *agapic* relationship has been between created persons. While relationship with God in Christ is constitutive of the definition of the human person, so also is relationship with the other in-Christ. It is in this sense that the Greek Orthodox theologian, John Zizioulas, speaks of the person as an 'ecclesial' being and hypostasis.[42]

Third, a 'perichoretic' (mutually indwelling) logic of giving and receiving is intrinsic to intersubjective relationships that are 'in-Christ', relationships marked by a radical giving of oneself to the other and the receiving of oneself from the other in accordance with the logic of the 'non-being out of love in order to be love' that we see in Christ on the Cross. Establishing such relationships involves both the work of the Holy Spirit and our attunement to the paschal dynamic of death-resurrection, living a certain 'inexistence', opening ourselves to full self-possession in the freedom of relationship to the O/others. In reading personhood within this Trinitarian ontology, relationship is central, not only with those with whom I am directly in contact but with 'everyone without face' (as Ricoeur puts it) that I meet through the mediation of structures and institutions.

It is clear that theologically we need to be careful in speaking of human personhood in terms of participation in the Trinitarian rhythm of love and life. As created persons, the 'non-being' of love[43] found in the heart of the Triune God in whom we can participate through faith, can only be lived intentionally. Only in God do being and *agape* coincide (the mutual love that is total Self-giving [non-being out of love]). Human beings cannot deprive themselves ontologically. They can give of themselves in knowing and loving. But only God 'is' Love. It will only be in death that we will be able to commit everything totally, the whole of our creaturely being, into the hands of God. For now, however, we find fulfilment in identifying ourselves with Jesus Christ who clothes us with personhood that is expressed in relationship to the O/others. And this can occur wherever people, prompted by the Spirit, open in conscience to the Truth and Light present in each other and within the multiple strands of history, cultures and traditions.[44]

CONCLUSION

In this article, I have attempted to outline some elements of Chiara Lubich's thought in particular with reference to the notion of being and human personhood. In one of his works, *The Drama of Humanity: Towards a Philosophy of Humanity in History*, Brendan Purcell concludes by quoting her in terms he believes are urgent for a new politics and a new civilisation of communion: 'Love gives us our being. We do not exist only because of love; we exist because we love. If we do not love – and in all the moments in which we do not love, we no longer are – we do not exist.'[45]

Chiara Lubich proposes that the relationships constitutive of human being find their measure in the Trinitarian nothingness/all of love that is disclosed in Jesus Christ, especially in his abandonment on the Cross. And this is the root of a culture of giving that is essential to human development. Writers such as Klaus Hemmerle and Piero Coda have drawn on her writings to develop their avenues of research in terms of Trinitarian ontology. There is a timeliness in their intuitions. In his encyclical letter on integral human development, Pope Benedict XVI wrote: 'The Christian revelation of the unity of the human race presupposes a metaphysical interpretation of the "humanum" in which relationality is an essential element.'[46] Chiara Lubich provided an original insight into the relationality that opens up in the Christ event. We can be grateful also to Brendan Purcell for dedicating his intellectual endeavour, influenced not least by Chiara Lubich, to the interpretation of humanity as 'we-wards'. And doing so in dialogue with history and with the explorers of human origins.

NOTES

1. For a biography of Chiara Lubich's life, see Jim Gallagher, *A Woman's Work: Chiara Lubich: A Biography of the Focolare Movement and Its Founder* (London: HarperCollins Publishers, 1996; Canada: New City Press, 1997; New York: New City Press, 2002). For a compendium of her writings, see Chiara Lubich, *Essential Writings: Spirituality, Dialogue, Culture* (New York: New City Press, 2007).
2. Eric Voegelin, 'The Origins of Totalitarianism', *Review of Politics* 15 (1953), pp. 68–85, p. 68.
3. Eric Voegelin, *The Political Religions, The Collected Works of Eric Voegelin*, Vol. 5, *Modernity Without Restraint*, Manfred Henningsen, ed. (Columbia, MO: University of Missouri Press, 2000), p. 24.
4. See Piero Coda, *Il negativo e la trinità: Ipotesi su Hegel* [*Negation and Trinity: Hypotheses on Hegel*] (Rome: Città Nuova, 1987). Cyril O'Regan, in his *The Heterodox Hegel* (Albany, NY: SUNY Press, 1994) refers several times to Coda's work.
5. The current editors are Giuseppe Maria Zanghí and Antonio Maria Baggio. More recently, an English online version of this review has been launched: *Claritas, Journal of Dialogue and Culture*. It is hosted by Purdue University e-Pubs (http://docs.lib.purdue.edu/claritas/).
6. See Chiara Lubich et al., *An Introduction to the Abba School: Conversations from the Focolare's Interdisciplinary Study Center* (New York: New City, 2002).
7. See *Il Patto del '49 nell'esperienza di Chiara Lubich: percorsi interdisciplinari* (*The Pact of '49 in the Experience of Chiara Lubich: Interdisciplinary Pathways*) (Rome: Città Nuova, 2012).
8. Accredited by the Holy See, the credits and degrees conferred by the Institute are recognised and transferable in accordance with international agreements, such as the Lisbon Convention of 1997, and the parameters set by the Bologna Process (for ECTS).
9. David Walsh, *The Modern Philosophical Revolution: The Luminosity of Existence* (Cambridge: Cambridge University Press, 2008), p. xiv.
10. See Lubich, *Essential Writings*, p. ixiii.
11. Ibid., xxiv.
12. Ibid., xxviii.
13. Ibid. The key ideas of this spirituality: 'God, the new ideal of our life, who manifested himself in the midst of the horrors of the war, fruit of hatred, for what he truly is, Love; doing the will of God and living his word as our possibility to respond to his love with our love; love of neighbour, especially of the needy, as the commandment which sums up all the law and prophets; carrying out this love reciprocally and radically by living Jesus' characteristic new commandment; consequently, accomplishing unity with him and with our brothers and sisters, as it is understood from his prayer for unity; living with the presence of Jesus among us, promised to those, even two or three, who are united in his name, that is, in his love; loving the cross, fixing our gaze on Jesus crucified in his terrible abandonment, which we discovered as the key to unity. See Chiara Lubich, 'For a Philosophy that Stems from Christ', *Communio* 25.4 (1998), pp. 746–56.
14. Piero Coda, 'L'esperienza e l'intelligenza della fede in dio trinità da sant'Agostino a Chiara Lubich', *Nuova Umanità* 167 (2006), pp. 527–52. See also the editorial article, 'Contextualising Paradise '49', *Claritas: Journal of Dialogue and Culture* [online journal] 1.1 (March 2012), pp. 13–23

15. See Chiara Lubich, 'For a Philosophy that Stems from Christ', *Communio* 25 (1998), pp. 746–56. Part of the text is reprinted slightly modified in *Essential Writings*, pp. 209–14.
16. 'A Philosophy', p. 750.
17. Ibid., p. 751.
18. Ibid.
19. Ibid., p. 752.
20. Ibid.
21. Ibid.
22. Ibid., p. 751.
23. Ibid., p. 753.
24. 'A Philosophy', p. 753.
25. Ibid.
26. Ibid., p. 754.
27. 'A Philosophy', p. 755.
28. Ibid.
29. Ibid.
30. Pope John Paul II, Encyclical Letter of the Relationship between Faith and Reason, *Fides et Ratio* (14 September 1998), n. 93.
31. Joseph Cardinal Ratzinger, *Introduction to Christianity*, J. R. Foster, trans. (San Francisco: Ignatius Press, 2004), p. 184.
32. *Thesen zu einer trinitarischen Ontologie*, Freiburg: 1976. Five volumes of selected writings (*Ausgewählte Schriften*) of Klaus Hemmerle's have been assembled by Herder 1995–1996. The *Thesen* are found in Volume II, pp. 124–61. For a detailed presentation of Hemmerle's Trinitarian ontology, see Bernhard Körner, 'Theology constituted by Communication in Multiple Causality: Klaus Hemmerle's Trinitarian Ontology and Relational Theology', *Theology and Conversation*, J. Haers and P. De Mey, (Leuven: Leuven University Press, 2003), pp. 255–68.
33. See Klaus Hemmerle, *F. Von Baaders philosophischer Gedanke der Schöpfung* (Freiburg: Verlag K. Alber, 1963) and *Gott and das Denken nach Schellings Spätphilosophie* (Freiburg: Herder, 1968).
34. See Klaus Hemmerle, *Theologie als Nachfolge Bonaventura – ein Weg für heute* (Freiburg: Herder, 1975).
35. *Thesen*, p. 132.
36. See Hans Urs von Balthasar, *Glory of the Lord: A Theological Aesthetics*, vol. 5: *The Realm of Metaphysics in the Modern Age* (Edinburgh: T&T Clark, 1991), p. 23.
37. *Thesen*, p. 139.
38. Ibid., p. 151.
39. For a recent work of Piero Coda on this theme see, *Dalla Trinità: l'avento di Dio tra storia e profezia*, (*From the Trinity: The Advent of God Between History and Prophecy*), (Rome: Città Nuova, 2011).
40. See Piero Coda, *Il logos e il nulla: Trinità, religioni, mistica* (*Logos and Nothingness: Trinity Religions Mysticism*) (Rome: Città Nuova, 2003).
41. Coda, *Dalla Trinità*, p. 561.
42. See J. Zizioulas, *L'être ecclesial* (Geneva: Labor et Fides, 1981).
43. Coda develops a reflection on creation and human personhood aware that recent philosophy and theology have considered the resources of negativity for understanding being and existence. See his own work on Hegel. He recognises also

the influence of Ghislain Lafont in his *Peut-on connaître Dieu en Jésus Christ?* (Paris: Cerf, 1969) and Giuseppe Zanghì, *Dio che è Amore. Trinità e vita in Cristo* (Rome: Città Nuova, 1991) and *Gesù Abbandonato maestro di pensiero* (Rome: Città Nuova, 2008).
44. See the Second Vatican Council Constitution on the Church in the Modern World, *Gaudium et Spes*, n. 22.
45. Frankfurt am Main: Peter Lang, 1996, p. 270, quoting Lubich, *On the Holy Journey* (New York: New City, 1988, p. 89).
46. Pope Benedict XVI, Encyclical Letter on Integral Human Development in Charity and Truth, *Caritas in Veritate* (29 June 2009), n. 54.

Brendan Purcell Bibliography

'The Horseshoe and the Ring', *The Black Book: An Analysis of Third Level Education*, R. Kearney and B. Fitzpatrick, eds. (Dublin, 1975), pp. 67–79.

'Newgrange: Between Sun and Stone', *The Crane Bag* 2, 1.2 (1978), pp. 89–95.

'Solzhenitsyn's Struggle for Personal, Social and Historical Anamnesis', *Philosophical Studies* 28 (1981), pp. 62–88.

'Cuore per cuore: educazione reciproca nella famiglia', *Nuova Umanità* 3.18 (1981), pp. 32–43.

'La persona come comunione. Riflessioni in chiave psicologica', *Nuova Umanità* 5.30 (1983), pp. 87–98.

'In Search of Newgrange: Long Night's Journey into Day', *The Irish Mind: Exploring Intellectual Traditions*, R. Kearney, ed. (Dublin: Wolfhound Press, 1985), pp. 39–55, pp. 319–23.

'Church, State and Society', *Irish Philosophical Journal* 3.1 (1986), pp. 58–79. (Expanded as 'Church and State', *Philosophical Studies* 31 (1987), pp. 380–403.)

'Reflections on Education in the light of *Learning for Life*', *Institute of Guidance Counsellors' Journal*, 14.1 (1988), pp. 23–6.

'Understanding the Human Mystery: Human Origins in Palaeoanthropology and Philosophy', *At the Heart of the Real*, F. O'Rourke, ed. (Dublin: Irish Academic Press, 1992), pp. 339–71.

The Drama of Humanity: Towards a Philosophy of Humanity in History, Frankfurt am Main: Peter Lang, 1996.

'Universal Viewpoint and Universal Humanity: Attunement or Discord in the Philosophies of Voegelin and Lonergan?', *Lonergan Workshop 12: In Tune with the Divine Ground: Cultural and Social Conditions for Political Order*, Fred Lawrence, ed., 12 (1996), pp. 227–49.

'Darwinism: Dangerous Idea or Deconstructed Myth?', *The Philosophy of Science: Proceedings of the Irish Philosophical Society*, Thomas Kelly, ed. (Maynooth: Irish Philosophical Society, 1997), pp. 40–54.

'The Philosophical Context of the "Hitler and the Germans" Lectures', *Hitler and the Germans: The Collected Works of Eric Voegelin, Vol. 31*, Eric Voegelin, translated and edited with an introduction by Detlev Clemens and Brendan Purcell (Columbia, MO: University of Missouri Press, 1999), pp. 21–40.

Hitler and the Germans: The Collected Works of Eric Voegelin, Vol. 31, Eric Voegelin, translated and edited by Detlev Clemens and Brendan Purcell (Columbia, MO: University of Missouri Press, 1999).

'What Would Socrates Say? Towards a Foundation in Media Ethics', *Media in Ireland: The Search for Accountability*, Damian Kiberd, ed. (Dublin: Open Air, 1999), pp. 19–32.

'Reflections on Evolution in the Light of a Philosophical Biology', *Thomas Aquinas: Approaches to Truth*, James McEvoy and Michael Dunne, eds. (Dublin: Four Courts Press, 2002), pp. 77–113.

'*Faith & Reason*: Charter for the Third Millennium', *The Challenge of Truth: Fides et Ratio*, James McEvoy, ed. (Dublin: Veritas, 2002), pp. 240–53.

'L'Opposition du principe anthropologique et de la bêtise extreme dans l'individu et la société', *Hitler et les Allemands*, Eric Voegelin, Mira Köller and Dominique Seglard, trans. (Paris: Du Seuil, 2003), pp. 21–5.

'*Amor amicitiae* in the *Bhagavad* Gita', *Amor Amicitiae: On the Love that is Friendship: Essays in Medieval Thought and Beyond, in Honor of Professor James McEvoy*, Thomas Kelly and Phillipp Rosemann, eds. (Leuven: Peeters, 2004), pp. 347–77.

'The Big Mystery: Human Emergence as Cosmic Metaxy', *Philosophy, Literature and Politics: Essays Honoring Ellis Sandoz*, Charles R. Embry and Barry Cooper, eds. (Columbia, MO: University of Missouri Press, 2005), pp. 102–25.

'Eric Voegelin', *Catholic Social Thought, Social Science, and Social Policy: An Encyclopedia*, Joseph A. Varacalli, Stephen M. Krason, Richard S. Myers & Michael L. Coulter, eds. (Lanham, MD: Scarecrow Press, 2007), pp. 1128–29.

'Culture and Values: The Contemporary Crisis', *Culture and Values: Towards a Common Humanity*, John McNerney, ed. (Dublin: Quinn School of Business, UCD, 2007), pp. 25–9.

'Foundations for a Judgement of the Holocaust: Etty Hillesum's Standard of Humanity', *Spirituality in the Writings of Etty Hillesum: Proceedings of the Etty Hillesum Conference at Ghent University, November 2008*, Klaas A. D.

Smelik, Ria van den Brandt, and Meins G. S. Coetsier, eds. (Leiden: Brill, 2010), pp. 125–46.

'Alexander Solzhenitsyn's Overcoming Personal, Political and Historical Amnesia Through Literary-Aesthetic Anamnesis', *History of Communism in Europe*, Vol. 1 (Bucharest: Zeta Books, 2010), pp. 33–46.

'From Big Bang to Big Mystery', *Having Life in His Name: Living, Thinking and Communicating the Christian Life of Faith*, Brendan Leahy and Séamus O'Connell, eds. (Dublin: Veritas, 2011), pp. 17–40.

From Big Bang to Big Mystery: Human Origins in the Light of Creation and Evolution (Dublin: Veritas, 2011; Hyde Park, NY: New City Press, 2012).

'Dawkins' Fear of Reason', *Human Destinies: Philosophical Essays in Memory of Gerald Hanratty*, Fran O'Rourke, ed. (Notre Dame: Notre Dame University Press, 2012), pp. 337–65.

'Towards a Trinitarian Humanism: Piero Coda's Development of a Heuristic of Radical Fraternity as a Lived Theology of History', *Sophia: Ricerche su i fondamenti e la correlazione dei saperi* IV.20 (Rome, 2012), pp. 247–71.

'The Focolare Movement', *Australasian Ecclesiastical Record* (June, 2012).

'Long Night's Journey into Eternal Day', *Treasures of Irish Christianity: People and Places, Images and Texts*, Salvador Ryan and Brendan Leahy, eds. (Dublin: Veritas, 2012), pp. 269–71.

'Reflections on Philosophical and Theological Historiography in Aleksandr Solzhenitsyn's *The Red Wheel*', *Life and Work of Aleksandr Solzhenitsyn: The Way to The Red Wheel*, Ludmila Saraskina, ed. (Moscow: Russian Literature Abroad Press, 2013).

'Finnegan's Waiting for God?', *Treasures of Irish Christianity: A People of the Word*, Salvador Ryan and Brendan Leahy, eds. (Dublin: Veritas, 2013).

List of Contributors

Gerard Casey is a professor of philosophy at University College Dublin. His *Murray Rothbard* (Volume 15 of the *Major Conservative and Libertarian Thinkers*) appeared in 2010 and his *Libertarian Anarchy: Against the State* was published in 2012.

Eoin Cassidy is a lecturer in philosophy and head of the philosophy department at the School of Humanities, Mater Dei Institute of Education, Dublin. He has served in executive positions in the Irish Philosophy Society, the Irish Theological Association and the Royal Irish Academy (philosophy committee) and was formerly executive secretary of the Irish Centre for Faith and Culture. Recent publications include *The Taylor Effect: Responding to a Secular Age* (2010; with Ian Leask) and *Community, Constitution and Ethos: Democratic Values and Citizenship in the Face of Globalization* (2008).

Piero Coda is president of the Sophia University Institute, Loppiano, Florence, and formerly professor of fundamental theology at the Lateran University, Rome. He is a consultor of a number of Pontifical Councils and formerly secretary of the Italian Theological Association. Recent publications include *Dalla Trinità. L'avvento di Dio tra storia e profezia* (2012); *Ontosofia. J. Maritain in ascolto dell'essere* (2009); *I comandamenti. Io sono il Signore Dio tuo* (2009).

Barry Cooper, FRSC, professor of political science at the University of Calgary, has published nearly two hundred articles and over twenty-five books, mostly on political philosophy, Canadian politics and military and security issues. His most recent books are *It's the Regime, Stupid! A Report from the Cowboy West on Why Stephen Harper Matters* (2009), and *Beginning the Quest: Law and Politics in the Early Work of Eric Voegelin* (2009).

James Greenaway, assistant professor of philosophy at St Mary's University in San Antonio, Texas, received his PhD from University College Dublin under Brendan Purcell's supervision. He is the author of *The Differentiation of Authority: The Medieval Turn Toward Existence* (Catholic University of America Press, 2012), and has written about convergences and divergences among legal, political and metaphysical problems.

Glenn Hughes, professor of philosophy at St Mary's University, San Antonio, Texas, is the author of *A More Beautiful Question: The Spiritual in Poetry and Art* (2011), *Transcendence and History* (2003), and *Mystery and Myth in the Philosophy of Eric Voegelin* (1993); and editor of *The Politics of the Soul: Eric Voegelin on Religious Experience* (1999). His poetry has appeared in many national literary journals, and in the chapbooks *Sleeping at the Open Window* (2005) and *Erato* (2010).

Brendan Leahy is Bishop of Limerick and formerly professor of systematic theology, St Patrick's College, Maynooth. He is a member of the Pontifical Theology Academy. Recent publications include *Treasures of Irish Christianity: People and Places, Images and Texts* (with Salvador Ryan, 2011); *Ecclesial Movements: Origins, Significance and Issues* (2011); *Priests Today: Reflections on Identity, Life and Ministry* (2010).

Joseph McCarroll, father and grandfather, is chairperson of the Pro-Life Campaign and a retired educational welfare officer in Ireland. He is an independent scholar who has lectured in the Milltown Institute of Theology and Philosophy and elsewhere. His publications include *Is the School Around the Corner Just the Same?* (1987), *Marriage or Divorce, Journey to the Centre of the Person* (1988) and *Meeting You in Scripture* (1999).

John McNerney is a priest of the Archdiocese of Dublin and head of chaplaincy services at University College Dublin. He is attached to the Quinn School of Business and Smurfit Graduate School of Business in University College Dublin. He is a member of the Irish Commission for the Economy of Communion project, linked to the international Economy of Communion project that has United Nations recognition. He is author of *John Paul II: Poet and Philosopher* (2004). His doctoral thesis was entitled *Towards an Economic Philosophical Anthropology: An Austrian Perspective*.

Emese Mogyoródi is associate professor at the University of Szeged, Hungary. She has published articles in English or Hungarian on Homer, Greek tragedy, Presocratic philosophy and Plato. She has translated into Hungarian and written commentaries to Plato's *Apology* and *Euthyphro* and published a collection of her essays written in Hungarian, entitled *Achilles and Socrates: Moral Psychology and Political Philosophy from the Archaic to the Classical Age* (2012).

Timothy Mooney is senior lecturer in philosophy at University College Dublin, has co-edited *The Phenomenology Reader* with Dermot Moran (2002), and has authored a number of studies on phenomenology, deconstruction and process philosophy. His major teaching and research interest is the philosophy of embodiment, with particular reference to Husserl and Merleau-Ponty.

Thomas Norris is a priest of the Diocese of Ossory, formerly associate professor of systematic theology at Maynooth, Paluch Visiting Professor at the University of St Mary of the Lake, Mundelein, and currently spiritual director at the Irish College in Rome. He is a member of the International Theological Commission. Most recent books are *Mary in the Mystery: The Woman in Whom Divinity and Humanity Rhyme*; *The Trinity: Life of God, Hope for Humanity: Towards a Theology of Communion* (2009); and *A Fractured Relationship: Faith and the Crisis of Culture* (2007).

Cyril O'Regan is the Huisking Professor of Theology at the University of Notre Dame, where he teaches courses in systematic, fundamental and historical theology. He is the author of *The Heterodox Hegel* (1994), *Gnostic Return in Modernity* (2001), *Gnostic Apocalypse* (2002), *Theology and the Spaces of Apocalyptic* (2009), *Anatomy of Misremembering: Balthasar and the Specter of Hegel* (2013).

Fran O'Rourke is associate professor of philosophy at University College Dublin. He is author of *Pseudo-Dionysius and the Metaphysics of Aquinas* (2005) and *Allwisest Stagyrite: Joyce's Quotations from Aristotle* (2005); and editor of a number of books, including *Human Destinies: Philosophical Essays in Memory of Gerald Hanratty* (2013). He is preparing for publication a collection of essays entitled *Aristotelian Interpretations*, and completing a book on James Joyce, Aristotle and Aquinas.

David Walsh is professor of politics at the Catholic University of America in Washington, DC, and the author of a trilogy on the nature of modernity that includes *After Ideology* (1990), *The Growth of the Liberal Soul* (1997), and *The Modern Philosophical Revolution* (2008). He is currently completing a study of the new philosophical language required of any account of the person, tentatively titled *Politics of the Person*.